Investing in Crypto with Confidence

Javier Pineda

Investing in Crypto with Confidence

How to Analyze, Select and Manage Digital Assets

Javier Pineda
Madrid, Spain

ISBN 978-3-032-07833-9   ISBN 978-3-032-07834-6 (eBook)
https://doi.org/10.1007/978-3-032-07834-6

"I don't have time to try to convince you, sorry."
(Satoshi Nakamoto)

Contents

1

Introduction

I started investing in cryptocurrencies more than five years ago and have evolved my approach to managing both medium- to long-term investments and short-term trading.

In March 2022, in the middle of the bear market, I had the idea of creating the first crypto investment fund in Europe within a regulated market, noticing that there were increasingly more institutional clients (investment banks, private banking, etc.), and that support for the crypto market and blockchain technology was on the rise. In March 2024, the fund was launched as a hedge fund, and only professional clients can invest; retail investors cannot participate yet. The truth is, it filled me with pride to see my dream come true, as it marks a before-and-after moment in the crypto world by being the first investment fund in Spain with 100% exposure to cryptocurrencies by investment policy. The fund is **Renta 4 Crypto FIL Fund** (a free investment fund).

After many years of trading and investing in cryptocurrencies, I have compiled everything you need to know about investing in this asset into a book. This book provides the essentials for understanding how cryptocurrencies behave and how to profit from this technology.

This book aims to provide you with the fundamental knowledge you need to navigate the world of cryptocurrencies. We will first cover basic concepts to lay the foundation and then move on to various tools and techniques for evaluating and investing in this sector.

Many think cryptocurrencies are like stocks (equity), but this asset class is entirely different. Techniques and indicators for stocks do not necessarily

© The Author(s), under exclusive license to Springer Nature Switzerland AG 2026
J. Pineda, *Investing in Crypto with Confidence*,
https://doi.org/10.1007/978-3-032-07834-6_1

work for cryptocurrencies, and vice versa. I intend not to fill this book with complex concepts and definitions, as many other books do, which only complicate understanding cryptocurrencies. Instead, I want to provide the most critical insights to help you understand how this market operates.

I hope you find this book useful and that, after reading it, you can successfully invest in cryptocurrencies. Let's dive in!

2

Bitcoin

2.1 How Did Bitcoin Originate?

To better understand Bitcoin, we must consider the financial framework in which it was created. In September 2008, Lehman Brothers became the largest company to file for bankruptcy in the history of the United States. At the same time, the major insurance company AIG had problems and had to be bailed out on September 15, since it was ¨too big to fail¨, by the Fed and US treasury with an injection of $85 billion.

In November 2008, the Federal Reserve announced a stimulus program of $600 billion called QE to purchase mortgage-backed debt securities to help lower mortgage rates. This plan pursued two targets:

* **Lower interest rate**: As there is greater demand for these, the bond price rises and the yield, therefore, falls.
* **Creation of liquidity** to facilitate credit to consumers and companies. Due to the massive purchase of state and corporate bonds, the latter, particularly the banks, increase their liquidity reserves. The other effect is for banks to send this liquidity to their clients through loans at reduced rates to individuals and companies.

During this financial crisis, where there was no belief in the financial system, Satoshi Nakamoto sought to create a form of electronic money without depending on any entity or financial intermediary, and thus, Bitcoin was born. He wrote the following email to a crypto mailing list:

© The Author(s), under exclusive license to Springer Nature Switzerland AG 2026
J. Pineda, *Investing in Crypto with Confidence*,
https://doi.org/10.1007/978-3-032-07834-6_2

I've been working on a new electronic cash system that's fully peer-to-peer, with no trusted third party.

The main properties are:

- *Double-spending is prevented with a peer-to-peer network.*
- *No mint or other trusted parties.*
- *Participants can be anonymous.*
- *New coins are made from Hashcash-style proof-of-work. The proof-of-work for new coin generation also powers the network to prevent double-spending.*

The paper is available at: https://www.bitcoin.org/bitcoin.pdf.
In this link, you will find the white paper where you can find *A Peer-to-Peer Electronic Cash System called Bitcoin.*

A purely peer-to-peer version of electronic cash would allow online payments to be sent directly from one party to another without the burdens of going through a financial institution. Digital signatures provide part of the solution, but the main benefits are lost if a trusted party is still required to prevent double spending. We propose a solution to the double-spending problem using a peer-to-peer network. The network timestamps transactions by hashing them into an ongoing chain of hash-based proof-of-work, forming a record that cannot be changed without redoing it. The longest chain not only serves as proof of the sequence of events witnessed, but also proof that it came from the largest pool of CPU power. As long as honest nodes control the most CPU power on the network, they can generate the longest chain and outpace any attackers. The network itself requires minimal structure. Messages are broadcast on a best effort basis, and nodes can leave and rejoin the network at will, accepting the longest proof-of-work chain as proof of what happened while they were gone.

Source: Nakamoto, Bitcoin P2P e-cash paper, 2008.

Satoshi Nakamoto built on a digital cash system called b-money, which Wei Dai proposed in 1998 on the cypherpunk mailing list. It was designed to create a distributed and anonymous electronic cash system.

He created an alternative monetary system that did not depend on any financial entity, so the crisis the current world was experiencing could not occur.

The root problem with conventional currency is all the trust that's Required to make it work. The central bank must be trusted not to debase the currency, but the history of fiat currencies is full of breaches of that trust. Banks must be trusted to hold our money and

*transfer it electronically, but they lend it out in waves of credit
bubbles with barely a fraction in reserve. We have to trust them with
our privacy, trust them not to let identity thieves drain our accounts.
Their massive overhead costs make micropayments impossible.*

Source: Nakamoto, Bitcoin open-source implementation P2P currency, 2009.

Satoshi described Bitcoin as "a purely peer-to-peer version of electronic cash that would allow online payments to be sent directly from one party to another without the burdens of going through a financial institution".

Peer-to-peer means that all the computers on the network are equal and no one has any privileges or other functions.

2.2 Most Important Events

Among the most important events in the history of Bitcoin, we have:

On October 31st, 2008, Satoshi Nakamoto published the Bitcoin whitepaper to the cryptography mailing list.

On January 3rd, 2009, the first block (known as the genesis block) of the Bitcoin blockchain was mined. Also, on this day, the peer-to-peer network was launched.

On January 10th, 2009, Hal Finney became the second person to join the Bitcoin network.

On October 5th, 2009, Bitcoin began to have an exchange price for a traditional currency, such as the dollar. New Liberty Standard is the first P2P platform for buying and selling bitcoins that publishes an exchange rate of 1309.03 bitcoins for one dollar, that is, 0.00764 USD for one bitcoin.

On October 12th, 2009, Martin Malmi made the first Bitcoin sale for dollars, selling 5050 bitcoins for $5.02.

On May 22nd, 2010, Laszlo Hanyecz paid 10,000 Bitcoin for two pizzas from Papa John's. This was considered the first purchase made with Bitcoin, so May 22nd is now celebrated annually as Bitcoin Pizza Day.

In February 2014, Mt.Gox, the largest bitcoin exchange at that time, was hacked after a theft of between 650,000 and 950,000 bitcoins, and it suspended all trading. Mt Gox centralized 70% of the bitcoin trading volume, and bitcoin was quoted at around 600 USD. After 10 years, today those stolen bitcoins are still being recovered and returned to their owners.

In January 2016, Joseph Poon and Thaddeus Dryja published the Lightning Network paper. It is a scaling solution for Bitcoin.

2.3   What Is Bitcoin?

Bitcoin is a digital currency in which transactions are recorded in a hash-linked data structure called blockchain, which is secured through a consensus mechanism called Proof of Work (PoW).

Andreas M.Antonopoulos indicates in his book *Mastering Bitcoin* that Bitcoin is composed of 4 items:

1. A distributed and decentralized peer-to-peer network (P2P)
2. A ledger called blockchain
3. Consensus Algorithm: Proof of work
4. A decentralized transaction verification system

* How does the Bitcoin network work?

When a transaction is made, it has to be validated by a validator or miner node, which are participants that validate and transmit transactions. They record the transaction in a block, which is linked together as a chain, creating a huge record of all transactions made, forming a record book. Therefore, it is called blockchain.

A node is a data structure unit, and a block is where the data is permanently recorded.

The size of each block is between 1 and 2 Mb; that is, about 2000 transactions can be recorded in each block.

A block is mined (created) every 10 minutes, and Bitcoin processes an average of 3 to 5 transactions per second.

For a transaction to be irreversible, you must wait for six confirmations, that is, five more blocks have been added to the block where the transaction was recorded. The computational effort of changing a transaction after six blocks is so great that it does not compensate for the effort for the reward received. Therefore, blockchain technology is secure and immutable.

The characteristics of this digital cash system are secure, borderless, decentralized, public, open access, and open source.

In general, money has three functions:

1. **Unit of Account**: a measurement of the value of goods or services to set prices
2. **Store of Value**: Money can be saved for later use, making savings possible
3. **Medium of Exchange**: Acquiring goods and services

Today, Bitcoin's **primary function is as a store of value**, which is why it is called digital gold. However, it is still not 100% a haven value, since when there is an event in the market that negatively affects it, it is gold that rises, and bitcoin does not always rise, since for now it is considered an asset with greater risk and volatility than equities, and if this event affects equities negatively, bitcoin will be affected more, and if it affects equities positively, bitcoin will benefit to a greater extent. For example, when Iran attacked Israel on October 1st, 2024, Gold rose 0,8% but bitcoin fell 4%. This is because Bitcoin is still in the early stages of adoption as a store of value.

If the US government creates a Bitcoin reserve, other countries could adopt the same measure, reducing Bitcoin's volatility and making it a safe haven like Gold.

2.4   Bitcoin vs Gold

As we can see in the following graph, historically, when Bitcoin fell, Gold rose, and in periods when Bitcoin rose, Gold remained stable or even rose. However, that relationship is changing, and since 2023, both have been more correlated than before, although not always, as with the October 1st event.

Bitcoin and gold have a low correlation, sometimes even negative, although this is less frequent. The ten-year average correlation was 9%, which is minimal. A strong dollar and higher real interest rates would create a bearish case for gold. If you believe that will happen, position yourself in BTC instead of gold.

As shown in Chart 2.1, the correlation between the two assets remains low and occasionally becomes negative (red bars), even when focusing on the last few years.

Gold vs Bitcoin Correlation

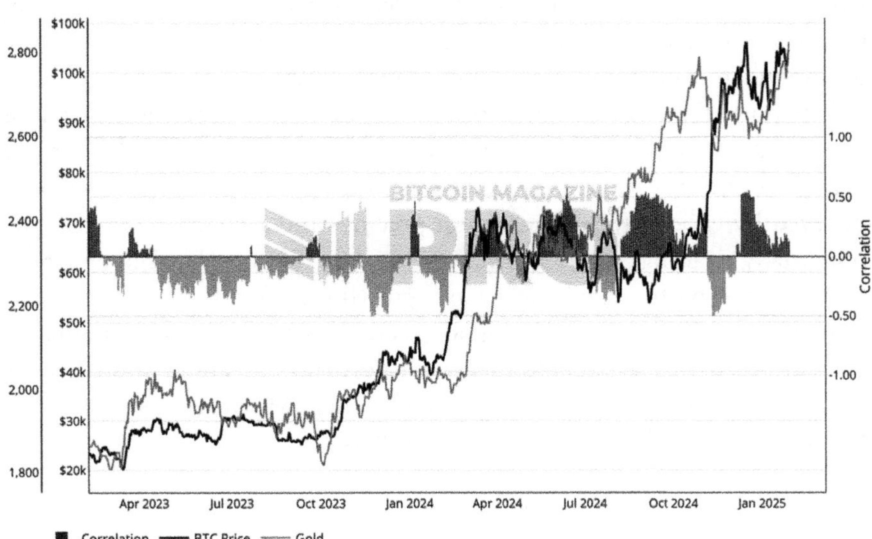

Chart 2.1   *Source* Bitcoin Magazine Pro (from Oct 2023 to Oct 2025)

In the current context (October 2025), where the U.S. dollar is experiencing a period of declining purchasing power, gold and Bitcoin stand out as the most attractive investment options.

This loss of the dollar's purchasing power is driven by three main factors:

- The progressive devaluation of the dollar
- The exponential growth of U.S. public debt
- The ongoing phase of interest rate cuts by the Federal Reserve

The interest rate cuts make borrowing cheaper, increase market liquidity, weaken the dollar, and boost demand for scarce assets such as gold and Bitcoin. Both tend to react positively in a scenario of rate cuts and monetary expansion.

Gold's scarcity is determined by the physical limitations of extraction, while Bitcoin's scarcity stems from its fixed and unchangeable supply of 21 million coins.

Technically, Bitcoin is inflationary, since new coins are created with each validated transaction. However, given that its total supply is capped at 21 million, with more than 19.5 million already in circulation, Bitcoin is barely affected by inflation and tends to appreciate in value over time.

If we compare these two assets in terms of inflation, gold is more inflationary than Bitcoin. Gold's inflation rate is around 1.8%, as its supply remains almost stable due to the lack of significant new discoveries. Bitcoin's inflation, on the other hand, is programmed through the halving (the event in which the block reward received by miners is cut in half), which decreases with each cycle. It currently stands at about 0.85% per year but will drop to 0.425% after the 2028 halving. For this reason, Bitcoin would be a better option when it comes to protecting against inflation.

The potential of Bitcoin is enormous compared to other safe-haven assets, such as gold. While gold can be affected by discoveries such as the new deposit found in China (October 2025), valued at over 83 billion USD and believed by experts to be the largest precious metal reserve ever discovered, potentially leading to a significant increase in supply, Bitcoin remains a scarce asset with a fixed supply and growing demand.

In the previous cycle, when gold reached its peak in 2020, similar to its current levels in October 2025, we witnessed a capital rotation from gold (yellow line) to Bitcoin (orange line), after which Bitcoin experienced a prolonged bullish rally, as shown in Chart 2.2:

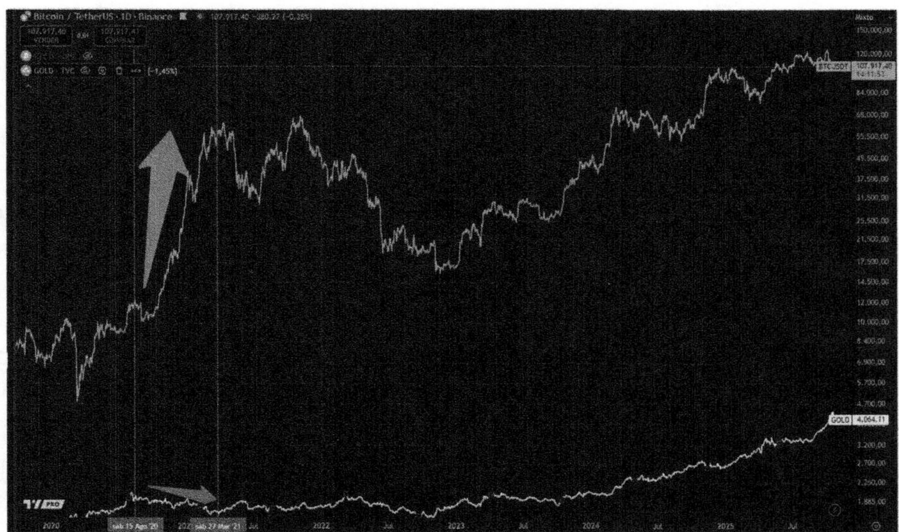

Chart 2.2 *Source* Tradingview (from 2020 to 2025)

Bitcoin is better than gold for several reasons:

* It is easier to transport (in 10 minutes, it can be anywhere in the world).
* It is more divisible than gold (it can be divided into up to eight decimal places).
* It is more verifiable than gold.

The adoption of Bitcoin is increasing. It is seen as digital gold due to its scarcity, low volatility, and superior transferability compared to physical gold. The yellow metal is considered the primary safe-haven asset, but Bitcoin's technological advantages and adoption trends suggest it could challenge gold's status over the long term.

Regarding diversification, gold remains a strong hedge against market downturns, while bitcoin is more volatile and offers higher returns during recoveries. Bitcoin also has a lower correlation with U.S. Treasuries, making it a valuable diversification tool, particularly as a hedge against sovereign defaults. A balanced allocation between Bitcoin and gold can optimize risk-adjusted returns.

The creation of the Gold ETF in its day had a very positive impact on the price of Gold, causing it to multiply by 5x in 8 years. With the creation of the Bitcoin ETF, it can also have a very positive impact, as it has already begun to show, rising from levels of 40,000 in January 2024 to over 120,000 USD a year and a half later.

2.5   Bitcoin Specifications

Today, Bitcoin is not a massively adopted medium of exchange globally since it only processes between 3 and 5 transactions per second, while Visa can process more than 40,000 transactions per second.

Bitcoin's limitations come from the size of the blocks (1–2 Mb) and the block time, which is 10 minutes; that is, a new block is generated every 10 minutes.

The problem is that we cannot increase the size of the blocks or decrease the time per block, as this would lead to the centralization of the network. Very few entities could mine due to the necessary hardware and bandwidth.

Joseph Poon and Thaddeus Dryja solved the Bitcoin scalability problem in January 2016 with the publication of his report called The Bitcoin Lighting Network: Scalable Off-Chain Instant Payments. This document proposes a second layer, a second network, where payments can be made between users, and only the initial deposit and final settlement transactions must be registered and validated by the Bitcoin nodes.

All transactions and blocks take up space on the blockchain. To group and verify large amounts of data efficiently and securely, Satoshi used the Merkle tree, which was created by Ralph Merkle in 1979.

A Merkle tree is a data structure that summarizes and verifies data in a block. It is a binary tree in which each leaf node represents a data block hash, and each non-leaf node is a hash of its child nodes. This structure culminates in a single hash known as the Merkle root.

The Merkle root is included in the block header of each block in the Bitcoin blockchain. It serves as a cryptographic summary of all transactions in the block, allowing for efficient and secure verification.

The benefits of Merkle Trees are:

- Data Integrity: Using cryptographic hashes, Merkle trees ensure that any alteration in the transaction data will result in a different Merkle root, making it easy to detect tampering.
- Efficiency: Merkle trees allow for efficient verification of transactions. Instead of verifying each transaction individually, the Merkle root can be used to verify the entire set of transactions in a block.
- Scalability: The hierarchical structure of Merkle trees reduces the amount of data that needs to be stored and processed, enhancing the scalability of the Bitcoin network.

Merkle trees enable simplified payment verification (SPV) in Bitcoin, allowing lightweight clients to verify transactions without downloading the entire blockchain.

In short, Merkle trees provide a secure and efficient method for transaction verification and data integrity.

There are two types of nodes:

- Full nodes: store an updated copy of the blockchain and verify transactions without the help of other nodes.
- Light nodes: store only a part of the blockchain and need the full nodes to verify transactions. These nodes are also known as simplified payment verification (SPV) nodes.

A mining node is a type of full node. All mining nodes are full nodes, but not all full nodes are mining nodes. A mining node stores an updated copy of the blockchain, validates transactions and blocks, and participates in the mining process. Non-mining full nodes do not create new blocks and don't receive rewards for their work. On the other hand, mining nodes create blocks and receive rewards for their work.

The blockchain is made up of different blocks that are linked together, and each block is divided into two parts: the header and the transactions. Full nodes store both, and light nodes only the header. They are united because each block saves the previous block's header, and thus the chain cannot be broken, since you would have to break all the blocks in the chain, and doing that is such a large computational and energetic effort that it would not compensate. Therefore, once the blocks have a considerable number of blocks above them, they are considered immutable.

A transaction is considered irreversible when it is five blocks older, that is, when there have been six confirmations.

We said earlier that Bitcoin transactions are recorded in the blockchain, which is secured through a consensus mechanism called Proof of Work (POW)

As Andreas M. Antonopoulos explains in chapter 10 of the *Mastering Bitcoin* book, consensus arrives by four processes happening independently across the network:

1. Independent verification of each transaction.
2. Independent aggregation of those transactions into new blocks by mining nodes.

3. Independent verification of the new blocks by every node and assembly into a chain.
4. Independent selection, by every node, of the chain with the most cumulative computation demonstrated through Proof of Work.

Cryptography (the art of secret writing) is essential in Bitcoin because private keys are used to sign transactions. Cryptography can be symmetrical or asymmetric.

The first protocol for asymmetric encryption was introduced by Ralph Merkle in 1978.

Bitcoin uses asymmetric cryptography to create both keys (private and public).

In Symmetric cryptography, the sender and the receiver use the same key.

In Asymmetric cryptography, two different keys are used. The public key is used to encrypt, that is, to go from plaintext into ciphertext. And the private key is used for decryption, that is, to go from ciphertext into plaintext.

Public keys can be derived from private keys, but private keys cannot be derived from public keys.

The private key is used to generate digital signatures. With the public key, you can verify that this digital signature is valid and was created with the private key.

The digital signatures also help us verify that the content has not changed after signature generation.

Hash algorithms transform plain text into a ciphertext. These algorithms scramble data into a hash that is a fixed-length alphanumeric reproducible fingerprint. Hashes are used to ensure the confidentiality and integrity of information.

Bitcoin uses two hashes: SHA-256 and RIPEMD-160. SHA (Secure Hash Algorithm) is used in the proof-of-work mining process, and RIPEMD-160 (Race Integrity Primitives Evaluation Message Digest) helps turn public keys into Bitcoin addresses.

To finish this section, I will comment on a series of nomenclatures that we must be clear about:

- Bitcoin with uppercase refers to the network or community.
- Bitcoin with a lowercase, "b" refers to the currency.
- The smallest unit is Satoshi; one bitcoin equals 100 million Satoshi.

1 bitcoin is 1000 millibit (mbit)
1 bitcoin is 1,000,000 bit
1 bitcoin is 100,000,000 satoshi (sat)
Bitcoin has a fixed supply of 21 million bitcoins

There are three historical challenges around money that Bitcoin can fix:

1. Prone to inflation and debasement given a non-fixed supply: Bitcoin has a fixed maximum supply of 21 million units, with supply growth declining every 4 years.
2. Difficult to transact across borders: Bitcoin is digitally native and borderless, permitting near-instantaneous, global transfers of value.
3. Access is limited to one's particular country and controlled by a central authority: Bitcoin is a truly open-access global monetary system.

Due to its decentralized, counterparty risk-free characteristics and increasing scarcity, Bitcoin can be used as insurance against the risk of a sovereign default and also in a hyperinflation scenario.

The US public debt has recently surpassed 36 trillion USD, approximately 123% of GDP, the highest level ever recorded. The same situation occurs in the UK, France, and other countries.

Since Bitcoin is a decentralized currency, it does not face counterparty risks, as no intermediary can censor or confiscate any transaction. Bitcoin's supply is also limited, and its annual inflation rate is below 1%.

2.6   Bitcoin vs Real Estate

In this section, I would like to comment on Bitcoin's evolution compared to real estate, which many investors consider a safe-haven asset.

Given the significant currency devaluation over the past 10 years, many assets such as property and Bitcoin have increased in value. This is because investors look to protect their dollars by moving from cash into assets more likely to retain or grow in value as governments continue debasing their currencies.

Chart 2.3 Illustrates the general increase over time, with $BTC shown in black and the U.S. Median House Sales Price in blue. While both have increased over time, the magnitude and pace of that growth differ significantly between the two assets.

BTC vs US Property

Chart 2.3   *Source* Bitcoin Magazine Pro

Chart 2.4 Shows House Prices in Bitcoin terms.

We can see how the value of house prices in the U.S. has continued to plummet relative to Bitcoin.

Property Priced in BTC

Chart 2.4   *Source* Bitcoin Magazine Pro

This chart shows that although both assets have appreciated in recent years, one has done so significantly more than the other. Bitcoin has appreciated much more than housing prices.

As shown in Chart 2.5, this becomes even clearer, which shows the house cost expressed in BTC vs. USD.

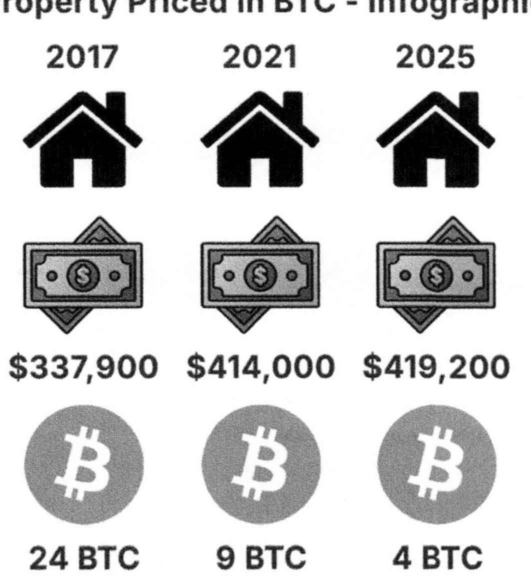

Chart 2.5 *Source* Bitcoin Magazine Pro

In 2017, an investor would have needed 24 bitcoins to purchase a US property with a median house price of $337,900. In 2021, you only required nine bitcoins to buy a house. And today, an investor would need just four bitcoins to purchase a US property with a median house price of $419,200.

While property value has increased in US dollar terms, it has crashed relative to bitcoin.

Therefore, the next time you consider investing in a house, keep this comparison in mind

2.7   Microstrategy

MicroStrategy, currently branded as Strategy, is a company led by Michael Saylor that has been purchasing Bitcoin using its available liquidity since August 2020. Over time, the company has become more associated with Bitcoin than its original core business.

The orange dots in Chart 2.6 represent the Bitcoin purchases made by MicroStrategy.

Strategy: Acquisitions

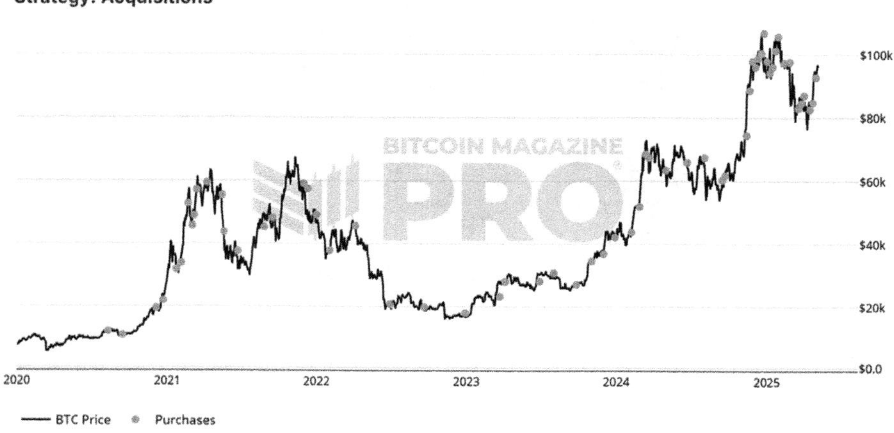

Chart 2.6   *Source* Bitcoin Magazine Pro April 2025

As of April 2025, MicroStrategy holds more than 550,000 BTC, representing approximately 2.64% of the total Bitcoin supply.

In Table 2.1, we can see the BTC holdings and return since the adoption by Microstrategy as of April 2025.

Table 2.1   *Source* Bitcoin Magazine Pro April 2025

BTC holdings	Return since adoption	MSTR price	% of 21m
553,555	3090%	$396.00	2.64%

This acquisition campaign has been methodical, with regular weekly purchases totaling billions of dollars in dollar-cost-averaged BTC. The company's average acquisition cost is nearly $68,500 (April 2025), translating to a mark-to-market profit of almost $15 billion. With their total spending now around $37.9 billion, Strategy has become the largest corporate holder of Bitcoin by a wide margin, positioning itself not just as a participant in this cycle but as a defining player. Chart 2.7 shows that the average acquisition cost is significantly lower than Bitcoin's current market price as of May 2025.

Chart 2.7 *Source* Bitcoin Magazine Pro

Furthermore, in May 2025, Michael Saylor announced that the Strategy company plans to raise over $84 billion to purchase more Bitcoin.

Since Strategy (MSTR) began its Bitcoin strategy in 2020, its performance closely mirrored that of BTC until February 2024 as we can see in Chart 2.8. At that point, the launch of Bitcoin ETFs revealed strong institutional demand for Bitcoin. This led other investors and investment funds, many of whom were unable to invest directly in Bitcoin or via ETFs, to turn to MSTR to gain exposure to Bitcoin.

As mentioned earlier, Strategy is increasingly viewed as a proxy for Bitcoin, but it trades on a regulated exchange like Nasdaq, making it more accessible to traditional investors. It's also worth noting that MSTR's Bitcoin purchases have accelerated since then.

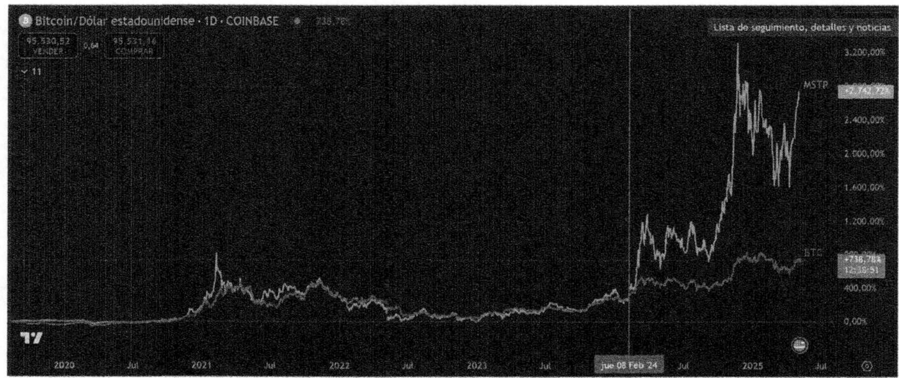

Chart 2.8 *Source* Tradingview

But since that moment (May 2025), Strategy has significantly outper-formed Bitcoin (691% vs. 172%) as shown in Chart 2.9, largely due to its leveraged exposure. However, it has also consistently been more volatile than Bitcoin, as shown in Chart 2.10:

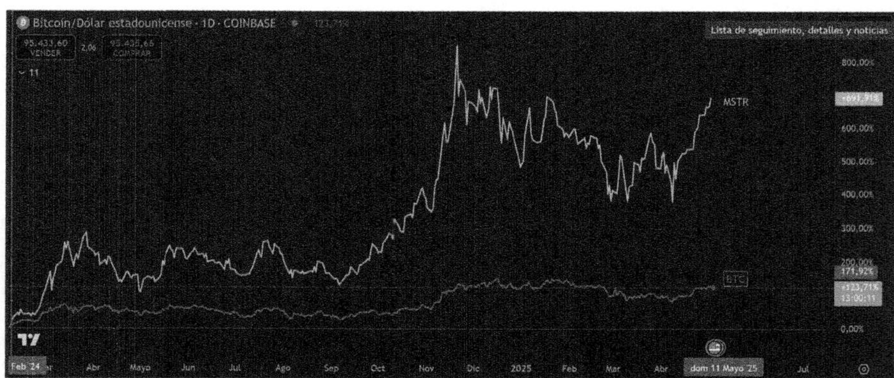

Chart 2.9 *Source* Tradingview (May 2025)

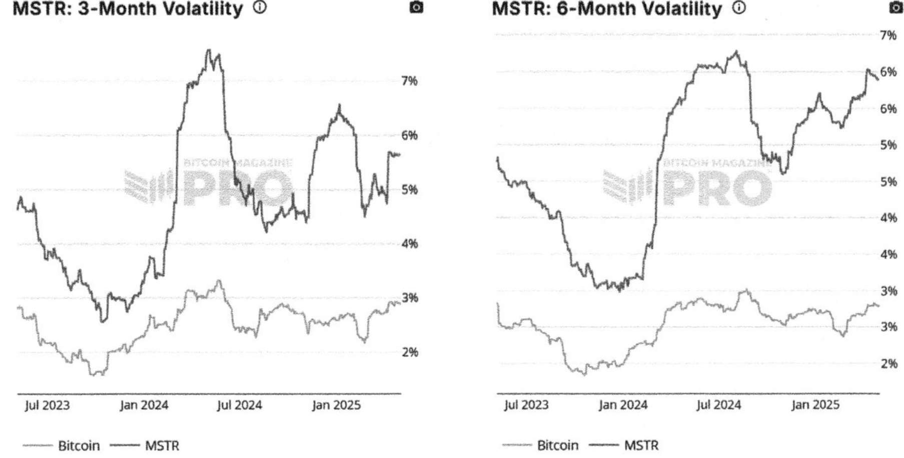

Chart 2.10   *Source* Bitcoin Magazine Pro

Using the Dollar Cost Averaging strategy, which means investing the same amount of money at regular time intervals—such as daily—you can see, as shown in Chart 2.11, that if you had invested $10 daily into Bitcoin over the past five years, you'd have contributed a total of $18,260, now (May 2025) worth over $61,000. You would have beaten every other asset class, including Gold, which has recently surged to new all-time highs.

The same $10/day strategy applied to Strategy stock since its first BTC purchase in August 2020 would have resulted in an investment of $11,850. That position would now be worth approximately $108,000, significantly outperforming Bitcoin over the same window.

Dollar Cost Average Strategies

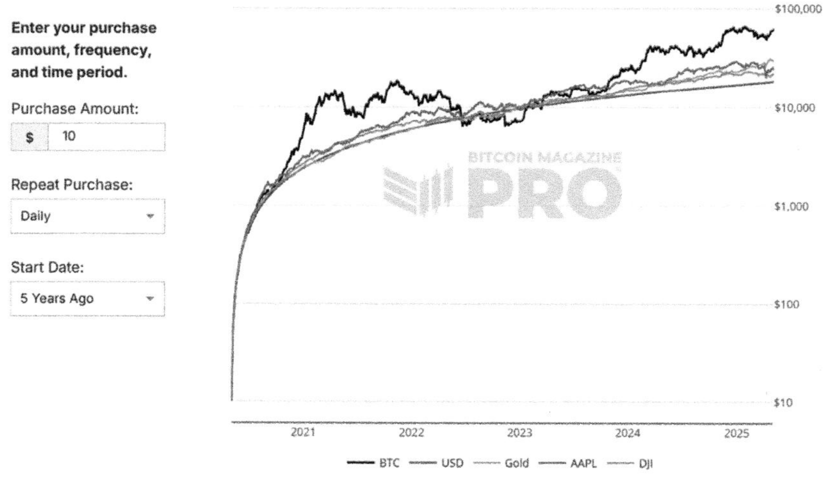

Asset	Total Invested	Total Value	Percent Change
BTC	$18,260	$61,235.06	235.35%
Gold	$18,260	$29,757.91	62.97%
AAPL	$18,260	$24,608.50	34.77%
DJI	$18,260	$22,078.26	20.91%

Chart 2.11 *Source* Bitcoin Magazine Pro

It is essential to recognize that Strategy is effectively a high-beta instrument tied to Bitcoin. For better or worse, this correlation amplifies both gains and losses. If Bitcoin were to experience a sharp drop, Strategy's correction would be even more pronounced.

An investor in MSTR must be aware of and prepared for this high volatility, which means enduring significant drawdowns during Bitcoin's downturns and enjoying substantial gains during bullish rallies.

So, is Strategy worth considering as part of a diversified crypto-forward investment portfolio? The answer is yes, but you must remember that it's essentially like being leveraged in Bitcoin. Therefore, you need to be an investor who can withstand those swings and high volatility and has a long-term investment horizon.

How long will this strategy remain profitable?

In principle, as long as there are investment funds and investors who cannot directly access spot Bitcoin or Bitcoin ETFs, this strategy will likely remain more profitable in the long term than investing directly in spot Bitcoin.

This is due to the indirect demand channeled through MSTR, its leverage effect, and its presence in regulated markets, making it an accessible proxy for Bitcoin exposure.

However, since July 2025, when Bitcoin reached its peak, we've seen the trend begin to shift. Bitcoin Treasuries Companies (BTCs) have been falling more sharply when Bitcoin declines (−34% vs −11%) but are not rising proportionally when Bitcoin goes up (+17% vs +13%), as shown in Chart 2.12:

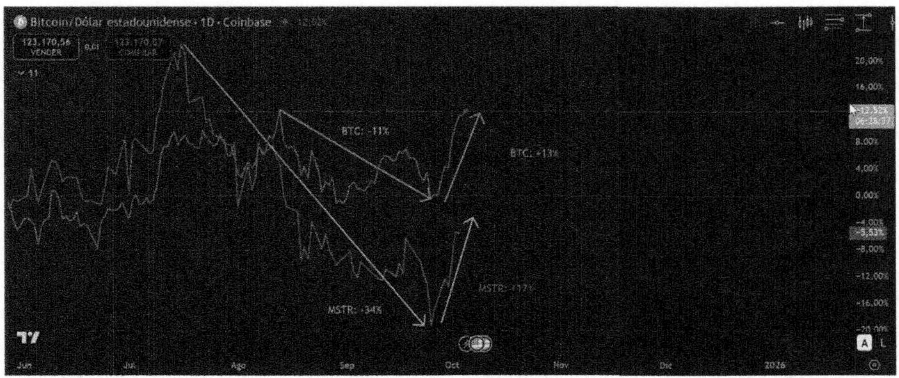

Chart 2.12   *Source* Tradingview (from July´25 to Oct´25)

2.8   Bitcoin Treasury Companies

I'm going to take a closer look at how Bitcoin Treasury Companies (BTCs) behave to provide a clearer understanding of their performance and their relationship with Bitcoin.

These types of companies raise liquidity to buy Bitcoin, MicroStrategy being a prime example. Retail investors often believe that such companies provide a way to gain leveraged exposure to Bitcoin, but in reality, they are volatility products.

BTCs are structured products, in other words, machines designed to sell optionality and recycle volatility.

As long as retail investors believe they are buying leveraged Bitcoin exposure, the stock trades above its book value (mNAV > 1). That premium enables accretive issuance, the issuance drives asset growth, and that growth in turn justifies the premium.

Leverage means using debt or derivatives to multiply exposure to the price of an asset. Optionality is different, instead of directly multiplying exposure, it creates asymmetric rights over price movements (as in an option).

Bitcoin Treasury Companies (BTCs), such as MicroStrategy or similar firms, do not leverage themselves directly through traditional debt. Instead, they create financial structures that introduce optionality into the market.

Here's how they work:

1. They issue hybrid instruments such as convertible bonds, warrants, or ATM (At-The-Market) equity.
2. Hedge funds subscribe to these instruments and hedge their positions (delta hedging): when they buy those bonds, they hedge by shorting the underlying shares. This hedging activity puts pressure on the stock price and increases realized volatility.
3. That pressure amplifies realized volatility.
4. With a more volatile stock, BTCs can issue new instruments at higher prices or with a premium.
5. They then use the capital raised to buy more Bitcoin.

The result is that BTCs sell optionality to hedge funds and recycle that volatility to increase their Bitcoin treasury without taking on linear leverage.

The effect of optionality and leverage is similar, meaning that if Bitcoin's price rises, the value of BTCs rises even more, not because they have taken on more direct debt, but because the market pays a premium for their wrapped crypto exposure.

For example, MicroStrategy issues convertible bonds (which include the option to convert into shares):

* Hedge funds buy them and short the stock to hedge, which increases volatility.
* MicroStrategy uses the proceeds from the issuance to buy more BTC.
* When the price rises, the stock surges (due to the effect of optionality).

There is no direct leverage; instead, there is implicit leverage through a derivative structure.

But what happens when volatility decreases?

Hedge funds stop trading, issuance dries up, and the accumulation of coins comes to a halt, the mNAV collapses, and retail investors are the ones who bear the losses.

When mNAV > 1, BTCs generate cash above the value of their underlying assets, but when mNAV < 1, the sale of new shares destroys value.

For example, Metaplanet's market capitalization fell from 7 billion (July 3, 2025) to 3.5 billion (October 2025), as shown in Chart 2.13:

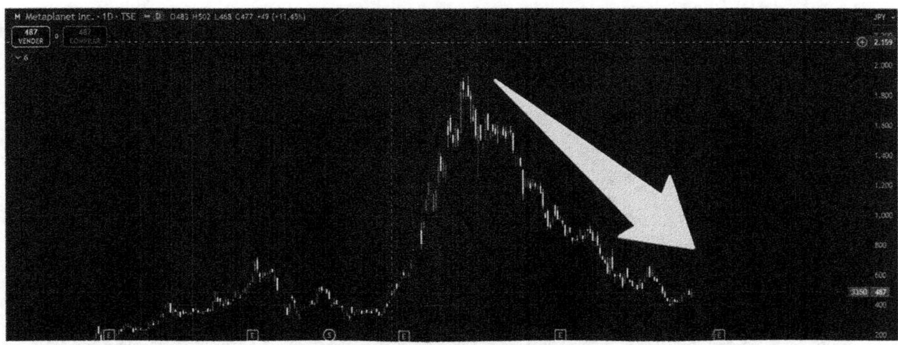

Chart 2.13   *Source* Tradingview (from July'25 to Oct'25)

Retail investors were the ones who bore the brunt of this decline, while hedge funds ended up profiting. BTCs are volatility factories, these structures only work when the mNAV is rising.

If you want exposure to Bitcoin, buy Bitcoin itself, not these kinds of companies.

Below, we can see how four of the main BTCs (MicroStrategy—pink, Metaplanet—purple, Capital B/Blockchain Group—red, and Semler Scientific—blue) have performed since Bitcoin (orange line) peaked in July 2025, showing declines ranging between 39% and 74%, as shown in Chart 2.14:

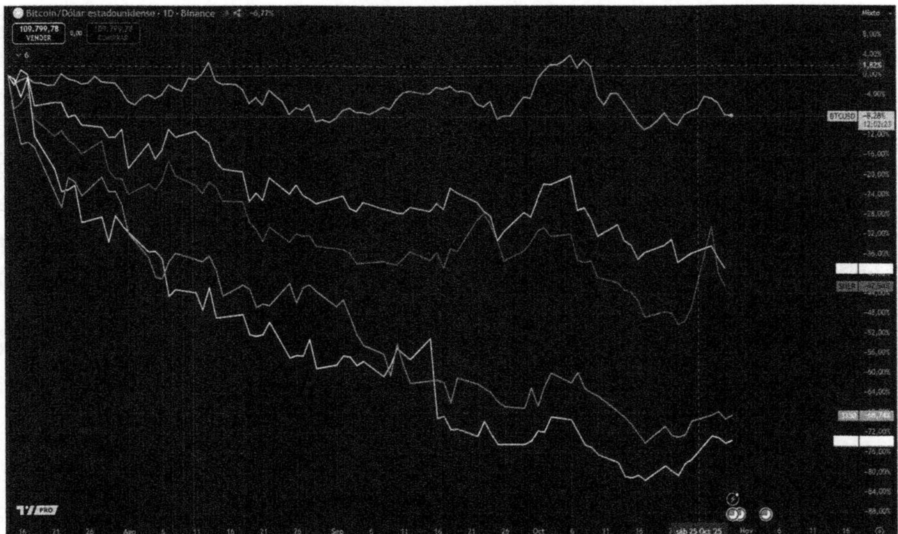

Chart 2.14   *Source* Tradingview (from July'25 to Otc'25)

In contrast to the poor performance of the treasury companies, Bitcoin mining companies have surged sharply.

If we look at how Bitcoin miners have performed compared to Bitcoin since mid-July, all of them have outperformed Bitcoin to varying degrees, the exact opposite of BTCs. Hive (blue line) rose by 141%, Hut (green line) by 134%, and Riot (red line) by 77%, while Bitcoin fell by more than 8%, as shown in Chart 2.15:

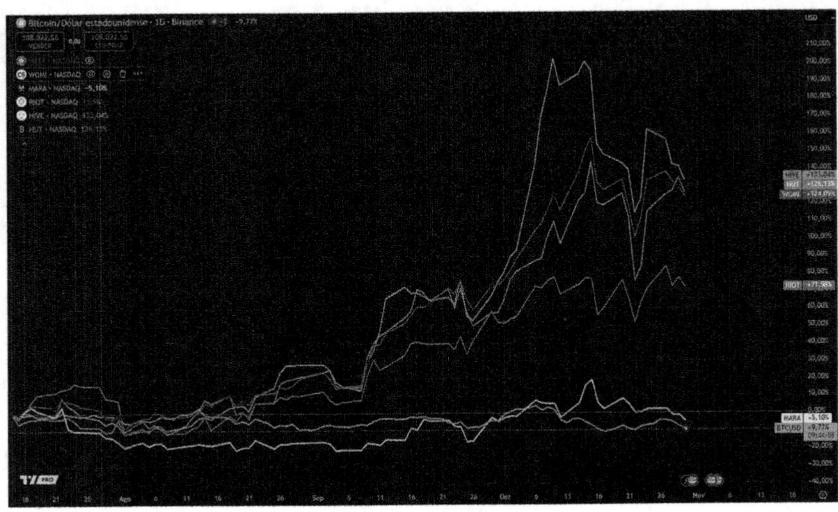

Chart 2.15 *Source* Tradingview (from July'25 to Oct'25)

The Bitcoin Mining ETF WGMI (purple line), which includes the main publicly traded mining companies, has risen by 123% since mid-July, outperforming Bitcoin by 75% since September.

Mining companies are experiencing one of their strongest periods of relative performance in years, which often signals that market momentum could continue.

One useful metric for understanding miners' behavior is the **Puell Multiple**, which tracks miners' revenues. When it rises sharply, it indicates that miners are generating disproportionately high income. In previous cycles, these periods have coincided with heightened market enthusiasm and Bitcoin's cyclical peaks.

Currently (Oct'25), this metric remains far from the overheating zone (red area), as shown in Chart 2.16, suggesting there is still room for Bitcoin to reach new cycle highs.

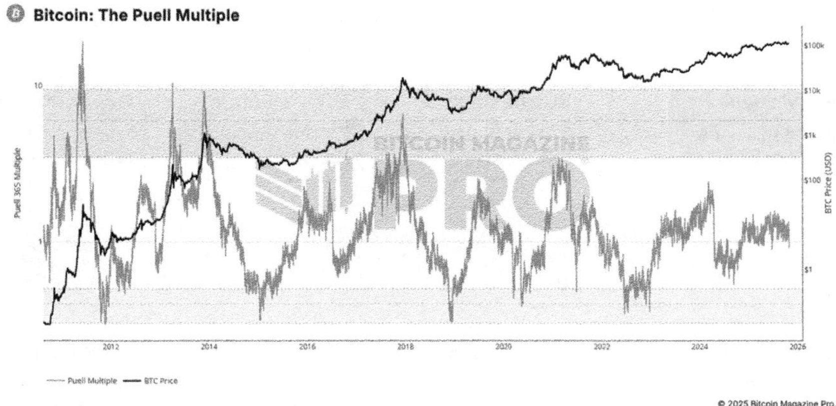

Chart 2.16   *Source* Bitcoin Magazine Pro Oct´25

2.9   Bitcoin Distribution

An important aspect to take into account is understanding the concentration of Bitcoin, since a very high concentration in the hands of a single entity could allow the market to be moved at will. For this reason, the Bitcoin ownership distribution is shown below, which is highly distributed and decentralized, with retail investors holding more than 60%, while the share of the remaining participants is below 10%.

The distribution of Bitcoin as of the end of August 2025 would be as follows, as shown in Fig. 2.1:

- Retail: 65.9%
- ETF: 7.8%
- Lost coins: 7.6%
- Corporate Treasuries: 6.2%
- Satoshi: 4.6%
- Governments: 1.5%
- Other Entities: 1.4%
- To Be Mined: 5.2%

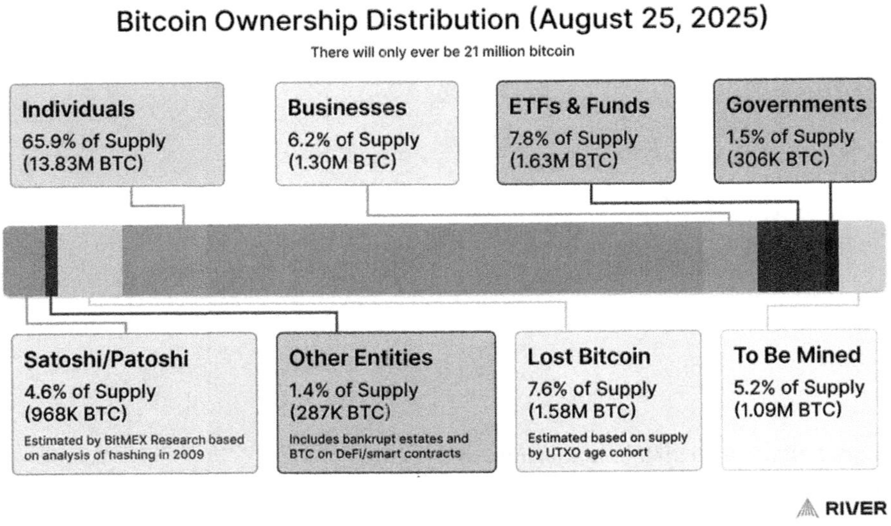

Bitcoin Ownership Distribution (August 25, 2025)

There will only ever be 21 million bitcoin

Individuals
65.9% of Supply
(13.83M BTC)

Businesses
6.2% of Supply
(1.30M BTC)

ETFs & Funds
7.8% of Supply
(1.63M BTC)

Governments
1.5% of Supply
(306K BTC)

Satoshi/Patoshi
4.6% of Supply
(968K BTC)
Estimated by BitMEX Research based on analysis of hashing in 2009

Other Entities
1.4% of Supply
(287K BTC)
Includes bankrupt estates and BTC on DeFi/smart contracts

Lost Bitcoin
7.6% of Supply
(1.58M BTC)
Estimated based on supply by UTXO age cohort

To Be Mined
5.2% of Supply
(1.09M BTC)

⛰ **RIVER**

Fig. 2.1 *Source* River, Bitcointreasuries.Net, Wublockchain (Aug'25)

Lastly, I'd like to share a reflection:

There is a common belief that Bitcoin would become inoperative in a blackout scenario (a widespread electricity outage affecting multiple countries simultaneously), such as the one that occurred in Europe on April 28, 2025.

I want to make it clear that Bitcoin will continue to operate. While we're used to thinking of Bitcoin as something "purely digital," the truth is that its underlying technology is designed to be resilient and adaptable, even in the face of such extreme situations.

How could we transmit and make Bitcoin payments in a blackout scenario?

1. **Via radio signals**: Bitcoin transactions can be transmitted using radio waves until they reach a node connected to the internet.
2. **Through text messages (SMS)**: Some services allow Bitcoin transactions to be sent via SMS. Examples include SMSPushTX or Machankura, especially in Africa.
3. **Using mesh networks**: These are small local networks between devices that communicate without needing the internet, passing the transaction from one node to another until it reaches its destination.

4. **Signing transactions offline**: You can sign a transaction on an offline device and physically transfer it (via USB drive or even on paper) to a connected device to broadcast it later.
5. **Using satellites**: Satellites are already broadcasting the Bitcoin time chain, enabling access to the network even in completely disconnected areas.

Of course, these methods are not commonly used in everyday life, but it's good to be aware of them in case of a global blackout or extreme scenario.

3

Basic Concepts

In this chapter, we will cover a series of definitions and concepts that are essential for understanding the cryptocurrency market.

3.1 What Is a Cryptocurrency?

* A **cryptocurrency** is a digital asset that uses cryptography to provide a secure payment system. It is not regulated or controlled by any institution and does not require transaction intermediaries.

3.2 Blockchain

What is Blockchain technology used for?

* Blockchain technology enables the secure transfer of digital data using sophisticated encryption through a chain of blocks, each containing information about individual transactions.

  It has **three key characteristics:**

  - **Secure:** Resistant to external attacks.
  - **Decentralized:** No single entity can alter the chain.
  - **Scalable:** Fast and adaptable to handle increasing demand.

© The Author(s), under exclusive license to Springer Nature Switzerland AG 2026
J. Pineda, *Investing in Crypto with Confidence,*
https://doi.org/10.1007/978-3-032-07834-6_3

3.3   Types of Networks

Within the world of cryptocurrencies, there are two types of networks: the main network and the secondary network.

- La **Relay-Chain** is the **main network**.
- La **Parachain** is a **secondary blockchain network** integrated into a main network or relay chain.

When it comes to validating (mining) transactions, there are primarily two methods:

- **PoW (Proof of Work)**: The miner needs powerful hardware to verify/validate transactions and receive a reward. This method consumes a lot of energy.

  - This validation method is:

    Secure
    Descentralized
    Slow
    Polluting, due to the high energy demand

- **PoS (Proof of Stake)**: The miner must own the cryptocurrency to validate the transaction. The coins are locked in staking, and the validator is rewarded in that currency.

  - This validation method is:

    Fast
    Descentralized
    Not as secure as PoW
    Much less polluting than PoW

A third method derived from PoS would be **Delegated Proof of Stake (DPoS)**. It is a consensus model based on democracy. Network users vote to elect delegates who validate the next block, to make the process more democratic.

The **Blockchain Trilemma** refers to the idea that no cryptocurrency can fully achieve all three of the following characteristics simultaneously:

- **Security** (resistance to hacking)
- **Scalability/Speed** (TPS—transactions per second)
- **Decentralization** (no single entity can control the network or manipulate the blockchain)

Any blockchain-based solution tends to fulfill **two of these three factors**, leaving the third in the background.

- Example: **Bitcoin** is **secure** and **decentralized**, but **slow**.

3.4   Types of Brokers

There are two main categories of brokers where cryptocurrencies can be traded: **centralized brokers (CEX)** and **decentralized brokers (DEX)**.

Centralized Exchanges (CEX) are online platforms that act as brokers, providing clients access and liquidity to trade in the crypto market.

In this model, the broker supplies the liquidity, and the cryptocurrencies are deposited with the broker. Examples include Binance, Coinbase, KuCoin, and Huobi. These platforms enforce anti-money laundering (AML) regulations and store private keys in users' wallets.

- Advantages:

  - High trading volume and high liquidity—greater than DEXs
  - Allows exchange between FIAT currencies (EUR, USD, GBP, etc.) and cryptocurrencies—not possible on most DEXs
  - Lower slippage compared to DEXs
  - User-friendly interfaces

- Disadvantages:

  - Higher risk of hacking compared to DEXs
  - Operates under government regulation (requires KYC)
  - High transaction fees

One crucial aspect to consider with this type of broker is Proof of Reserves:

Proof of Reserves verifies that the institution holds sufficient reserves to back all client balances. Ideally, this should be conducted by an independent external auditor.

It serves as a way to assess the solvency and liquidity of the institution.

Proof of Reserves' main goal is to enhance transparency and client trust. It assures users that the platform is liquid and solvent enough and that funds are readily accessible should clients withdraw them.

Proof of Reserves (PoR) involves several steps:

Please verify that the audited company owns the assets it claims to hold on behalf of its clients.

Please verify that the audited company's assets match the total client assets reflected in their balances.

Build a verification tool that allows clients to individually confirm that their account balances were included in the PoR.

The most common way to verify that client balances are fully backed is to construct a Merkle Tree data structure.

A Merkle Tree is a data structure built by repeatedly hashing a dataset.

The Merkle Tree allows the auditor to aggregate the account balance data of all clients into a single Merkle root without publicly exposing any individual client's account balance, thereby preserving privacy.

- **CURRENT STATUS OF PROOF OF RESERVES:**

Table 3.1 illustrates the situation of the proof of reserves of the main centralized brokers (CEX) and if they are audited or not:

Table 3.1 Current status of the main CEXs in relation to proof of reserves and whether they are audited or not

Exchange	Proof of reserves	Audit
Kraken	Yes	Yes
Coinbase	Yes	Yes
Gate.io	Yes	Yes
Binance	Yes	Yes
Crypto.com	Yes	Yes
Kucoin	Yes	Yes

Let me give you the example of **KuCoin**, where you can see in Table 3.2 that the reserve they hold is greater than the amount deposited by users.

Table 3.2 *Source* KuCoin

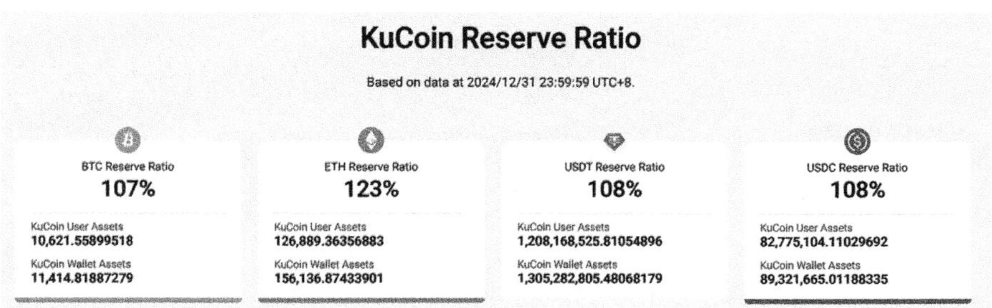

Decentralized Exchanges (DEX) are digital platforms that operate similarly to CEXs, but unlike centralized exchanges, a smart contract sits at the core of the service. This essentially eliminates intermediaries, making them more secure and transparent.

* In this case, users provide the liquidity, and the coins are deposited directly into their wallets. Examples include PancakeSwap (BSC network), Uniswap (Ethereum network), and SushiSwap (Polygon network).
* The AMM (Automated Market Maker) sets the price of assets. Users supply liquidity through liquidity pools; the tokens are stored in their personal wallets, not on the platform.

* **Advantages**:

    – More secure and transparent than CEXs
    – Not regulated (No KYC required)
    – More cryptocurrencies listed compared to CEXs
    – Does not store wallet private keys
    – No intermediaries involved

* **Disadvantages**:

    – Lower trading volume and liquidity compared to CEXs
    – Cannot exchange FIAT currencies for cryptocurrencies
    – Higher slippage than on CEXs

How It Works An Automated Market Maker (AMM):

Figure 3.1 shows the flow of how AMM works.

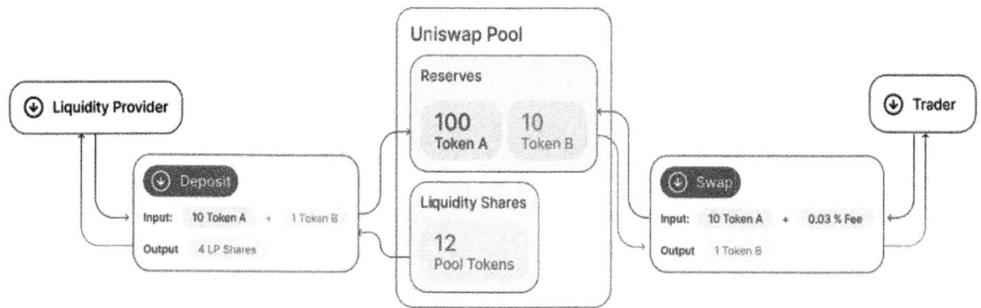

Fig. 3.1 *Source* Uniswap

An AMM (Automated Market Maker) is a type of decentralized exchange (DEX) protocol that relies on a mathematical formula to determine the price of assets. Instead of using an order book like traditional exchanges, asset prices are set by a pricing algorithm.

These protocols use smart contracts to define the price of tokens and to provide liquidity. The protocol aggregates liquidity into smart contracts.

Essentially, users are not trading against other participants, but rather against the liquidity locked in smart contracts.

These smart contracts are also known as liquidity pools.

For example, to become a liquidity provider for the ETH/USDT pair, you must deposit a specific amount of both assets into the pool.

How the Price is calculated:

AMMs use predefined mathematical equations to ensure that the ratio of assets in liquidity pools remains as balanced as possible and to eliminate price discrepancies between asset pools.

A standard formula that Uniswap and many other DEXs use is $x^*y = k$ to establish the mathematical relationship between the assets in the liquidity pool.

- **X** = quantity of one asset in the pool (e.g., ETH)
- **Y** = quantity of the other asset (e.g., USDT)
- **K** = **a** constant value that remains unchanged

Uniswap liquidity pools always maintain a relationship where the constant remains unchanged

Liquidity pools work as shown in Fig. 3.2:

When traders buy ETH, they add USDT to the pool and remove ETH. This decreases the amount of ETH in the pool, and therefore, its price increases to balance the equation and maintain the constant. On the other hand, adding USDT to the pool decreases the price of the different assets.

When a trader sells ETH, the opposite happens: the price of ETH falls as its quantity in the pool increases, and the price of USDT rises as its amount decreases.

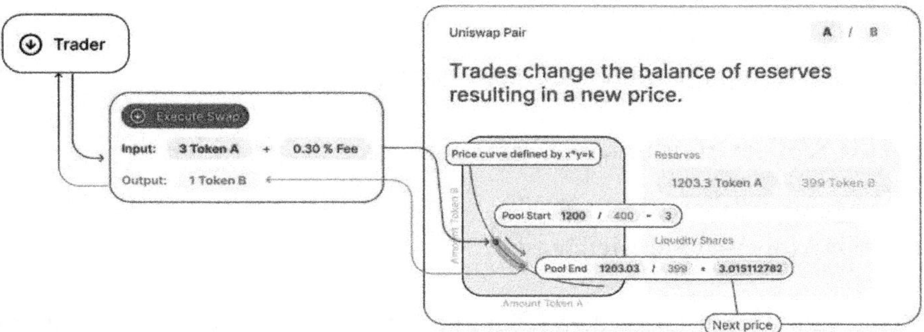

Fig. 3.2 *Source* Uniswap

Price Discrepancies:

When large orders are executed on AMMs and a significant amount of a token is added to or removed from a pool, substantial discrepancies can arise between the asset's pool price and its market price.

For example, the market price of ETH might be $3000, while in the pool it's $2850 due to a large amount of ETH being added to the pool.

These imbalances are corrected by arbitrage traders, who seek out such market inefficiencies to profit, thereby bringing the pool price back in line with the market price.

3.5   Types of Wallets

What is a Wallet?

The software application allows you to send, receive, and store cryptocurrencies. You access it using a set of seed keys (seed phrases).

Satoshi originally referred to a wallet as a single Bitcoin address. Years later, a wallet became known as a collection of addresses, keys, and the software that manages them.

There are two types of wallets:

- **Cold Wallets**: store private keys and sign transactions offline

  - Trezorstore
  - Ledger Nano

If a cold wallet is stolen or destroyed, the private keys can be restored to a new wallet using the mnemonic seed backup.

- **Hot Wallets**: runs on an internet-connected device (riskier)

  - Mobile Wallets: Trust Wallet
  - Desktop Wallets: Metamask

If you want to transfer a token from one network to another, you can use the website **chainport.io**. The steps are as follows:

- Go to https://www.chainport.io
- Connect your wallet
- Select the token you want to transfer
- Choose the two networks (from and to)
- Enter the amount of the token to be transferred
- Approve, grant permission, and confirm
- Click the "Burn xxx on source network" button, confirm, and pay the fee
- Switch your wallet's network to the destination chain and pay the fee
- Click "Release xxx on destination network" and confirm
- Add the token to your wallet on the destination network

3.6   Market Knowledge Data

Regarding **market knowledge data**:

- PRICE = MARKET CAP/CIRCULATING SUPPLY
- MARKET CAP = PRICE × CIRCULATING SUPPLY
- FULLY DILUTED MARKET CAP = PRICE × MAXIMUM SUPPLY

- Circulating Supply: the number of coins currently circulating in the market.
- Total Supply: the number of coins created minus the coins that have been burned.
- Max Supply: the maximum number of coins that will ever exist over the cryptocurrency's lifetime.
- Fully Diluted Market Capitalization: the market cap if the maximum supply were already in circulation.
- Dominance: a metric representing an asset's market capitalization relative to the total market capitalization.

- **Why is Circulating Supply used to determine Market Capitalization instead of Total Supply?**

Coins locked, reserved, or otherwise unavailable for public trading cannot influence the market price and should not be allowed to impact market capitalization.

Using Circulating Supply is analogous to using free float when calculating the market capitalization of companies in traditional investing.

A website where you can view all market data and information for any cryptocurrency: http://www.coinmarketcap.com

- **Total Value Locked**: The total amount of assets locked within a specific protocol.

  - This is a key metric used to assess the overall health of the DeFi market and the yielding market (farming/staking).
  - TVL reflects how much value is currently being staked, lent, or used within DeFi protocols.
  - There are three main factors considered when calculating TVL:

    Current price of the locked assets
    Supply
    Maximum Supply

Websites where you can check the TVL of different coins: https://defillama.com/

3.7 Metrics

- **HASH RATE**: is the number of computational operations a miner—or the entire network of miners—can perform.

  - It refers to a cryptocurrency network's overall capacity or power to solve the cryptographic puzzles required by the Proof of Work (PoW) mechanism.
  - Currently, the Bitcoin network has a global hash rate of approximately 800 million PH/s, as shown in Chart 3.1.
  - The hash rate value indicates how secure a cryptocurrency's mining network is: **the higher the hash rate, the more secure the network.**

Bitcoin: Bitcoin Hashrate

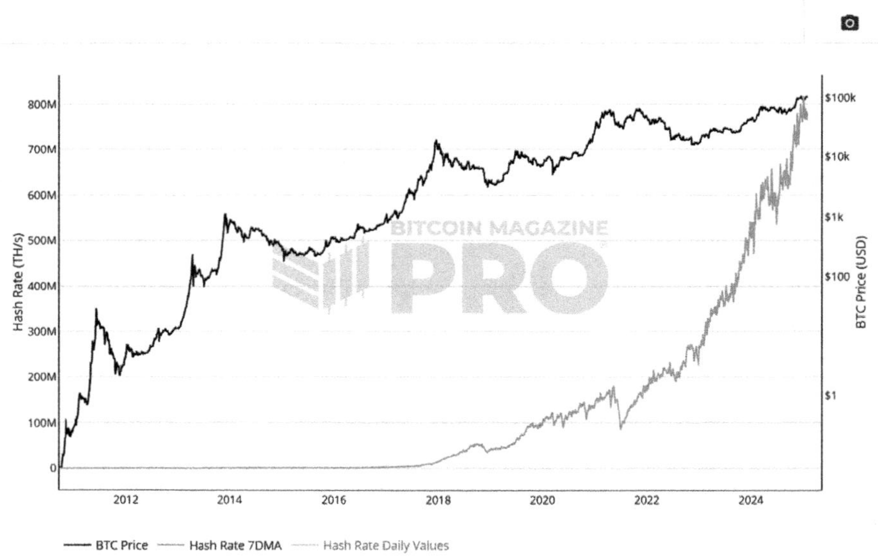

Chart 3.1 *Source* Bitcoin Magazine Pro

- **UNSPENT TRANSACTION OUTPUT(UTXO):**

  - It is the amount of cryptocurrency left over after a transaction, like the change you receive after making a purchase.
  - For example, you have 1 BTC and buy something worth 0.3 BTC. You send the entire 1 BTC to the recipient and receive 0.7 BTC as change. You now have a UTXO (Unspent Transaction Output) valued at 0.7 BTC.

3.8   What is a Fork?

- A fork is a divergence in software code.
- There are two types of forks:

  - Soft Fork is a tightening of the rules
  - Hard Fork: is a loosening of the rules

- The most common type of fork is a code fork. Someone copies a software, makes changes, and runs it separately from scratch. Examples of Bitcoin code forks would be Litecoin, Dogecoin, etc.

4

Ethereum

4.1 Definition

Ethereum is the second most important and largest cryptocurrency after Bitcoin.

If Bitcoin is considered digital gold, then Ethereum would be digital oil, as it facilitates economic activity. Through the Ethereum Virtual Machine (EVM), developers can deploy smart contract computer programs that run on the network.

Ethereum is designed as a general-purpose programmable blockchain that operates a virtual machine capable of executing code of arbitrary and unbounded complexity.

It is a decentralized, open-source blockchain platform with smart contract functionality.

The main innovation of Ethereum was the introduction of smart contracts.

Ethereum is a platform for building and launching software applications known as dApps (decentralized applications). It was the first smart contract platform.

4.2 What are Smart Contracts?

It is a self-executing contract with the terms of the agreement directly written into code. These contracts run on blockchain networks, ensuring that transactions are executed automatically when predetermined conditions are

© The Author(s), under exclusive license to Springer Nature Switzerland AG 2026
J. Pineda, *Investing in Crypto with Confidence*,
https://doi.org/10.1007/978-3-032-07834-6_4

met, without the need for intermediaries. Smart contracts can control digital assets and send or receive them.

The creation of the smart contract revolutionized the cryptocurrency market and introduced new forms of investment, such as farming and staking (which we will explain later).

It also enabled developers to create decentralized applications (dApps) in areas like DeFi, gaming, and more.

Smart Contract Platforms function as blockchain software protocols that allow global transfer of value without requiring permissions. These platforms form the basis for decentralized applications (dApps).

Smart Contract Platforms can be classified into three types:

1. **Layer 0**: is the infrastructure on which blockchains are built—layer 1. These are not built on top of other chains. Examples: Cosmos and Polkadot.
2. **Layer 1**: They have their structure, are independent, and can work without relying on other chains. Examples: Solana, Ethereum, Cardano.
3. **Layer 2** is built on top of Layer 1 and designed to solve the scaling problem of Layer 1. Examples: Arbitrum, Optimism, Polygon.

The Ethereum Virtual Machine is the **computation engine for Ethereum, managing the state of the blockchain and enabling smart contract functionality.**

4.3 Road Map

When Ethereum (ETH) was created, it used Proof of Work (PoW), but with the process known as **The Merge**, it transitioned **from Proof of Work (PoW) to Proof of Stake (PoS).**

* The different upgrade phases (Roadmap) proposed by Vitalik Buterin (the creator of Ethereum) for Ethereum are:

  - **The Merge**: upgrades relating to the switch from proof of work to proof of stake.
  - **The Surge**: upgrades related to scalability by rollups and data sharding
  - **The Scourge**: upgrades related to censorship resistance, decentralization, and protocol risks from MEV.
  - **The Verge**: upgrades related to verifying blocks more easily.
  - **The Purge**: upgrades related to reducing the computational costs of running nodes and simplifying the protocol.

  – **The Splurge**: other upgrades that don't fit well into the previous categories.

According to the Ethereum Foundation, they decided not to use this terminology because they wanted to adopt a simpler and more user-centric model.

Although they use more accessible, user-friendly language, the vision remains aligned with the one proposed by Vitalik.

As a result, they created new names for the phases within the upgrade stages originally designed by Vitalik.

Below, I will explain only the first two stages—The Merge and The Surge—as they are the most important and impactful.

The Merge began with the Beacon Chain phase, as shown in Fig. 4.1, which involved creating a separate network from Ethereum and a consensus layer where ETH staking was possible.

In PoW networks, staking is not possible.

They burned ETH on the PoW chain and then minted it on the Beacon Chain so it could be staked.

Technically, you weren't truly staking at the blockchain level, as it was more of a bridge or simulation to prepare for the transition.

It ends the PoW chain, which is merged with the PoS chain (Beacon Chain); from that point forward, only the PoS chain exists.

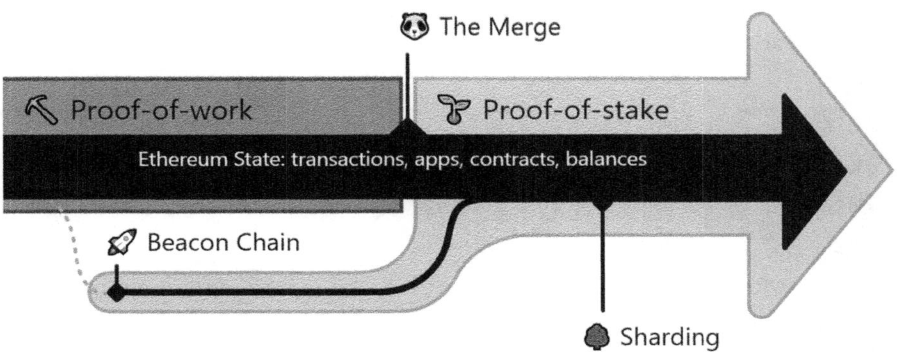

Fig. 4.1 *Source* https://www.ethereum.org

The Beacon Chain, which previously couldn't process transactions or store smart contracts, has now become fully functional, enabling both.

The Merge is the most critical point in the roadmap because it merges the PoW and PoS chains.

The Merge's sole objective is to transition Ethereum from Proof of Work to Proof of Stake, primarily to reduce energy consumption.

It does not significantly improve scalability (it is only about 10% faster) or reduce fees. Those improvements will come with the Sharding update.

To be able to withdraw your staked ETH, you'll need to wait for an update that comes after The Merge.

If you're an ETH holder, a PoS network is better for you than a PoW one, because in a PoW network, the real stakeholders—that is, those who benefit from the network—are the miners, since they earn money every time a transaction is made on Ethereum. On the other hand, in a PoS network, the people who stand to gain more as the network is used are ETH holders.

When you stake, you're delegating your crypto to a validator node so it can validate more transactions, and you earn network fees in return.

The Merge was Ethereum's most significant upgrade. It reduced the energy consumption required to secure Ethereum by 99.95%, creating a more secure network for a much smaller carbon cost. Ethereum is now a low-carbon blockchain while boosting its security and scalability. Chart 4.1 illustrates annual energy consumption, and Ethereum PoS consumes less than gold mining, Google, Netflix, etc.

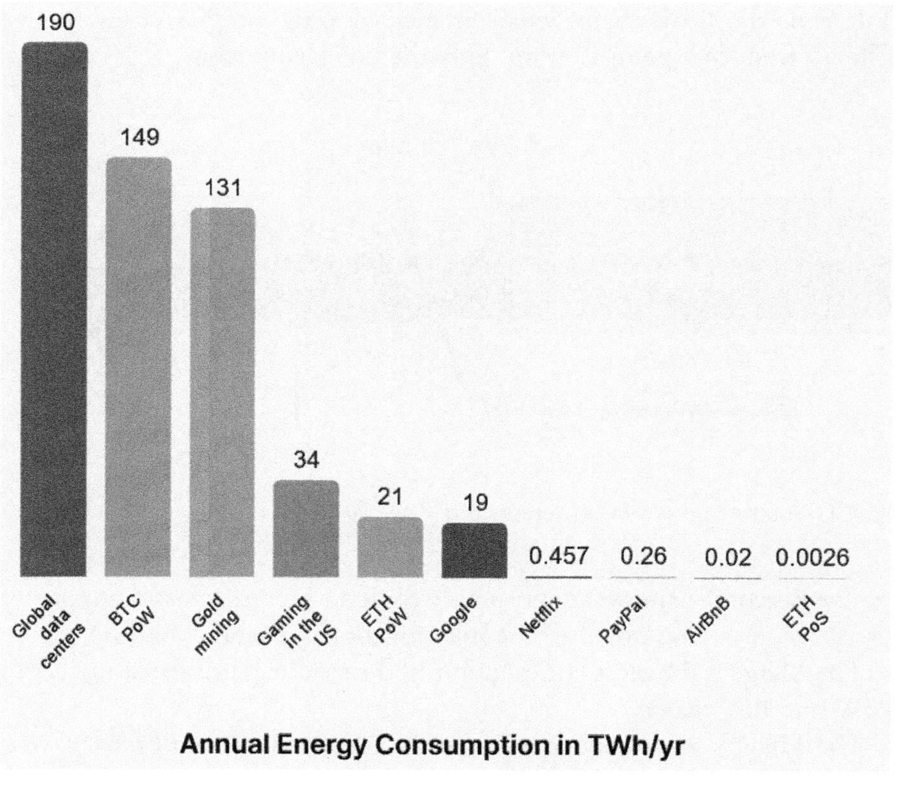

Chart 4.1   *Source* https://www.ethereum.org

- **The Surge:**

This stage will change everything, and it's the one Ethereum is currently in. It brings low fees and infinite scalability to the Ethereum ecosystem. Data storage will be redistributed across multiple networks to make the ETH network much more scalable (faster transactions).

The problem with blockchain is data storage. Currently, there is only Layer 1 (Ethereum). Still, rollups like Optimism, Arbitrum, etc. (Layer 2) are being created so that this storage can be redistributed among them, rather than handled solely by Layer 1. This reduces the load and prevents Layer 1 from becoming slower over time.

Rollups will group multiple transactions into a package and send them to Ethereum. Once this phase is completed, the ETH network will be capable of handling 100,000 transactions per second (TPS), but this will take years to implement fully. Figure 4.2 illustrates the process to achieve 100,000 transactions per second using rollups.

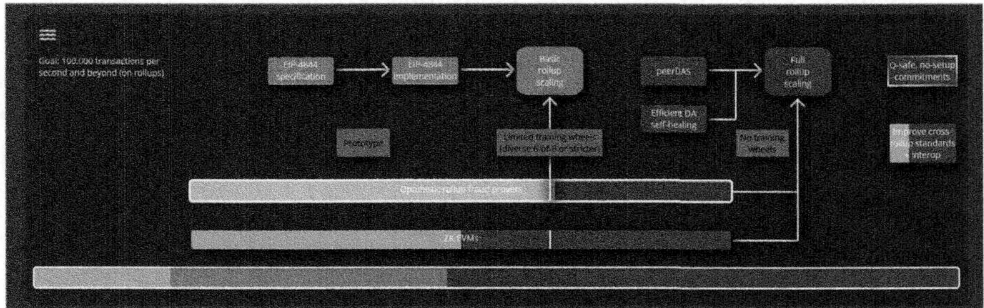

Fig. 4.2 *Source* https://ethroadmap.com/

Within this stage, we have the following phases. Here is the expected timeline based on recent updates and the roadmap:

- Q1 2024—**Dencun** Upgrade (Proto-Danksharding Launch):
- Introduced Proto-Danksharding (EIP-4844) to improve data availability through data "blobs." Lays the foundation for further rollup scaling.
- Ethereum's Layer 2 solutions leverage improved data availability for faster and cheaper transactions.
- 2024–2025—Rollup Expansion and Maturing Proof Systems. Rollups like Arbitrum, Optimism, and zkSync will implement updates to enhance scalability.

- New cryptographic proofs (e.g., SNARKs) will improve the trustworthiness of rollups.
- Data Availability Sampling (DAS) systems, such as PeerDAS and 2D DAS, will expand to support higher transaction throughput.
- 2025 Pectra: It is an Ethereum protocol upgrade that brings new functionality and changes to the Ethereum network. Following Dencun, this is another major upgrade to both the execution and consensus layer of Ethereum. The shortened name Pectra is a combination of Prague, the execution layer hard fork, and Electra on the consensus layer fork, both of which will be activated at the same time. Together, they bring several improvements to the Ethereum core protocol, such as how it works under the hood and how we can use it. There are many benefits to Ethereum users, developers, and validators.

- Pectra will be divided into two phases:

  - **Part one (early 2025)**: The first phase will focus on immediate improvements like account abstraction and validator upgrades. These changes will make Ethereum more user-friendly and improve staking rewards.
  - **Part two (expected in 2026)**: The second part will bring in more technical improvements, like the EVM Object Format (EOF), which will make smart contracts more efficient, and PeerDAS, which will supercharge Layer 2 scalability.

- The major improvements that Pectra brings are:

  - Account abstraction
  - Smart contract efficiency
  - Improvements for validators
  - Scalability improvement (Verkle trees)
  - PeerDAS (Peer Data Availability Sampling)

- These significant improvements will result in enhanced scalability, a restructured staking system with higher limits and more flexible withdrawals, a better user experience, improved developer tools, and reduced gas fees associated with network congestion.
- Ultimately, Pectra focuses on validator efficiency, data availability, and user experience, while preparing Ethereum for future innovations such as Verkle Trees and stateless clients.

- 2026 Fusaka: By late 2025 or early 2026, the Fusaka hard fork is expected to arrive. This Ethereum hard fork aims to increase the mainnet gas limit by 4x. The proposal (EIP-9678) would raise the current limit from 36 million to 150 million gas per block.
- The goal is to scale the base layer without introducing new features, only by optimizing the current protocol limits.
- Raising the gas limit brings more pressure, increased operational complexity, greater demands on nodes, and a risk of bugs if not adequately tested. The key question is how far Layer 1 execution can be scaled without compromising sustainability.
- Ethereum core developers have decided to remove the EVM Object Format (EOF) from the upcoming Fusaka network upgrade, following a decision made during the ACDT 34 developer call. This move reflects a shift in consensus regarding the direction of improvements to the Ethereum Virtual Machine (EVM).
- Several key factors drove the decision to exclude EOF from Fusaka:

  - Risks to the upgrade timeline.
  - Technical uncertainties related to the impact of the Option D variant of EOF.
  - Considerations regarding prioritization processes within Ethereum's development roadmap.

With this decision, the team will focus on other critical improvements, such as PeerDAS—a technology designed to enhance Ethereum's scalability. Despite EOF's exclusion from Fusaka, its advocates may still propose it for future upgrades, with the next likely candidate being the Glamsterdam hard fork. This decision has been documented in proposal EIP-7607 and reflects the ongoing discussions within the Ethereum community on how to balance addressing technical debt with expanding the network's capacity.

This timeline reflects Ethereum's phased approach, ensuring stability and smooth adoption throughout the transition. Each step in The Surge builds on the previous one, aiming for a blockchain to support global-scale applications while maintaining decentralization and security.

Forks are when major technical upgrades or changes need to be made to the network. They typically stem from Ethereum Improvement Proposals (EIPs) and change the protocol's "rules."

When **upgrades** are needed in traditional, centrally controlled software, the company publishes a new version for the end-user. Blockchains work differently because there is no central ownership.

To understand the names of the different **upgrades,** I will show you in the following tables:

In Table 4.1, we have the **execution** upgrades:

Table 4.1 *Source* https://www.ethereum.org

Upgrade name	Devcon year	Devcon number	Upgrade date
Berlin	2014	0	Apr 15, 2021
London	2015	I	Aug 5, 2021
Shanghai	2016	II	Apr 12, 2023
Cancun	2017	III	Mar 13, 2024
Prague	2018	IV	TBD-Next
Osaka	2019	V	TBD
Bogota	2022	VI	TBD

Figure 4.3 shows a sequence of **execution** layer hard forks for Ethereum:

Fig. 4.3 *Source* https://www.ethroadmap.com

In Table 4.2, we have **Consensus** upgrades:

Table 4.2 *Source* https://www.ethereum.org

Upgrade Name	Upgrade Date
Beacon Chain genesis	Dec 1, 2020
Altair ↗	Oct 27, 2021
Bellatrix ↗	Sep 6, 2022
Capella ↗	Apr 12, 2023
Deneb ↗	Mar 13, 2024
Electra ↗	TBD - Next
Fulu ↗	TBD

And in Fig. 4.4, we see a sequence of **consensus** layer hard forks for Ethereum:

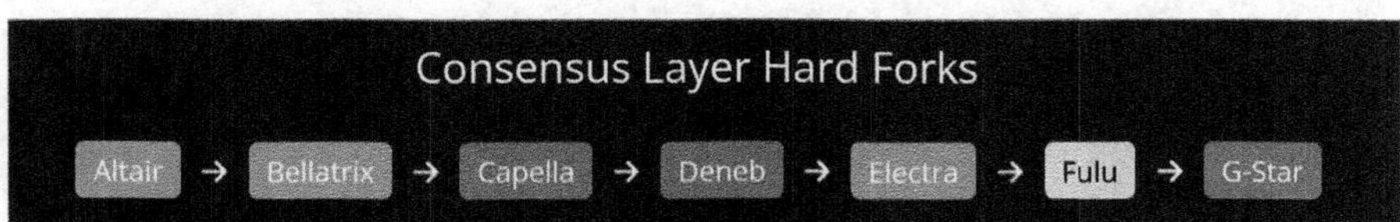

Fig. 4.4   *Source* https://www.ethroadmap.com

Table 4.3 illustrates the combined name of the upgrade:

Table 4.3 *Source* https://www.ethereum.org

Execution upgrade	Consensus upgrade	Short name
Shanghai	Capello	"Shapella"
Cancun	Deneb	"Dencun"
Prague	Electra	"Pectra"
Osaka	Fulu	"Fusaka"

4.4   Ethereum 2.0 vs Polkadot

Ethereum is following a development path somewhat similar to Polkadot's, so I will make a comparison to highlight the similarities and differences in their roadmaps:

Ethereum's rollups are comparable to Polkadot's parachains, but rollups lack interoperability—something parachains on DOT already have.

ETH is adopting DOT's technology, but DOT is far ahead regarding technical implementation; however, ETH benefits from its massive community. There will be a race to see who can achieve a network with this advanced technology while attracting a large user base.

4.5   Rollups

All ETH scalability solutions currently being developed are listed on the website https://www.l2beat.com as shown in Table 4.4.

Table 4.4 *Source* https://www.l2beat.com - August 2025

#	NAME	RISKS	PROOF SYSTEM	STAGE	TOTAL VALUE SECURED	PAST DAY UOPS
1	Arbitrum One		Optimistic BoLD	STAGE 1	$19.43B ▲0.35%	32.05 ▲0.53%
2	Base Chain		Optimistic OP OPFP	STAGE 1	$15.75B ▲3.41%	110.25 ▲2.76%
3	OP Mainnet		Optimistic OP OPFP	STAGE 1	$3.74B ▲1.43%	26.78 ▲121%
4	ZKsync Era		Validity Boojum	STAGE 0	$1.27B ▲1.49%	0.44 ▲28.9%
5	Linea		Validity Linea	STAGE 0	$1.03B ▲46.8%	2.24 ▲5.43%
6	Unichain		Optimistic OP OPFP	STAGE 1	$1.03B ▲0.50%	10.85 ▲17.2%
7	Starknet		Validity Stone	STAGE 1	$574.74M ▲1.43%	7.27 ▲19.4%
8	Katana		Validity SP1	STAGE 0	$466.10M ▼1.64%	0.62 ▲25.4%
9	Scroll		Validity OpenVM	STAGE 1	$283.07M ▼1.00%	1.15 ▲25.3%

There are two types of rollups:

- **Optimistic Rollups:** These assume all transactions are valid unless someone reports an error within a specific period. This approach keeps things fast, as it doesn't require every transaction to be verified immediately. *This method has the potential for quicker transaction processing.*

- **ZK-Rollups:** These assume all transactions are false until proven valid. They use advanced mathematics called zero-knowledge proofs to confirm that transactions are valid immediately. *This method provides instant and secure verification* and potentially enhances privacy and security.

One of the consequences Ethereum faces with the rise of Layer 2 solutions (rollups) is that, while they reduce congestion and increase the number of transactions processed per second, they also result in lower fee revenue. Much of the activity has shifted from Layer 1 to Layer 2, leading to fewer fees being collected on the base layer.

This trend became even more noticeable after Ethereum's Dencun upgrade in March 2024 drastically reduced fees per transaction on L2s.

Table 4.5 shows that the number of transactions has decreased, and Ethereum is now the sixth-ranked cryptocurrency in the Ethereum ecosystem.

Table 4.5 *Source* https://www.growthepie.com—August 2025

Chain	last 30d ↓	1 month	6 months	1 year
Base Chain	260.66M	+1.6%	+15%	+137%
Arbitrum One	79.89M	+12%	+58%	+51%
Celo	36.69M	+6.0%	-4.5%	+6.9%
OP Mainnet	34.71M	-6.8%	+32%	+146%
Gravity	14.64M	-22.4%	-39.5%	-46.8%
Ethereum Mainnet	48.90M	+16%	+34%	+53%

In terms of transaction cost, that means the median amount that a user pays to execute a transaction on a chain, which is measured in gas, Ethereum is in sixth place, as shown in Table 4.6.

Table 4.6 *Source* https://www.growthepie.com—August 2025

Average

Daily Monthly

Chain	last 30d↓	1 month	6 months	1 year
Arbitrum One	$0.0044	+10.6%	-26%	-32%
Base Chain	$0.0032	+42.3%	-36%	+21.6%
Gravity	$0.0019	-3.7%	-36%	+63.8%
Celo	$0.0011	-0.3%	+72.2%	+729.6%
OP Mainnet	$0.0004	-13%	-75%	-87%
Ethereum Mainnet	$0.2334	-26%	-41%	-63%

Table 4.7 illustrates the throughput, which means the amount of gas used per second, reflecting how much computational work the network is handling.

Table 4.7 *Source* https://www.growthepie.com—August 2025

Average

Daily Monthly

Chain	last 30d↓	1 month	6 months	1 year
Base Chain	24.96 Mgas/s	-0.3%	+2.0%	+152%
OP Mainnet	7.98 Mgas/s	-17.6%	+80%	+219%
Arbitrum One	5.25 Mgas/s	+3.0%	+36%	+19%
Celo	2.10 Mgas/s	+4.7%	-8.7%	+28%
Gravity	0.49 Mgas/s	-24.4%	-39.9%	-88.2%

In terms of active addresses, the two rollups with the highest numbers are Base and Arbitrum, as shown in Table 4.8:

Table 4.8 *Source* https://www.growthepie.com—August 2025

Distinct

Daily Monthly

Chain	last 30d ↓	1 month	6 months	1 year
Base Chain	23.02M	-12.7%	+20%	+78%
Arbitrum One	3.86M	-25.8%	-19.9%	+5.0%
OP Mainnet	1.40M	-32.1%	-6.4%	+30%
Gravity	1.36M	+34%	+37%	+9999%
Celo	1.27M	+3.1%	—	—

Table 4.9 illustrates the Total Value Secured, which means the sum of all assets secured by the chain, including canonically bridged, externally bridged, and natively issued tokens. Arbitrum and Base are the first two by a large margin:

Table 4.9 *Source* https://www.growthepie.com—August 2025

Average

Daily Monthly

Chain	last 30d ↓	1 month	6 months	1 year
Arbitrum One	$18.56B	+18%	+27%	+18%
Base Chain	$14.90B	+12%	+12%	+125%
OP Mainnet	$3.72B	+14%	-31.1%	-35.8%
Celo	$408.42M	+4.4%	—	—
Gravity	$69.28M	-0.8%	-33.5%	+6546%

As a rollup, Base processes transactions off the Ethereum main net (Layer 1), which benefits developers and customers by improving scalability and efficiency, increasing transaction speeds, and reducing gas fees.

Taking a closer look at Base, we can see in Chart 4.2 that in the last year (from Jul 24 to Aug 25), active addresses have almost doubled going from 750k to 1.3 M, transactions have more than doubled from 4 M to 9 M, revenue has increased from \$42k to \$179k, and the Total Value Secured (the sum of all funds secured by the chain) has grown almost 3x, rising from \$6.2B to \$16.3B.

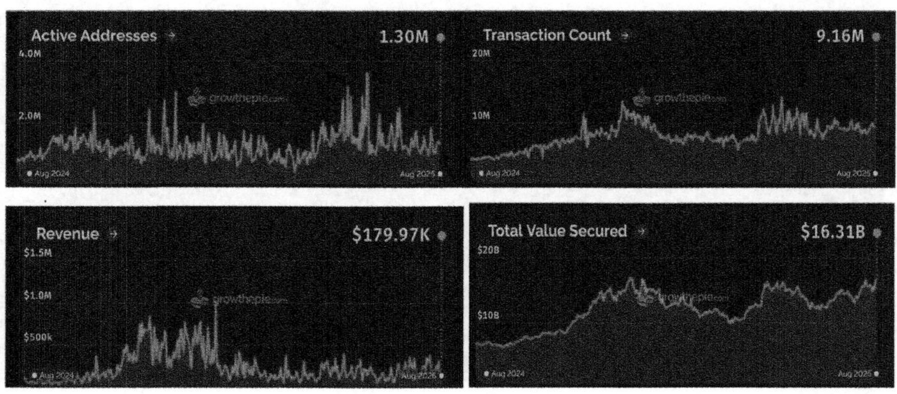

Chart 4.2   *Source* https://www.growthepie.com—From August 24 to August 2025

Examining the Ethereum ecosystem, the revenue generated, as shown in Chart 4.3, is \$42 million; however, more than 85% of the income comes from the Ethereum mainnet. This is because the token transfer fees on Ethereum Layer 1 (mainnet) are 0.33, while those on rollups Layer 2 are 0.007 as of August 2025.

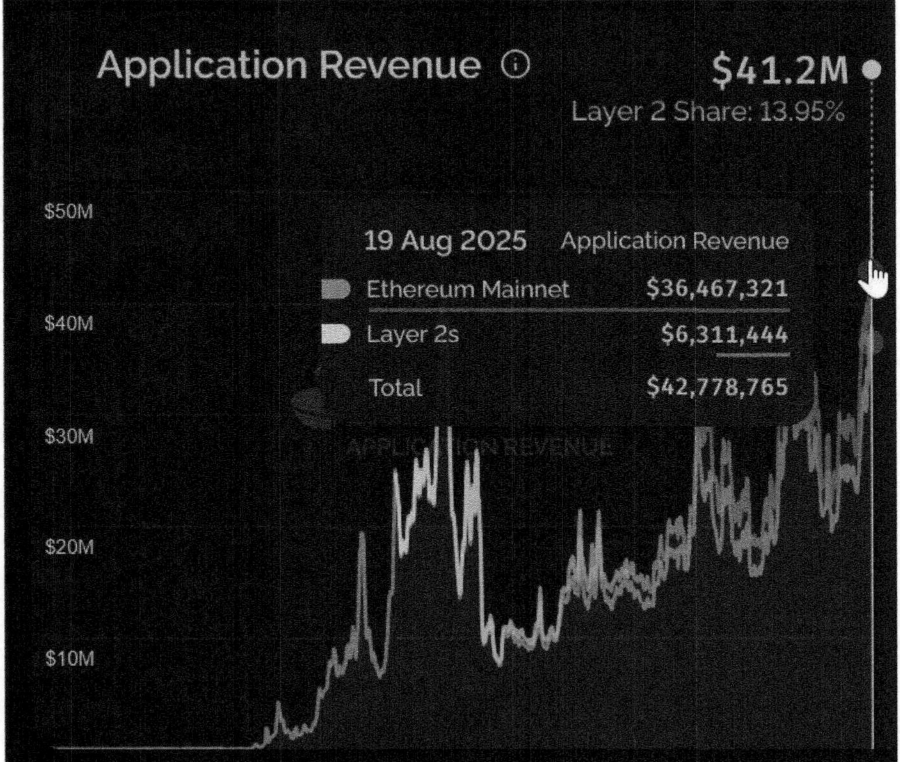

Chart 4.3 *Source* https://www.growthepie.com—August 2025

After the Merger and Ethereum's transition to Proof of Stake (PoS), the resulting asset was referred to as Ethereum 2.0. It was ultimately classified as a commodity rather than a security and, therefore, is not subject to SEC regulation.

Had it been classified as a security, cryptocurrency exchanges listing ETH and operating in U.S. markets would have automatically been dealing in an asset legally defined as a security. As a result, exchanges would have been forced to either delist Ethereum from their platforms or register as securities brokers with the SEC. This scenario would have been very damaging to ETH's value.

However, this previously negative outlook for cryptocurrencies has shifted entirely since Donald Trump came to power.

Another major event for Ethereum was the launch of its ETF, which took place in July 2023. It was the second cryptocurrency ETF to be launched, following Bitcoin's. Since its launch, performance has been mixed, with strong inflows and outflows until July'25, where entries increased exponentially, as we can see in Chart 4.4:

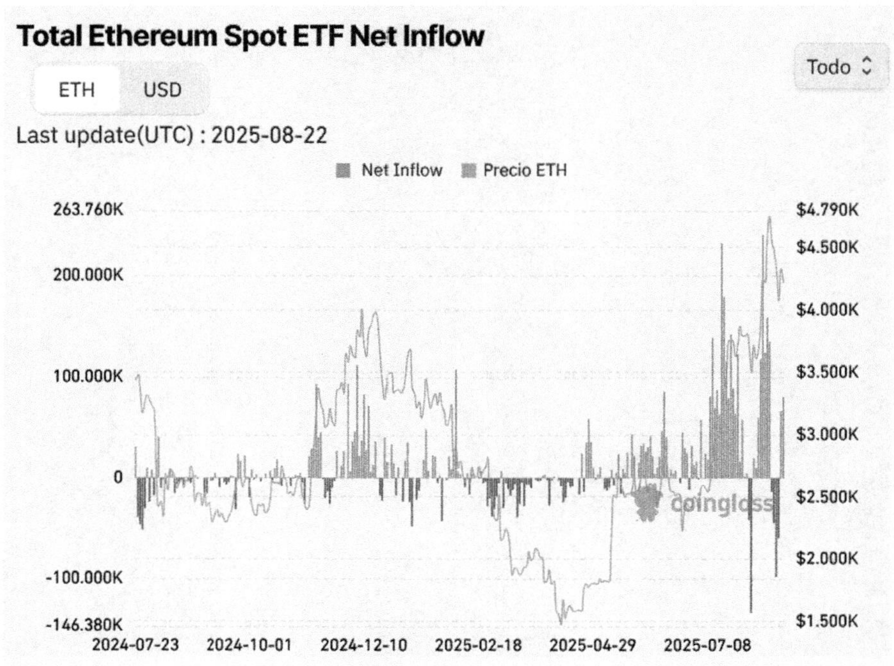

Chart 4.4   *Source* Coinglass—From Jul'23 to Aug'25

Lastly, I'd like to discuss different ways to evaluate altcoins. The easiest way to assess Smart Contract Platforms and DeFi dApps is through metrics. The simplest method is to compare a coin with its peers to determine whether it has high or low potential.

The demand-side metrics are indicators of how the platform is currently performing:

- Total Value Locked (TVL): total value of cryptoassets staked on a particular blockchain network via decentralized finance (DeFi) applications (dApps).
- Fees are an indicator of the growth of the platform
- Number of Developers
- Active Addresses: An increase in this indicator means a higher demand, and the expectation of an increase in its price should be higher.
- Market cap to TVL ratio

DeFiLlama is a website where you can check the TVL (Total Value Locked) of each cryptocurrency, as Table 4.10 illustrates, the first positions are Lido and Aave:

Table 4.10 *Source* https://defillama.com/ - August 2025

Name	Category	TVL	1d Change	7d Change	1m Change	Mcap/TVL
1 Lido 5 chains	Liquid Staking	$40,147b	-4.52%	+6.24%	+18.54%	0.03
2 Aave 17 chains	Lending	$39,44b	-4.08%	+7.47%	+17.53%	0.13
3 EigenLayer 1 chain	Restaking	$20,807b	-4.55%	+5.35%	+13.04%	0.02
4 Binance staked ETH 2 chains	Liquid Staking	$15,21b	-3.81%	+11.32%	+36.59%	
5 Ethena 1 chain		$12,227b	+0.40%	+6.36%	+64.99%	0.34

An essential aspect when evaluating a cryptocurrency is its tokenomics. This refers to the token economy structure, which outlines its distribution, utility, incentive mechanisms, token burning strategies, etc.

Token allocation shows how the token has been distributed among stakeholders, and this distribution will directly impact its growth. For example, if no portion is allocated to marketing and network development, it will be much harder for that token to grow.

5

Altcoins

5.1 What Is an Altcoin?

An alternative coin, or altcoin, is a cryptocurrency created after and separate from Bitcoin. The first altcoin was Ethereum, and many others have followed since then.

It's essential to ensure that the smart contract you select is correct and not a scam when trading on a DEX. Websites like CoinMarketCap or CoinGecko do not guarantee that the listed smart contracts are scam-free. Be cautious when trading on a DEX.

My recommendation is: if the contract doesn't appear directly in the DEX, don't trade that token. Even visiting the token's official website can be risky, as it might be fake. That's why the safest approach is always to trade on reputable CEXs.

Solana is the altcoin currently capturing market share and TVL from Ethereum, primarily due to the growing interest in launching meme coins on its network.

© The Author(s), under exclusive license to Springer Nature Switzerland AG 2026
J. Pineda, *Investing in Crypto with Confidence*,
https://doi.org/10.1007/978-3-032-07834-6_5

As we can see in Fig. 5.1, from Nov'24 to Feb'25, Solana has nearly four times the number of transactions compared to Ethereum and its rollups combined.

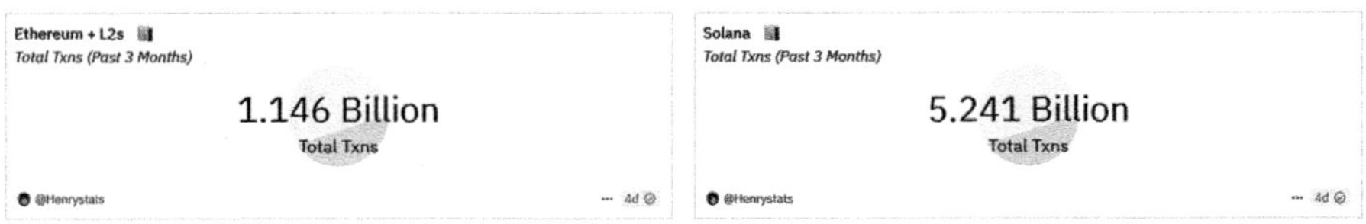

Fig. 5.1 *Source* Dune

In terms of active addresses in that period, as shown in Fig. 5.2, Solana has 5 times more than Ethereum.

Fig. 5.2 *Source* Dune—Feb´25

In terms of DEX volume, as shown in Fig. 5.3, Solana has four times more than Ethereum. While Ethereum still leads in market capitalization, Solana is winning in terms of activity. Its network is cheaper and faster for launching tokens than Ethereum's.

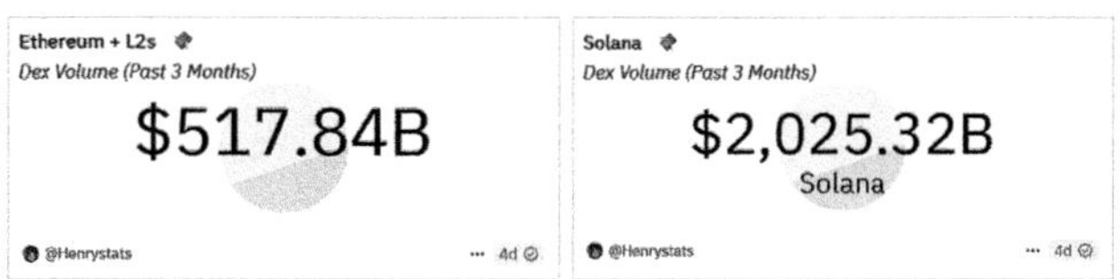

Fig. 5.3 *Source* Dune

Solana, as shown in Chart 5.1, generated more revenue in Q1 2025 than other L1 & L2 chains combined:

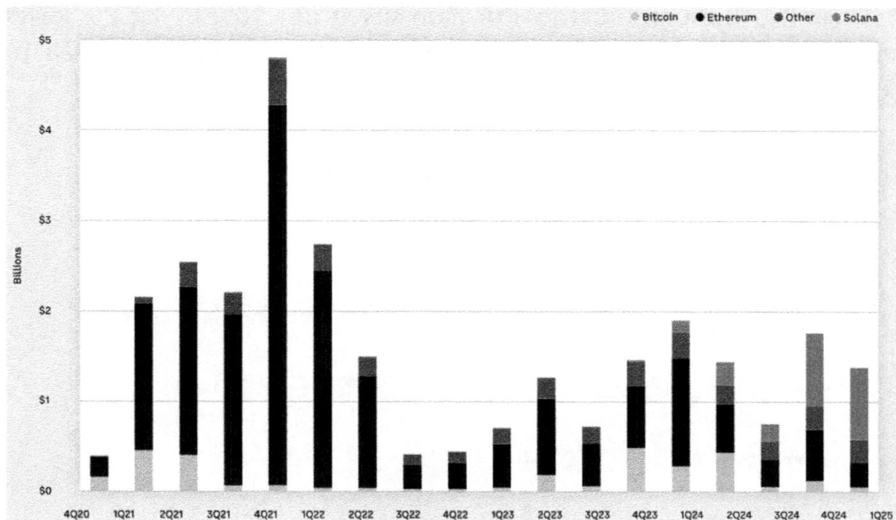

Chart 5.1   *Source* Coinbase

The most important metric isn't how much capital is locked, it's how actively that capital is used. By comparing 12-month DEX volume per $1 of TVL, we measure throughput per unit of capital. And here, as shown in Chart 5.2, Solana dominates. This level of efficiency underscores Solana's real strength: it's not just attracting capital, **it's putting it to work**. The result is outsized economic activity on a leaner capital base, positioning Solana as a chain designed for real usage thanks to its high throughput and low friction.

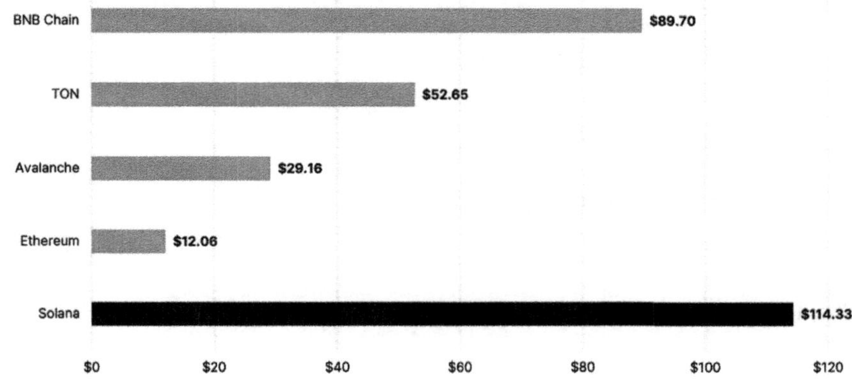

Chart 5.2   *Source* 21shares Tokenterminal May'25

Chart 5.3 Illustrates that its P/F ratio sits at just 165, by far the lowest among major Layer 1s. That compares to 708 for Ethereum, 1828 for Avalanche, and over 2000 for TON.

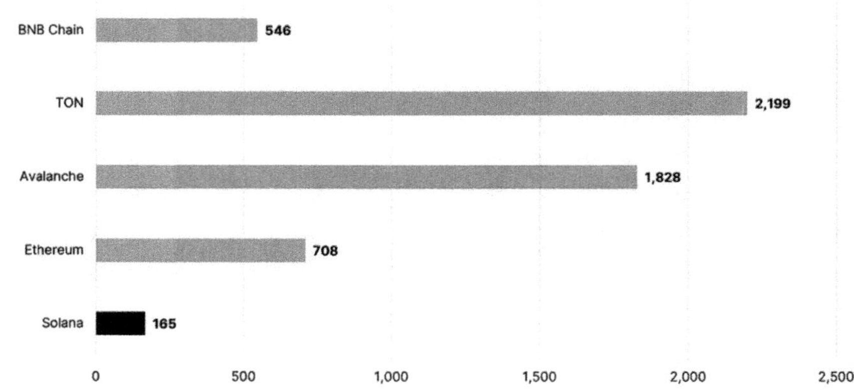

Chart 5.3 *Source* 21shares tokenterminal may´25

While, as shown in Chart 5.4, its P/S ratio, at 1906, is still well below peers like BNB Chain (5413) and TON (4398), and remains in line with Avalanche and Ethereum.

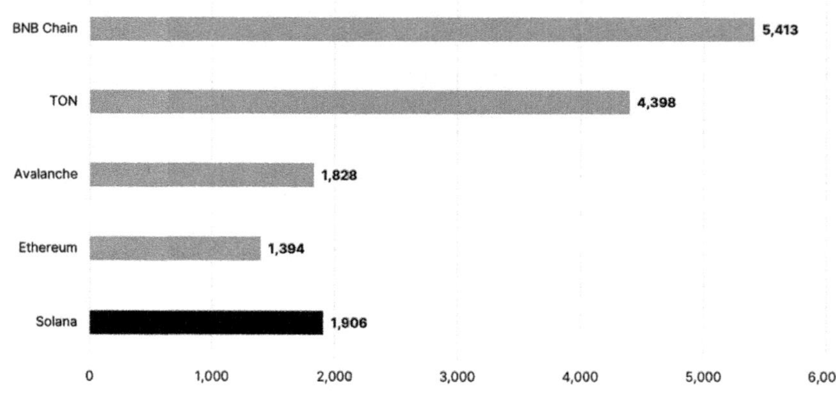

Chart 5.4 *Source* 21shares tokenterminal may´25

Looking at all these metrics, we can say that Solana is driving real economic activity, yet its network is still valued at a significant discount compared to its peers.

5.2 Key Aspects to Consider When Investing

When investing in altcoins, one crucial factor is the phase of the market cycle we are in. The main stages of the crypto cycle are Halving → Bull Run → Bear Market. However, within the Bull Run, there are additional internal phases.

From the bottom of the bear market to the start of the Bull Run, Bitcoin rose the most since it is the largest and most stable, and serves as a haven when the market is uncertain.

However, once the Bull Run begins, Bitcoin dominance tends to decrease—even if its price continues to rise, which indicates that the new money entering the market is starting to flow into other coins. That's when the following phases typically occur.

Figure 5.4 Shows the phases of the bull run. The first is the Bitcoin phase, which I just explained. Once Bitcoin's dominance starts to fall but its price keeps rising, capital typically shifts toward Ethereum, the second-largest cryptocurrency on the market. In this phase, Ethereum is outperforming Bitcoin.

The third phase is when other large-cap altcoins (such as Solana, XRP, etc.) begin to surge. When these coins experience substantial gains, that momentum spreads to the rest of the market, specifically to mid-cap and small-cap coins.

This final phase usually signals that the bull cycle is about to end, and the bear market is approaching. As a result, capital starts flowing back into Bitcoin as a safe haven.

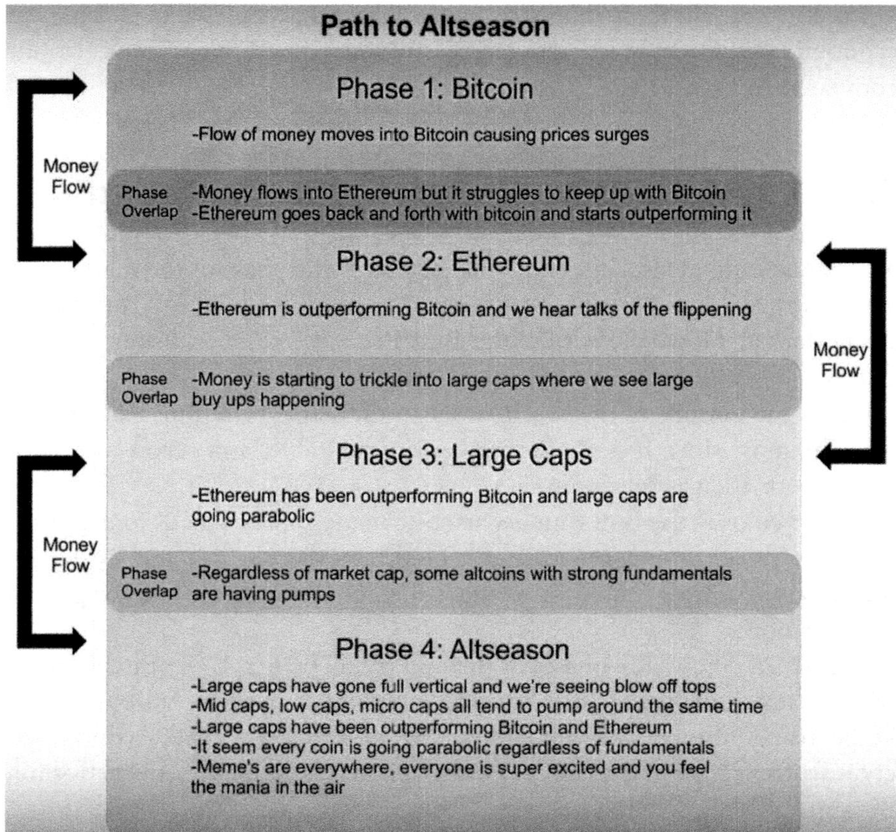

Fig. 5.4 Phases of capital rotation in crypto markets, from Bitcoin to Ethereum, then to large cap altcoins and ultimately to medium and small altcoins

A handy index to follow is the Altcoin Season Index by CoinMarketCap, which helps you track whether altcoins are starting to rise strongly or are still far from doing so. The index includes a kind of "thermometer," if it goes above 75, it indicates that we are in Altseason, as shown in Fig. 5.5 and Chart 5.5.

This index provides real-time insights into whether the cryptocurrency market is currently in Altcoin Season. It is based on the performance of the top 100 altcoins relative to Bitcoin over the past 90 days, with detailed charts and metrics for tracking market trends and altcoin dominance.

The CoinMarketCap 100 Index (CMC100) measures the performance of the top 100 cryptocurrency projects by market capitalization, as ranked by CoinMarketCap. It excludes stablecoins (USDT) and tokens tied to other crypto assets (such as WBTC or stETH).

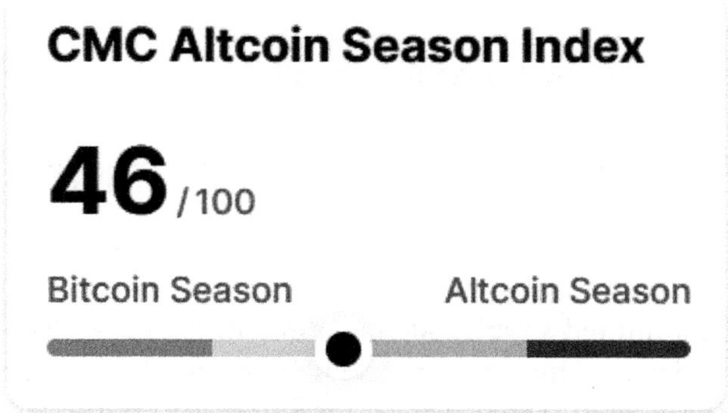

Fig. 5.5 *Source* Coinmarketcap

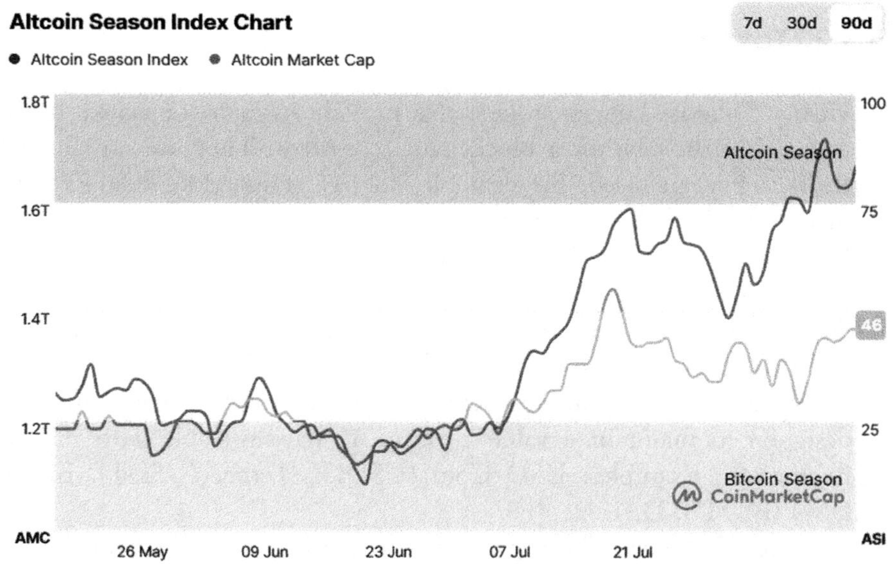

Chart 5.5 *Source* Coinmarketcap

5.3   Tokenomics

It is a combination of two words: **Token** and **Economics**. It refers to the economic model that defines how a cryptocurrency or token functions within its ecosystem. It is the set of rules that determines the supply, demand, distribution, utility, and incentives of a cryptocurrency or blockchain token.

It's like the financial system or financial infrastructure behind the token.

5.3.1 Token Supply

There are two key concepts regarding supply:

- Circulating Supply: This refers to the number of tokens currently in circulation and available for trading.
- Max Supply: This is the total number of tokens that will ever exist.

If a token has a limited supply, such as Bitcoin, it can be deflationary. This means that as demand increases, the value may rise due to scarcity.

On the other hand, tokens with an unlimited supply may experience inflation, which could erode their value over time.

This aspect is essential to understanding the token price.

5.3.2 Token Types

- **Utility Tokens**: They are tokens that provide access to a product, service, or functionality within a blockchain ecosystem. They are not financial assets. They are used, for example, to pay transaction fees. Examples include BNB, MATIC, and others.
- **Governance Tokens**: They grant voting rights on protocol decisions. Examples: Maker Dao, AAve, and others.
- **Security Tokens**: They are digital representations of traditional financial assets (such as stocks, bonds, or real estate) on a blockchain.
- **Stablecoins**: are a coin representing a fiat currency, usually the USD, designed to maintain a value close to 1, staying stable with minimal fluctuation. Examples: USD Coin (USDC), Tether (USDT), Binance USD (BUSD), DAI, etc.
- **Payment Tokens**: Whose primary purpose is to serve as a medium of exchange, that is, as digital money. Examples: Bitcoin, Litecoin.
- **NFT**: They are non-fungible tokens, meaning they are not divisible. They represent intellectual property that is tamper-proof, transparent, and immutable.
- **Reward/Incentive Tokens**: These are designed to compensate users for participating in a blockchain ecosystem. These tokens are typically distributed as rewards for actions such as staking, providing liquidity, and validating transactions. Examples: CAKE, UNI.

A token with a strong utility often attracts more users and increases demand, which can positively affect its value.

5.3.3 Token Distribution

How tokens are distributed is another crucial part of tokenomics.

It refers to how a cryptocurrency or token is allocated among different stakeholders when it is launched.

An example of a Token distribution could be:

- Team and Founders
- Investors
- Community Rewards
- Advisors
- Treasury
- Liquidity
- Airdrops

Some tokens are distributed through mining or staking, while others are sold through Initial Coin Offerings (ICO) or Initial DEX Offerings (IDO).

It is essential to understand how tokens are allocated to early investors, the team, and the community.

An unfair distribution can lead to centralization, where a few wallets control the majority of the supply, potentially leading to market manipulation.

5.3.4 Incentives and Burn Mechanisms

Many projects implement incentive structures to encourage long-term holding or participation in their ecosystems:

- Staking rewards are given to users who lock their tokens, reducing the circulating supply.
- Participating in governance.

Some projects even have token burn mechanisms, where a portion of tokens is permanently removed from circulation, increasing scarcity. It is a deflationary tool.

5.3.5 Errors in Tokenomics

- **Unclear Utility**: Are launched without a well-defined purpose or real use case.
- **Poor Token distribution**: Concentration in the hands of a few token distributors.
- **Uncontrolled inflation**: Leads to price dilution and long-term devaluation.
- **Low circulating supply**: Token price may be artificially inflated, creating future dump risks.

Tokenomics is an essential part of any cryptocurrency project, and understanding it can give you a better idea of a project's potential for success.

Whether it is the supply, utility, or distribution, every aspect of tokenomics plays a role in determining a token's value.

6

Crypto Classification

Before explaining the classification of cryptocurrencies, let's understand what a token is.

6.1 Token

A token is any unit of account on a blockchain. The difference between a token and an altcoin is that an altcoin is essential to the functioning of its blockchain—the blockchain could not exist without it. In contrast, a token can disappear, and the blockchain would still operate normally.

6.2 Cryptocurrency Classifications

There are several types of cryptocurrency classifications.

Categories of crypto tokens:

* Cryptocurrencies are a digital form of money
* Utility tokens: used for a specific purpose
* Stablecoins: represent one unit of another fiat currency
* Security tokens: represent a security, like a company share

© The Author(s), under exclusive license to Springer Nature Switzerland AG 2026
J. Pineda, *Investing in Crypto with Confidence*,
https://doi.org/10.1007/978-3-032-07834-6_6

Blockchain Infrastructure Classification:

- Smart Contract Platforms: Ethereum, Solana, etc.
- Scaling Protocols: Polygon, Arbitrum, Optimism
- Interoperability protocols: Cosmos, Polkadot
- Bridges: Celer, etc. Source: Coingecko

Digital Assets categories:

- DeFi: Uniswap, Aave
- Exchange (CEX): Binance, OKX
- Infrastructure Applications: Chainlink, Filecoin
- Media and Entertainment (Metaverse): Decentraland, Axie Infinity
- Payments: Bitcoin cash, Litecoin, XRP
- Smart Contract Platforms: Ethereum, Polkadot, Solana
- Stablecoins: Tether, USDC
- Store of Value: Bitcoin. Source: Marketvector

6.3   Stablecoins

- **What is a stablecoin?**

Stablecoin: is a coin representing a fiat currency—usually the USD—designed to maintain a value close to 1, staying stable with minimal fluctuation. These coins provide excellent stability and liquidity to the market.

Examples: USD Coin (USDC), Terra USD (UST), Tether (USDT), Binance USD (BUSD), DAI, etc.

The difference lies in how the coin is backed by physical assets, other cryptocurrencies, or algorithms.

One of the cheapest networks for sending USDT is the TRC20 network, which charges only a 2.5 USDT fee per transfer.

Types of Stablecoins:

1. Stablecoins backed by real-world assets, such as U.S. dollars. Examples: USDT, BUSD, USDC

- Advantage: Backed by real assets.

- Disadvantages:

  - Regular audits are required to verify those reserves.
  - They are centralized, as private companies hold the equivalent fiat reserves for each token issued. This makes the reserves vulnerable to being frozen or targeted by governments.

2. Stablecoins backed by cryptocurrencies, usually ERC-20 tokens. Example: DAI (backed by Ether)

- DAI requires a minimum collateralization ratio of 150%, meaning the dollar value of ETH deposited into a smart contract must be at least 1.5 times greater than the amount of DAI borrowed. For example, to borrow $1000 in DAI, a user must lock up $1500 worth of Ether.
- Advantage: A reliable decentralized system (e.g., BTC and ETH).
- Disadvantage: Risk of price volatility.

3. Stablecoins backed by commodities. These stablecoins are pegged to the value of a physical asset, such as gold. They are not very common, and there are only a few of them. For example, PAX Gold.

- Advantage: In the case of gold, it offers stable value and serves as a hedge against inflation.
- Disadvantage: Risk of price volatility and the difficulty in quickly converting large amounts of those tokens into gold or fiat currency.

4. Algorithmic stablecoins: These use mathematical algorithms to maintain their value over time. The algorithm links two tokens to adjust the price based on supply and demand. Example: Terra (UST).

- Disadvantage: Not backed by a real asset, making it inherently risky.

The TERRA (UST) Case:

- UST was a hybrid between an algorithmic stablecoin and a crypto-backed stablecoin (LUNA).
- The value of UST was backed solely by LUNA.
- Its role was to act as a twin token to absorb any price deviations of the algorithmic stablecoin on the TerraUSD (UST) blockchain. It was intended that UST would maintain its peg to the U.S. dollar by minting and burning UST tokens to balance supply and demand and keep the price at $1.

How It Worked:

- When UST > 1: There was high demand for UST, so LUNA was burned to mint more UST. This increased the supply of UST, lowering its price and stabilizing it.
- When UST < 1: UST was burned to mint LUNA, increasing demand for UST and raising its price, bringing it back to $1.
- Anchor offered very high yields (20%) for depositing UST. When UST was created, LUNA was burned, which pushed LUNA's price higher.
- However, a critical point came when UST's market cap ($19 billion) exceeded LUNA's, meaning there was more UST in circulation than LUNA was backing.
- Terra began purchasing other cryptocurrencies like BTC to use them as collateral.
- However, the reserves did not grow proportionately to the amount of UST in circulation, and the system lost its stability.
- Neither LUNA's market cap nor the reserves in other assets were sufficient to back the volume of UST being issued.
- When Anchor Protocol reduced the interest rate for UST deposits from 20 to 15%, it triggered a massive sell-off of UST.
- The peg started to break as UST was sold off, and there wasn't enough liquidity.
- The first major sell-off happened on the DeFi platform Curve, where 85 million UST were exchanged for USDC. More sales followed, which ultimately broke the peg completely. LUNA was printed to support UST, but this led to a collapse in LUNA's value due to oversupply.
- As LUNA dropped and UST lost its peg to the USD, people sold UST, which led to the minting of even more LUNA, pushing its value down even further.
- More and more, LUNA was created to try to support UST's value. Confidence in LUNA was lost, triggering a sell-off of both LUNA and UST.
- As LUNA crashed, the Luna Foundation Guard (LFG)—which held reserves of 80,394 BTC and 39,914 BNB (worth around USD 3.193 billion)—sold nearly all of its BTC, leaving reserves of just $89 million. Selling BTC to buy UST triggered a drop in BTC's price, which then dragged down the entire crypto market.

For all these reasons, I recommend using stablecoins backed by real assets, such as USDT—but only if they undergo regular audits to ensure that real (USD) reserves properly back each token issued (Table 6.1).

Table 6.1 Shows the main stablecoins in the market

#	Name		Price	1h %	24h %	7d %	Market Cap ⓘ	Volume(24h) ⓘ	Circulating Supply ⓘ
4	Tether USDT	Buy	$0.9997	▲0.01%	▲0.00%	▼0.08%	$167,101,328,511	$169,277,589,894 169.30B	167.15B USDT
7	USDC USDC	Buy	$0.9997	▲0.01%	▼0.01%	▼0.02%	$67,296,476,019	$21,902,230,501 21.90B	67.31B USDC
15	Ethena USDe USDe	Buy	$1.00	▲0.01%	▲0.01%	▼0.07%	$12,097,023,683	$198,896,618 198.80M	12.09B USDe
25	Dai DAI	Buy	$0.9999	▲0.00%	▲0.00%	▼0.00%	$5,365,330,240	$21,069,504,565 21.06B	5.36B DAI
43	World Liberty Financial USD	USD1 Buy	$0.9996	▲0.01%	▼0.01%	▼0.01%	$2,454,930,102	$335,961,895 336.07M	2.45B USD1

Source CoinMarketCap.com—Aug´25

The two main stablecoins, as shown in Chart 6.1, are Tether (USDT) and USD Coin (USDC), both in terms of market cap and supply:

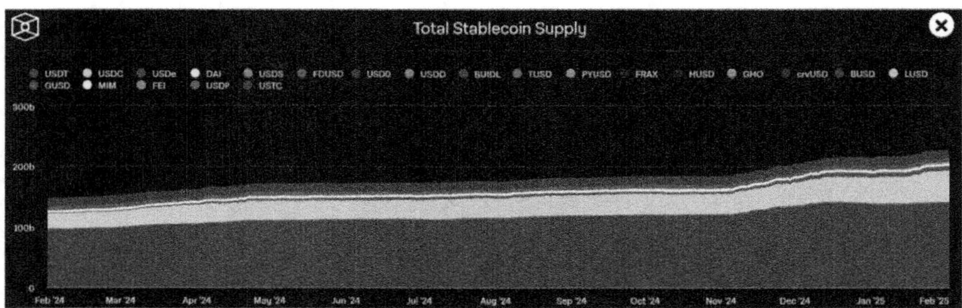

Chart 6.1   *Source* theblock.co

- USDT (Tether)—Issued by Tether Limited, USDT is a centralized stablecoin backed by fiat reserves. While widely used in trading and DeFi, it faces transparency concerns due to unclear reserve audits.
- USDC (USD Coin)—Managed by Circle and Coinbase, USDC offers full USD collateralization with regular audits, making it a highly trusted stablecoin for payments and DeFi.
- DAI—A decentralized stablecoin governed by MakerDAO, backed by crypto assets like ETH and USDC. Its smart contract-based stability makes it a preferred choice for DeFi applications.

Which stablecoin do you trust the most? In my opinion, USDT and USDC, they have fiat reserves. Table 6.2 shows a comparison between USDT, USDC and DAI.

Table 6.2 Comparison of major USD pegged stablecoins, comparing centralized and decentralized issuance models, collateral backing, regulatory transparency and adoption metrics.

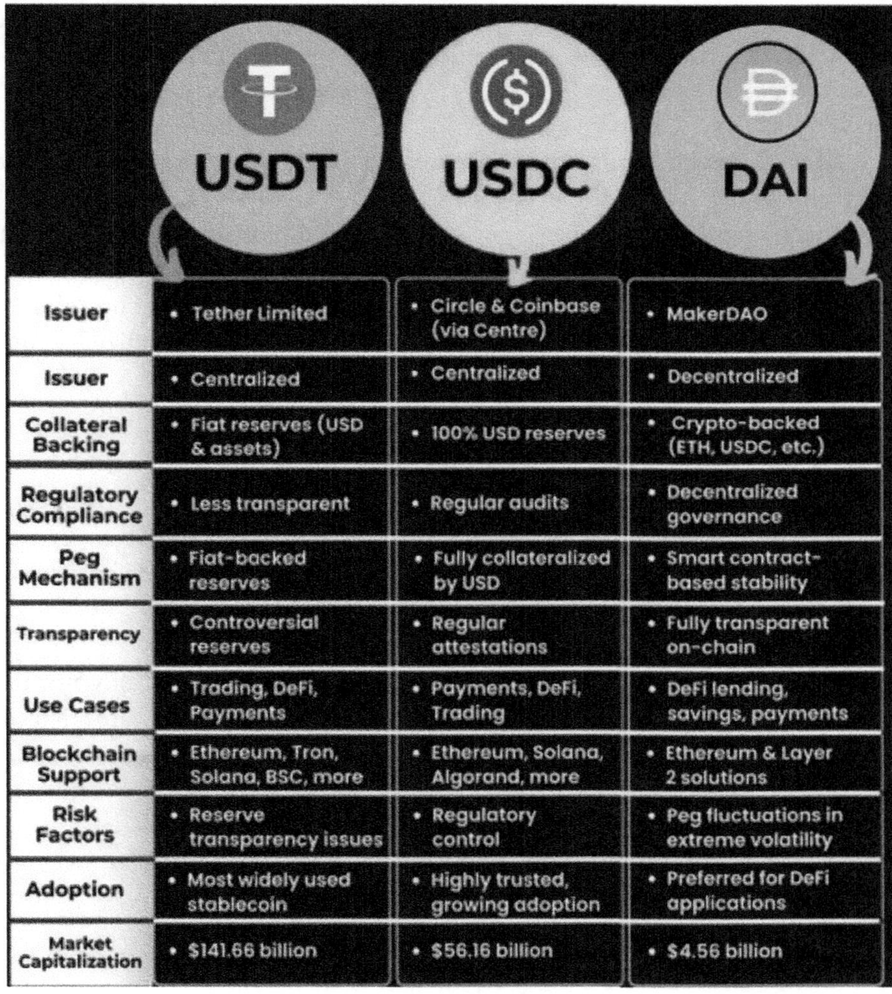

	USDT	USDC	DAI
Issuer	• Tether Limited	• Circle & Coinbase (via Centre)	• MakerDAO
Issuer	• Centralized	• Centralized	• Decentralized
Collateral Backing	• Fiat reserves (USD & assets)	• 100% USD reserves	• Crypto-backed (ETH, USDC, etc.)
Regulatory Compliance	• Less transparent	• Regular audits	• Decentralized governance
Peg Mechanism	• Fiat-backed reserves	• Fully collateralized by USD	• Smart contract-based stability
Transparency	• Controversial reserves	• Regular attestations	• Fully transparent on-chain
Use Cases	• Trading, DeFi, Payments	• Payments, DeFi, Trading	• DeFi lending, savings, payments
Blockchain Support	• Ethereum, Tron, Solana, BSC, more	• Ethereum, Solana, Algorand, more	• Ethereum & Layer 2 solutions
Risk Factors	• Reserve transparency issues	• Regulatory control	• Peg fluctuations in extreme volatility
Adoption	• Most widely used stablecoin	• Highly trusted, growing adoption	• Preferred for DeFi applications
Market Capitalization	• $141.66 billion	• $56.16 billion	• $4.56 billion

Covered stablecoins maintain a 1:1 value with the U.S. dollar and can be redeemed for dollars at a 1:1 ratio—low-risk, highly liquid reserve assets back them.

The issuing entity does not use these reserve assets for operational purposes, nor are they lent out or pledged. They are protected from third-party claims and are not used for trading or speculation.

Additionally, the interest generated from these assets is not used to compensate tokenholders.

According to the SEC's Division of Corporation Finance, the offering and selling of this type of stablecoin do not involve securities trading. Therefore, entities involved in their issuance, redemption, or distribution are not required to be licensed under securities law since their design and commercialization are based on fulfilling functions such as payment, money transfer, or stable value storage.

Finally, what is a CBDC?

CBDC (Central Bank Digital Currency) is a new form of money issued electronically by a central bank.

Central banks can surveil every single transaction an individual makes, and they can shut down your bank account if you start doing something they disagree with. Through CBDCs, governments aim to gain control over citizens. In contrast, Bitcoin is a decentralized ledger that no one controls.

Stablecoins are much better than CBDC for several reasons:

- **Authority that regulates them:**
  CBDCs are controlled by a central authority (government or central bank), whereas Stablecoins are decentralized, created by private enterprises

- **Accessibility**
  Stablecoins can operate across borders, making them perfect for countries without robust financial infrastructure, whereas CBDCs are tied to a single nation and its regulations, limiting their global utility.

- **Innovation**
  Stablecoin innovation is moving quickly but faces obstacles, whereas CBDC development is slower due to central bank oversight.

- **Control**
  Private companies and foundations manage stablecoins, whereas with CBDCs, the central bank has complete control over issuance, distribution, and monetary policy.

6.3.1 Genius Act

The bill that establishes a regulatory framework for stablecoins is called the Guaranteed and Uniform Stablecoin Issuance Act. Informally, it is referred to as the Genius Act. That acronym comes from the following words:

Guaranteed
Emission (Electronic Money)
National
Issuance for
Uniform
Standardization

On June 17, 2025, the U.S. Senate officially passed the Genius Act with a vote of 68 in favor and 30 against.

This is just the first step, as the bill must now be approved by the House of Representatives (Congress), and once passed, it must be signed into law by the President of the United States (Donald Trump).

The Act will come into effect on whichever of the following dates occurs first:

- 120 days after the relevant federal regulators (such as the Treasury, the Fed, or the FDIC) publish the final implementing regulations.
- 12 months after enactment by Congress.

Its entry into force is therefore expected in 2026.

Among the different types of stablecoins that exist, the decision was made to include only those backed by liquid assets—specifically, U.S. dollars and/ or Treasury bills (T-bills).

The **objectives** of this law include:

- **Establishing a regulatory framework for stablecoins**
- **Requiring mandatory annual audits for issuers with over $50 billion USD in circulation**
- **Strengthening the U.S. Dollar:**

  - International adoption: Since many people outside the U.S. lack access to U.S. dollars because they don't have a bank account or access to the banking system
  - Each issued token must be backed by a physically held U.S. dollar or Treasury bill

- **Ensuring compliance with anti–money laundering laws**
- **Reducing the government's borrowing costs**
- **Helping to curb the growth of the federal deficit and national debt**

Regarding this last point, the current Secretary of the Treasury, Scott Bessent, stated that stablecoins could help reduce the government's borrowing costs by encouraging sustained purchases of Treasury bills (T-bills) by stablecoin issuers, which would allow the Treasury to finance itself under more favorable conditions.

The Secretary has affirmed that the regulatory framework proposed under the Genius Act would have a positive impact on federal debt and the deficit, due to the way stablecoins are expected to stimulate demand for government debt.

Stablecoin issuers will be required to purchase T-bills as collateral, which will increase demand for these instruments. As demand rises, the cost of financing for the Treasury decreases. In turn, this lowers government spending on interest payments, helping to slow the growth of the deficit and national debt.

For all these reasons, the Genius Act could contribute to easing the fiscal pressure associated with debt costs, thanks to the structural and steady demand for T-bills as collateral for stablecoins.

An essential aspect of this law is that **it prohibits issuers from paying a yield on stablecoins**; in other words, it does not allow users to earn returns from holding them. The intention is for stablecoins to serve strictly as payment instruments or stores of value, not as investment products, in order to minimize systemic risks. As a result, the benefits for users or consumers are limited, while the advantages appear to favor banks and large corporations.

Since yields cannot be paid, activities such as farming or staking—earning returns by depositing and locking stablecoins—will not be allowed.

For these reasons, four major banks (JP Morgan Chase, Bank of America, Citigroup, and Wells Fargo) are working on launching a joint USD-backed stablecoin. Their goal is to reduce the cost of cross-border and interbank payments, thereby improving profit margins (through lower fees) and increasing banking efficiency via instant settlements.

What they aim to do is avoid falling behind and prevent tech giants from taking over parts of their business. In this way, they aim to lead the transformation, modernize their model, capture new sources of revenue, and secure the future of digital finance—ultimately avoiding disintermediation.

Major corporations, such as Amazon, Walmart, Expedia, and Alibaba, are also interested in creating their stablecoins. Their goals include optimizing payment systems, reducing transaction costs, increasing customer loyalty, and gaining access to consumer behavior data.

Currently, Visa and Mastercard charge fees ranging from 1.5 to 3.5%. In contrast, stablecoins operating on networks like Solana, Polygon, or Ethereum Layer 2 solutions charge a maximum fee of around $0.30 per transaction, regardless of the transfer amount. Sending \$1000 costs the same as sending \$1 million.

6.3.2 Tether: USDT vs USAT

Tether, the largest stablecoin in the crypto market, was not included in the Genius Act, and the reasons for this can be summarized as follows:

* Tether, which is domiciled outside the USA, does not have all of USDT's reserves in cash or Treasury bonds, which is an essential requirement for the Genius Act, and in addition, some of these reserve assets may not meet the liquidity standards required by U.S. regulation.
* The Genius Act requires full audits and regular disclosures with strict transparency, and although USDT does perform quarterly audits, it does not necessarily meet all the auditing criteria required by law.

Due to this opacity from Tether and the assets used as reserves, it was not included in the Genius Act, and therefore Tether chose to create the stablecoin USAT so as not to lose part of the U.S. market share.

USAT is a new U.S.-regulated asset, which will be a stablecoin backed by the dollar and designed to comply with U.S. regulation, particularly the new Genius Act.

The goal is to serve the U.S. market with a digital currency that meets stricter regulatory standards from its design.

What is the difference between USDT and USAT?

* USDT will continue to exist as a foreign stablecoin but will not be subject to primary U.S. regulation.
* USAT will be issued by Anchorage Digital Bank, a federally licensed crypto bank in the U.S., and its reserves will be managed by Cantor Fitzgerald. Bo Hines, former advisor to the U.S. government, will be appointed as CEO of the new product.

The official launch of USAT is scheduled for the end of 2025, and the main differences between the two stablecoins will be:

* USDT is the most widely used stablecoin globally. It operates on multiple blockchains (Ethereum, Tron, Solana, etc.). It is not directly regulated by the U.S., although Tether claims to maintain audited reserves. It has faced

criticism for a lack of transparency and for not complying with U.S. regulatory frameworks.

- USAT will be issued exclusively for the U.S. market. It will comply with the Genius Act and other U.S. financial regulations. It will have more controlled reserve backing and management: Anchorage Digital Bank (a regulated U.S. bank) as issuer, and Cantor Fitzgerald as reserve custodian. It will be aimed at institutional clients and regulated entities in the U.S.

What implications will the creation of USAT have for USDT?

- Coexistence in the short/medium term:

    - USDT will remain the dominant stablecoin outside the U.S.
    - USAT will cover the institutional and regulated space within the U.S.
    - This will allow Tether to expand its market without putting USDT at risk in less strict jurisdictions.

- Market segmentation:

    - USDT → retail users, global traders, emerging markets.
    - USAT → banks, funds, regulated companies in the U.S.

- Regulatory pressure on USDT:

    - With the arrival of USAT, there could be more pressure from regulators for U.S.-based exchanges to stop listing USDT and move to USAT.
    - Internationally, USDT would remain strong (especially in Asia, Latin America, and Africa).

As for the future, it is most likely that they will not merge and that both will coexist:

- USAT will be a regulated product with traceability required by the U.S., while USDT offers more flexibility and fewer restrictions, which makes it attractive for international traders and countries without strong regulation.

In this way, Tether would maintain its global leadership.

7

Mass Adoption

We are immersed in the second most important revolution of the last 40 years. The first was the **Internet of Information (TCP/IP)**, which gave us a series of protocols/capabilities, such as **email and web pages** that were free, and that certain companies generated value by creating applications such as e-commerce, online banking, etc. Those companies that captured the value were Facebook, Google, Amazon, etc.

Now we are in a second revolution, the Internet of Value (Blockchain), which does not copy information or a record from one place to another but **moves that record** that represents money, and is done immediately and securely. Blockchain technology provides a **single centralized record of transactions**, instead of exchanging records as before, and having many separate records. So that there is only **one accounting book** that no one can modify or falsify.

These records are entered into blocks through validator nodes, which are participants that validate and transmit transactions. These blocks are linked as a chain, creating a huge record of all transactions. Therefore, it is called blockchain.

But **inserting these transactions into the blocks has a cost**. Therefore, in this case, this technology is not free like the Internet of Information was. The protocols that capture that value are cryptocurrencies, **which are listed protocols.**

J. Pineda, *Investing in Crypto with Confidence,*
https://doi.org/10.1007/978-3-032-07834-6_7

Bitcoin, Ethereum, Binance, etc., are listed protocols. It is as if HTTP costs money to use, and on top of that, they are listed on the stock market. That is, they have a cost and generate value. Using the Internet costs money, but you can be a shareholder in that Internet and therefore benefit.

For all this, I believe that these protocols have a great future, and the time to invest is now, since, at the user level, we are in the 1999 era of the Internet, just before the beginning of the exponential growth that the Internet had. But many of these protocols will disappear. Therefore, it is essential to know which protocols to invest in and do so with professionals who know how to value these protocols.

As with the dot-com companies, many disappeared after the boom, and mainly the five big ones, FAANG (Facebook/Meta, Amazon, Apple, Netflix, Google/Alphabet), remained.

Everett M. Rogers, in 1962, created the Diffusion of Innovations model, also known as the **Technology Adoption Lifecycle**, in his book Diffusion of Innovations.

This model, or lifecycle, follows a normal distribution and divides adopters, meaning individuals or organizations that decide to incorporate a new idea or technology, into five groups within the innovation or technology adoption process:

- Innovators (2.5%): within this group are the tech enthusiasts
- Early Adopters (13.5%): these are the visionaries
- Early Majority (34%): this group includes the pragmatists
- Late Majority (34%): these are the conservatives
- Laggards (16%): this group represents the skeptics

In 1991, Geoffrey A. Moore observed that many technological innovations failed when transitioning from the "**early market**" (Innovators + Early Adopters) to the "**mainstream market**" (Early + Late Majority + Laggards). He introduced the concept of **The Chasm**, expanding Rogers' model, and published it in his book Crossing the Chasm (1991).

In my opinion, the crypto market is currently in The Chasm phase, a crucial point in the life of any innovation and an early stage of adoption.

This model, with its different adopter groups, can be seen in Chart 7.1:

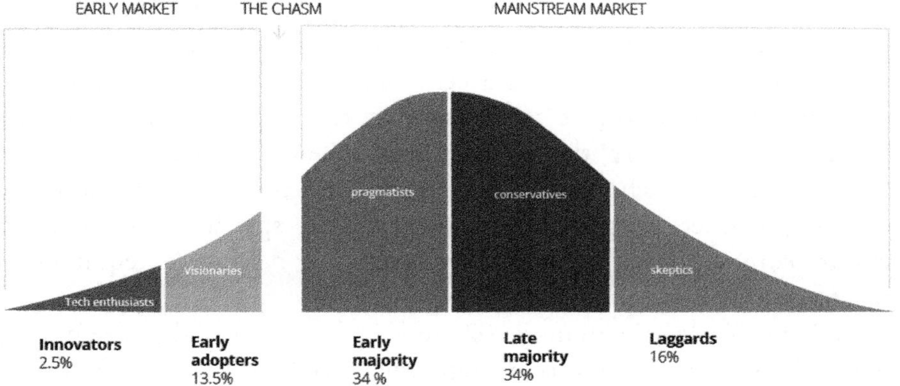

Chart 7.1 The technology adoption life cycle. *Source* Moore (1991) *crossing the chasm*. HarperCollins Publishers

7.1   Regulation

The following chart shows which countries are most advanced in cryptocurrency adoption. The top two are the UAE and Singapore.

Table 7.1 shows the top 30 Countries with the Highest Cryptocurrency Ownership Rate in 2024.

Table 7.1 *Source* Triple-A

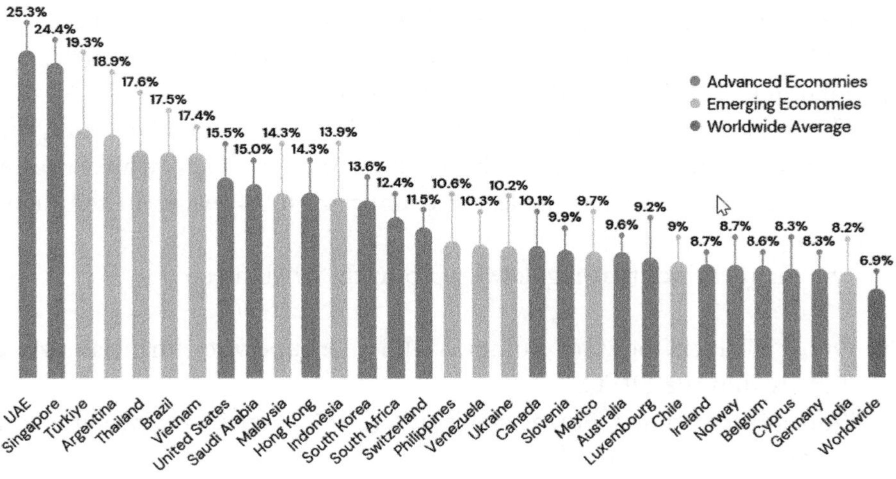

In first place is the United Arab Emirates, which is implementing pro-crypto regulations, attracting many high-net-worth individuals and crypto companies to develop their businesses in the country.

The SCA and the UAE Central Bank play the most important roles in regulating and supervising Crypto UAE. The SCA (Securities and Commodities Authority) plays a central role in regulating crypto commodities in the UAE. It is responsible for implementing rules and guidelines that govern the trading and issuance of digital assets. The SCA's approach is characterized by a focus on protecting investors and ensuring market integrity. It has introduced specific regulations for crypto commodities, including licensing and disclosure requirements to enhance transparency.

Emirates Blockchain Strategy 2021 seeks to have 50% of the government's transactions on blockchain technology, which could be the nation's effort to transform the digital world.

Creating the Dubai Virtual Assets Regulatory Authority and signing the Virtual Assets Law proves Dubai actively develops rules governing virtual assets such as cryptos and NFTs.

The RAK Digital Assets Oasis is a free zone dedicated exclusively to digital and virtual asset companies. Its launch makes the UAE a go-to jurisdiction for global crypto firms.

Therefore, by adopting friendly tax policies, including no taxation on capital gains, business income in the Dubai region cements its position and attracts investors and firms in the decentralized economy.

The introduction of legislative measures in financial free zones such as ADGM (Abu Dhabi Global Market), DIFC (Dubai Multi Commodities Centre), and Ras Al Khaimah Digital Assets Oasis also proves the UAE's attitude to developing novelties in the sphere of professional activity and maintaining economic stability and legislation.

These changes may be attributed to the UAE's comprehensive strategy for managing digital currencies, which prioritizes innovativeness while ensuring security. This strategy has made the country a global leader in the digital economy.

The main entities that regulate crypto in the UAE are:

- Dubai Financial Services Authority (DFSA): supervises financial services firms within the DIFC.
- Dubai International Financial Center (DIFC): *offers services for a new company to establish itself.*
- Securities and Commodities Authority (SCA): is tasked with monitoring and regulating the UAE's financial markets, including the Dubai Financial Market ("DFM"), the Abu Dhabi Securities Exchange ("ADX"), and the Dubai Gold & Commodities Exchange ("DGCX").

- The Virtual Assets Regulatory Authority (VARA) is responsible for regulating and overseeing the provision, use, and exchange of virtual assets in and from the emirate of Dubai.

The DIFC is more than just a financial center; it offers a wide range of business services for virtually any company.

The DFSA explicitly regulates financial services firms operating within the DIFC and supervises institutions composed of banks, insurance firms, fund managers, and other financial institutions. Its focus is ensuring compliance with stringent regulatory requirements related to financial conduct, risk management, and anti-money laundering practices.

The *SCA* and *VARA* will establish rules and procedures for licensing and supervising virtual asset service providers (VASPs) and related activities.

Regulation is essential for the adoption of institutional clients. Precise and reliable regulation is required for institutional investors to enter this market.

Singapore comes in second. The Monetary Authority of Singapore (MAS) enhances cryptocurrency operations with clear guidelines. MAS has defined the legal status of digital assets, set responsibilities for service providers, and imposed stringent anti-money laundering (AML) practices and consumer protections, boosting transaction security and investor appeal.

That is why Singapore ranks as the second country in the previous chart.

7.2 Institutional Adoption

A clearer regulatory environment has also led to increased institutional interest. With defined rules, financial institutions are more willing to offer crypto-related products, making these assets accessible to a broader audience. This is evident from the introduction of Spot BTC ETFs.

The lack of regulation is the primary barrier preventing institutional clients from entering the cryptocurrency market and developing a digital asset strategy.

Both crypto businesses (70%) and financial institutions (52%) report that regulatory uncertainty and a lack of clarity around compliance requirements hinder their progress in developing digital asset strategies.

Anti-money laundering (AML) and Know Your Customer (KYC) regulations come in second place after the lack of regulation.

Globally, cryptocurrency legislation is gaining momentum—not only in the UAE but also in the USA, Russia, Japan, Qatar, and other countries. Some examples include:

1. The **UAE** has officially removed Value Added Tax (VAT) on all crypto-currency transactions:

VAT Exemption: Services provided by fund managers to licensed funds are now exempt from VAT.

No VAT on Transfers: VAT will not be charged on the transfer and conversion of virtual assets, including cryptocurrencies.

2. **Japan's Financial Services Agency (FSA)** has announced it will reform the country's cryptocurrency regulations to stimulate growth in the blockchain gaming industry.
3. **Qatar** has officially launched a digital asset regulatory framework to position itself as a financial hub.
4. **Dubai** has approved the payment of salaries in BTC and other cryptocurrencies.
5. **Russia** has passed a law allowing companies to use cryptocurrencies as a means of payment for international trade.
6. **Donald Trump** is taking several measures to make the USA the global capital of cryptocurrencies. He has appointed crypto-friendly figures to key positions, such as **Paul Atkins** as SEC Chair and **Mark Uyeda** as interim, and announced plans to:

- Create a **national strategic Bitcoin reserve**
- Hold **100% of any BTC owned by the government**
- **Reject the implementation of a CBDC** as long as he is president

Institutional ownership of Bitcoin has surged over the past year with the creation of the ETF. This adoption has been facilitated through ETFs, publicly listed companies, and government initiatives.

Is this growing institutional presence a good thing for Bitcoin? On the one hand, the entry of institutional investors into the Bitcoin and crypto market is positive because it brings more stability. On the other hand, it's not entirely positive because it compromises Bitcoin's independence and lack of correlation.

Due to this type of investor entering the space, Bitcoin is increasingly seen as a risk asset rather than a safe haven, which makes it more correlated with the stock market.

This institutional bet on Bitcoin is reflected in:

- BTC Treasury holdings of publicly listed Companies
- ETF Cumulative Flows (BTC)
- Governments

Table 7.2 shows the Treasury of Public Listed Companies:

Table 7.2 *Source* Bitcoin Magazine Pro—August 2025

BTC treasury holdings of publicly traded companies.

Where possible, Bitcoin Treasuries are updated live.
Help update the data here.

BITCOIN MAGAZINE PRO

Public Companies with > 100BTC	Combined BTC Holdings	USD Value of Holdings	% of 21m
75	**930,143**	**$110.162B**	**4.38%**

Company Name	Exchange:Symbol	Country	# of BTC	Value Today (USD)	% of 21m	Membership	Website	Active Strategy
Strategy	NASDAQ:MSTR		628,946	$74,489,463,550	2.99%	Bitcoin CORPS		✓
Marathon Digital Holdings	NASDAQ:MARA		50,639	$5,997,449,614	0.24%			✓
XXI	XXI		43,514	$5,153,597,474	0.21%			
Riot Platforms, Inc	NASDAQ:RIOT		19,239	$2,278,578,430	0.09%			
Trump Media & Technology Group	DJT		18,430	$2,182,764,201	0.09%			
Metaplanet Inc.	TYO:3350		18,113	$2,145,220,183	0.09%	Bitcoin CORPS		✓
Galaxy Digital Holdings	TSE: GLXY		17,102	$2,025,482,006	0.08%			
CleanSpark Inc.	NASDAQ:CLSK		12,703	$1,504,484,734	0.06%			
Coinbase Global, Inc	NASDAQ:COIN		11,776	$1,394,695,129	0.06%			
Tesla, Inc.	NASDAQ:TSLA		11,509	$1,363,072,881	0.05%			
Hut 8 Mining Corp	NASDAQ:HUT		10,667	$1,263,350,284	0.05%			
Block Inc.	NYSE:SQ		8,584	$1,016,649,371	0.04%			
Next Technology Holding Inc.	NXTT		5,833	$690,833,618	0.03%			

Major companies, including Strategy, MetaPlanet, and others, have accumulated over 700,000 BTC. Considering that Bitcoin's total hard-capped supply is 21 million, this represents roughly 3.41% of all BTC that will ever exist. This indicates that the institutions are making long-term bets.

Chart 7.2 illustrates that ETFs control a substantial portion of the market. At the time of writing, spot Bitcoin ETFs hold approximately 1,000,000 BTC, just under 5% of the total supply.

When we combine corporate treasuries and ETF holdings, the number climbs to over 1.67 million BTC, or roughly 8% of the total theoretical supply.

ETF Cumulative Flows (BTC)

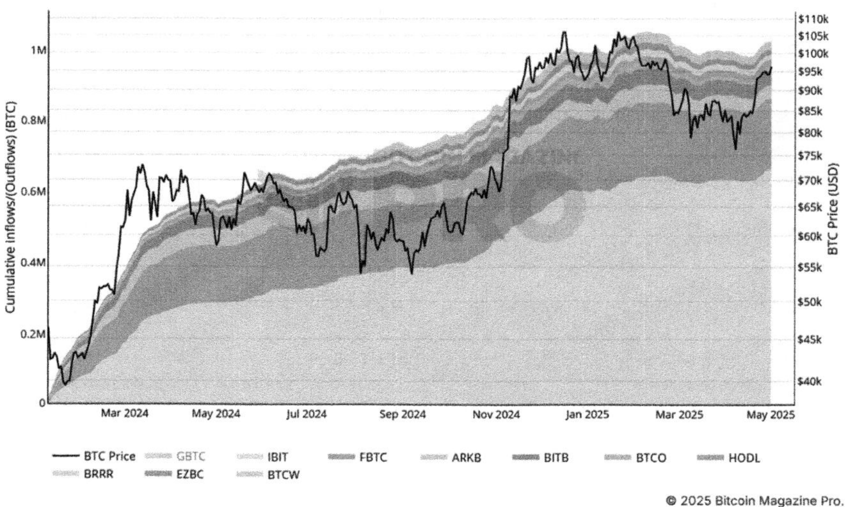

Chart 7.2 *Source* Bitcoin Magazine Pro—From January 2024 to May 2025

As we can observe in Chart 7.3, the price of the Bitcoin ETF spikes when there are significant inflows. Likewise, a clear correlation exists between downward price action and net outflows.

Bitcoin: ETF Daily Flows (USD) - Total

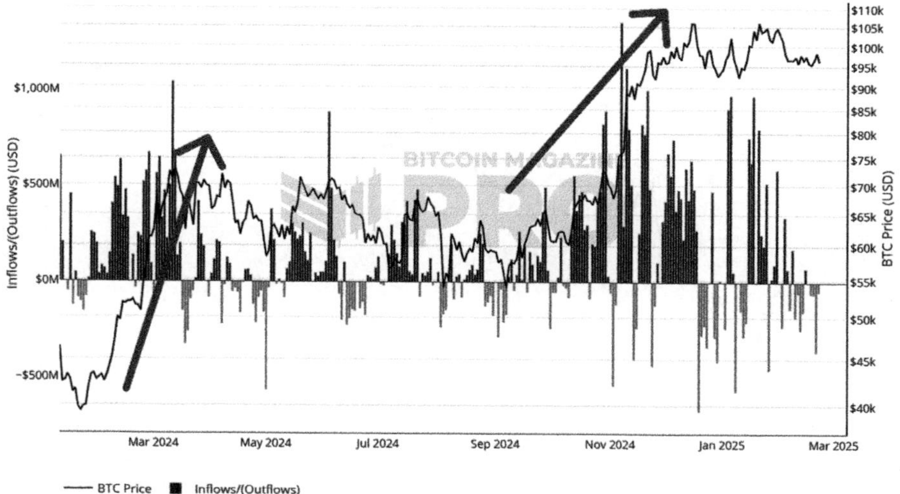

Chart 7.3 *Source* Bitcoin Magazine Pro—From January 2024 to May 2025

Some governments are now active players in the Bitcoin space. Through sovereign purchases and reserves under initiatives like the Strategic Bitcoin Reserve, nation-states collectively hold approximately 542,000 BTC. Add that to the previous institutional holdings, and we arrive at over 2.2 million BTC in the hands of institutions, ETFs, and governments. On the surface, that's about 10.14% of the total 21 million BTC supply.

More than 3.4 million BTC are likely lost forever, as those coins have not moved in over a decade. This can be verified using the following metric shown in Chart 7.4:

Bitcoin: 10+ Years HODL Wave

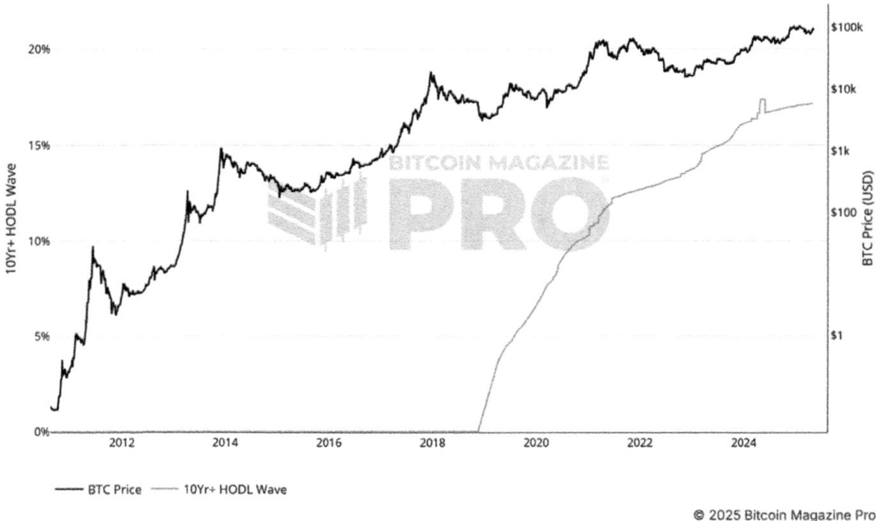

Chart 7.4 *Source* Bitcoin Magazine Pro—From October 2010 to May 2025

Considering that approximately 19.8 million BTC are currently in circulation, 3.4 million are lost (17.15%), the effective supply is closer to 16.45 million BTC. Suppose the percentage of BTC held by institutions (2.2 million BTC) rises to roughly 13.40%. This means that institutions, ETFs, or sovereigns have already locked up approximately one in every 7.4 BTC available.

As governments and financial institutions incorporate crypto assets into their strategies, we can expect to see a stronger correlation with the traditional financial system. A government-held Bitcoin reserve could help solidify BTC as a strategic financial asset, although it may also undermine its narrative as a purely decentralized one.

The market is currently at an inflection point due to the measures taken by the Trump administration. These measures could catalyze greater institutional adoption, but they may also lead to stricter regulation that could reshape the cryptocurrency ecosystem as we know it today.

News like the following represents another step toward institutional adoption: BNY Mellon received SEC 'non-objection' approval to offer Bitcoin custody services to clients beyond Bitcoin ETFs. As the world's largest custodian bank, managing $2 trillion in assets and holding $48.8 trillion under custody as of June 2024, this approval marks a significant milestone for institutional Bitcoin adoption. It signals a growing acceptance of Bitcoin within traditional financial institutions, making it more accessible to a broader range of investors and further promoting mainstream adoption.

Lastly, it's worth noting that brokers' exposure to BTC is not very high. Major brokerages still restrict client exposure to bitcoin ETFs, as shown in Table 7.3. If a 2% allocation to bitcoin were instituted across these platforms, it would imply 22 times the net ETF inflows in 2024.

Table 7.3 *Source* Coinbase—Total AUM reflects investable assets as of Q4 2024

Brokerage	Allows exposure	Allowed in all accounts	Limitations	Advisor recs allowed	Investment ($B)	Total AUM ($B)
Fidelity	Yes	Yes	No	Yes	$5,900	$15,100
Vanguard	No	No	n/a	n/a	$4,000	$10,400
Schwab	Yes	Yes	No	Yes	$5,062	$10,101
Morgan Stanley	Yes	No	Yes	Yes	$6,194	$7,860
UBS	Yes	No	Yes	No	$4,182	$6,087
JP Morgan	Yes	No	Yes	No	$5,932	$5,932
Merrill/ BofA	Yes	No	Yes	No	$1,888	$4,252
Goldman Sachs	Yes	No	Yes	No	$1,600	$3,137
Wells Fargo	Yes	Yes	No	Yes	$2,293	$2,293
Citi	No	No	n/a	n/a	$587	$587

8

Crypto in Your Portfolio

Bitcoin and crypto have considerable volatility, but they have produced returns commensurate with it. In other words, crypto assets have compensated investors for the higher risk with higher returns, and their attractiveness is evident in the Sharpe ratio, which is higher for Bitcoin than for the DJIA and the S&P 500, indicating that it continues to maintain its appeal despite its high volatility.

In Chart 8.1, we can see how Bitcoin's Sharpe ratio (yellow line) over the past six years has been significantly higher than that of the DJIA (blue line) and the S&P 500 (purple line) by a wide margin.

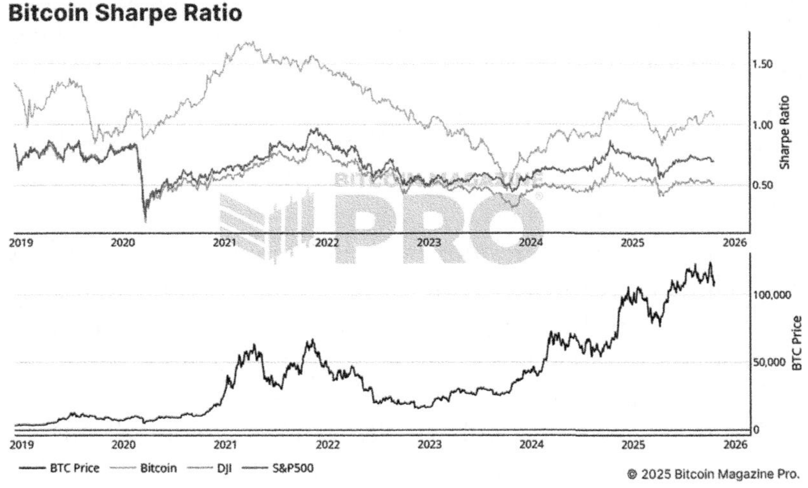

Chart 8.1 *Source* Bitcoin Magazine Pro (from 2019 to 2025)

J. Pineda, *Investing in Crypto with Confidence*,
https://doi.org/10.1007/978-3-032-07834-6_8

Including cryptocurrencies in a global portfolio can enhance returns and provide diversification benefits, but it also introduces higher volatility. Institutional adoption and regulatory developments are paving the way for broader integration of digital assets into traditional investment strategies. Investors should consider these factors and align their portfolios with their risk tolerance and investment goals.

There is positive skewness of the returns distribution, which means that extensive periods of excess positive returns far outweigh the drawbacks of negative return periods.

8.1   Correlations

Bitcoin's correlation with other assets, although it has increased in recent years, remains low and provides strong diversification to a global portfolio, as we will see in Sect. 8.2.

Table 8.1 displays a correlation heatmap of USD **weekly returns** between Bitcoin and a diverse range of traditional assets, including equities, bonds, commodities, and alternatives, over the past 10 years. Most asset classes in the table correlate with at least one other asset class, but this is not the case for digital assets.

The correlation between Bitcoin and any traditional asset class remains below 24%.

BTC's correlation with U.S. bonds is 6.2%, while gold has a 38.3% correlation with U.S. bonds. The same applies to U.S. long-term Treasuries: Bitcoin has a very low correlation of 2.3%, whereas gold's correlation with that asset is 29.5%.

Examining the 10-year correlation, Bitcoin is the most uncorrelated asset among the rest. This is crucial to understand when adding a new asset class, such as BTC, to your portfolio.

Examining the 4-year correlation between Bitcoin and traditional assets in USD weekly returns, we observe in Table 8.2 that the picture has changed only slightly, with BTC exhibiting a somewhat higher correlation with U.S. equities and U.S. tech. However, the core insight remains the same: the assets currently most uncorrelated with the rest are Bitcoin and Gold.

The historical correlation with the S&P 500 is very low (17%), but it's true that since institutional investors have entered the market and Bitcoin ETFs have been created, that correlation has increased in the short term. This is because cryptocurrencies are perceived as even riskier assets than equities.

Table 8.1 *Source* Bloomberg from May 2015 to May 2025

	BITCOIN	US equity	US tech equity	Dev equity	Emerging equity	US Bonds	US bond LT treasury	Real estate	Gold
BITCOIN	-								
US equity	17.1%	-							
US tech	23.2%	74.7%	-						
Dev equity	15.8%	84.4%	64.9%	-					
Emerging equity	12.1%	71.6%	60.3%	81.4%	-				
US bonds	6.2%	22.9%	23.6%	27.2%	19.0%	-			
US bond LT	2.3%	−7.4%	3.4%	−4.0%	−4.8%	85.3%	-		
Real estate	9.3%	74.7%	52.5%	68.4%	52.7%	46.9%	17.7%	-	
Gold	9.9%	13.7%	10.6%	20.5%	23.9%	38.3%	29.5%	26.5%	-

US Equity: SPDR SP500
US Tech Equity: ARK Innovation (ARKK)
Developed Equity: iShares MSCI EAFE ETF (EFA)
Emerging Equity: iShares MSCI Emerging Markets ETF (EEM)
US Bond: iShares Core US Aggregate Bond ETF (AGG)
US Long Term Treasury: iShare 20 + year treasury Bond ETF (TLT)
Real Estate: vanguard real estate Etf (VNQ)
Gold: Spdr gold shares Etf (GLD)

Table 8.2 *Source* Bloomberg from May 2021 to May 2025

	BITCOIN	US equity	US tech equity	Dev equity	Emerging equity	US Bonds	US bond LT treasury	Real estate	Gold
BITCOIN	-								
US equity	32.9%	-							
US tech	38.6%	78.1%	-						
Dev equity	22.7%	78.8%	64.8%	-					
Emerging equity	16.8%	63.5%	57.7%	79.0%	-				
US Bonds	7.0%	28.0%	26.9%	30.4%	22.5%	-			
U S bond LT	0.8%	11.4%	15.1%	11.5%	8.4%	91.8%	-		
Real estate	26.2%	73.2%	60.8%	66.9%	48.1%	52.9%	39.6%	-	
Gold	14.9%	14.1%	8.4%	25.9%	31.6%	17.8%	7.2%	22.2%	-

As a result, Bitcoin performs even worse when equities perform poorly, but when equities do well, Bitcoin tends to perform much better.

This is also due to Bitcoin's maturation. Bitcoin is evolving into a global asset class that will ultimately be more aligned with other international markets, but it's only partially there for now (in the short term).

Table 8.3 illustrates the evolution of the correlation between USD weekly returns of Bitcoin and traditional assets since the launch of Bitcoin ETFs. As we can see, Bitcoin is no longer the most uncorrelated asset; that position now belongs to Gold, which is seen as a safe-haven asset.

As mentioned earlier, Bitcoin is still perceived more as a volatile asset than a safe haven. As a result, its correlation with tech stocks stands at 55,2%. Once Bitcoin is viewed more as a store of value, its correlations will begin to resemble those of Gold.

Table 8.4 compares the evolution of Bitcoin's correlation with other asset classes throughout its history. We can see that, over time, the correlation has increased, but Bitcoin remains an uncorrelated asset relative to the rest.

The correlations that have increased the most are with U.S. equity, U.S. tech equity, and real estate. With the rest of the asset classes, correlations have remained relatively stable over time.

As observed in the following tables, when a geopolitical event occurs, Bitcoin underperforms other assets in the short term but outperforms them in the long term.

Table 8.5 shows how, in the early days, Bitcoin drops more than the rest of the assets, but over the long term, it recovers and outperforms all of them. This is due to the short-term volatility of the asset, which causes sharp fluctuations in the immediate aftermath of news or events. However, once things stabilize or the initial reaction fades, Bitcoin tends to recover and surpass other assets, delivering higher medium- to long-term returns as shown in Chart 8.2.

Table 8.3 *Source* Bloomberg Jan 24 to May 25

	BITCOIN	US equity	US tech equity	Dev equity	Emerging equity	US Bonds	US bond LT treasury	Real estate	Gold
BITCOIN	-								
US equity	35.3%	-							
US tech	55.2%	81.2%	-						
Dev equity	26.3%	70.0%	57.1%	-					
Emerging equity	21.6%	66.8%	59.9%	77.8%	-				
US bonds	3.0%	6.6%	7.3%	4.4%	1.7%	-			
US bond LT	−0.9%	−1.9%	0.6%	−8.6%	−6.8%	95.2%	-		
Real estate	36.4%	52.4%	42.7%	48.6%	37.0%	54.0%	44.5%	-	
Gold	6.6%	2.5%	-3.9%	23.6%	23.2%	−6.3%	−8.8%	6.6%	-

Table 8.4 *Source* Bloomberg

	BITCOIN	US equity (%)	US tech equity (%)	Dev equity (%)	Emerging equity (%)	US bonds (%)	US bond LT treasury (%)	Real estate (%)	Gold (%)
BITCOIN	**10 Y**	**17.1**	**23.2**	**15.8**	**12.1**	**6.2**	**2.3**	**9.3**	**9.9**
BITCOIN	**4 Y**	**39.2**	**38.6**	22.7	16.8	7.0	0.8	26.2	14.9
BITCOIN	**Jan`24**	**35.3**	**55.2**	26.3	21.6	3.0	-0.9	36.4	6.6

- **COVID:**

Table 8.5 *Source* Bloomberg

COVID (02/03/2020)	1 MONTH (%)	3 MONTHS (%)	12/31/2020 (%)
GOLD	4.07	7.95	20.40
NASDAQ	−6.67	−1.79	27.75
BITCOIN	**−5.78**	**−3.80**	**212.66**
S&P 500	−8.39	−11.23	4.58

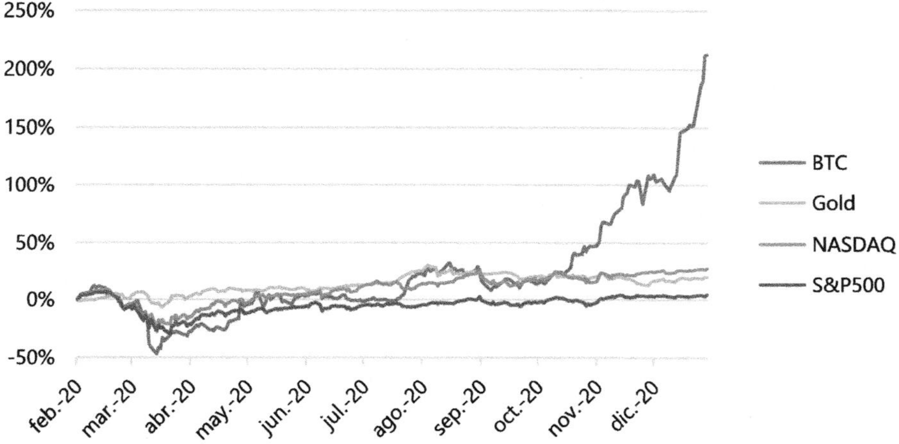

Chart 8.2   *Source* Bloomberg

- **TARIFF LIBERATION DAY:**

A similar situation arose in another case, where Donald Trump imposed tariffs on various countries as shown in Table 8.6 and its graphic representation in Chart 8.3.

Table 8.6 *Source* Bloomberg

LIBERATION DAY (04/02/2025)	1 WEEK (%)	1 MONTH	2 MONTHS
GOLD	1.45	3.41	5.36
NASDAQ	−9.21	−1.58	4.20
BITCOIN	**−11.02**	**7.20**	**15.40**
S&P500	−9.97	−3.87	−0.33

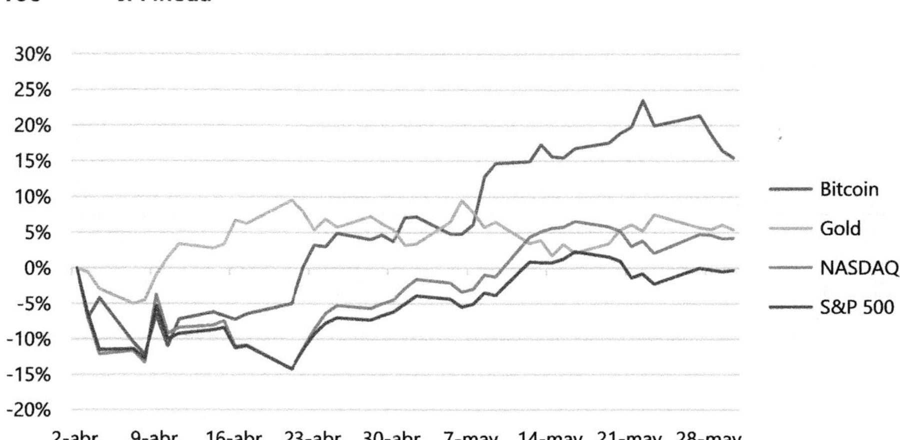

Chart 8.3 *Source* Bloomberg

We can also observe a performance correlation with the S&P 500 in Chart 8.4, showing that Bitcoin is a riskier asset.

Portfolio Monthly Returns

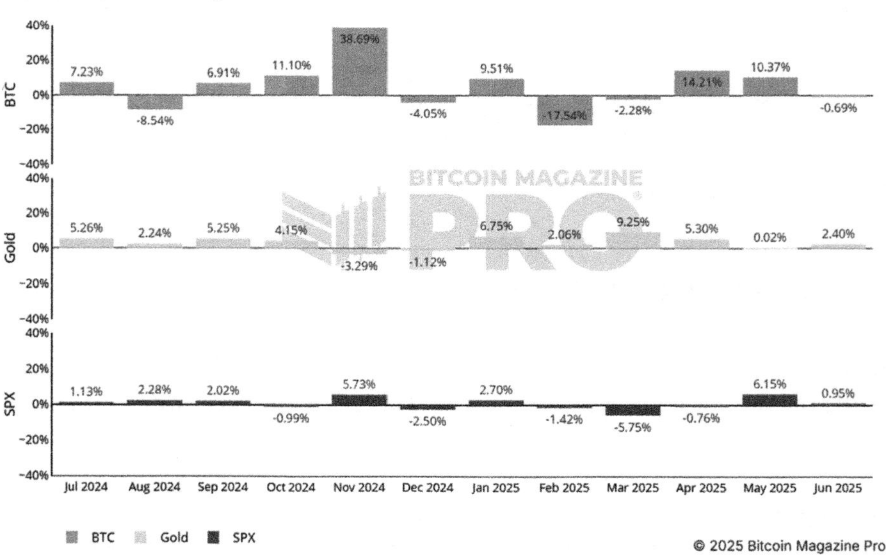

Chart 8.4 *Source* Bitcoin Magazine Pro

Bitcoin is still a risky asset:

None of the prior analyses negates the fact that Bitcoin remains a highly risky asset. It is an emerging technology that is still in its early stages of adoption on the path to becoming a global payment asset and store of value. Bitcoin has also been volatile and subject to numerous risks, including regulatory challenges, uncertainty over its adoption path, and an immature ecosystem.

However, over the years, Bitcoin has gained maturity, resulting in a gradual decrease in its volatility as shown in Chart 8.5. At the same time, its correlation with the S&P 500 has slowly increased, although it remains an uncorrelated asset compared to the U.S. stock market index.

Bitcoin Volatility

Chart 8.5 *Source* Bitcoin Magazine Pro

8.2 Crypto in Portfolio

Nowadays, no one doubts that crypto should be included in a portfolio. The real question lies in what percentage should be allocated to it.

Even though the volatility and drawdown of bitcoin or crypto in general is elevated on a single asset basis when added in a small quantity to a multi-asset portfolio, the relative risk (volatility) created is relatively minor and has been historically very richly rewarded.

Even conservative investors with a low risk tolerance could benefit from a small (1%) allocation to bitcoin, as the added volatility is minimal.

Bitcoin's positive aspect is that it offers a strong risk-return ratio for your portfolio. Although it is a highly volatile asset in the short term, its historically high returns offset this.

Another positive aspect of Bitcoin is its low correlation with other assets. Since the launch of ETFs a year ago, this correlation with equities has increased, as Bitcoin is currently seen more as a risk asset than a safe haven.

However, as more countries begin to incorporate Bitcoin into their balance sheets and reserves, this correlation is expected to decrease again gradually, and Bitcoin will increasingly be viewed as a safe-haven asset, similar to gold, providing substantial diversification benefits to a portfolio.

Digital assets represent 2.87% of the market portfolio. Multi-asset allocations that don't invest in cryptocurrencies effectively underweight the asset class and bet against it.

By market cap, a global 60/40 portfolio should include 2.87% of digital assets, as shown in Chart 8.6. Of all the listed assets accessible to investors, we have a total market capitalization of approximately $119 trillion. Cryptocurrencies, also known as digital assets, have a market capitalization of $3.41 trillion. (June 2025)

To achieve market neutrality, the investor should allocate 2.87% to digital assets. **If you don't include crypto in your portfolio, you're incurring an opportunity cost.**

Market Portfolio: 2.87% is a neutral position

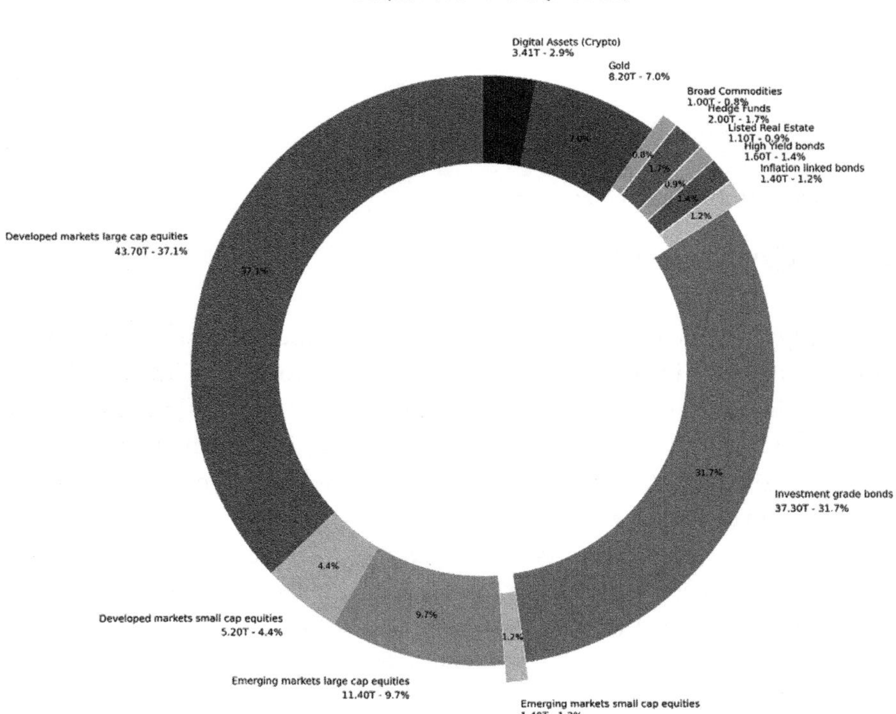

Chart 8.6 *Source* Bloomberg, June 2025

The approximate composition of this global portfolio would be.

- Digital Assets 2.87%
- Gold 7%
- Broad Commodities 0.8%
- Hedge Funds 1.7%
- Real Estate 0.9%
- High Yield Bonds 1.4%
- Inflation Linked Bonds 1.2%
- Investment Grade Bonds 31.7%
- Emerging Markets Large Cap equities 9.7%
- Developed Markets Small Cap Equities 4.4%
- Developed Markets Large Cap Equities 37.1%

The big question is: ***How much crypto should be added to your portfolio?***
Next, we will review a 7-year, 5-year, and 3-year analysis to assess the positive impact of adding a percentage of Bitcoin to a traditional global portfolio composed of 60% Equity and 40% Fixed Income.
Each simulation includes four scenarios:

- The first scenario is a standard portfolio with 60% Equity and 40% Fixed Income.
- The second scenario includes 59% Equity, 40% Fixed Income, and 1% Bitcoin.
- The third scenario consists of 58% Equity, 39% Fixed Income, and 3% Bitcoin.
- The final scenario allocates 57% Equity, 38% Fixed Income, and 5% Bitcoin.

Table 8.7 shows a simulation showing this effect from **seven years** ago (May'18–May'25):

Table 8.7 *Source* Bloomberg (May 2018–May 2025)

	60/40 (%)	59/40/1 (%)	58/39/3 (%)	57/38/5 (%)
Cumulative return	83.52	89.30	102.70	116.76
Annualized return	**9.94**	**10.43**	**11.55**	**12.67**
Annualized volatility	**12.64**	**12.64**	**12.89**	**13.25**
Downside risk	90.24	9.26	9.48	9.76
Sharpe ratio	**0.59**	**0.63**	**0.70**	**0.77**

Equity: SPDR SP500
Fixed Income: iShares Core US Aggregate Bond ETF (AGG)

If you add 5% Bitcoin to a global 60% equity/40% fixed income portfolio, annual volatility increases by 0.61%, while annualized returns increase by 2.73%. Therefore, adding BTC to your portfolio provides an optimal risk-return ratio (4.5x). This means that adding Bitcoin to your portfolio increases portfolio return by more than the volatility increases.

As you can see, the Sharpe ratio increases in all three scenarios. This is due to Bitcoin's strong performance over the past seven years and its low correlation with the other assets held in these 60–40 portfolios.

The most optimal multi-asset portfolios would include Bitcoin.

Table 8.8 compares the results over the past **five years**. We see that they are similar.

Table 8.8 *Source* Bloomberg (May 2020–May 2025)

	60/40 (%)	59/40/1 (%)	58/39/3 (%)	57/38/5 (%)
Cumulative return	54.38	58.23%	67.38	76.91
Annualized return	**9.78**	**10.32%**	**11.61**	**12.91**
Annualized volatility	**11.28**	**11.33%**	**11.65**	**12.06**
Downside risk	8.07	8.12%	8.36	8.67
Sharpe ratio	**0.62**	**0.66**	**0.75**	**0.84**

Equity: SPDR SP500
Fixed Income: iShares Core US Aggregate Bond ETF (AGG)

In this case, adding 5% Bitcoin to your global portfolio results in a 0.78% increase in volatility and a 3.13% increase in annualized returns, leading to a risk-return ratio of 4.01x—meaning the return it adds is four times greater than the risk it introduces to the portfolio. In all scenarios, the Sharpe ratio also improves.

If we analyze the **past 3 years**, the return added is **five times** greater (0.60% volatility vs. 3.13% annualized return) as illustrated in Table 8.9, since the bear market bottomed out in November 2022. Therefore, from the time the portfolio was created, Bitcoin has been rising almost continuously.

Table 8.9 *Source* Bloomberg (May 2022–May 2025)

	60/40 (%)	59/40/1 (%)	58/39/3 (%)	57/38/5 (%)
Cumulative return	43.33	45.39	50.24	55.19
Annualized return	**13.49**	**14.04**	**15.32**	**16.62**
Annualized volatility	**11.49**	**11.52**	**11.77**	**12.09**
Downside risk	7.86	7.88	8.05	8.27
Sharpe ratio	**0.77**	**0.82**	**0.91**	**0.99**

Equity: SPDR SP500
Fixed Income: iShares Core US Aggregate Bond ETF (AGG)

Looking at the 7-year, 5-year, and 3-year scenarios, we can conclude that:

- Risk decreases over time, which reflects the maturing of the market.
- The Sharpe ratio increases as the allocation to BTC rises.
- Optimal risk-return ratio: over 4x with a 5% BTC allocation.

As we have seen, adding Bitcoin to the classic 60/40 (Equity/Fixed Income) portfolio in small increments initially increases the expected Sharpe Ratio. The reason is that, although Bitcoin is a volatile asset, it may offer high returns and low correlation with traditional assets, thus providing diversification benefits.In the following simulation, I analyze how increasing the allocation of Bitcoin from 1% to 10% affects the Sharpe Ratio of a 60/40 (Equity/Fixed Income) portfolio.

Analyzing the last 10 years, the Sharpe Ratio rises until Bitcoin reaches approximately a 7% share of the total portfolio, then begins to level off. After that point, increasing the Bitcoin allocation is no longer expected to improve risk-adjusted returns. This can be observed in the Sharpe Ratio delta, which reflects the increase in the Sharpe Ratio from one scenario to the next. Table 8.10 shows the relationship between these two variables:

Table **8.10** *Source* Bloomberg

	0%	1%	2%	3%	4%	5%	6%	7%	8%	9%	10%
Sharpe ratio	0.65	0.71	0.78	0.84	0.90	0.95	1.00	1.05	1.09	1.13	1.17
Delta sharpe	0%	9.23%	9.86%	7.69%	7.14%	5.56%	5.26%	**5.00%**	**3.81%**	3.67%	3.54%

In Chart 8.7, the Sharpe Ratio is represented by a line, and the Sharpe Ratio delta is shown as a histogram. On the Y-axis, we have the different scenarios of Bitcoin allocation increases, ranging from 0% to 20%.

As we can observe, the Sharpe Ratio delta drops sharply from 7% to 8%. **Therefore, a 7% allocation is considered the most optimal scenario.**

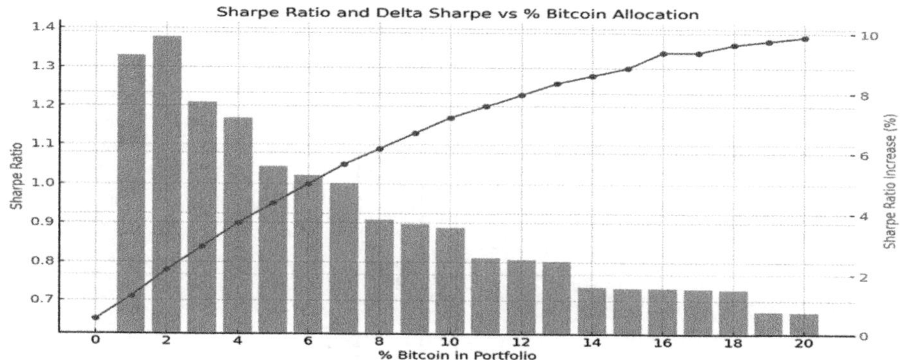

Chart 8.7   *Source* Bloomberg

However, when we perform a 5-year analysis, we find that the optimal Sharpe Ratio corresponds to a 6% allocation, as shown in Table 8.11:

Table 8.11 *Source* Bloomberg

	0%	1%	2%	3%	4%	5%	6%	7%	8%	9%	10%
Sharpe ratio	0.62	0.67	0.72	0.76	0.80	0.84	0.88	0.91	0.94	0.97	1.00
Delta sharpe	0%	8.06%	7.46%	5.56%	5.26%	5.00%	**4.76%**	**3.41%**	3.30%	3.19%	3.09%

As shown in Chart 8.8, the Sharpe Ratio delta drops sharply from 6% to 7%. **Therefore, a 6% allocation is considered the most optimal scenario.**

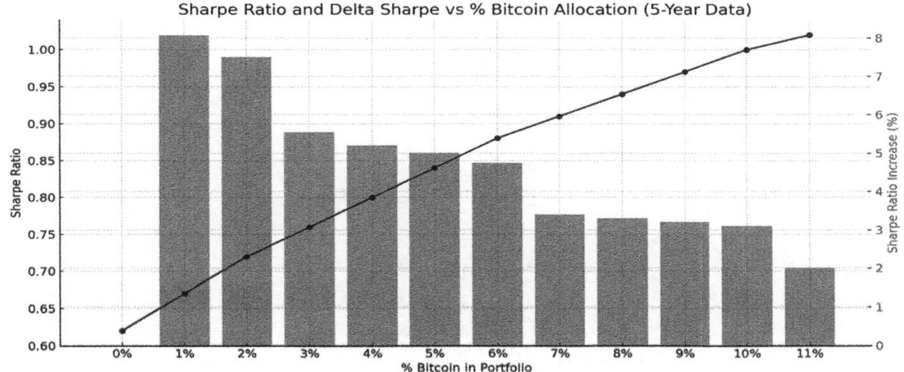

Chart 8.8   *Source* Bloomberg

Based on these two analyses, we can conclude that the **optimal allocation of Bitcoin in a global portfolio should be between 6% and 7%.**

On the other hand, as we can see, Bitcoin has had the best Sharpe ratio since 2019 compared to the S&P 500 and DJI. According to the Sharpe ratio, Bitcoin's risk-adjusted returns are double those of the Dow Jones Industrial Average and significantly outperform the S&P 500.

As of April 2025, Bitcoin's Sharpe ratio is 0.89, compared to 0.62 for the S&P 500 (purple line) and 0.45 for the Dow Jones Industrial Average (DJIA) (blue line), as shown in Chart 8.9:

Bitcoin Sharpe Ratio

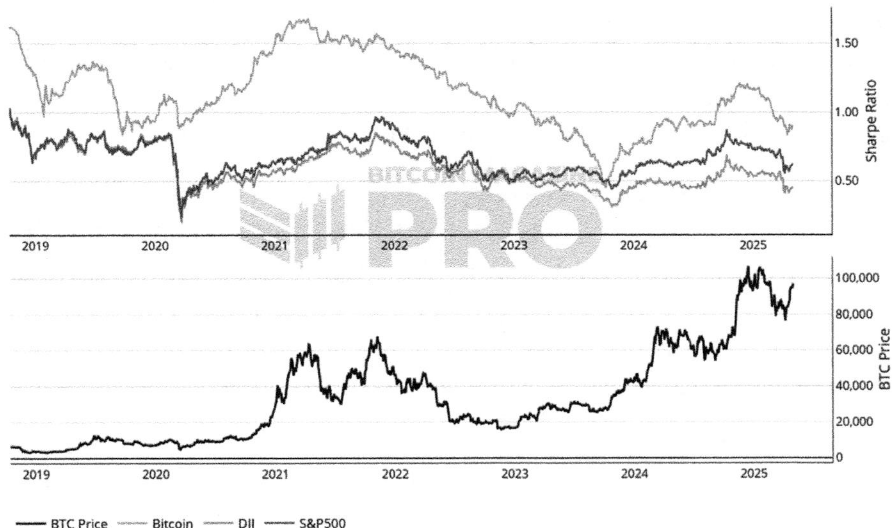

Chart 8.9   *Source* Bitcoin Magazine Pro

As we mentioned earlier, as Bitcoin grows and matures, its market cap and investor conviction increase, and its volatility will continue to decline. The impact of Bitcoin on portfolio volatility has decreased with each cycle, as illustrated in Chart 8.10:

Portfolio Volatility

Chart 8.10 *Source* Bitcoin Magazine Pro

But this doesn't mean Bitcoin won't continue to experience significant drops, even during a bull run.

To understand just how volatile Bitcoin is, we can observe that from bull run peaks to bear market bottoms, the average decline across all cycles has been around 80% as shown in Chart 8.11.

Chart 8.11 *Source* Tradingview (2012–2025)

In the most recent cycle (2021–2024), the decline was approximately 78%.

Another critical aspect is **diversification**: A well-diversified portfolio can help manage risk. The optimal cryptocurrency portfolio should be more evenly distributed across various assets, rather than heavily weighted toward major cryptocurrencies like Bitcoin and Ethereum.

However, over-diversification is not ideal in the crypto market, as it can introduce more risk than benefit, mainly when concentrating your investment in the most profitable, secure, and sector-leading protocols.

By considering these strategies and tools, investors can better assess their risk tolerance and make informed decisions when incorporating cryptocurrencies into their investment portfolios.

An essential factor to consider in portfolios is the timing of rebalancing, as it significantly impacts performance and risk, particularly since cryptocurrencies are highly volatile assets.

The impact of transaction costs (market impact cost) is irrelevant, as fees are typically below 0.2%. However, I would opt for quarterly or monthly rebalancing.

I have included a Chart of Bitcoin's monthly returns since 2012. Table 8.12 illustrates that October and November are the best-performing months.

Table 8.12 *Source* Bitcoin Magazine Pro

Monthly Returns Heatmap

Select which asset you want to view from the Asset dropdown box.

Month	2012	2013	2014	2015	2016	2017	2018	2019	2020	2021	2022	2023	2024	2025
January	17.48%	51.43%	10.10%	-32.22%	-14.74%	-0.05%	-27.81%	-7.51%	30.55%	14.25%	-17.03%	39.98%	0.78%	0.00%
February	-12.02%	62.71%	-31.37%	17.31%	19.50%	22.71%	2.56%	11.23%	-8.28%	36.80%	12.26%	0.07%	43.63%	-9.41%
March	0.35%	181.34%	-17.40%	-4.01%	-4.98%	-8.97%	-32.84%	7.95%	-25.05%	29.61%	5.52%	23.20%	15.80%	
April	1.07%	48.17%	-1.42%	-3.43%	8.16%	27.75%	33.32%	28.63%	34.51%	-1.79%	-17.23%	2.97%	-14.36%	
May	4.85%	-8.13%	39.88%	-2.91%	18.01%	66.39%	-18.96%	62.46%	9.03%	-35.38%	-15.60%	-7.30%	11.07%	
June	28.92%	-29.99%	1.76%	14.99%	27.00%	6.67%	-14.75%	26.72%	-3.07%	-6.02%	-39.26%	12.00%	-7.03%	
July	39.53%	9.55%	-8.92%	7.86%	-7.34%	16.71%	21.17%	-7.23%	24.00%	19.19%	20.81%	-4.15%	3.10%	
August	8.38%	30.97%	-17.78%	-18.94%	-8.41%	65.60%	-9.06%	-4.51%	3.00%	12.98%	-14.26%	-11.17%	-8.84%	
September	22.66%	-1.78%	-18.65%	2.62%	6.39%	-8.56%	-5.99%	-13.77%	-7.76%	-7.28%	-2.94%	3.94%	7.26%	
October	-10.05%	61.22%	-13.38%	32.69%	14.79%	48.31%	-4.51%	10.54%	28.17%	40.32%	5.43%	28.39%	11.10%	
November	12.92%	450.61%	12.31%	20.14%	6.20%	55.51%	-36.99%	-17.47%	42.42%	-7.06%	-16.17%	8.88%	37.36%	
December	7.62%	-34.82%	-15.32%	13.85%	30.55%	39.26%	-7.20%	-5.15%	47.59%	-18.81%	-3.80%	12.22%	-3.11%	
Annual	187.33%	5285.96%	-56.05%	34.00%	125.51%	1336.73%	-73.51%	94.39%	304.93%	59.72%	-64.35%	156.11%	120.95%	-9.41%

It uses color coding: green for positive monthly returns, amber for neutral, and red for negative returns.

The heatmap helps investors quickly assess Bitcoin's historical volatility and performance patterns month by month. It allows investors to track and understand Bitcoin's cyclical behavior, highlighting potential seasonal trends in price movements.

8.3   Risk Management

A good strategy for acquiring Bitcoin is dollar-cost averaging. This strategy consists of systematically buying the same amount of Bitcoin every week. This decreases the impact of volatility and eliminates the need for any complex purchasing strategy.

If you had invested $50 weekly in Bitcoin over the past nine years, your total investment of $23,550 would be worth more than $500,000 with substantially eased periods of drawdown. This approach allows investors to accumulate Bitcoin gradually without the pressure to time the market. Chart 8.12 shows that performance should be more than 2118% Versus 106% in Gold, 43% in DJI, and 221% in Apple (April 2025).

Dollar Cost Average Strategies

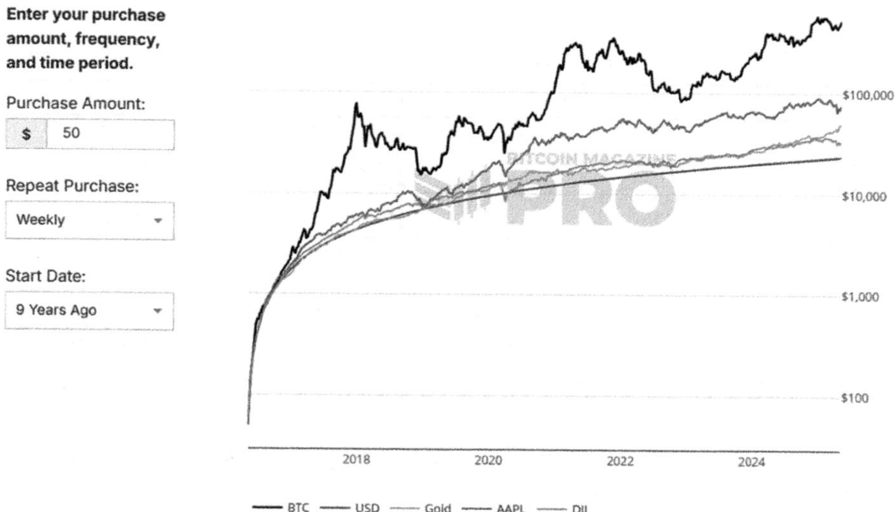

Asset	Total Invested	Total Value	Percent Change
BTC	$23,500	$521,381.52	2,118.64%
Gold	$23,500	$48,447.05	106.16%
AAPL	$23,500	$75,486.22	221.22%
DJI	$23,500	$33,634.45	43.13%

Chart 8.12   *Source* Bitcoin Magazine Pro

Bitcoin outperforms other assets even if you select different time frames, such as 5 years, 4 years, 3 years, 2 years, or 1 year.

Table 8.13 shows a 5-year scenario:

Table 8.13 *Source* Bitcoin Magazine Pro

Asset	Total invested	Total value	Percent change
BTC	$13,100	$44,124.44	236.83%
Gold	$13,100	$22,073.69	68.50%
AAPL	$13,100	$18,176.07	38.75%
DJI	$13,100	$15,452.35	17.96%

Table 8.14 shows a 2-year scenario:

Table 8.14 *Source* Bitcoin Magazine Pro

Asset	Total invested	Total value	Percent change
BTC	$5250	$10,419.92	98.47%
Gold	$5250	$7687.42	46.43%
AAPL	$5250	$5574.54	6.18%
DJI	$5250	$5503.28	4.82%

In summary, it's simply too risky not to hold Bitcoin.

Not having it may be riskier than holding it, due to the opportunity cost.

In seven out of the last ten years, bitcoin was the best-performing asset, often by a large margin, as shown in Table 8.15. While bitcoin was also the worst-performing asset in the remaining three years, this still highlights how powerful this cryptocurrency can be in generating extra performance for multi-asset managers. Looking more closely, those negative years are placed exactly midway between halvings, the periodic events where bitcoin's supply issuance is reduced, and miners' block rewards are halved.

Asset classes ranked by calendar year performance:

Table 8.15 *Source* Bloomberg, WisdomTree

2014	2015	2016	2017	2018	2019	2020	2021	2022	2023
REITS (15.9%)	Bitcoin (36.2%)	Bitcoin (120.3%)	Bitcoin (1403.2%)	Treasuries (-0.4%)	Bitcoin (94.8%)	Bitcoin (305.1%)	Bitcoin (59.8%)	Commodities (16.1%)	Bitcoin (152.9%)
Infrastructure (7.4%)	REITS (0.1%)	High Yield (14.3%)	Equities (24.0%)	Gold (-0.5%)	Equities (26.6%)	Gold (24.6%)	REITS (27.2%)	Gold (0.4%)	Equities (22.2%)
Equities (4.2%)	Small Caps (-1.0%)	Commodities (11.8%)	Small Caps (23.8%)	IG Bonds (-1.2%)	Small Caps (24.7%)	Small Caps (16.3%)	Commodities (27.1%)	Infrastructure (-4.7%)	Small Caps (16.8%)
Corporates (2.9%)	Equities (-2.4%)	Small Caps (11.6%)	Gold (12.7%)	Corporates (-3.2%)	REITS (23.1%)	Equities (16.3%)	Equities (18.5%)	High Yield (-12.7%)	Gold (14.6%)
Small Caps (1.8%)	High Yield (-2.7%)	Gold (8.1%)	REITS (11.4%)	High Yield (-4.1%)	Infrastructure (21.6%)	Corporates (10.0%)	Small Caps (16.1%)	IG Bonds (-16.2%)	High Yield (14.0%)
IG Bonds (0.6%)	IG Bonds (-3.2%)	Infrastructure (8.0%)	High Yield (10.4%)	REITS (-4.7%)	Gold (18.4%)	Treasuries (9.5%)	Infrastructure (6.3%)	Corporates (-17.0%)	REITS (10.9%)
Gold (0.1%)	Treasuries (-3.3%)	Equities (7.9%)	Infrastructure (9.8%)	Infrastructure (-5.3%)	High Yield (12.6%)	IG Bonds (9.2%)	High Yield (1.0%)	Treasuries (-17.5%)	Corporates (9.2%)
High Yield (0.0%)	Corporates (-3.6%)	REITS (5.0%)	Corporates (8.9%)	Equities (-9.4%)	Corporates (10.7%)	High Yield (7.0%)	Corporates (-3.2%)	Equities (-18.4%)	IG Bonds (5.7%)
Treasuries (-0.8%)	Infrastructure (-6.2%)	Corporates (3.7%)	IG Bonds (7.4%)	Commodities (-11.2%)	Commodities (7.7%)	Infrastructure (0.1%)	Gold (-4.3%)	Small Caps (-18.7%)	Treasuries (4.2%)
Commodities (-17.0%)	Gold (-12.1%)	IG Bonds (2.1%)	Treasuries (7.3%)	Small Caps (-14.4%)	IG Bonds (6.8%)	Commodities (-3.1%)	IG Bonds (-4.7%)	REITS (-24.4%)	Infrastructure (3.4%)
Bitcoin (-57.5%)	Commodities (-24.7%)	Treasuries (1.7%)	Commodities (1.7%)	Bitcoin (-74.3%)	Treasuries (5.6%)	REITS (-8.2%)	Treasuries (-6.6%)	Bitcoin (-64.2%)	Commodities (-7.9%)

Table 8.16 shows a comparison of Bitcoin with Nasdaq, Gold, and the S&P 500:

Table 8.16 *Source* Bloomberg 2015–2024

2015	2016	2017	2018	2019	2020	2021	2022	2023	2024
BTC 37,30%	BTC 118,88%	BTC 1317,22%	NDX -2,79%	BTC 85,03%	BTC 316,57%	BTC 47,74%	GOLD 0,78%	BTC 152,24%	BTC 108,38%
NDX 8,58%	SPX 11,24%	NDX 30,24%	GOLD -3,12%	NDX 37,29%	NDX 45,27%	SPX 28,79%	SPX -19,95%	NDX 54,90%	NDX 27,01%
SPX -0,69%	NDX 8,13%	SPX 18,42%	SPX -7,01%	SPX 28,71%	GOLD 23,90%	NDX 28,56%	NDX -33,71%	SPX 24,73%	GOLD 26,96%
GOLD -11,06%	GOLD 6,53%	GOLD 11,93%	BTC -74,52%	GOLD 17,78%	SPX 15,29%	GOLD -6,24%	BTC -63,93%	GOLD 11,76%	SPX 24,01%

When it comes to risk assessment methods, I use the **Sortino Ratio**. This measure of risk-adjusted return distinguishes between upside (good) and downside (bad) volatility, making it helpful in evaluating investment performance in cryptocurrency portfolios.

The **Sharpe Ratio** measures the return of an investment against the risk taken. It is calculated as the return minus the risk-free rate, divided by the standard deviation of the portfolio's return.

The **Sharpe Ratio** penalizes investments for their volatility on both the downside and the upside. This is less of an issue in traditional asset management but a meaningful one in crypto. The **Sortino Ratio** adjusts the Sharpe Ratio to consider only downside deviations.

Unlike the more common Sharpe ratio, the **Sortino Ratio** focuses exclusively on downside volatility, a more relevant metric for long-term wealth accumulation and preservation, as it does not penalize upside volatility.

8.4   Limited Supply Versus Monetary Expansion

* A limited supply of 21 million bitcoins, of which nearly 20 million have already been issued, contrasts with the continuous growth of the money supply in centralized currencies.
* When liquidity expands, Bitcoin's price appreciates, although this effect typically occurs with a 10-week lag, as shown in Chart 8.13.

As of June 2025, global liquidity is at an all-time high.

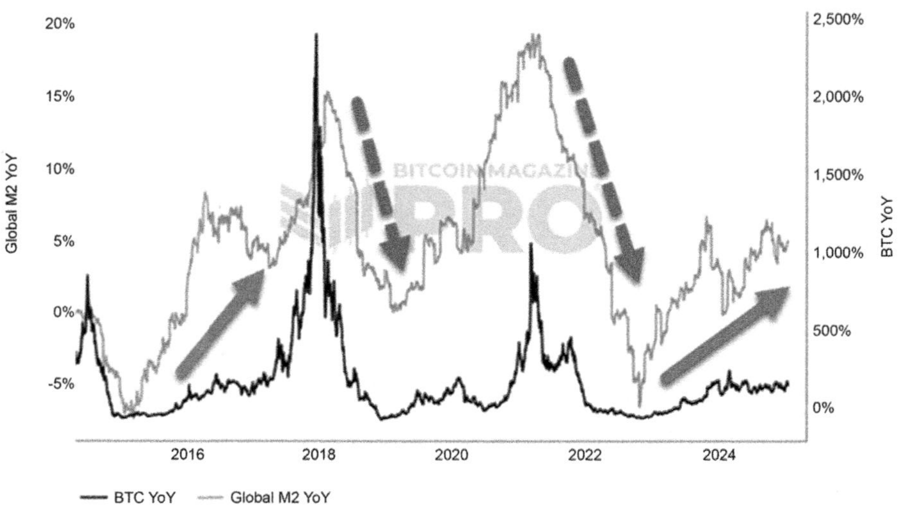

Chart 8.13 *Source* Bitcoin Magazine Pro

8.5   Hedge Against Inflation and Fiat Currency Depreciation

There are two types of inflation:

- **Physical Inflation**: caused by a shortage of goods (due to natural disasters like floods, tornadoes, etc.)
- **Monetary Inflation**: caused by the uncontrolled issuance of money by central banks.

Approximately 90% of the inflation generated is due to monetary inflation, which drives up prices without proportionally increasing wages.

As of February 2025, the U.S. public debt stood at $36 trillion, representing 123% of the country's GDP.

Since September 2024, U.S. public debt has increased by more than $1 trillion.

Then, you need a solution: **seek shelter in alternative assets, such as Bitcoin.**

The median home price in the U.S. continues to rise in USD terms, but it **declines when measured in BTC**, as shown in Chart 8.14.

It's becoming more expensive to buy a house in dollars, but cheaper in Bitcoin, due to the **depreciation of the USD and the appreciation of BTC.**

Bitcoin is technically inflationary, as new coins are created with each validated transaction. However, since its total supply is capped at **21 million**, Bitcoin is **barely affected by inflation** and tends to **increase in value over time**.

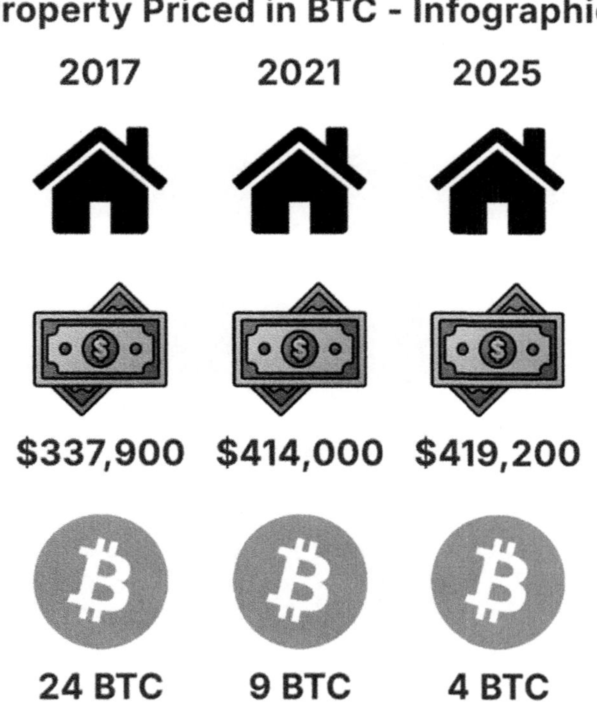

Chart 8.14 *Source* Bitcoin Magazine Pro

8.6 Why add Crypto to Your Portfolio?

Here are several reasons:

- A distinct and established asset class
- Institutional adoption: ETFs, Bitcoin treasury companies
- Limited supply vs. ongoing monetary expansion

- Hedge against inflation and fiat currency depreciation
- Low correlation with other asset classes
- Improves the portfolio's risk-return ratio
- High short-term volatility, but strong long-term performance
- The best-performing asset in 8 of the last 10 years.

9

Crypto Cycle

The cryptocurrency market follows a cycle of three phases in the following order: Halving → Bull Run → Bear Market. Among these three phases, the most important is the Halving.

9.1 Halving

What is the halving?

In the cryptocurrency market, all transactions are recorded in a public ledger, and the miner validates and records those transactions. For performing this function, the miner receives a reward, which comes in two forms:

1. Transaction fees are paid with each transaction.
2. Block reward for generating a new block.

These rewards can be spent after 100 confirmations.

The block reward is reduced every time 210,000 blocks are mined (approximately every 4 years) Table 9.1 Shows the halvings that have taken place so far:

J. Pineda, *Investing in Crypto with Confidence*,
https://doi.org/10.1007/978-3-032-07834-6_9

Table 9.1 Historical evolution of Bitcoin's block reward following each halving event, illustrating how the reward is progressively reduced by half and how the marginal impact of each halving diminishes over time

BTC block reward	Date	Block number at halving
50 BTC	January 2009	
25 BTC	Nov 2012	210.000
12,5 BTC	July 2016	420.000
6,25 BTC	May 2020	630.000
3,125 BTC	April 2024	840.000

As we can see, the reward decreases each time, and therefore, the impact and influence of each halving also become smaller over time.

Halving reduces the Bitcoin supply. Together with the fact that BTC demand has increased in 2024 because Institutional investors can access this asset class via regulated vehicles, exchange-traded products, or exchange-traded funds, this has caused Bitcoin to rise from 64k USD to 109k USD.

Increasing institutional demand and reducing supply due to halving have caused a positive price momentum.

Historically, the Bitcoin bull cycle begins on average 170 days after a halving and peaks 480 days following the halving event. The most recent Bitcoin halving happened on April 19, 2024. Counting 170 days from April 19, 2024, we are approximately October 6, 2024. As we can see in Chart 9.1, the rally began in mid-October and took Bitcoin from $60K to $109K by mid-December.

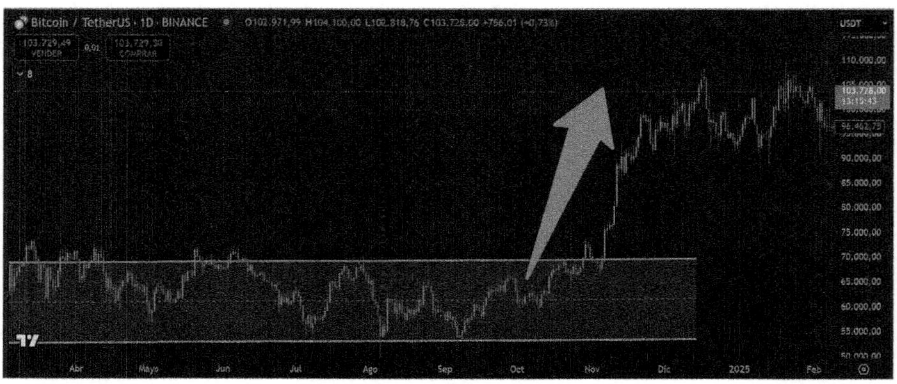

Chart 9.1 *Source* Tradingview

Consequently, 480 days from April 19, 2024, lead us to July 14, 2025. We will be at the top of this cycle, but this cycle is different.

The current cycle shows similarities to the 2017 cycle (blue line), the second line starting from the top. The period following the halving began with accumulation and no significant price increases. About a year after the halving, Bitcoin started to rise exponentially.

After the halving, which usually lasts about a year and is considered an **accumulation** period, comes the bull run, which typically lasts around a year and a half, followed by the bear market, which lasts for a similar duration as the bull run.

This halving has been different from all the previous ones, since in January 2024, **Bitcoin ETFs were launched,** driving Bitcoin's price higher during a period that normally does not see such strong appreciation. **In** just **three months** (January to March), **Bitcoin went from $40,000 to nearly $70,000.**

The bull run starts in April 2025 and has four phases, as discussed in the Altcoins chapter, sect. 5.2:

* The **first phase** is when all the money flows into Bitcoin.
* The **second phase** is when Ethereum starts outperforming Bitcoin.
* The **third phase** is when Ethereum continues to outperform Bitcoin, and large-cap altcoins go parabolic.
* The **final phase** is when mid-cap and low-cap altcoins tend to pump and go parabolic.

The first three phases can be seen in Charts 9.2 and 9.3.

In Chart 9.2, we can observe that from the bottom of the bear market, the Ethereum/Bitcoin pair follows a downtrend, meaning Bitcoin is outperforming Ethereum until April 2025.

From May 2025 onward, this trend changes, as shown within the green upward channel, and Ethereum begins to outperform Bitcoin until August 2025.

* BTC winner: from Sept 22 to April 25.
* ETH winner: from May 25 to August 25
* Sideways: Oct'25 to Nov'25

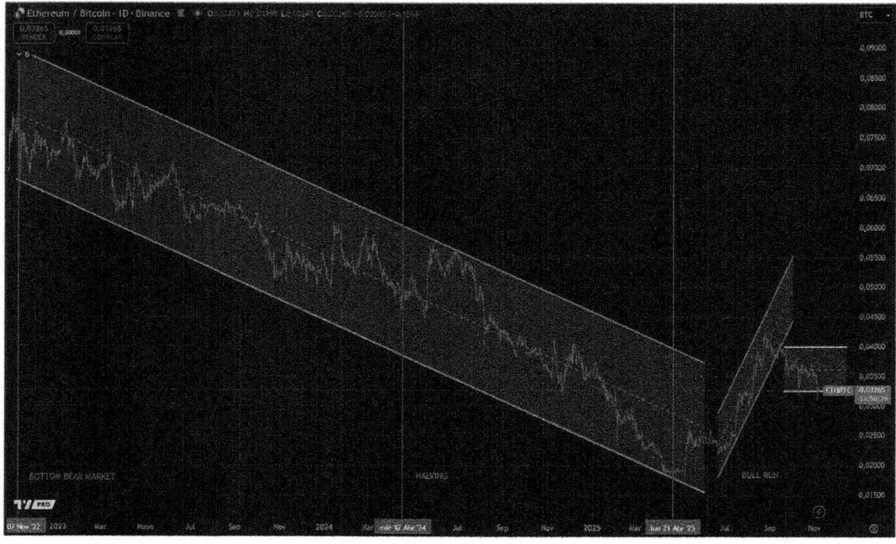

Chart 9.2   *Source* Tradingview (Nov´25)

In Chart 9.3, we can observe that starting from August 2025, Solana is outperforming Ethereum, as shown within the green upward channel. The same is happening with other top altcoins, such as Binance, which are also outperforming Ethereum.

* ETH winner: from Apr'25 to Aug'25
* SOL winner: from Aug'25 to Sept'25
* Sideways: Oct'25 to Nov'25

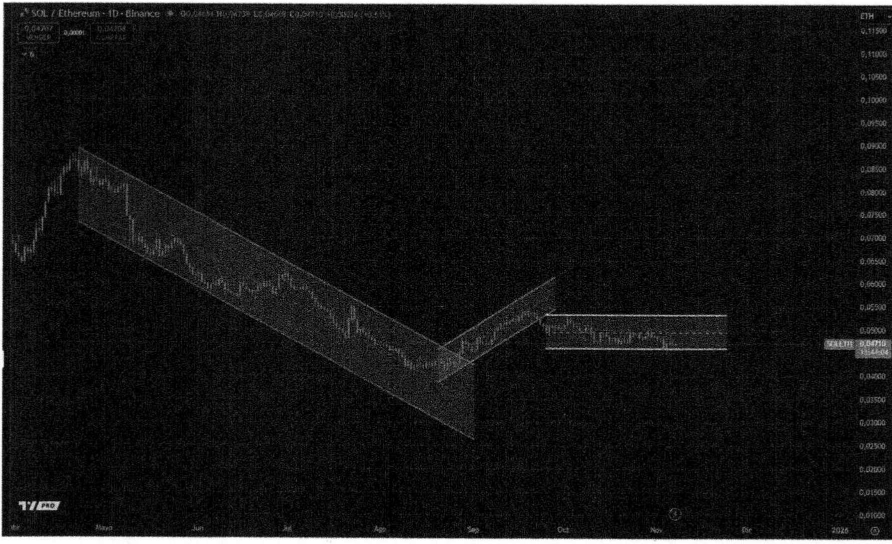

Chart 9.3   *Source* Tradingview

In the previous cycle, the same thing happened: Ethereum started outperforming Bitcoin (from Feb'20 to Aug'20), then there were a few sideways months (from Aug'20 to Apr'21), and afterward a final rally (from Apr'21 to Nov'21), as we can see in Chart 9.4:

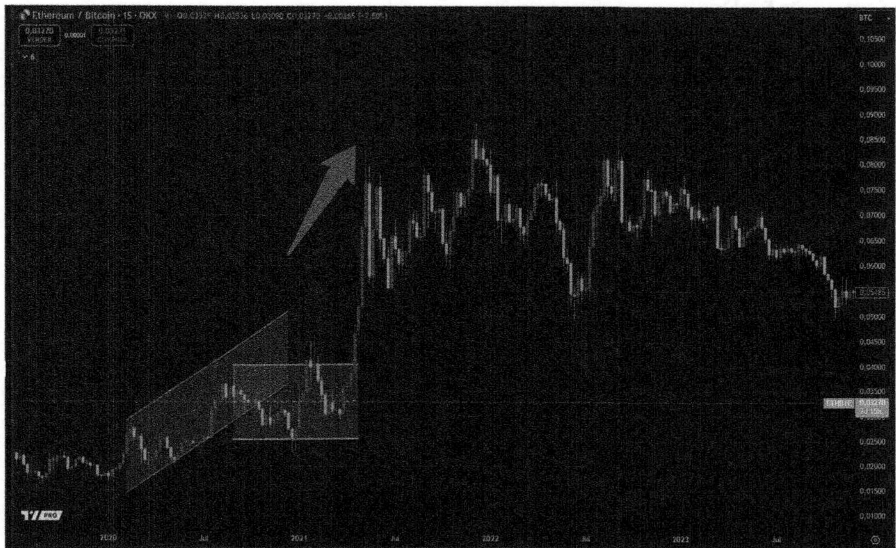

Chart 9.4 *Source* Tradingview

The same thing happened, as we can see in Chart 9.5, with the SOL/ETH pair: Solana outperformed Ethereum (from Jan'21 to Apr'21), then moved

Chart 9.5 *Source* Tradingview

sideways for a few months (from May'21 to Aug'21), and finally had the last bullish rally (from Aug'21 to Nov'21) before the bear market began.

9.2   Cycle

Chart 9.6 illustrates the different Bitcoin cycles that have occurred since each halving event:

Chart 9.6 *Source* Bitcoin Magazine Pro

It's essential to compare the current cycle with previous ones to gain a better understanding of the context.

However, it's also crucial to consider that **the market has matured over time**. The three aspects that reflect this market maturity are:

- Decline in volatility
- Diminishing returns
- Lower drawdowns

This evolution has made the **cryptocurrency market more attractive to institutional investors**.

At the same time, it's important to understand that the **entry of this type of investor** has **caused these three factors to occur.** In the end, it's a self-perpetuating cycle, or as we'd say in Spanish, *"a snake biting its own tail."*

This evolution is reflected in two key aspects:

- The following chart shows how Bitcoin's rate of appreciation from cycle lows has decreased with each new cycle.
- The drawdown size is also decreasing, meaning Bitcoin is less volatile than in previous cycles.

In the last two cycles, as shown in Chart 9.7, the peak occurred 1070 days after the bear market bottom. In the current cycle, that date would fall in early November 2025. However, this cycle is entirely different from the previous ones due to the entry of institutional investors and the launch of Bitcoin ETFs, which have distorted both the cycle and the phase we are currently in.

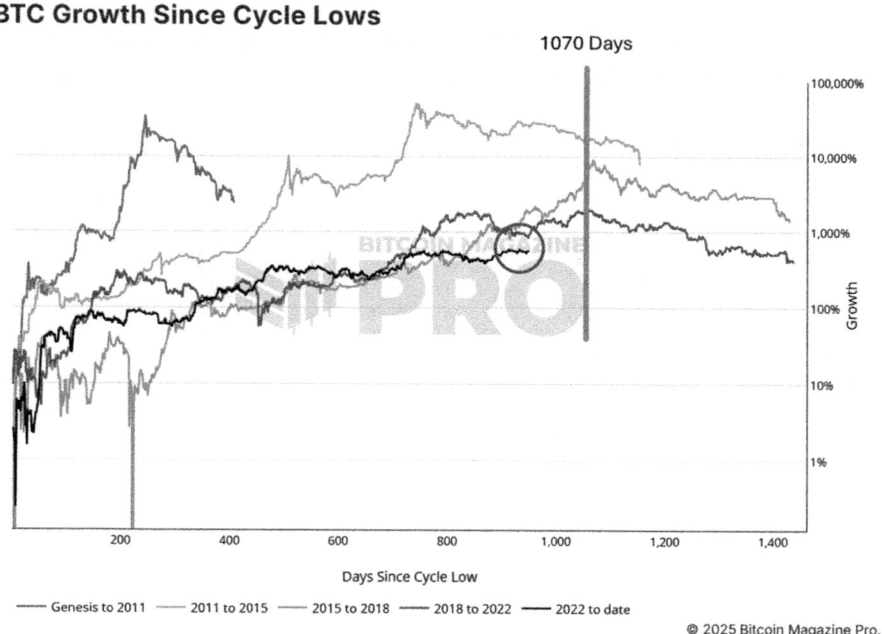

Chart 9.7   *Source* Bitcoin Magazine Pro (June 2025)

In Chart 9.8, we can observe how drawdowns have been decreasing within the bull market. We can see that within each bull market, there are more than eight corrections per cycle, but the magnitude of those declines has been shrinking over time. The current cycle is represented in black.

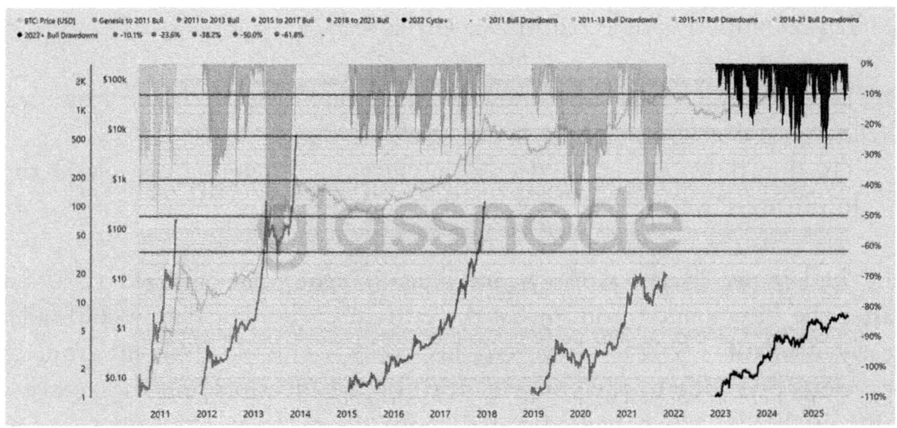

Chart 9.8   *Source* Glassnode (Sept´25)

As mentioned earlier, **volatility has been decreasing over time**, as we can observe in Chart 9.9, which shows the 3-month, 6-month, and 1-year volatility.

Bitcoin Volatility

Chart 9.9   *Source* Bitcoin Magazine Pro

An important point is that these three aspects contribute to making Bitcoin a more investable and attractive asset for institutions. This market maturation means that the days of cycles with gains above 2000% are likely behind us. However, the era of Bitcoin as an institutional and widely used asset is just beginning and will probably continue to deliver unmatched returns in the coming years.

This market maturity doesn't reduce Bitcoin's attractiveness, quite the opposite, as we can see in Chart 9.10. Bitcoin's Sharpe ratio is twice that of the Dow Jones and more than 30% higher than that of the S&P 500.

Bitcoin still offers superior returns relative to its risk, even as the market stabilizes. However, even as Bitcoin matures, its upside remains extraordinary compared to traditional markets.

Bitcoin Sharpe Ratio

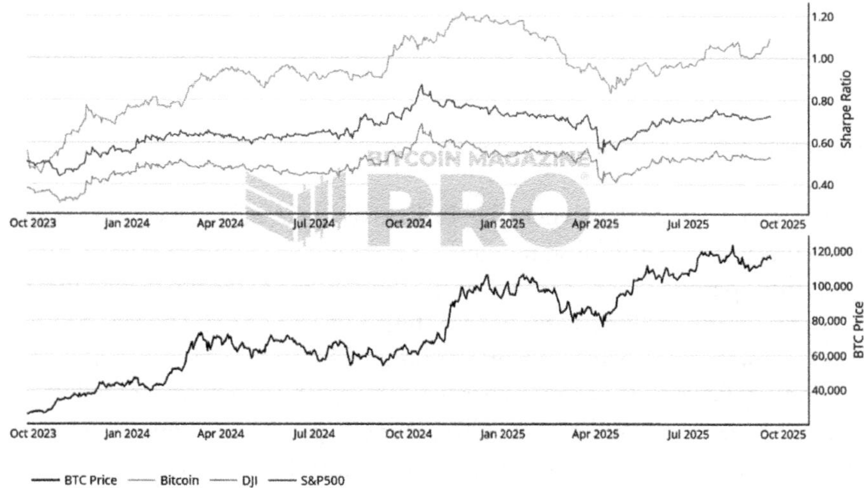

Chart 9.10 *Source* Bitcoin Magazine Pro (Sept'25)

Up to now, the Bitcoin cycle has been driven by the halving, which was the key element that made the cycle last four years. However, its effect is becoming weaker. The impact of the halving is increasingly marginal because the new supply is already small compared to the total circulating volume.

The new dominant factor is the debt structure, meaning **debt maturity and its refinancing**.

In Chart 9.11, we can see the relationship between the **Federal Reserve's balance sheet** and **Bitcoin's price rallies**.

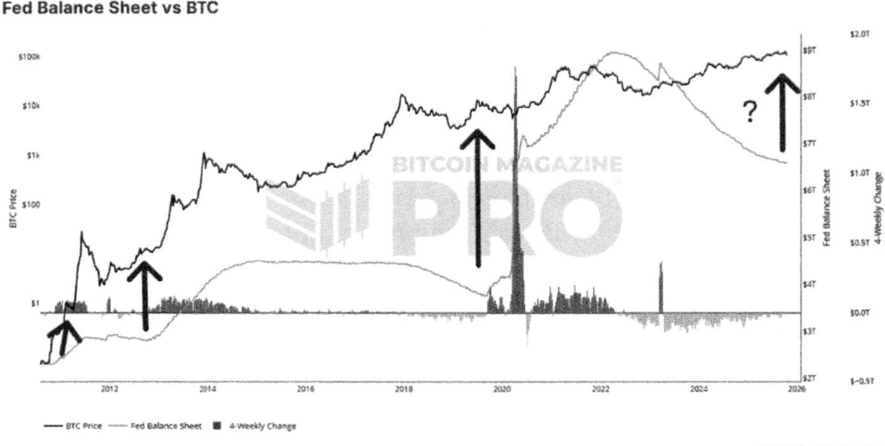

Chart 9.11   *Source* Bitcoin Magazine Pro

We can observe that when the Fed expands its balance sheet (red line), it coincides with strong bullish markets for Bitcoin. Throughout history, there have been three periods when increases in the 4-week rate of change (green histogram) occurred simultaneously with balance sheet expansion (red line). In each of these cases, it marked the beginning of a prolonged bullish trend in Bitcoin.

The "4-Weekly Change" refers to the variation in the Federal Reserve's balance sheet measured over a rolling 4-week period. It shows how much the Fed's balance sheet increases or decreases every four weeks.

- If the green bar is positive, the Fed is expanding its balance sheet → injecting liquidity into the system (buying bonds, conducting QE, lending to banks, etc.).
- If the bar is negative, the Fed is reducing its balance sheet → withdrawing liquidity (selling assets, letting bonds mature, QT).

A single weekly change can be very volatile; by using a 4-week moving average, the noise is smoothed out, providing a clearer view of the monthly liquidity trend. This indicator is widely used by macro traders to identify turning points in monetary policy.

- When the Fed observes that inflation is very high, it first raises interest rates, and if inflation persists, the Fed begins QT (Quantitative Tightening) to cool down the economy.

QT: Quantitative tightening (liquidity contraction): The Fed allows the bonds it holds to mature without reinvesting or sells assets, thereby withdrawing liquidity from the financial system and reducing its balance sheet.

* When the Fed observes that inflation is very low, there is high unemployment, and the economy is in recession, it first lowers interest rates, and if the economy does not improve, the Fed initiates QE (quantitative easing) by expanding its balance sheet to stimulate economic activity.

QE: Quantitative easing (liquidity expansion): The Fed injects money into the financial system by buying assets, thereby increasing its balance sheet.

During the previous cycles, as liquidity flowed into the system and risk premiums compressed, Bitcoin rose aggressively. When the Fed tightened its policy by raising interest rates, Bitcoin's price declined.

If we look at Bitcoin's peaks and troughs, they align much more closely with liquidity expansion or contraction (QE, M2 growth, negative real rates, etc.) than with the halving dates, as shown in Table 9.2.

Table 9.2 Relationship between U.S. monetary policy regimes, Federal Reserve interest rates, and major Bitcoin market peaks and troughs, showing that Bitcoin cycle extremes have historically aligned more closely with liquidity conditions than with halving dates

Date	Fed	Interest rate	Bitcoin
2013	QE3	0%	DIC 2013 peak bull run
2017	Accommodative policy —low interest rates	1,25%	DIC 2017 peak bull run
2020–2021	QE Covid	0%	NOV 2021 peak bull run
2022	QT	5%	NOV 2022 bottom bear market

In Chart 9.12, we can see all the above together and verify that when Bitcoin has experienced a bullish rally, it has coincided with low interest rates (blue line) and/or Fed balance sheet expansion (green line). Conversely, when Bitcoin has entered a bearish phase, it has been during periods of rising interest rates and/or Fed balance sheet reduction.

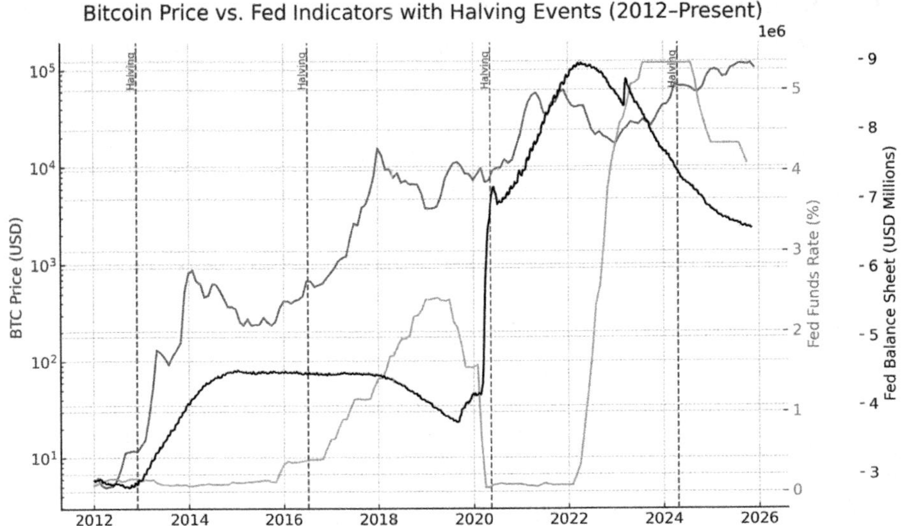

Chart 9.12 Combined view of Bitcoin price cycles, U.S. interest rates, and Federal Reserve balance sheet dynamics, highlighting that bullish Bitcoin phases have coincided with low interest rates and/or balance sheet expansion, while bearish phases have occurred during periods of monetary tightening

Now (Nov'25), as the Fed has begun cutting interest rates, putting an end to quantitative tightening (QT) and closing the chapter on the restrictive monetary policy in place since December 1st, a new phase of the current bull market could be beginning, especially considering that many metrics suggest BTC is still far from reaching its peak.

Many indicators remain well below overbought levels, as shown in Chart 9.13, which presents the MVRV Z-Score metric, an indicator that identifies periods when Bitcoin is extremely overvalued or undervalued relative to its fair value.

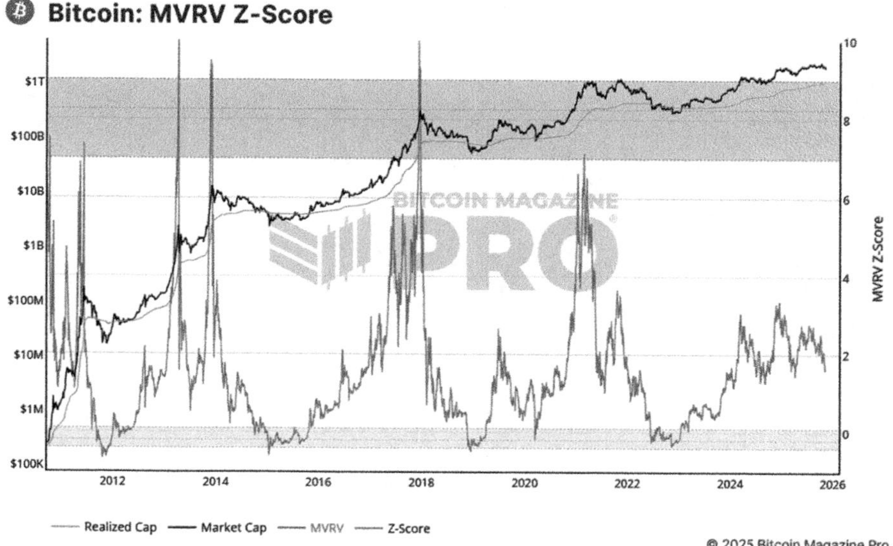

Chart 9.13   *Source* Bitcoin Magazine Pro

A metric that can give us an idea of how high the top of the bull market and the bottom of the bear market could reach is the **Bitcoin Cycle Master**. This metric is a combination of on-chain indicators, including coin value days destroyed and terminal price.

In previous cycles, Bitcoin has always reached the red line (overvalued) at the top, which currently sits around $274 K. However, since this market is more mature, a more conservative estimate would be the orange level (aggressively valued), which is around $170 K, as shown in Chart 9.14.

This metric has identified bear market bottoms with near-perfect accuracy, such as in Jan'15, Dec'18, and Nov'22. At present, the cycle low for the next bear market would be around $43 K.

Bitcoin: Bitcoin Cycle Master

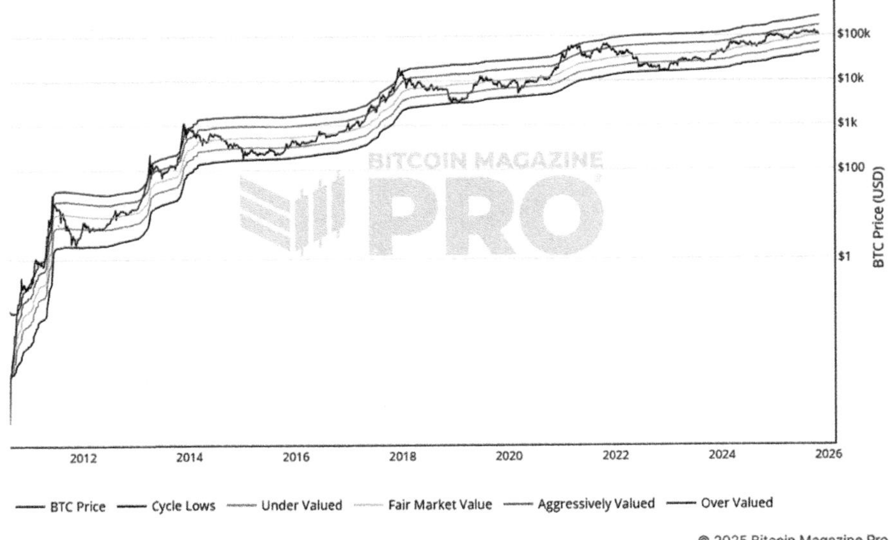

Chart 9.14 *Source* Bitcoin Magazine Pro

Therefore, the bull market is likely to extend beyond early 2026, stretching the current uptrend to almost two years in duration.

In Table 9.3, we can see how the time span between each halving and the subsequent market peak has been increasing with every cycle.

Table 9.3 Duration between each Bitcoin halving event and the subsequent bull market peak, illustrating the progressive lengthening of cycles as the market matures and institutional participation increases

Halving	Top bull market	Duration
NOV´12	DIC´13	1 YEAR
JUL´16	DIC´17	1,5 YEARS
MAY´20	NOV´21	1,5 YEARS
APR´24	¿?	2 YEARS?

It's important to remember that every bull run includes pullbacks, which are healthy and necessary to strengthen the overall trend. That's why, when you see Bitcoin dropping, zoom out and look at the bigger picture in the long term.

This cycle, in my opinion, will be selective, meaning **not all altcoins will rise,** but only a few in particular. It won't be like previous cycles where everything rises. Coins from certain narratives will rise, or those favored by the genius act, or those included in the US strategic reserve, or the network where most stablecoins are created (which so far is ETH the most used).

It will also influence the currencies selected by treasury companies, which currently include Bitcoin, Ethereum, Solana, and Hyperliquid.

BTC is a fundamentally different asset compared to the rest of the market. It is no longer marginal; it is maturing, evolving, and becoming increasingly institutionalized.

This, naturally, alters market behavior—but it does not invalidate the potential for explosive growth. Moreover, family offices and wealth managers have not yet begun to accumulate Bitcoin, and governments are gradually starting to integrate it into their reserves.

On another note, as of today (June 2025), Trump and his team are exploring a way to purchase Bitcoin to create a strategic reserve, without increasing the national debt and without impacting taxpayers. The approach being considered involves revaluing the U.S. gold reserves at current market prices ($3,300 per ounce), instead of the outdated official price of $42 per ounce that has remained unchanged since 1971.

By doing so, the Federal Reserve's balance sheet would increase by approximately $850 billion, allowing the Fed to borrow against the newly valued gold to purchase Bitcoin, potentially up to 1 million BTC, without adding to the national debt. This would form the foundation of a U.S. Strategic Bitcoin Reserve.

However, this measure requires approval from the U.S. Congress. Senator Cynthia Lummis has already introduced the proposal.

Another variable that is related to Bitcoin's cycles is high-yield credit.

Bitcoin prices are influenced by **global market liquidity, credit, and sentiment.**

High-yield credit rates can be seen as a reflection of investor sentiment toward the global economy.

- When optimistic about the economy, investors are more willing to take on risk and invest in high-yield bonds.
- Conversely, when investors are pessimistic about the economy, they are less willing to take on risk, and demand for high-yield bonds falls.

High-yield credit refers to corporate bonds that pay higher interest rates because they have lower credit ratings than investment-grade bonds. Although high-yield bonds are riskier, they can offer investors higher returns and diversification benefits.

As Chart 9.15 shows, when high yield rises, Bitcoin's price tends to increase as well, and when high yield falls, Bitcoin's price also declines. The chart is divided by halving dates.

High Yield Credit: Bitcoin Cycles

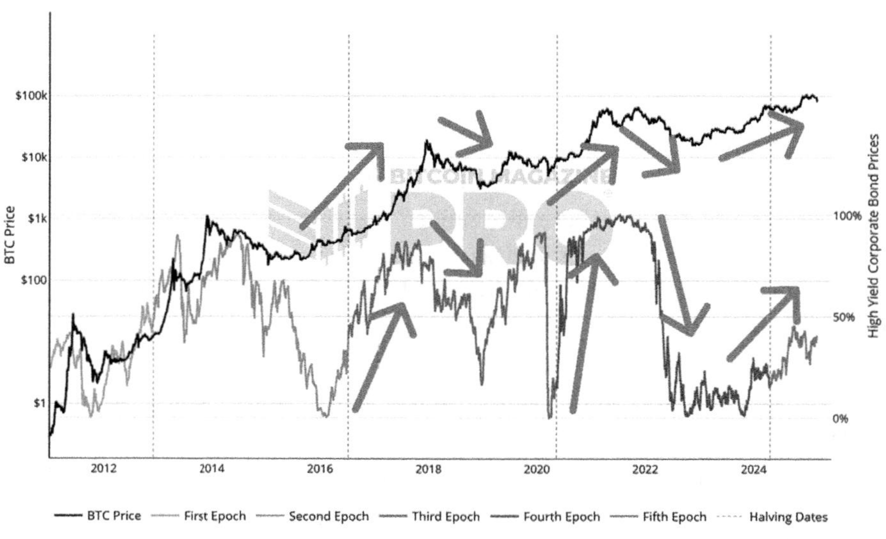

Chart 9.15 *Source* Bitcoin Magazine Pro

9.3   Miner's Metrics

Regarding metrics that reflect miner activity, one key indicator is the **Puell Multiple**, which measures Bitcoin miner sentiment by evaluating their earnings relative to historical data.

The Puell Multiple compares current miner earnings against the yearly average from the previous year.

As of February 2025, the Puell Multiple is at 1.04, meaning miners currently earn 104% of what they made on average over the past year.

This marks a significant improvement from just a few months ago. As shown in Chart 9.16, in September 2024, the multiple was as low as 0.53, indicating miners earned just over half of their previous year's average.

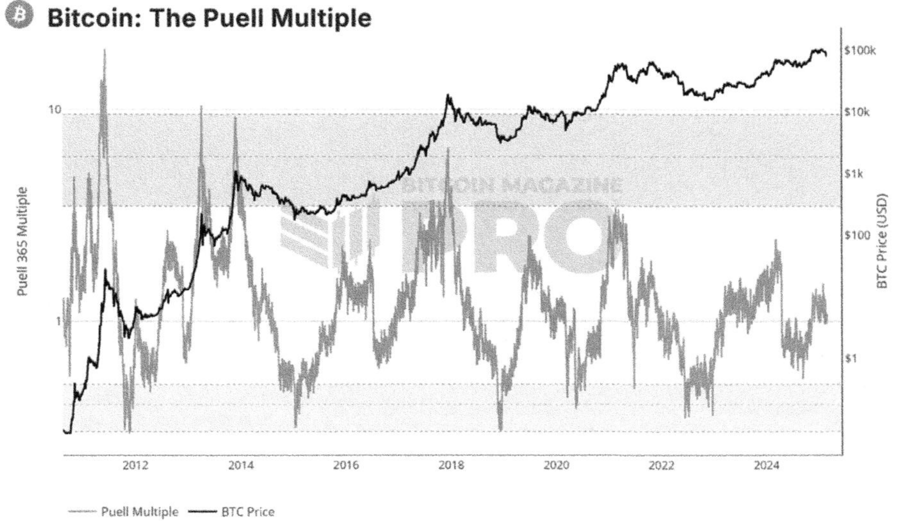

Chart 9.16   *Source* Bitcoin Magazine Pro

The fact that the Puell Multiple is recovering suggests that the outlook for miners is improving.

In Chart 9.17, we can see another miner metric **Bitcoin's hash rate,** which is the total computational power used to secure the network. This hash rate has steadily increased, indicating that more miners are entering the network or existing miners are upgrading their equipment to compete for block rewards.

Bitcoin: Bitcoin Hashrate

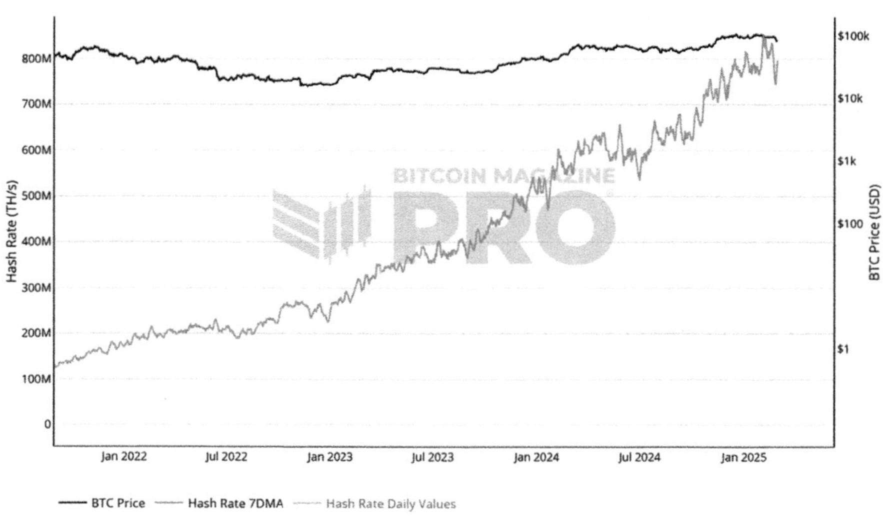

Chart 9.17 *Source* Bitcoin Magazine Pro

Hash Ribbons Indicator is a Bitcoin market signal designed to identify periods of miner distress, known as miner capitulation. It tracks the 30-day (blue line) and 60-day (purple line) moving averages of Bitcoin's hash rate. When the 30-day moving average crosses below the 60-day moving average, it means a miner capitulation, when miners, under financial stress, shut off their equipment, and it is a bearish outlook for the following days. During these times, Bitcoin miners may turn off their mining rigs due to unsustainable costs or low profitability. When miners capitulate, Bitcoin prices may be at or near major lows, potentially signalling a buying opportunity for long-term investors.

But I would buy after this situation occurs, that is, after the moving average crosses the 30-day moving average and the 60-day moving average, as we can see in Chart 9.18.

🅱 Bitcoin: Hash Ribbons Indicator

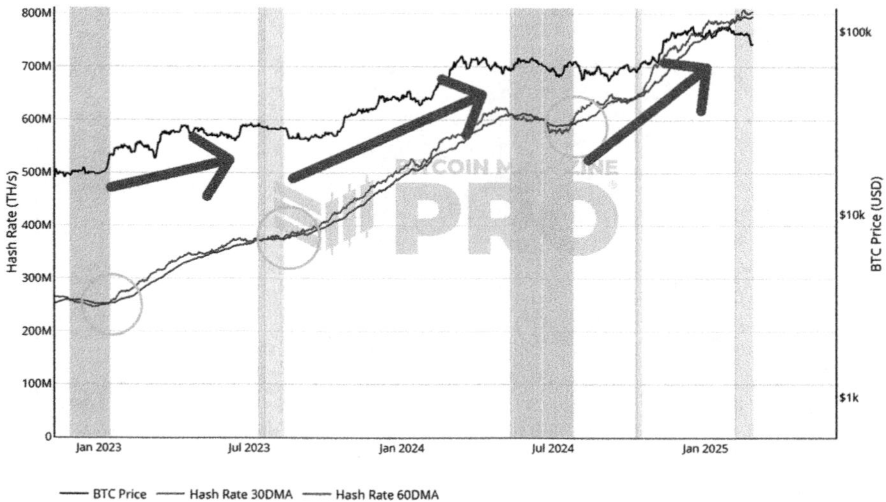

Chart 9.18 *Source* Bitcoin Magazine Pro

Miner capitulation often occurs after sharp declines in Bitcoin's price, making it a crucial signal for detecting potential market bottoms. Historically, this indicator has helped investors identify periods of accumulation where buying Bitcoin at depressed prices may offer significant upside in the future.

Another important miner metric is the **Hashprice,** the amount of BTC or USD miners can earn for each terahash (TH/s) of computational power they contribute to the network. It has a positive correlation with Bitcoin price and transaction fees.

And it has a negative correlation with changes in Bitcoin mining difficulty.

When the hash price declines, as shown in Chart 9.19, the miner's competitiveness increases.

Bitcoin: Hashprice

Chart 9.19   *Source* Bitcoin Magazine Pro

The **Hash price Volatility** tracks how stable or volatile miner earnings are over time. Historically, periods of low hash price volatility have preceded significant price movements for Bitcoin. As we can see in Chart 9.20, when

Bitcoin: Hashprice Volatility

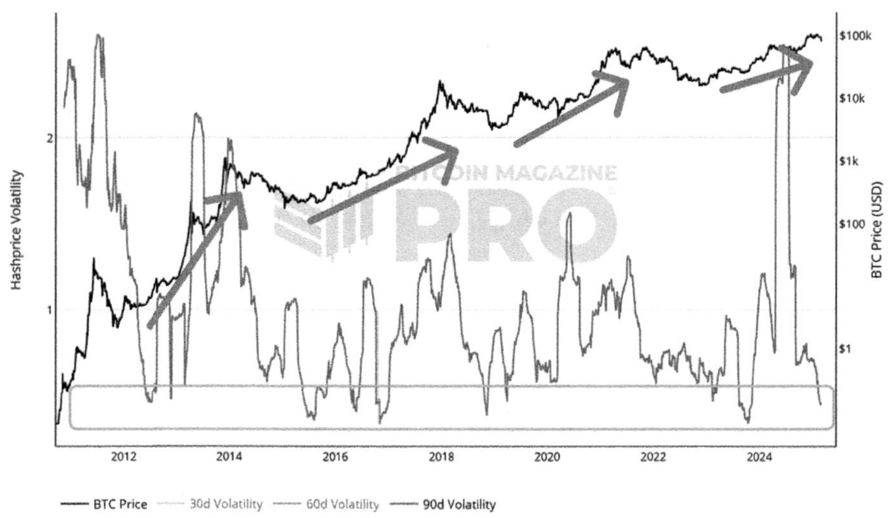

Chart 9.20   *Source* Bitcoin Magazine Pro

the 90-day hash price volatility is under 0.5, a substantial price movement for Bitcoin is coming.

9.4   Global M2 Money Supply

A variable that has shown a direct relationship with Bitcoin in previous cycles is the **Global M2 Money Supply.**

Global liquidity cycles deeply influence Bitcoin's price action, making macroeconomic conditions a fundamental pillar of this indicator. The correlation between Bitcoin and broader financial markets, especially regarding the Global M2 money supply, is optimistic. When liquidity expands, Bitcoin typically appreciates, as we can see in the following graph.

Another key observation is that Global Liquidity does not instantly impact Bitcoin, as shown in Chart 9.21. Research suggests that Bitcoin lags behind Global Liquidity changes by approximately 10 weeks. Shifting the Global Liquidity indicator forward by 10 weeks significantly strengthens the correlation with Bitcoin.

Global M2 vs BTC YoY

Chart 9.21   *Source* Bitcoin Magazine Pro

Lyn Alden mentions in her research Bitcoin: A global liquidity barometer," that *bitcoin's price has correlated more with various global liquidity measures over the past decade than any other asset class. For example, when the global broad money supply in dollar-denominated terms moves up or down in a given 12-month period, bitcoin's price moves in the same direction 83% of the time. This is a noticeably better correlation than equities, gold, or bonds of various types.*

This relationship exists because when more money is in the system, investors allocate capital to riskier assets that offer higher returns.

Additionally, as central banks create more money and inflation rises, the value of traditional assets tends to decline, prompting investors to seek out riskier assets in pursuit of better performance.

Historically, Bitcoin's bull cycles have coincided with periods of substantial expansion in the money supply (M2).

Ciclo 2013: + 26% M2

Ciclo 2017: + 22% M2

Ciclo 2021: + 49% M2

However, in this cycle, that relationship is not holding. Global M2 money supply has only grown by 0.5%, yet Bitcoin has reached new all-time highs.

This may be due to Bitcoin's growing maturity as an asset, suggesting that its price appreciation could enter a more structural phase and be less dependent on monetary policy.

The vast majority of existing Bitcoins have already been released.

This was designed so that most of the Bitcoin supply would be issued in the first 10 years, and from that point onward, Bitcoin's inflation would become minimal.

The result is a currency that increasingly tends toward zero inflation over time.

Many people may wonder why Satoshi limited Bitcoin's supply to 21 million. It wasn't an arbitrary number. Regarding this, Satoshi commented:

My choice for the number of coins and distribution schedule was an educated guess. It was a difficult choice, because once the network is going, it's locked in and we're stuck with it. I wanted to pick something that would make prices similar to existing currencies, but without knowing the future, that's very hard. I ended up choosing something in the middle. If Bitcoin remains a small niche, it'll be worth less per unit than existing currencies. If you imagine it being used for some fraction of world commerce, there will only be 21 million coins for the whole world, so that it would be worth much more per unit. Values are 64-bit integers with eight decimal places, so one coin is represented internally as 100,000,000. There's plenty of granularity if typical prices become small. For example, if 0.001 is worth 1 Euro, it might be easier to change where the decimal point is displayed, so if you had 1 Bitcoin, it's now displayed as 1000, and 0.001 is displayed as 1.

Source: Email from Satoshi Nakamoto to Mike Hearn in 2009.

Bitcoin is not a deflationary currency since its supply does not decrease. Its circulating supply continues to grow, but at an increasingly slower rate, meaning it is only slightly inflationary, and its inflation is now close to zero.

Bitcoin is inflationary, as new Bitcoins are created with each block generation. However, this inflation rate decreases over time, since the block reward gradually declines.

Combined with its fixed supply limit, Bitcoin is an asset barely affected by inflation and tends to increase in value over time.

Therefore, your purchasing power won't decrease if you hold Bitcoin. In contrast, it does decrease if your wealth is held in USD.

The dollar loses value over time, and your purchasing power declines as more money is printed and its value dilutes.

This can't happen with Bitcoin, since its supply is capped at 21 million—no more will ever be created.

There are two types of inflation. The first is caused by a shortage of goods (for example, a tornado or flood), leading to higher prices. This is called physical inflation.

The second type is monetary inflation, and over 90% of total inflation is caused by this second type.

The problem is that wages do not keep up with inflation, which leads to a decline in people's purchasing power over time.

On the other hand, U.S. debt continues to grow.

The interest expenses on the U.S. federal debt have reached a record high of $3 billion per day, tripling the amount paid 10 years ago and doubling the amount paid just 2.5 years ago.

The bubble keeps growing; the worst part is that the U.S. government has done nothing to stop it.

It's such a serious problem—with the national debt exceeding $35 trillion as of February 2025—that Elon Musk has warned: if they don't stop the increase in national debt, all tax revenue will go toward paying interest, and there will be nothing left for anything else.

As of February 2025, interest on the national debt is $1.4 trillion for the 2025 fiscal year. About 25% of U.S. government revenue will go toward paying interest on the debt.

The optimal debt-to-GDP ratio would be around 30%, while a level of 60% is already considered critical. The U.S. is currently at 106%—meaning that for every $1 of GDP, the country is borrowing $1.06.

The debt is growing by $1 trillion every 100 days.

In February 2025, the US total public debt surpassed 36 trillion USD, which amounts to around 123% of GDP, the highest level ever recorded.

According to the latest data from Bloomberg, US public debt appears to accelerate. Since the beginning of September 2024, the US total public debt has grown by almost + 1 trillion USD. More specifically, total US public debt has been growing at 7.43% p.a. since April 2020 until today.

For this reason, many investment banks recommend that their clients seek refuge in alternative assets like Bitcoin, which they describe as a unique diversifier to protect against economic and political risk.

10

Dominance

What is dominance? It refers to the weight or share a particular cryptocurrency holds within the overall market.

For example, Bitcoin dominance represents Bitcoin's share of the total crypto market, which is measured by comparing Bitcoin's market cap to the total market cap of all cryptocurrencies.

Since Bitcoin is the most crucial asset in the crypto space, any variation in its dominance or price significantly impacts the rest of the market Table 10.1.

Table 10.1 Illustrates the relationship between the two variables mentioned above (Bitcoin dominance and price) and the cost of altcoins, all other cryptocurrencies

Bitcoin dominance	BTC price	Altcoins price
UP	UP	DOWN
UP	DOWN	DOWN A LOT
UP	SIDEWAYS	SIDEWAYS
DOWN	UP	UP A LOT
DOWN	DOWN	SIDEWAYS
DOWN	SIDEWAYS	UP

The explanation for each scenario would be:

UP/UP/DOWN means that money is moving from altcoins to BTC, so BTC's dominance and price go up, and altcoins' prices go down. This happens **from the bottom of the bear market**. You can see it in Chart 10.4 (second arrow—the red arrow).

UP/DOWN/DOWN A LOT: since altcoins are more volatile than bitcoin, they will fall more than bitcoin when it (BTC) falls, and its dominance rises. This occurs when it makes highs in the bull run and begins a bear market. The money that has entered the altcoins during the bull run leaves the altcoins to go to the most stable and safe value, BTC. This happens **when a bear market begins**. You can see it in Chart 10.4 (first arrow—the green arrow).

UP/SIDEWAYS/SIDEWAYS: This situation hardly has any significance because this rise in BTC dominance is not reflected in its price, neither for better nor for worse.

DOWN/UP/UP A LOT: beginning of the bull run. As BTC dominance falls but the price of BTC rises, it implies that the dominance of altcoins rises because money goes more towards altcoins than towards BTC. Since altcoins are more volatile, the money goes to altcoins when the bull run begins, since you will obtain higher returns than in BTC. This happens **at the beginning of the bull run** (Jan'21). An example of this can be seen in Chart 10.1, where you can observe that in July'25, Bitcoin's dominance dropped by more than 8%, the price of Bitcoin rose by over 26%, and a top altcoin like Ethereum increased by more than 88%.

Chart 10.1 *Source* Tradingview

DOWN/DOWN/SIDEWAYS: As BTC's dominance falls, money leaves BTC and goes to altcoins. Even though the price of BTC drops, this negative factor is offset by the rise in altcoins' dominance.

DOWN/SIDEWAYS/UP: In this case, when the dominance of BTC falls, the dominance of the altcoins rises, and without the negative factor of the price of BTC falling, the altcoins will increase.

The following graphs show the Bitcoin and Ethereum price behavior vs Bitcoin dominance.

Chart 10.2 shows the Ethereum price (blue line, the higher one) and the Bitcoin price (red line, the lower one).

Chart 10.3 illustrates Bitcoin's dominance.

From January to May 2021, Dominance was down, but the price of Bitcoin and Ethereum was up significantly.

From May to August 2021: Dominance was up, Bitcoin price down, and Ethereum down more.

In November 2021, Dominance was down, Bitcoin price was down, and Ethereum price was sideways.

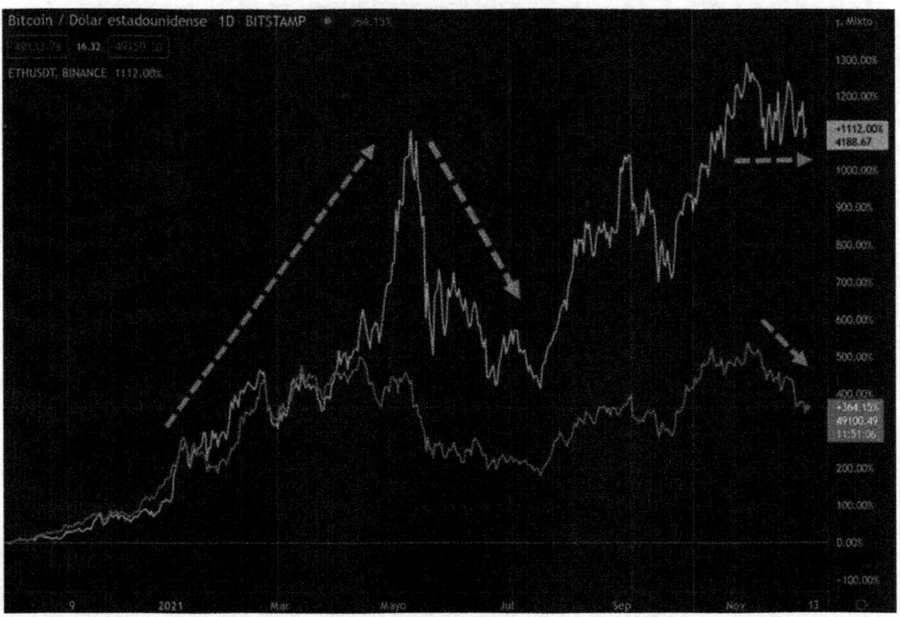

Chart 10.2 *Source* Tradingview—Year 2021

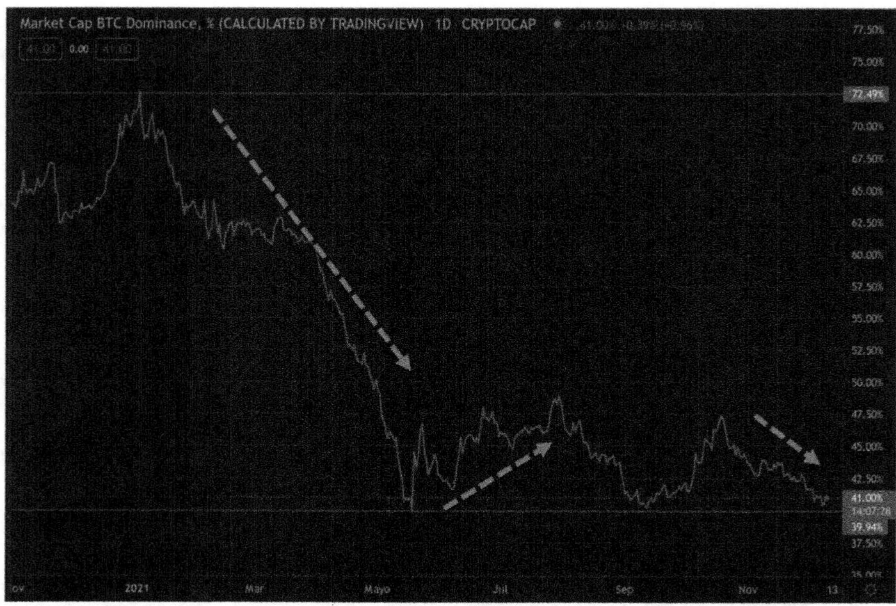

Chart 10.3 *Source* Tradingview—Year 2021

Chart 10.4 shows how Bitcoin's dominance decreases during bull runs and increases during bear markets.

This makes sense, as Bitcoin—the most significant asset in the market—acts as a safe haven, showing less volatility when the market enters a bearish phase.

Conversely, as more profitable investment opportunities emerge beyond Bitcoin during bullish phases, its dominance tends to decline.

The first arrow (green arrow) marks the top of the bull run (Nov'21), and we can see that Bitcoin's dominance had been decreasing since the start of the bull run in January'21.

The second arrow (red arrow) indicates the bottom of the bear market (Nov'22), and from that point onward, dominance began to rise.

Chart 10.4 *Source* Tradingview (March 25)

11

Ways to Invest in Crypto

In this chapter, we will explore the different ways (vehicles) available to gain exposure to Bitcoin, along with the advantages and disadvantages of each.

11.1 Hedge Fund vs ETP vs Spot vs Bitcoin Treasury Companies

When it comes to investing in crypto, there are four main ways to do it:

* Hedge Fund
* ETP (Exchange-Traded Product)
* Spot
* Bitcoin Treasury Companies

Each of these options has its advantages and disadvantages, which I summarize below:

* HEDGE FUND:

  - Professional management
  - Valuation and analysis using professional methods
  - Elimination of operational and custody risks
  - Risk management and control
  - Broad investment exposure, with access to any cryptocurrency

© The Author(s), under exclusive license to Springer Nature Switzerland AG 2026

J. Pineda, *Investing in Crypto with Confidence,*

https://doi.org/10.1007/978-3-032-07834-6_11

- – Professional-grade custody
- – Access to better trade execution (via market makers)
- – High management fees
- – High performance fees

- ETP:

  - – Low fees
  - – Professional custody
  - – Elimination of operational and custody risks
  - – Limited selection of cryptocurrencies
  - – You manage it yourself (selection and diversification)
  - – Worse trade execution than hedge funds
  - – Regulated market
  - – High liquidity

- SPOT:

  - – Unregulated market
  - – Low fees
  - – Worse trade execution
  - – Operational and custody risks
  - – Self-managed (you handle selection and diversification)
  - – Custody is your responsibility (DEX) or delegated to a broker (CEX), with the associated hacking risk
  - – Wide investment exposure with access to any cryptocurrency

- BITCOIN TREASURY COMPANIES:

  - – Investment is limited to Bitcoin only
  - – Low fees
  - – Regulated market
  - – Professional custody
  - – Traded at a premium over Net Asset Value (NAV)
  - – Exposed to a range of additional risks
  - – Worse risk-return ratio than a direct investment in Bitcoin as Spot or ETP

In my opinion, the best option is always a hedge fund. The only real drawback of this approach is the fees, but since it's professionally managed, the returns can fully offset the costs.

Investing with professional hands is extremely important, as cryptocurrencies are valued differently than other assets like equities.

Moreover, many of today's cryptocurrencies will disappear in a few years—only the most robust ones will survive: those with strong communities, solid projects, active developer ecosystems, and clear leadership in their sectors.

11.2 Bitcoin Treasury Companies

Among these companies, we have (Micro)Strategy, Metaplanet, etc. These are companies that actively purchase Bitcoin, despite their core business having nothing to do with cryptocurrency. Their goal is to hold Bitcoin as a reserve asset in their treasury.

Investors who buy shares in these companies are gaining exposure to Bitcoin, but that exposure comes at a cost: they trade at a premium to Net Asset Value (NAV). In other words, the market pays more for the company's shares than the value of their underlying assets. This premium reflects the present value of Bitcoin's expected future gains.

In addition, shareholders in Bitcoin treasury companies **are exposed to several additional risks**, including management execution, debt, share dilution, operational volatility, and high leverage, which makes their stock prices highly sensitive to fluctuations in the Bitcoin price.

For all these reasons, when comparing these companies to Bitcoin ETPs, the latter is generally the better choice. ETPs do not trade at a premium, provide a cleaner and more cost-effective way to gain exposure, and track the price of Bitcoin directly, without the added risks associated with Bitcoin treasury companies.

In Chart 11.1, we can see the premium at which these companies are trading:

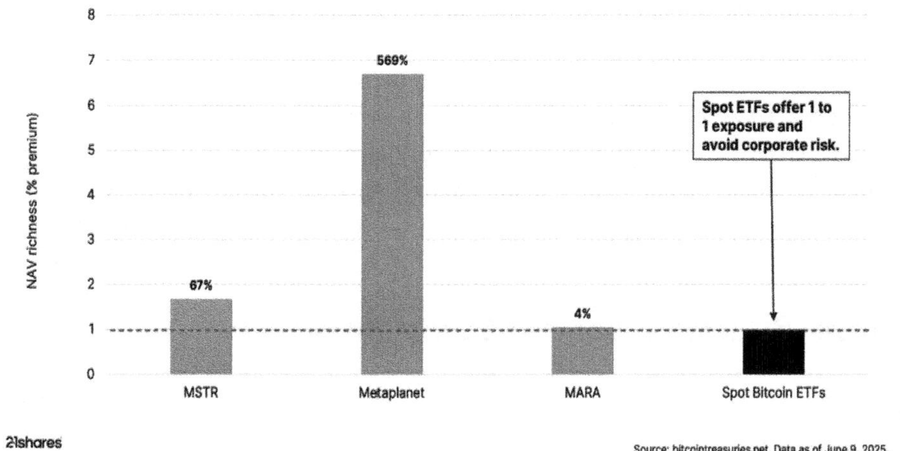

Chart 11.1 *Source* 21shares

Investing through (Micro)Strategy has delivered higher 3-month returns (1.60x more than spot Bitcoin), but also comes with significantly higher volatility (2.47x more than Bitcoin), as shown in Table 11.1:

Table 11.1 *Source* (Micro)Strategy June 2025

Asset	Price	3 Month Return	1 Year Return	BSE Return	Market Cap ($M)	Avg Trading Vol (30D) ($M)	Historic Volatility (30D)	Open Interest ($M)	Sharpe Ratio	Open Interest/ Market Cap	Avg Trading Vol/ Market Cap
MSTR	$379.76	45%	137%	2972%	$106,152	$4634	47%	$93,913	1.43	88.5%	4.4%
BTC	$106,936.02	28%	57%	799%	$2,129,595	-	19%	-	1.58	-	-

However, this increased volatility does not translate into proportionally higher returns, as the stock has a lower Sharpe ratio than a direct investment in Bitcoin (spot).

In other words, **Strategy has a worse risk-return ratio than Bitcoin.**

11.3 Bitcoin ETF

Since the launch of the Bitcoin ETF, adoption has continued to grow. ETFs now (Dec'24) hold over 1.1 million BTC, surpassing the wallet of Bitcoin's creator, Satoshi Nakamoto.

This is also why Bitcoin's dominance has not declined since 2024 (except for November), as more players—including investment funds, institutional clients, private banks, and central banks—are backing this asset.

BlackRock's Bitcoin ETF (IBIT) reached $70 billion in under a year, five times faster than the previous record held by the Gold ETF (GLD), which took 1691 days to reach the same amount.

By the end of 2024, the largest holders of Bitcoin are:

- ETFs: more than 1.2 million BTC
- Nakamoto: 1.1 million BTC
- Binance: 633.000 BTC
- Microstrategy: 439.000 BTC
- US Government: 207.000 BTC
- China Government: 194.000 BTC
- Tether: 82.500 BTC
- UK Government: 61.000 BTC

Chart 11.2 shows the accumulation of BTC in Bitcoin ETFs since their creation, showing that the largest holder is the iShares Bitcoin Trust ETF (IBIT).

ETF Cumulative Flows (BTC)

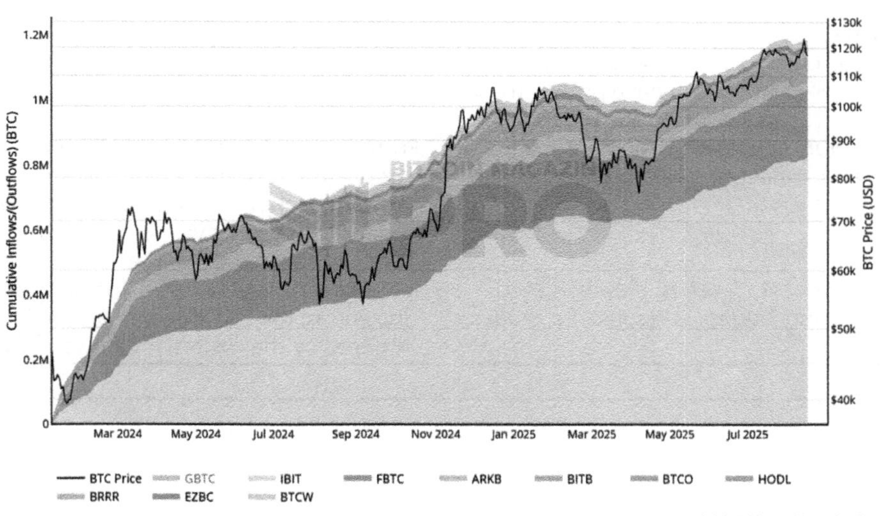

Chart 11.2 *Source* Bitcoin Magazine Pro—From January 2024 to August 2025

All underlying cryptoassets are stored in cold storage and segregated into separate accounts. Since there is clear and established legal ownership of assets, the level of legal protection would be equivalent to traditional ETPs.

The assets are also fully segregated, meaning each ETP has dedicated wallets containing only the assets that collateralize the specific ETP. Assets are never commingled and are bankruptcy remote. Because assets are diversified across custodians and wallets, it minimizes the risk of a single point of failure.

An additional layer of safety exists in the form of insurance that all custodians maintain over their business activities; independent audits and due diligence are performed on the custodians' security measures.

Table 11.2 summarizes the various asset protection mechanisms that have been put in place and their corresponding client benefits:

Table 11.2 *Source* 21 shares

Protection	Description	Benefits
Segregated assets	Assets are completely segregated	21 Shares can independently verify asset holdings on the blockchain
Cold storage	All assets are 100% physically backed in cold storage	Private keys stored offline to protect from risk of hacking. Most secure method for storing digital assets — requires both a public and a private key (as this private key is never connected to the internet it cannot be hacked)
Supervision	Custodians subject to supervision by regulatory bodies	Conformity to traditional custodial standards
Qualified custodian	Custodians are established and have proven track record	Meet institutional-grade standards for asset protection
Insurance arrangement	Custodians maintain insurance	Protection for client assets in the event of physical loss, fraudulent transfer, employee theft or cycle crime/hacking. Specific provisions vary by custodian and are subject to change
Financial & Security audits	Financial and tech audits of custodians	Independent reviews of custodian's set up ensure the activities and protections offered by the custodians are verified

12

Technical Analysis

In this chapter, my goal is to provide a concise and structured overview of the key points of technical analysis. I primarily use volatility and trend indicators, as well as chart patterns, and rely on technical analysis primarily for entry and exit timing.

Let's start by explaining what technical analysis is.

- **Technical Analysis** is the study of market movements, primarily through charts, to forecast future price trends.
- The philosophy behind Technical Analysis is based on three core principles:

  - The market discounts everything
  - Prices move in trends
  - History repeats itself

12.1 Dow Theory

Next, I will explain Dow Theory, which was developed by Charles Henry Dow and aims to analyze price trends in the market.

- **Dow Theory** is the cornerstone of technical analysis, and it is based on the following principles:

© The Author(s), under exclusive license to Springer Nature Switzerland AG 2026
J. Pineda, *Investing in Crypto with Confidence*,
https://doi.org/10.1007/978-3-032-07834-6_12

– The averages discount everything.
– The market has three types of trends:

> **Primary trend (the tide)**: lasts longer than one year
> **Secondary trend (the waves)**: corrections of the primary trend, lasting from 3 weeks to 3 months
> **Minor trend (ripples)**: fluctuations within the secondary trend, lasting less than 3 weeks

– Principle of confirmation: Two out of the three averages must confirm the trend direction (industrial, transportation, and utilities)
– Volume must confirm the trend
– Only closing prices are used
– A trend is assumed to be in effect until there are clear signals that it has reversed

- When it comes to chart types, we can find three main ones, as shown in Chart 12.1:

    – Line chart: uses only the closing price
    – Bar chart (OHLC): shows Open, High, Low, and Close prices
    – Candlestick chart

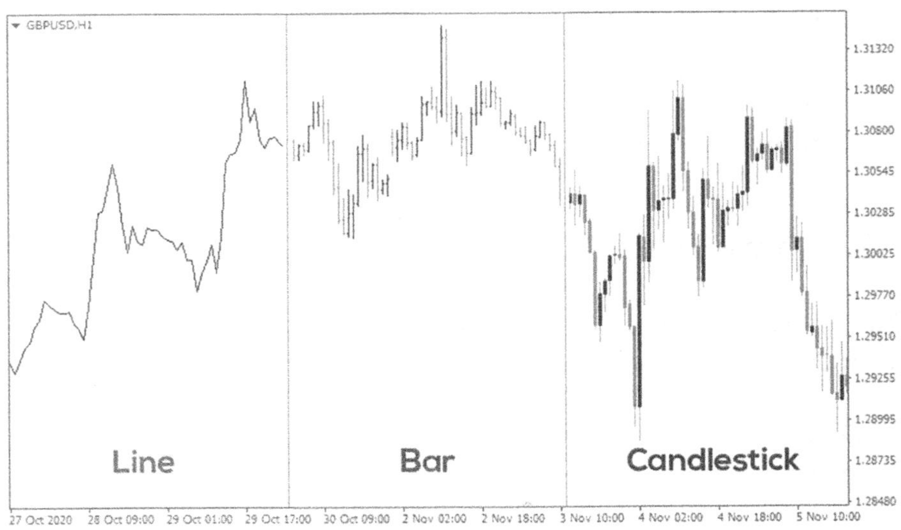

Chart 12.1 *Source* MetaTrader 4/5 (MetaQuotes Software)

Figure 12.1 shows the appearance of a bar chart and a candlestick with its interpretation.

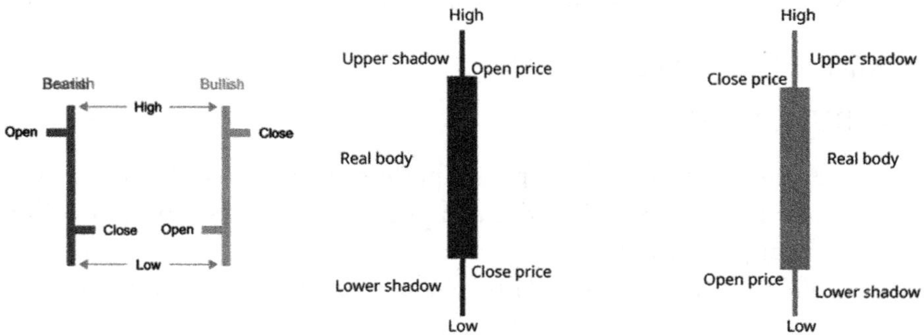

Fig. 12.1   *Sources* datavizcatalogue.com/xs.com

12.2 Basic Concepts

- Regarding basic concepts, I would like to highlight the following:

  - **TREND**: Simply the direction in which the market is moving.

    Uptrend
    Downtrend
    Sideways trend

- **TRENDLINE**: Two points are needed to draw or define a trendline. There are two types:

  - Uptrend line: connects two rising lows
  - Downtrend line: connects two falling highs

- **SUPPORT**: is the price level or zone below which buying pressure overcomes selling pressure, causing the price to bounce upward.
- **RESISTANCE**: is the price level or zone above which selling pressure overcomes buying pressure, causing the price to reverse downward.
- **CHANNEL**: consists of two parallel lines, one acting as support and the other as resistance. A trendline is drawn using two points, and then a parallel line is added—the parallel line does not need its own two reference points.
- **ROUND NUMBERS**: serve as psychological levels in the market.
- **TAKE PROFIT**: is an order that limits your profit. It is placed above the entry price for long positions and below the entry price for short positions.

- **STOP LOSS**: is an order that limits your loss. It is placed below the entry level in a long position and above the entry level in a short position.

  – When low volatility, place stop losses closer to the entry level.
  – When high volatility, place stop losses further away from the entry level.

- **MARKET PHASES**:

  – **BULL MARKET**:

    Accumulation: In this phase, professionals buy undervalued assets, often from essential service and primary industry sectors like utilities (energy, gas, water).
    Volume Expansion: This phase sees greater participation from investors, pushing both prices and volume higher.
    Euphoria: Excessive speculation takes place. People who have never invested before start entering the market.

  – **BEAR MARKET**:

    Distribution: Professionals sell their holdings while the general public still buys. Less experienced investors typically enter the market at this late stage.
    Panic: prices fall faster than in any bull market phase. There is an urgency to liquidate positions.
    Lack of Interest: The public loses interest in the market. The news is overwhelmingly negative.

- BULL/BEAR MARKET: How to identify the end of a bull or bear market.

  – **END OF A BULL MARKET**:

    Increase in trading volume
    Interest rates are high
    Rise in prices of the most popular stocks
    Stocks become a common topic of conversation
    News headlines discuss an overheating stock market

  – **END OF A BEAR MARKET**:

    Low trading volume
    Interest rates are low
    Falling commodity prices
    Low corporate earnings
    Falling stock prices and widespread negative news

- A **breakout** typically signals the beginning of a bear or bull market:

  Bear Market: triggered by a break below the previous correction low.
  Bull Market: triggered by a break above the previous rally high.
  Another signal: prices bounce 20% from their previous lows or highs.

- **TYPES OF GAPS**:

  - Gap: represents the price void between two successive quotes, caused by a lack of trading during a specific period.

    Common Gap: has little significance. It is small and occurs with low volume.
    Breakaway Gap: happens at the beginning of a trend, usually near a support or resistance level, and is the most profitable.
    Runaway Gap: occurs in the middle of a trend and is the most risky.
    Exhaustion Gap: appears at the end of a trend.

TYPES OF TECHNICAL ANALYSIS:

- CANDLESTICKS
- CHART PATTERNS/FORMATIONS
- INDICATORS
- FIBONACCI
- PIVOT POINTS
- ELLIOTT WAVES
- POINT AND FIGURE
- MARKET PROFILE

12.3 Candletiscks

- Strengths of Candlesticks:

  - Clear visualization of price action:

    A white body represents a bullish day
    A black body represents a bearish day
    The shadow is the line extending from the body, indicating the high or low price
    No shadow means the opening or closing price matches the high or low

– Easy to understand
– Can be combined with other types of technical analysis
– Allow for precise trendline drawing

- Weaknesses of Candlesticks:

    – A higher timeframe doesn't provide information about a lower timeframe
    – Doesn't show which came first—the high or the low
    – There are hundreds of candlestick patterns
    – Most candlestick patterns are reversal patterns

Single Candlestick Patterns:

- **Spinning Top**: small body (with or without shadows).
- **Marubozu**: large body with no shadows.
- **High Wave Candle**: small body with long shadows; indicates market confusion.
- **Doji**: no body; open and close are equal; indicates indecision.
- **Dragonfly Doji**: significant at market bottoms (bottom reversal); a doji with a long lower shadow and no upper shadow.
- **Gravestone Doji**: significant at market tops (top reversal); a doji with a long upper shadow and no lower shadow.
- **Hammer**: small body with a long lower shadow; bullish signal at a bottom; body color doesn't matter.
- **Hanging Man**: small body with a long lower shadow; bearish signal at a top; body color doesn't matter; requires confirmation.
- **Inverted Hammer**: small body with a long upper shadow; bullish signal at a bottom; body color doesn't matter; requires confirmation.
- **Shooting Star**: small body with a long upper shadow; bearish signal at a top; body color doesn't matter.

Double Candlesticks Patterns:

The color of the second candlestick indicates whether the pattern is bullish or bearish.

- **Harami**: the body of the second candle is entirely within the body of the first candle—bodies only, shadows are not considered (Fig. 12.2), as shown in Fig. 12.3.
- **Engulfing**: the body of the second candle completely engulfs the body of the first—bodies only, shadows are not considered, as shown in Fig. 12.4.

- **Tweezers Top**: two candles with matching highs, as shown in Fig. 12.2.
- **Tweezers Bottom**: two candles with matching lows, as shown in Fig. 12.2.
- **Piercing Line**: bullish formation—the second candle closes above the midpoint of the first candle, as shown in Fig. 12.5.
- **Dark Cloud Cover**: bearish formation—the second candle closes below the midpoint of the first candle, as shown in Fig. 12.6.

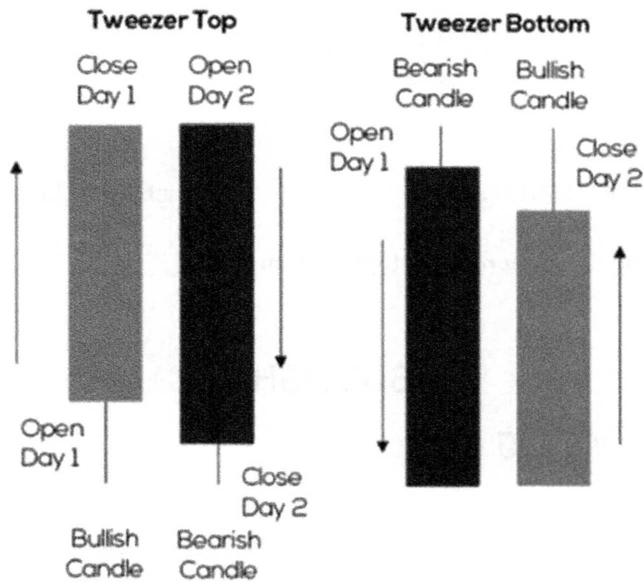

Fig. 12.2 Tweezer *Source* Investopedia.com

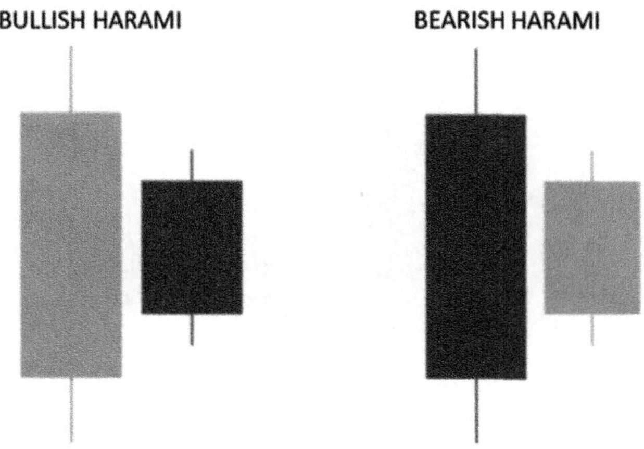

Fig. 12.3 Harami *Source* Investopedia.com

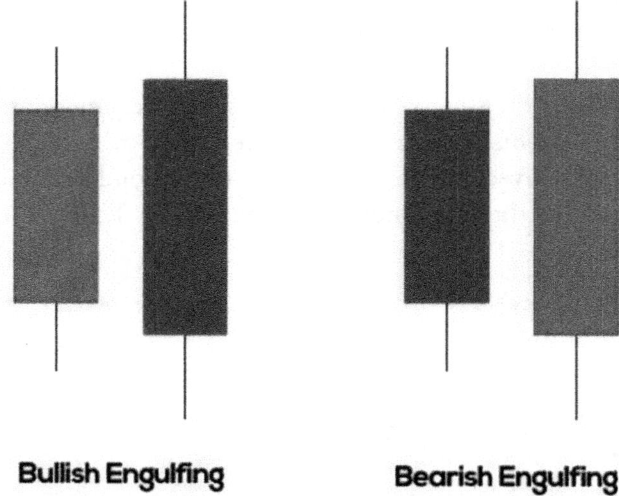

Fig. 12.4 Engulfing *Source* Investopedia.com

BULLISH:

Piercing Line

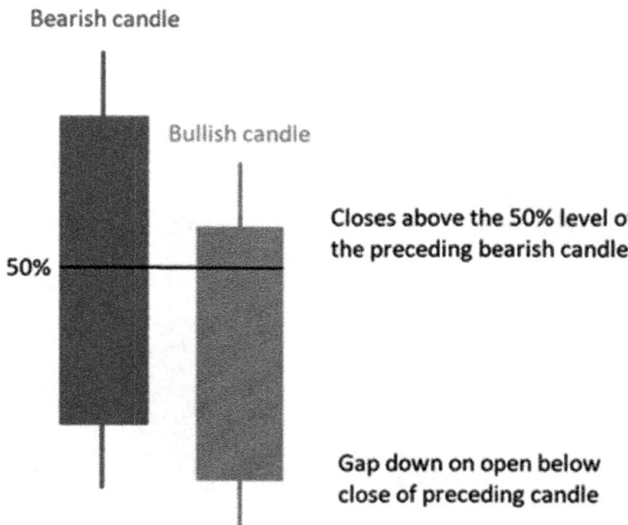

Fig. 12.5 Piercing Line *Source* Investopedia.com

BEARISH:

Dark Cloud Cover

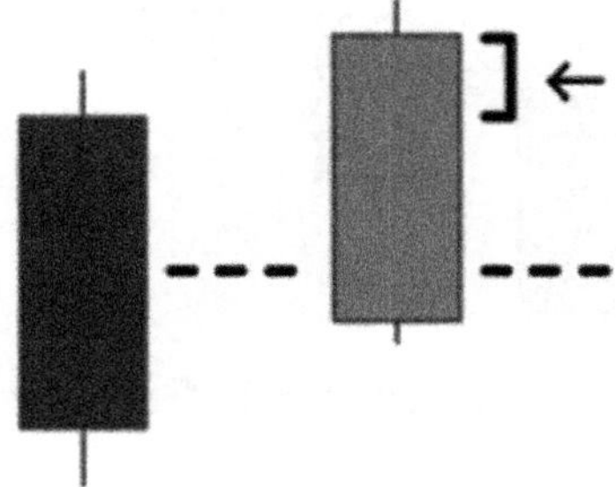

Fig. 12.6 Dark Cloud Cover. *Source* Investopedia.com

Triple Candlesticks Pattern:

BULLISH:

- **Morning Star**: the "star" (the second candle) opens below the shadow of the first candle, and its body does not overlap with the first candle's body, as shown in Fig. 12.7.
- **Three White Soldiers**: consists of three consecutive bullish candles, each opening within the previous candle's real body and closing above the previous candle's high, as shown in Fig. 12.8.

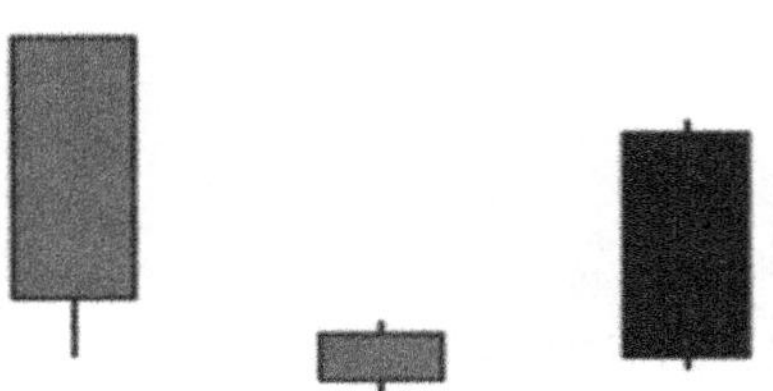

Fig. 12.7 Morning Star *Source* Investopedia.com

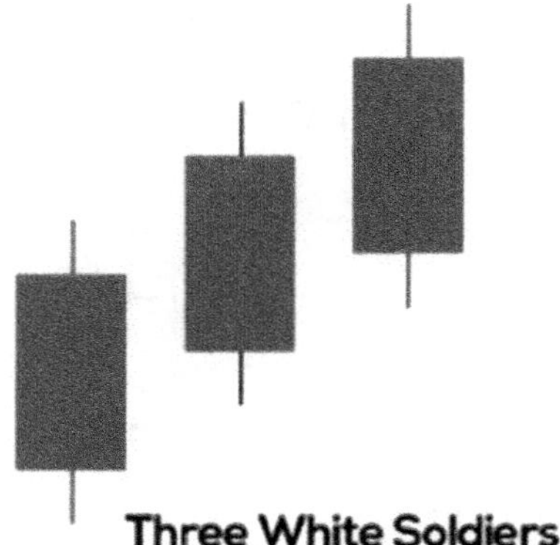

Fig. 12.8 Three White Soldiers *Source* Investopedia.com

BEARISH:

- **Evening Star**: the "star" opens above the shadow of the first candle, and its body does not overlap with the first candle's body, as shown in Fig. 12.9.
- **Three Black Crows**: consists of three consecutive bearish candles, each opening within the previous candle's real body and closing below the previous candle's low, as shown in Fig. 12.10.

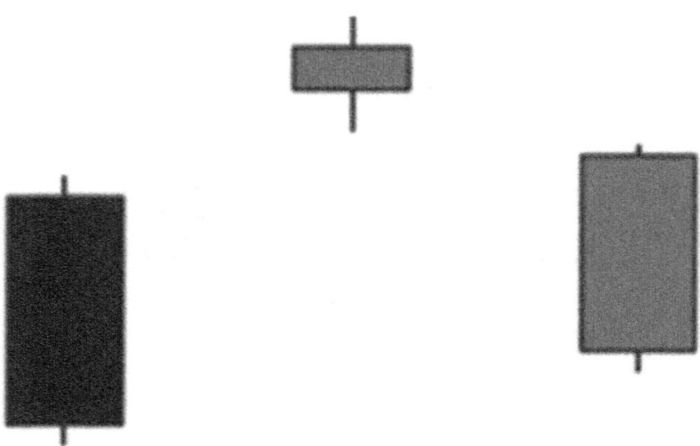

Fig. 12.9 Evening Star *Source* Investopedia.com

Fig. 12.10 Three Black Crows *Source* Investopedia.com

12.4 Chart Patterns & Formations

- **PULLBACK:** a retracement that occurs after breaking below a support level, as shown in Fig. 12.11.

  - Often seen as a second chance to enter a short position
  - Price breaks downward with **below-average volume**

- **THROWBACK:** a retracement that occurs after breaking above a resistance level, as shown in Fig. 12.11.

  - Often seen as a second chance to enter a long position
  - Price breaks upward with above-average volume

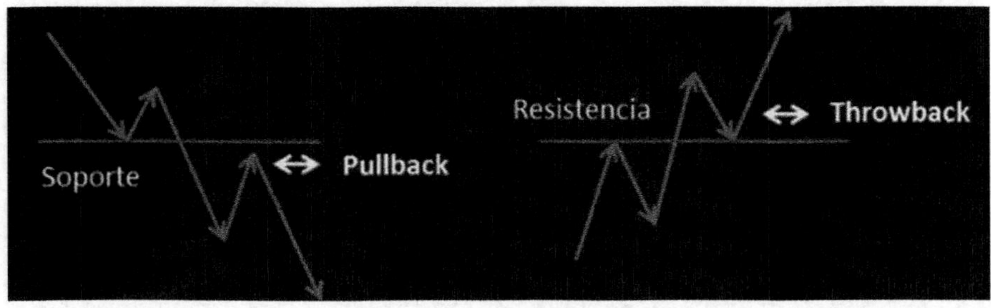

Fig. 12.11 *Source* Rankia.com

- **REVERSAL PATTERNS** (as shown in Fig. 12.12):

  - **Double Top and Double Bottom**: a formation that takes 2 to 6 weeks to develop. Volume is not a critical factor.

    There is typically a 5% difference between the two peaks.
    And a 10% difference between the peak and the valley.

  - **Head and Shoulders (H&S)**: one of the most reliable and profitable chart patterns. Volume typically decreases throughout the pattern and then increases at the breakout.

    H&S Top: usually followed by a pullback. It performs better when the neckline is ascending. This pattern appears at the tops of trends.
    H&S Bottom (Inverse H&S): usually followed by a throwback. It performs better when the neckline is descending. This pattern appears at the bottom of trends.

  - **WEDGE**: must have at least five reversal points $(3 + 2)$. It is a formation that typically takes 3 to 6 months to develop.

    Rising Wedge: less reliable; usually followed by a pullback. The lower trendline is steeper than the upper one.
    Falling Wedge: more reliable; usually followed by a throwback. The upper trendline is steeper than the lower one.

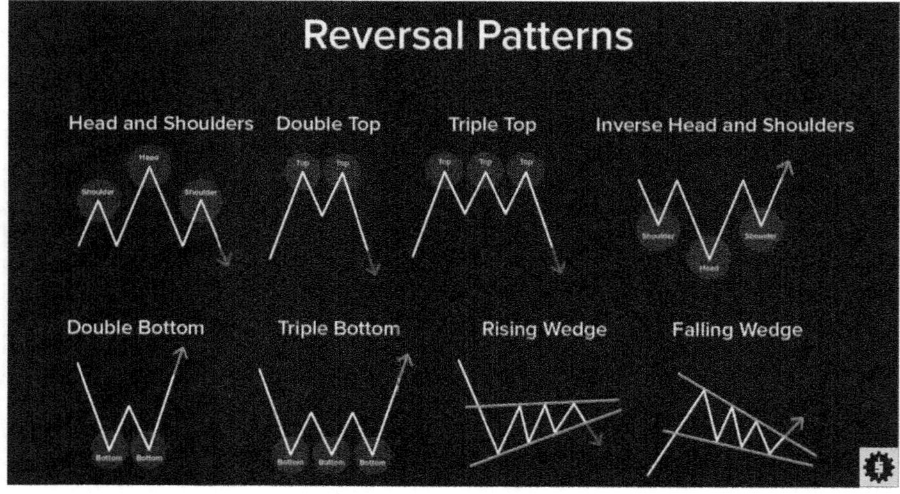

Fig. 12.12 *Source* Forextester.com

- **CONTINUATION PATTERNS** (as shown in Fig. 12.13):

  - **Flags**: considered the best pattern overall. Typically develops over 3 months.
  - **Pennants**: a shorter formation, usually lasting less than 3 weeks.

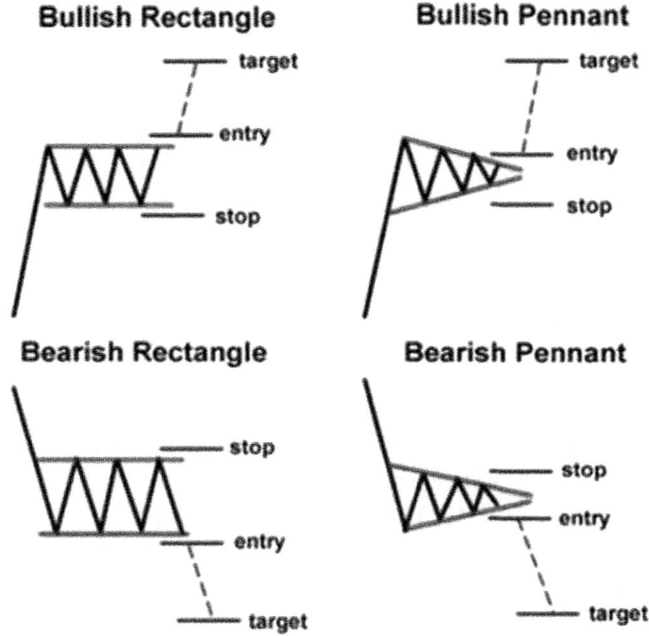

Fig. 12.13 *Source* Investopedia.com

- **BILATERAL PATTERNS** (as shown in Fig. 12.14):

  - **Triangle**:

    Each band must be touched at least twice
    Over 75% of breakouts are false
    As a reversal pattern, it occurs more frequently at bottoms
    Best performance occurs when the breakout happens between ½ and
    ⅔ of the distance from the base to the apex

Bilateral Patterns

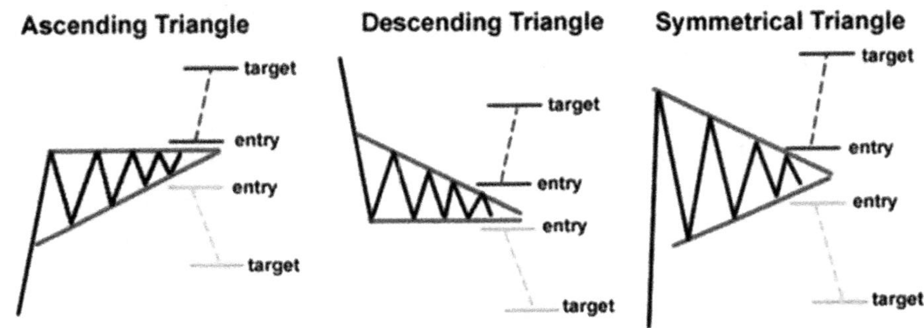

Fig. 12.14 *Source* Investopedia.com

12.5 Indicators

- There are several types:

  - **TREND INDICATORS**: Moving Average, ADX, DM, SAR, Donchian, ROC, Envelopes, Ichimoku.
  - **VOLATILITY INDICATORS**: ATR, Bollinger.
  - **OSCILLATORS**: Momentum, MACD, RSI, Stochastic, Williams
  - **VOLUME INDICATORS**: Force Index, OBV, MFI.

A common feature in indicators is divergence, which can be either bullish or bearish:

Bearish divergence occurs when the indicator shows two lower highs while the price shows two higher lows, as shown in Chart 12.2.

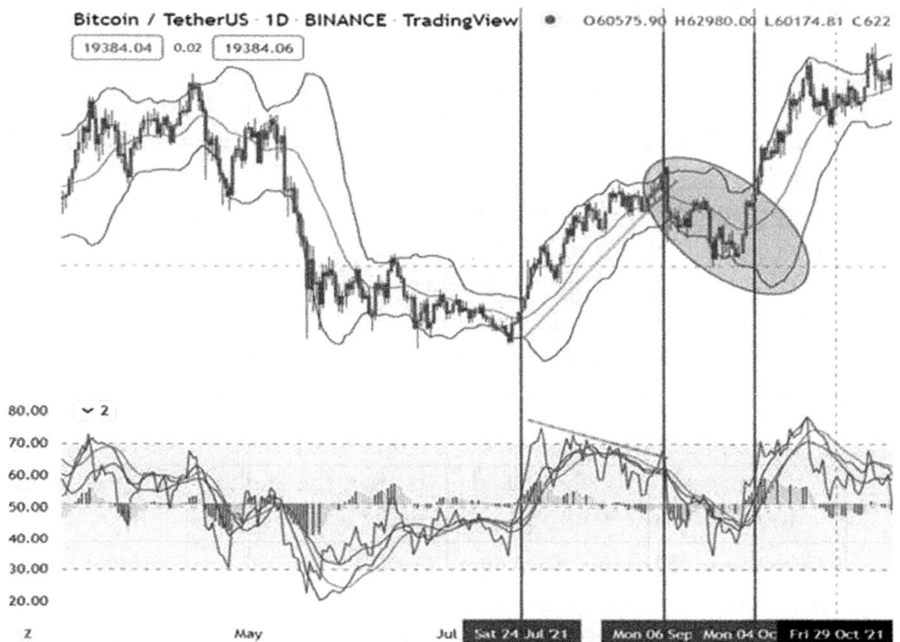

Chart 12.2   *Source* Tradingview

Bullish divergence occurs when the indicator shows two higher lows while the price shows two lower highs, as shown in Chart 12.3.

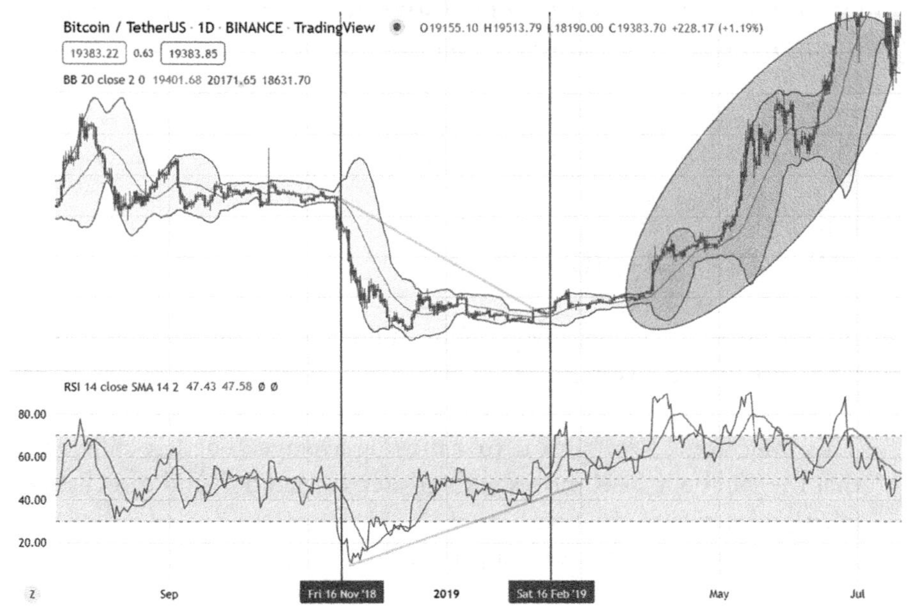

Chart 12.3   *Source* Tradingview

12.5.1 Trend Indicators

- **MOVING AVERAGES**: There are several types of moving averages

  - **Simple Moving Average**: assigns the same weight to each value in the period.
  - **Exponential Moving Average (EMA)**: a weighted price average over a set period, giving more weight to recent data. It avoids the drop-off effect (a sudden change in the current value when an older, significant value drops out of the calculation).
  - **Triangular Moving Average**: an average of a moving average, used for cycle analysis.

    Example: 20-day SMA of daily closes, smoothed with a 10-day SMA. From day 1 to day 20, day 10 has the highest weight—weights increase to the 10th value and decrease thereafter.

  - **Geometric Moving Average**: an SMA of the percentage changes between the previous and current bar over a set period. It's typically used for indices and gives more weight to lower values.

- **GOLDEN CROSS**: occurs when the 50-day moving average crosses above the 200-day moving average.
- **DEATH CROSS**: occurs when the 50-day moving average crosses below the 200-day moving average.

Another indicator is the **Directional Movement (DM)**, which measures the strength of a price trend, whether up or down.

- DM− when Today's Low < Yesterday's Low
- DM+ when Today's High > Yesterday's High
- DI+ = DM+/ATR
- DI− = DM−/ATR
- ADX = (DI+ − DI−)/(DI+ + DI−)

Parabolic SAR, developed by J. Wells Wilder, determines trend direction and potential price reversals.

- This indicator is very similar to a moving average. The key difference is that the Parabolic SAR moves with greater acceleration and can change its position relative to the price.
- In an uptrend, the indicator appears below the price.

- In a downtrend, it appears above the price.
- It is commonly used as a trailing stop line to protect profits during a trend.

ADX is another trend indicator:

- It determines whether prices are trending or not
- It is always positive
- Rising ADX indicates a trend is forming (up or down)
- Falling ADX indicates a sideways (range-bound) market
- ADX peaks: signal to close trend-following positions
- ADX valleys: may indicate an upcoming breakout in either direction
- When ADX starts to rise, a trend may be beginning
- The indicator ranges from 0 to 100

  - ADX < 20: weak trend
  - ADX > 40: strong trend

- Strategy:

  - BUY: when +DI crosses above −DI
  - SELL: when +DI crosses below −DI

Goichi Hosoda, a Japanese journalist, developed **ICHIMOKU**. It consists of five lines or calculations, two of which comprise a cloud in which the difference between the two lines is shaded.

It consists of five lines:

- Conversion Line/Turning Line (Tenkan-Sen): 9-period moving average (midpoint of high and low)
- Base Line/Standard Line (Kijun-Sen): 26-period moving average (midpoint of high and low)
- Leading Span A/Cloud Span A (Senkou Span A): average of the Conversion Line and Base Line, projected 26 periods forward
- Leading Span B/Cloud Span B (Senkou Span B): 52-period moving average (midpoint of high and low), projected 26 periods forward
- Lagging Span/Lagging Line (Chikou Span): current closing price plotted 26 periods back in time

Span A above Span B: prices are rising faster in the short term than in the long term → Bullish (Blue cloud).

Span A below Span B: prices are falling faster in the short term than in the long term → Bearish (Red cloud).

If the price is above the cloud: Bullish signal—there is an uptrend and prices are rising.

If the price is below the cloud: Bearish signal—there is a downtrend and prices are falling.

ICHIMOKU Signals:

- After a sustained price rise or fall, thick clouds may indicate an imminent trend reversal.
- If the price crosses the cloud, it is a preliminary and less reliable trend reversal signal.
- In an uptrend, if the Turning Line (9p) crosses above the Standard Line (26p) → BUY signal.
- In a downtrend, if the Turning Line (9p) crosses below the Standard Line (26p) → SELL signal.
- This indicator does not work well in sideways markets.
- It works best on daily and weekly charts.

Cloud boundaries act as support/resistance:

- If the price is above the cloud:

    - The upper edge is the first support level
    - The lower edge is the second support level

- If the price is below the cloud:

    - The lower edge is the first resistance level
    - The upper edge is the second resistance level

Lagging Line (Chikou Span):

- When it crosses the price, it signals a potential trend reversal:

    - If it crosses from below, it is a buy signal
    - If it crosses from above, it is a sell signal

- **Standard Line (26p)** is used as a **market movement indicator**:

    - If **price moves above** the Standard Line, prices will likely continue to rise, and a trend reversal may occur.

- **Turning Line (9p)** is used as a **trend direction indicator**:

  - If the line rises or falls, a trend is in place.
  - If the line is moving horizontally, it signals a sideways market.

Conversion Line = Turning Line (9p)
Base Line = Standard Line (26p)

12.5.2 Volatility Indicators

- As for VOLATILITY INDICATORS, we have:

ATR: Average True Range

  - It is the 14-day moving average of the True Range (TR)
  - ATR = ((Previous ATR × 13) + Current TR)/14
  - True Range (TR) is the greatest of the following three values:
  - ATR = ((ATRp x 13) + TR)/14
  - ATRp is the previous ATR
  - True Range is the greatest of the following values:

    Current high minus current low
    Absolute value of the current high minus the previous candle's close
    Absolute value of the current low minus the previous candle's close

BANDS:
More useful in commodity markets than in stocks.
They are profitable in trending markets.
There are three main types:

- **ENVELOPES**: fixed bands
- **BOLLINGER BANDS**: dynamic bands—20-day SMA ± 2 standard deviations
- **KELTNER CHANNELS**: dynamic bands—10-day SMA of typical price ± 10-day SMA of bar range
- **STARC BANDS**: dynamic bands—5-period ATR ± 5-period SMA

Typical price = C + H + L/3

Next, I'll explain Bollinger Bands in more detail, as they are the most important of the four.

- **BOLLINGER BANDS (BB):**

  - Consists of an upper band, a lower band, and a middle moving average line (also known as the middle band). The two outer bands react to market price action: they expand when volatility is high (**bulge**, moving away from the middle line), and contract when volatility is low (**squeeze**, moving closer to the middle line).
  - Middle line: 20-day Simple Moving Average (SMA)
  - Upper band: 20-day SMA + (20-day standard deviation × 2)
  - Lower band: 20-day SMA − (20-day standard deviation × 2)
  - Uses:

    Identify tops and bottoms
    Spot trend continuation
    Define trend ranges
    Recognize the squeeze

Since the value of standard deviation depends on volatility, the width of the bands adjusts automatically:

- Bands expand when the market is volatile (bulge)
- Bands contract during periods of stability (squeeze)

Squeeze: occurs when volatility drops to very low levels, causing the bands to tighten significantly. This signals that the market is preparing for a potentially explosive move.

The squeeze is triggered when the Bandwidth indicator reaches its lowest level in the last 6 months.

- **BOLLINGER BANDWIDTH** is derived from the standard Bollinger Bands indicator. It measures quantitatively the width between the Upper and Lower Bands.

  - Bollinger Bandwidth = (Upper BB- Lower BB)/Middle BB
  - It helps create trading systems and signals
  - It helps identify the squeeze
  - It is used to detect the beginning and end of trends

There are several types of signals for trading with this indicator:

METHOD 1:

- BUY: when the price breaks above the upper band
- SELL: when the price breaks below the lower band

METHOD 2:

- BUY: Bandwith > 0.8 y MFI > 80
- SELL: Bandwith < 0.2 y MFI < 20

12.5.3 Oscillators

- Another type of indicator is the OSCILLATOR:

It is said that the market moves sideways 80% of the time, making this indicator particularly useful.

There are several TRADING METHODS using oscillators:

METHOD 1:

- Enter and exit trades within the same zone (70–100/0–30)
- Buy when entering the overbought zone (around 70), and close the position when exiting the zone
- Sell when entering the oversold zone (around 30), and close the position when exiting the zone

METHOD 2:

- Enter a trade when exiting one zone, and close the position when entering the opposite zone (30–70)
- Buy when exiting the oversold zone (30), and close the position when entering the overbought zone (70)
- Sell when exiting the overbought zone (70), and close the position when entering the oversold zone (30)

MOMENTUM: It is the difference between two prices over a fixed interval. Example: 5-day Momentum = today's price minus the price from 5 days ago. When used as a leading indicator:

BUY: When momentum turns upward
SELL: When momentum turns downward

When used as a trend indicator:

BUY: When momentum crosses above the zero line
SELL: When momentum crosses below the zero line

HERRICK PAYOFF INDEX: It combines volume and open interest.
   Open interest refers to the total number of long or short positions currently open in the market.

   MACD: (Moving Average Convergence Divergence)
   It is used to detect momentum and trend.
   It shows the correlation between two moving averages.

* MACD Line (faster): difference between the 12-day and 26-day EMAs
* Signal Line (slower): 9-day EMA of the MACD Line
* Histogram = MACD Line – Signal Line

BUY: When the MACD Line crosses above the Signal Line
SELL: When the MACD Line crosses below the Signal Line

MACD is smoother than Momentum, using moving averages rather than price directly, as shown in Chart 12.4.

Chart 12.4   *Source* Tradingview

RSI: Relative Strength Index
   It measures an asset's momentum based on closing prices.
   It uses only closing prices.
   Key levels: 70/30, as shown in Chart 12.5.

It is more stable than Momentum because it incorporates all values within the calculation period (average), unlike Momentum, which only uses the first and last data points.

RSI > 70: Overbought zone → SELL
RSI < 30: Oversold zone → BUY

Chart 12.5 *Source* Tradingview

STOCHASTIC:

Use High, Low, and Close prices.
Key levels: 80/20, as shown in Chart 12.6.
Moves faster than RSI and tends to exaggerate price swings.

- %D = Kslow: the faster indicator
- %Dslow: the slower signal line

STOCHASTIC > 80: Overbought zone → SELL
STOCHASTIC < 20: Oversold zone → BUY

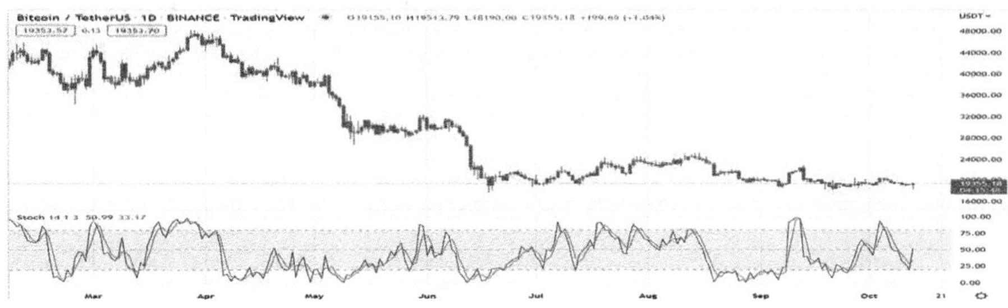

Chart 12.6 *Source* Tradingview

WILLIAMS (Accumulation/Distribution Oscillator):

BP + SP/2 x (H–L)
BP = Buying Power: High—Open
SP = Selling Power: Close—Low
WILLIAMS > −20: Overbought zone → SELL
WILLIAMS < −80: Oversold zone → BUY

12.5.4   Volume Indicators

They are not helpful in crypto or forex because these are not centralized markets. The volume data provided is that of the broker, not from a clearinghouse, meaning that volume is not representative of the entire market.

Although volume is not particularly important in this type of market, it is relevant in centralized markets such as stock exchanges. For this reason, the following tables present different scenarios in which volume interacts with other variables and provides useful confirmation signals.

In the first table, we can observe the interaction between volume and price, as shown in Table 12.1.

In the second table, we can observe the interaction between volume and open interest, as shown in Table 12.2.

In the third table, we can observe the interaction of all three variables together, as shown in Table 12.3.

To better understand how and when open interest changes, the different possible scenarios are presented, as shown in Table 12.4.

Table 12.1 Illustrates the relationship between price and volume, along with its interpretation

Volume	Price	Interpretation
Up	Up	Volume confirms an uptrend
Up	Down	Volume confirms downtrend
Down	Down	Volume indicates weak rally
Down	Up	Volume indicates a weak pullback

Table 12.2 Illustrates the relationship between volume and open interest, along with its interpretation

Volume	Open interest	Interpretation
UP	UP	Confirmation trend
UP	Down	Position liquidation
Down	Up	Slow accumulation
Down	Down	Congestion phase (consolidation)

Table 12.3 Illustrates the relationship between price, volume and open interest, along with its interpretation

Price	Volume	O.I.	Interpretation
Up	Up	Up	New buyers
Down	Up	Up	New sellers
Down	Down	Down	Long are being forced out
Up	Down	Down	Sellers covering positions

Table 12.4 Illustrates the relationship between the buyer and seller, along with its interpretation in terms of open interest.

Buyer	Seller	Change in OI
New	New	Open interest up
New	Old	No change OI
Old	New	No change OI
Old	Old	Open interest down

Elder FORCE INDEX (EFI): created by Dr.Alexander Elder
It is a price change multiplied by volume:
EFI = (Today's Close—Yesterday's Close) × Volume

A **2-period EMA** is applied to EFI for entry and exit timing:

- BUY: when the value is low
- SELL: when the value is high

A **13-period EMA** is applied for long-term analysis:

- BUY: when EFI crosses above the zero line
- SELL: when EFI crosses below the zero line

ON BALANCE VOLUME (OBV):
It relates volume to price changes that have accompanied that volume.

It is based on the principle that changes in OBV (On Balance Volume) precede price changes. According to this principle, an increase in OBV indicates that professional investors are entering the instrument.

- If the current bar's closing price is higher than the previous bar's close, the current volume is added to the previous OBV value.
- If the current bar's closing price is lower, the current volume is subtracted from the previous OBV value.

When the trend of the OBV indicator shifts from bullish to bearish, this is called a breakout.

Since OBV breakouts typically precede price breakouts, traders should:

- Take long positions when OBV breaks upward
- Sell when OBV breaks downward

Positions should be held until the direction of the OBV trend changes.

- OBV moves in the same direction as the price, as shown in Table 12.5

Table 12.5 Relationship between price and OBV, along with its interpretation

Price	OBV	Interpretation
Up	**Up**	**Clear uptrend**
Up	Down	Weak uptrend
Sideways	Up	Accumulation
Sideways	Down	Distribution
Down	Up	Weak downtrend
Down	**Down**	**Clear downtrend**

MONEY FLOW INDEX: uses price and volume data to identify overbought or oversold signals in an asset.

It measures money flow into and out of an asset over some time.

It analyzes price and volume to assess buying and selling pressure in a given market.

- MFI > 80: Overbought → SELL
- MFI < 20: Oversold → BUY

12.6 Fibonacci

Fibonacci was an Italian mathematician who introduced a famous numerical sequence in which each number is the sum of the two preceding ones (1, 1, 2, 3, 5, 8, 13, 21, 34, ...).

One of the technical analysis tools used to predict support and resistance levels in financial markets is the Fibonacci retracements and extensions.

The Fibonacci levels are:

0.0%, 23.6%, 38.2%, 61.8%, 100%, 138.2%, 161.8%, 261.8%, and 423.6%.

Although technically not a Fibonacci ratio, some traders also value the 50% level, as it represents the midpoint of the price range, and the 150% level.

12.7 Pivot Points

They are levels where the price is expected to react, meaning they act as support and resistance.

The Pivot Point is the strongest support/resistance level among them.

PIVOT POINT: $P = (H + L + C) / 3$

RESISTANCE 1: $R1 = Px2 - L$

SUPPORT 1: $S1 = Px2 - H$

RESISTANCE 2: $R2 = P + H - L$

SUPPORT 2: $S2 = P - H + L$

RESISTANCE 3: $R3 = H + 2x(P - L)$

SUPPORT 3: $S3 = L - 2x(H - P)$

- Pivot points often align with Fibonacci extensions.
- When a pivot point coincides with other pivot points from different timeframes, that level becomes more significant and harder to break.

  - Example: if the monthly S1 aligns with the daily S1 and hourly S1, that level becomes highly important.

- For day trading, use 5-minute and 15-minute timeframes—15 minutes to detect the signal, and 5 minutes to enter the trade.

Market Direction:

- It is a moving average of the pivot point from the last 3 periods.
- MD = (Pivot + Pivot + Pivot)/3.
- It acts as support in uptrends and resistance in downtrends.
- Es una media de del pivot point de los ultimos 3 periodos.

- After a downtrend:
  - If the price closes above the MD, and there is a sequence of higher highs and higher lows, → BUY or EXIT short position

- After an uptrend:

  - If the price closes below the MD, and there is a sequence of lower highs and lower lows, → SELL or EXIT long position

- Trend confirmation:
  - If the pivot point breaks above the MD, and both are sloping upward → Uptrend
  - If the pivot point breaks below the MD, and both are sloping downward → Downtrend

Use pivot points together with candlestick patterns (such as doji or hammer) and an indicator like Stochastic or MACD.

- BUY:
  - Enter at the close of the candle that makes a new high after the doji.
  - Set a stop loss below the low of the doji.
  - Exit the long position at the close of the candle that makes a lower low near the pivot point resistance.
- SELL:
  - Enter at the close of the candle that makes a new low after the doji.
  - Set a stop loss above the high of the doji.
  - Exit the short position at the close of the candle that makes a higher high near the pivot point support.

If the stop loss is far from the entry level, reduce the position size when entering.

12.8 Elliott Waves

Elliott Waves suggests that financial markets follow specific patterns regardless of the time frame.

They propose that market movements follow a natural sequence of mass psychology cycles.

Elliott Waves are used to identify market cycles and trends to predict market behavior.

The basic Elliott Wave pattern consists of 8 waves:

- 5 impulse waves (in the direction of the trend): 1, 3, 5, A, C
- 3 corrective waves: 2, 4, B

Figure 12.15 illustrates the Elliot wave in a bull market:

BULL MARKET:

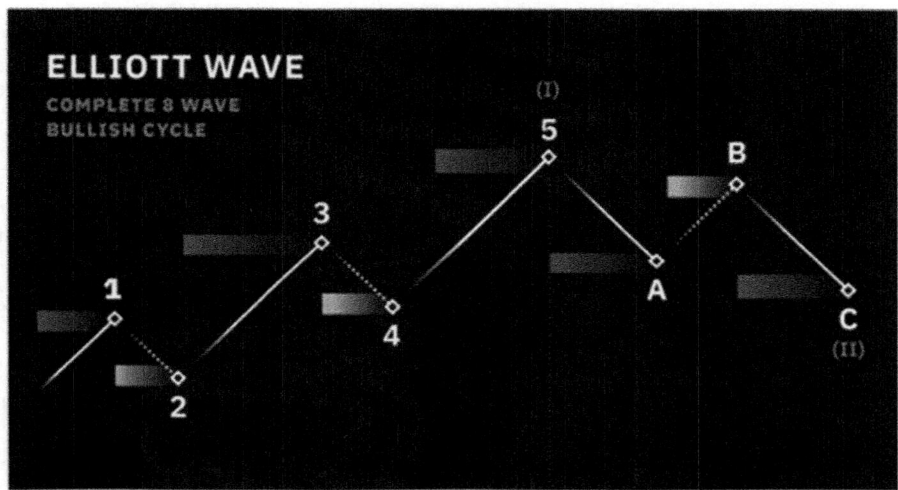

Fig. 12.15 *Source* Academy Binance

Figure 12.16 illustrates the Elliot wave in a bear market:

BEAR MARKET:

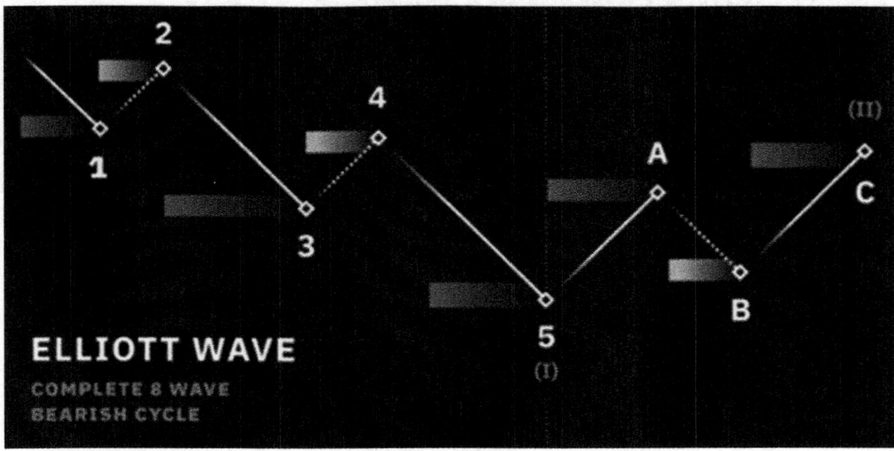

Fig. 12.16 *Source* Academy Binance

However, according to Elliott, financial markets form patterns of a fractal nature.

Therefore, if we zoom out the time frame, the movement from 1 to 5 could also be seen as a single Impulse Wave (i), while the A-B-C movement may represent a single Corrective Wave (ii), as shown in Fig. 12.17.

RULES:

- Wave 2 cannot retrace more than 100% of the previous Wave 1 movement.
- Wave 4 cannot retrace more than 100% of the previous Wave 3 movement.
- Wave 4 must not overlap with Wave 1.
- Among waves 1, 3, and 5, wave 3 cannot be the shortest, and it is often the longest.
- You should be able to draw a clean trendline between the end of wave 2 and the end of wave 4. This 2–4 line must not be breached.
- Waves 2 and 4 must not be equal in depth, duration, and shape—at least one of the three must differ.
- Wave 5 will generally exceed the high of wave 3, except in fifth-wave failures, where wave 5 must be at least 38% the length of wave 4.

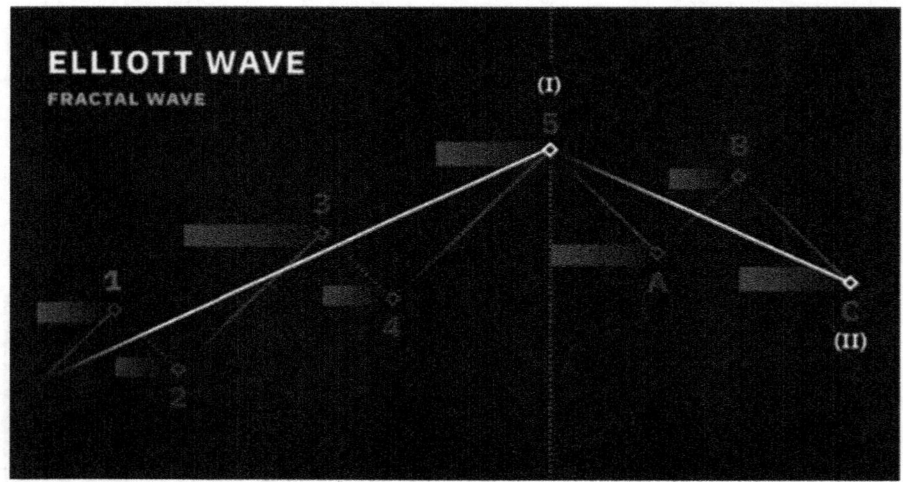

Fig. 12.17 *Source* Academy Binance

12.9 Point & Figure

It is a type of chart that represents the **price movements** and trends of an asset **without considering time.**

It is a chart that represents supply and demand dynamics.

The chart is made up of Os (price decreases) and Xs (price increases). There are two factors to determine:

* Box Size
* Box Reversal

Box Size:
If the Box Size is 1:

* If the price moves up by three units, it will be represented by 3 X's.

  – Example: price goes from 100 to 103.

* If the price moves down by four units, it will be represented by 4 Os.

  – Example: price goes from 100 to 96.

Box Reversal: It is the number of boxes required for a change in direction. Common reversal amounts are 1-box, 3-box, or 5-box.

If the Box Reversal is set to 3:

* If the price rises from 100 to 110 and starts to fall, a column of Os will not appear until the price drops to 107.
* If the price drops from 100 to 90 and starts to rise, a column of X's will not appear until the price reaches 93.
* A switch from X to O or O to X will only occur if prices reverse by the value of three boxes.

FIGURES:

The following figures are illustrated in Figs 12.18, 12.19, 12.20, and 12.21.

* **Bullish Signal**: A higher bottom followed by a higher top. This indicates that demand has exceeded supply. Higher lows with higher highs.
* **Bearish Signal**: A lower top followed by a lower bottom forms a bearish signal formation. This indicates that supply has exceeded demand—lower highs with lower lows.
* **Bullish Catapult**: A Triple Top Buy Signal, followed by a pullback that does not produce a bearish signal, and then a new Double Top Buy.

- This pattern consists of a Triple Top, a pullback, and a Double Top breakout to new highs.

This formation has three distinct buy points:

1. The Triple Top Buy Signal
2. The bottom of the pullback (with a stop, a bearish signal—if it should occur)
3. The Double Top Buy Signal.

- **Bearish Catapult**: Triple Bottom Sell Signal, a throwback that produces no bullish signal, followed by a new double bottom sell. Triple Bottom, Throwback, and Double Bottom with a breakout below the previous lows.
- **Long Tail Down**: must have at least twenty Os downward. A buy signal is given when there is a 3-box upside reversal. *(20 Os followed by 3 Xs reversal)*.
- **Long Tail Up**: must have at least twenty X's upward. A sell signal is given when there is a 3-box downside reversal. *(20 X's followed by 3 O's reversal)*.
- **High Pole**: starts with at least 3 X's above a previous top. The pattern is completed when there is a reversing column of Os that is at least 50% the length of the X column.
- **Low Pole**: begins with at least 3 Os below a previous bottom. The pattern is completed when there is a reversing column of X's that is at least 50% as long as the column of O's.

TERMINOLOGY:

- A **continuation** 3-box **DOUBLE** TOP/BOTTOM is equivalent to a 1-box SEMI-CATAPULT
- A **continuation** 3-box **TRIPLE** TOP/BOTTOM is equivalent to a 1-box SEMI-CATAPULT
- A **reversal** 3-box **DOUBLE** TOP/BOTTOM is equivalent to a 1-box FULCRUM
- A **reversal** 3-box **TRIPLE** TOP/BOTTOM is equivalent to a 1-box FULCRUM

Point and Figure can be combined with RSI, Fibonacci, Bollinger Bands, etc.
   Point and Figure can also be applied across different timeframes and with various box reversal sizes (1, 3, or 5).

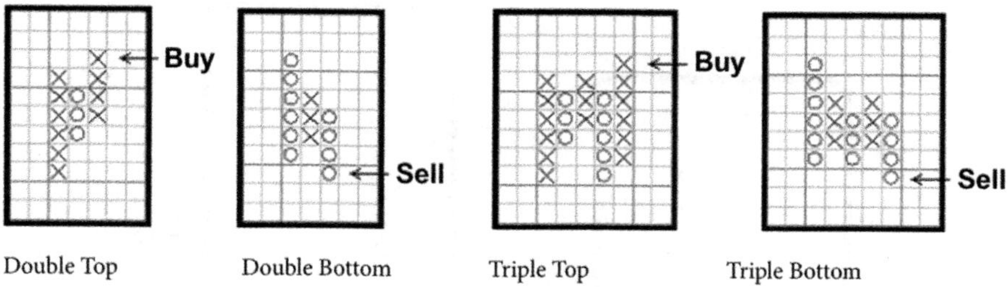

Fig. 12.18 *Source* Stockcharts.com—chartschool

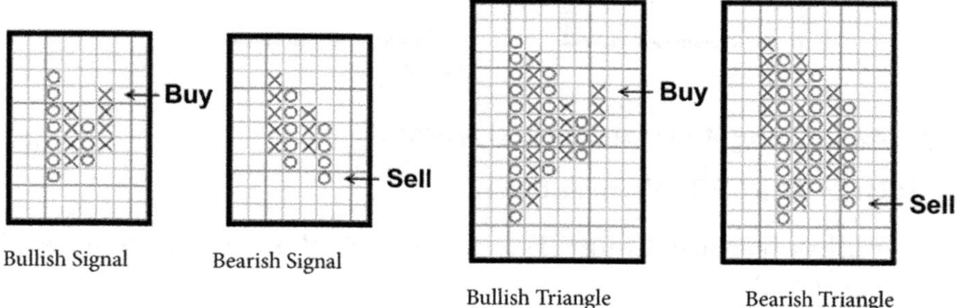

Fig. 12.19 *Source* Stockcharts.com—chartschool

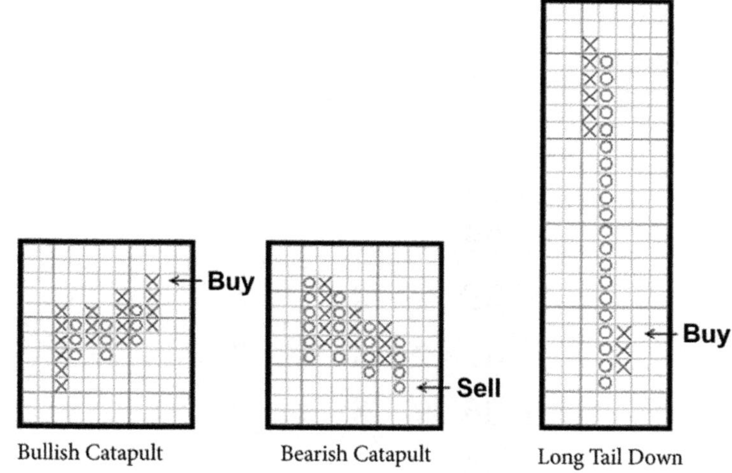

Fig. 12.20 *Source* Stockcharts.com—chartschool

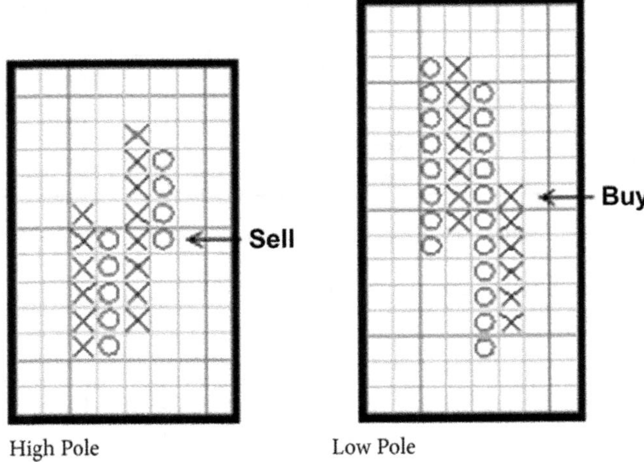

Fig. 12.21 *Source* Stockcharts.com—chartschool

- **PRICE TARGET**: Vertical Count

  - **Bullish Vertical Count**: Box reversal = 3, Box size = 1, as shown in Fig. 12.22.

Count the number of X's in the first upward move that generates a buy signal. Multiply it by the box size (1) and the box reversal (3), then add the lowest X value in the rightmost column.

$5 \times 1 \times 3 = 15$

$15 + 35 = 50$

Target Price: 50

Example of a Bullish Vertical Count

40				
39				X
38		X		X
37	O	X	O	X
36	O	X	O	X
35	O	X	O	X
34	O		O	
33				

Fig. 12.22 *Source* Stockcharts.com—chartschool

– **Bearish Vertical Count**: Box reversal = 3, Box size = 1, as shown in Fig. 12.23.

Count the number of Os in the first downward move that generates a sell signal. Multiply it by the box size (1) and the box reversal (3), then subtract the result from the highest O value in the rightmost column.

4 × 1 × 3 = 12

52–12 = 40

Target Price: 40

Example of a Bearish Vertical Count

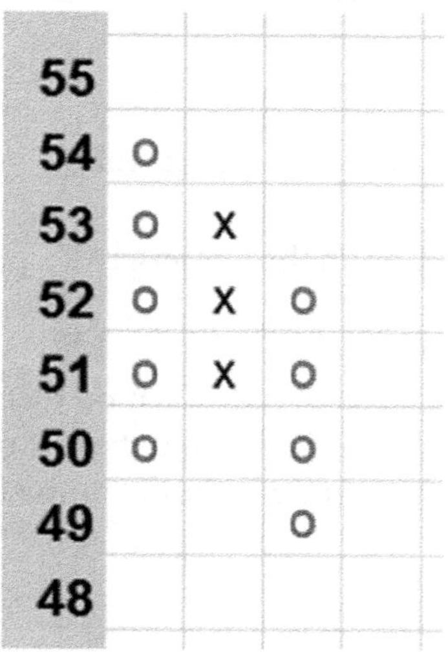

Fig. 12.23   *Source* Stockcharts.com—chartschool

• **TARGET PRICE: Horizontal Count**

– **Bullish Horizontal Count**: Box reversal = 3, Box size = 1, as shown in Fig. 12.24.

Count the number of boxes across the base of the formation that generated the buy signal. Multiply that value by the box size (1) and the box reversal (3), then add it to the price of the lowest point in the formation.

3 × 1 × 4 = 12

35 + 12 = 47

Target Price = 47

Example of a Bullish Horizontal Count

40			
39			X
38		X		X
37	O	X	O	X
36	O	X	O	X
35	O	X	O	X
34	O		O	
33				

Fig. 12.24 *Source* Stockcharts.com—chartschool

– **Bearish Horizontal Count**: Box reversal = 3, Box size = 1, as shown in Fig. 12.25.

Count the boxes across the top of the formation that generated the sell signal. Multiply that value by the box size (1) and the box reversal (3), then subtract it from the price of the highest point in the formation.

$3 \times 1 \times 3 = 9$
$54{-}9 = 45$
Target Price = 45

Example of a Bullish Horizontal Count

55			
54	O		
53	O	X	
52	O	X	O
51	O	X	O
50	O		O
49			O
48			

Fig. 12.25 *Source* Stockcharts.com—chartschool

12.10 Market Profile

MARKET PROFILE: TIME WITH PRICE

- Each letter represents a TPO (Time Price Opportunity)
- Each TPO corresponds to 30 minutes
- POC (Point of Control): the price level with the highest number of TPOs
- The Value Area (VA) contains over 70% of the day's traded volume
- Midpoint = (High + Low)/2

STRATEGY:

- Avoid trading inside the Value Area
- BUY: when price breaks above the Value Area High (VAH)
- SELL: when price breaks below the Value Area Low (VAL)
- If Midpoint > POC:

  - Projection = Low − (Midpoint − POC) × 2

- If Midpoint < POC:

  - Projection = High + (Midpoint − POC) × 2

- Look for an asset about to break the Value Area in different timeframes
- Always consider Daily, Weekly, and Monthly POCs, as they serve as important support and resistance levels

- **TAS INDICATORS**:
- TAS Boxes: a dynamic visual representation of Market Profile using three lines (VAH, VAL, and POC)
- TAS Navigator: shows whether trend momentum is increasing or decreasing. Useful for spotting divergences
- TAS Vega: helpful for exit strategies and used in combination with TAS Boxes
- TAS Ratio: provides short-term price movement forecasts and counter-trend trading opportunities
- Thin TAS Boxes indicate low volatility, while thick boxes indicate high volatility
- The longer the TAS Boxes, the more significant they are

- If the POC is near the VAL or VAH, that support or resistance level becomes more important
- Stop Loss should be placed a few pips below the VAL or above the VAH

A software where you can access the Market Profile is **Pro Real Time**, as shown in Chart 12.7, in which:

- The Red Triangle represents the POC (Point of Control)
- The Red Line indicates the Value Area (VA)
- The Green Triangle marks the day's opening price
- The Blue Triangle marks the day's closing price

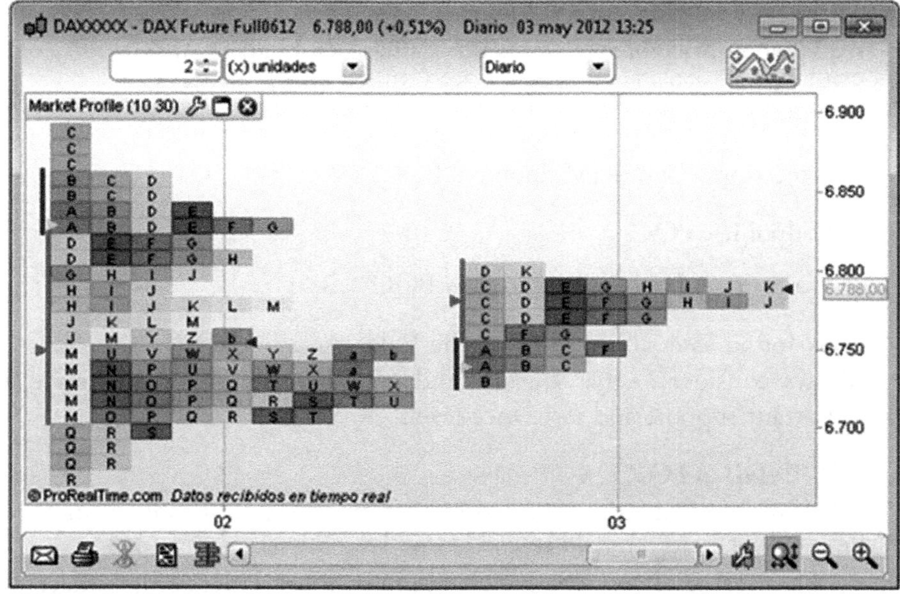

Chart 12.7   *Source* Pro Real Time

12.11 Volume Profile

- **VOLUME PROFILE: VOLUME WITH PRICE. Time is not taken into account**

VOLUME PROFILE is not helpful for non-centralized products such as crypto and forex, since it analyzes volume, and the volume provided by the broker is not representative of the entire market.

This is why it is only beneficial when trading futures, which are centralized and backed by a clearinghouse—in this case, the CME (Chicago Mercantile Exchange).

That means Volume Profile is valid if you're trading forex futures (CME) or bitcoin futures (CME), even though bitcoin futures are also traded on platforms like Binance, whose volume is not reflected on the CME.

- Value Area: it is the acceptance area. Prices tend to move toward this area because it accumulates the highest volume.
- Value Area (VA) comprises 68.2% of the total volume (1 standard deviation of a **normal distribution**).
- VAH (Value Area High): Resistance.
- VAL (Value Area Low): Support.
- VPOC (Volume Point of Control): It is the price level with the highest concentration of volume. It is the most accepted price by both buyers and sellers and serves as the reference point from which the VA is calculated.
- Price > VPOC: indicates buyer control.
- Price < VPOC: indicates seller control.
- VWAP (Volume Weighted Average Price): It is the average price of all contracts traded during a specific time period.

  - Number of contracts traded × asset price/total number of contracts traded
  - Above the VWAP, there is the same traded volume as below it. It represents the equilibrium level.

- Acceptance zones are profit-taking zones: Value Area
- Rejection zones (low volume) are entry zones
- **Breakout of VAH or VAL should occur with volume**
- Stop-loss for long positions: below the VPOC
- Stop-loss for short positions: above the VPOC

Note: The most recent acceptance areas are more important than the more distant ones/Volume Profile does not use letters (TPO).

Figure 12.26 illustrates the representation of a normal day would have a bell-shaped curve:

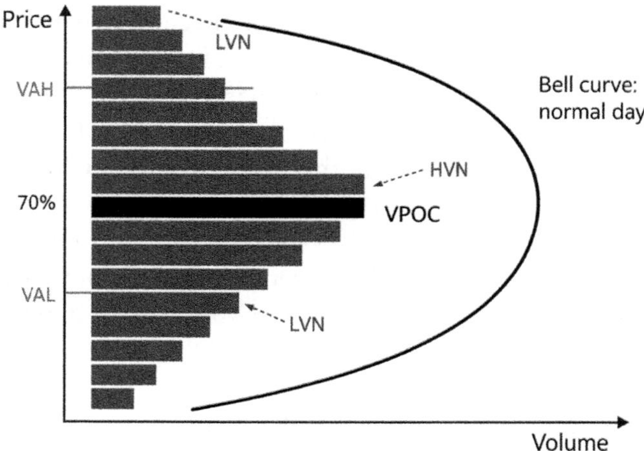

Fig. 12.26 *Source* Tradingview—Volume Profile Guide

Below are several representative types of market days, as shown in Fig. 12.27, including:

- **P-Shaped Volume Profile**: This is a normal day with upward variation. It occurs when a market rises sharply and then consolidates. It typically happens during uptrends. A P-shaped profile can also mark the end of a downtrend, indicating a possible short covering rally, which is seen as a bullish signal.
- **b-Shaped Volume Profile**: This is a normal day with downward variation. It occurs when a market crashes sharply and then consolidates. It is the opposite of a P-shaped profile and is often seen during downtrends. However, when a b-shape appears during an uptrend, it may potentially signal a reversal. This pattern is considered a bearish signal.
- **D-Shaped Volume Profile**: This represents a neutral day. It occurs when there is a temporary balance in the market. The Point of Control (POC) is located at the center of the profile, indicating equilibrium between buyers and sellers. It may indicate a sideways market, often preceding a breakout in one direction.
- **B-Shaped Volume Profile**: This type of day is formed by two D-shaped profiles. You need to pay attention to where the POC is located—whether it's in one area or the other. Identifying this is important as it shows which of the two zones is dominant. This pattern is generally interpreted as a continuation of a trend.

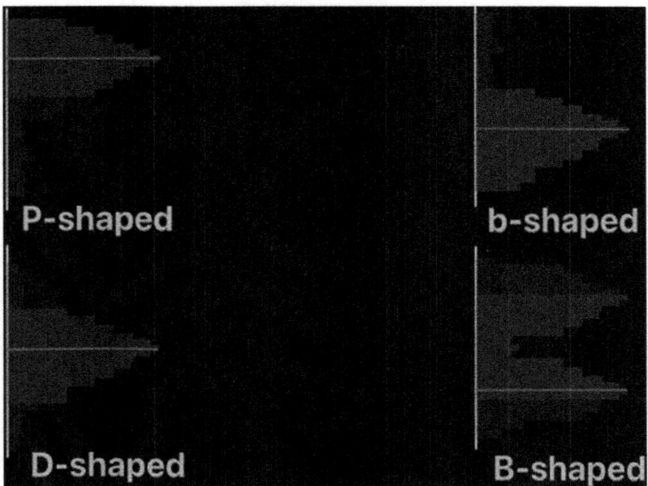

Fig. 12.27 *Source* Tradingview

- **Use Volume Profile to track Order Flow**.
- Volume Cluster: It is the exact level where the highest volume has occurred within a single candlestick.

  - Green indicates buyers
  - Red indicates sellers

- High Volume Node (HVN): It is a price area with high volume (a peak in the volume profile). It is considered a target price due to the high consensus between buyers and sellers.
- Low Volume Node (LVN): It is a price area with low volume (a valley in the volume profile). It is considered an entry level (supports/resistances).

Figure 12.28 illustrates the interpretation of volume clusters.

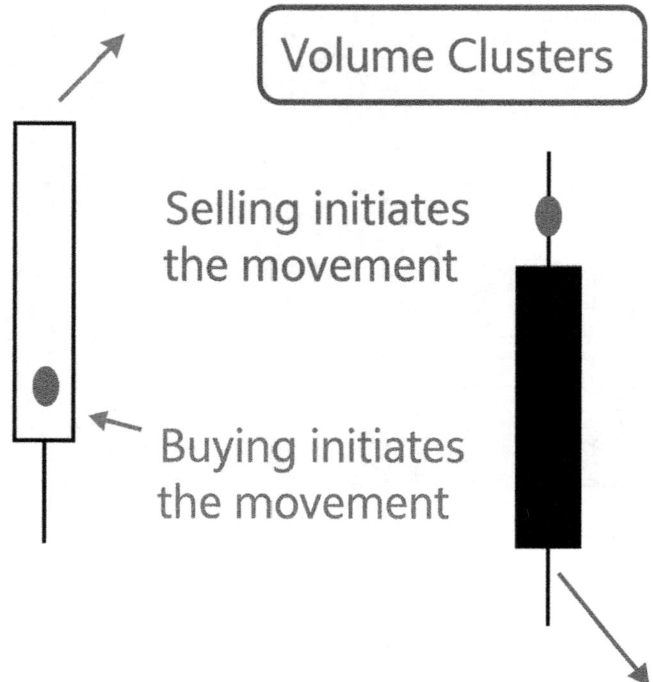

Fig. 12.28 *Source* Trade-Dale.com

12.12 Order Flow

Order Flow is the study of the flow of orders.

Figure 12.29 illustrates the appearance of the order flow.

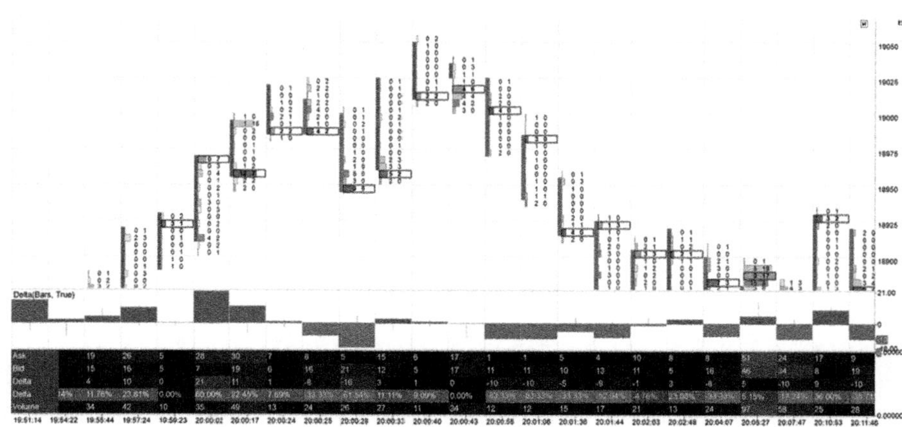

Fig. 12.29 *Source* Atas Software

- **OFA (8,3)**: it means a movement of 8 ticks and a reversal of 3 ticks in order to generate a new candle.

Figures 12.30 and 12.8 illustrate the appearance of the order flow with the OFA Analytics software.

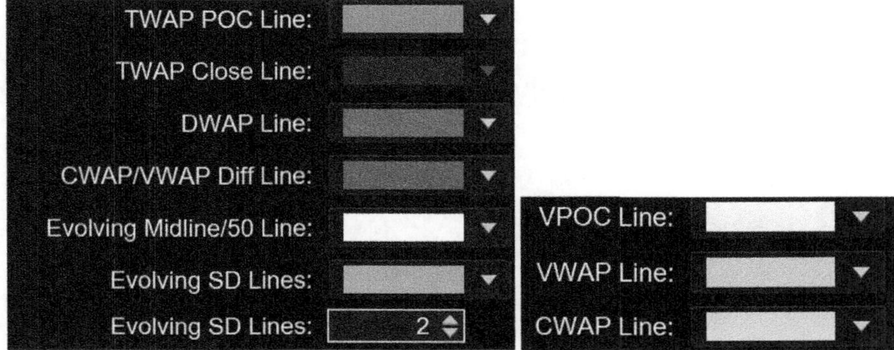

Fig. 12.30 *Sources* OFA Analytics

Chart 12.8 *Source* Order Flow Analytics with Motivewave software

Among the ORDER FLOW SOFTWARES we have:

- **ORDER FLOW ANALYTICS (OFA)**: You need to have MotiveWave or NinjaTrader to launch their program.

  - For data, you can choose between CQG/Rithmic. And finally, you need to choose a broker (e.g., AMP Futures). Figure 12.31 explains the features inclucs software.

Order Flow Analytics Software Includes:

Order Flow Charting Bars	Drag & Drop Volume Profile Analysis
• OFA Probe and Rotation Bars	• Decision Point Profiles
• OFA Minute-Based Bars	• Range Profiles
• OFA Second-Based Bars	• Swing Profiles
• OFA Volume-Based Bars	• Fixed Bar Width Live Profiles
• OFA Tick-Based Bars	• Right & Left Margin Alignment
• Dynamic Volume Cluster Analysis	• Dynamic Neutral/Buy/Sell Color Logic
• Order Flow / Structure Chart Toggle	• Adjustable Value Area Calculation
• Order Flow Volume Print	• Adjustable Cluster Area Calculation
• Order Flow Bid and Offer Alerts	• CWAP Indicator
• Toxic Order Flow Sequence Alerts	• Value Area Lines
• Order Flow Exhaustion Markers	• Cluster Area Lines
• Net Delta / COT numbers	• VPOC Line
• Best Bid/Offer Highlight	• VWAP Line
• Last Price Highlight	• VWAP History Line
• Zero Print Filter	• Standard Deviation Lines

Fig. 12.31 *Source* OFA Analytics Software

- Another software would be **ATAS**:

  - You can have free data in crypto.
  - Data provider can be: CQG, but you need a broker (e.g., AMP Futures).

Figure 12.32 illustrates the appearance of the order flow with the Atas software.

Fig. 12.32 *Source* ATAS

Lastly, here is all the software I use for the different types of trading:

- TECHNICAL ANALYSIS—CRYPTO

  - https://www.tradingview.com/gopro/#plans

- POINT AND FIGURE:

  - https://www.bullseyebroker.com/
  - https://www.multicharts.com/net/features/chart-analysis/
  - https://www.esignal.com/add-ons/most-popular

- MARKET PROFILE:

  - https://www.esignal.com/add-ons/most-popular
  - https://www.prorealtime.com/en/new-features-ProRealTime-v11-1
  - https://www.tasmarketprofile.com/

- ORDER FLOW:

  - https://atas.net/es/
  - https://orderflowanalytics.com/
  - https://motivewave.com/
  - https://ninjatrader.com/es/Order-Flow-Trading

13

On-Chain Metrics

The valuation of cryptocurrencies is conducted in a manner distinct from that of stocks. In stocks, you analyze performance through ratios such as P/E and ROE. In contrast, to analyze and assess the activity of the network (blockchain) in cryptocurrencies, we use these metrics.

On-chain metrics are indicators that analyze transactions and movements occurring within the blockchain, and there is a wide variety of them.

Below, I will explain the most relevant ones.

13.1 Fear & Greed Index

This metric, as shown in Fig. 13.1, measures Bitcoin's sentiment in the crypto market.

The components are:

- Volatility—25%
- Market Momentum—25%
- Social Media—15%
- Surveys—15%
- Dominance—10%
- Trends—10%

J. Pineda, *Investing in Crypto with Confidence*,
https://doi.org/10.1007/978-3-032-07834-6_13

There are four levels:

- Extreme Fear (0–24): Buying Opportunity
- Fear (25–49)
- Greed (50–74)
- Extreme Greed (75–100): Selling Opportunity

Fig. 13.1 *Source* https://www.Alternative.Me

It aggregates various metrics to provide a snapshot of market sentiment. These metrics include:

- Price Volatility: Large price swings often evoke fear, especially during downturns.
- Momentum and Volume: Increased buying activity generally signals greedy sentiment.
- Social Media Sentiment: Public discourse about Bitcoin across platforms reflects collective optimism or pessimism.
- Bitcoin Dominance: A Higher dominance of Bitcoin relative to altcoins usually indicates cautious market behavior.
- Google Trends: Interest in Bitcoin search terms correlates with public sentiment.

By synthesizing this data, the index provides a simple visual representation: red zones signify fear (lower values), while green zones indicate greed (higher values), as illustrated in Chart 13.1.

Chart 13.1 *Source* Bitcoin Magazine Pro

You'll also immediately notice that this tool outlines how mass psychology is almost always best acted on as a contrarian. If everyone is bearish, you should probably be more bullish, and vice versa.

The Fear and Greed Index is rooted in human psychology. Markets tend to overreact in both directions. The strategy is to **buy when there is extreme fear** and **sell when there is extreme greed**.

You can find this metric at the following link:

* https://alternative.me/crypto/fear-and-greed-index/

13.2 Currency

DXY is the US Dollar Index, a basket of foreign currencies. It is a weighted geometric mean of the dollar's value relative to the following select currencies:

* Euro (EUR), 57.6% weight
* Japanese yen (JPY), 13.6% weight
* Pound sterling (GBP), 11.9% weight
* Canadian dollar (CAD), 9.1% weight
* Swedish krona (SEK), 4.2% weight
* Swiss franc (CHF), 3.6% weight

The DXY increases when the U.S. dollar gains "strength" (value) compared to other currencies.

It can be useful to monitor trends in DXY relative to Bitcoin because a strengthening US Dollar may also put Bitcoin's price under pressure. Conversely, a weakening US Dollar may, over time, allow for an upside opportunity in Bitcoin's price.

Throughout Bitcoin's history, we've seen an inverse correlation between the $BTC price and US Dollar Strength (DXY).

During Q4, we've seen DXY move significantly higher, and Bitcoin has rallied to new all-time highs. This has outlined the demand for $BTC even in less favorable macroeconomic conditions for more volatile assets.

In Chart 13.2, we can see that a declining DXY often creates favorable macroeconomic conditions for Bitcoin price appreciation.

BTC vs DXY

Chart 13.2 *Source* Bitcoin Magazine Pro

The drop experienced by the DXY index since the beginning of 2025 has not yet, as of April 2025, been reflected in an appreciation of Bitcoin's value. For now, a consolidation phase is taking place in the BTC price.

To understand the potential impact of this DXY signal, let's examine the three prior instances when this sharp decline in the US dollar strength index occurred:

- 2015 Post-Bear Market Bottom
  The first occurrence was after BTC's price had bottomed out in 2015. Following a period of sideways consolidation, BTC's price experienced a significant upward surge, gaining over 200% within months.

- Post-COVID Market Crash
  The second instance occurred in early 2020, following the sharp market collapse triggered by the COVID-19 pandemic. Similar to the 2015 case, BTC initially experienced choppy price action before a rapid upward trend emerged, culminating in a multi-month rally.

- 2022 Bear Market Recovery
  The most recent instance happened at the end of the 2022 bear market. After an initial period of price stabilization, BTC followed with a sustained recovery, climbing to substantially higher prices and kicking off the current bull cycle over the following months.

In each case, the sharp decline in the DXY was followed by a consolidation phase before BTC embarked on a significant bullish run.

13.3 Addresses

13.3.1 Daily Active Addresses

Daily active addresses are the number of addresses on the Bitcoin blockchain that either sent or received transactions. They show the amount of activity happening on the Bitcoin network. This metric is shown in Chart 13.3.

It is a "superficial metric," easily manipulated. People should not trust it to gather insights into a chain's user base or fundamental value.

"Daily Active Addresses" is one of the most misused metrics in the crypto space, often creating confusion with "Daily Active Users." Experts have urged people to stop using "DAA" when evaluating users' activity for fundamental analyses, and recent data shows why.

Often referred to as "daily active users," the Daily Active Addresses (DAA) indicator measures the number of crypto wallet addresses that performed at least one activity (or transaction) in a day.

The problem with this metric is that it doesn't measure the size of each wallet and gives the same weight to a whale's wallet as to a retail client's.

At first glance, this could be a valuable metric for crypto fundamental analyses, considering users are essential for any ecosystem. However, "addresses" are not the same as "users".

A user can control hundreds, thousands, or millions of addresses, artificially inflating the number of daily active addresses.

Chart 13.3 *Source* Bitcoin Magazine Pro

13.3.2 Percent Addresses in Profit

This metric shows the number of Bitcoin addresses that are in profit, meaning their average purchase price is below the current market value, as illustrated in Chart 13.4.

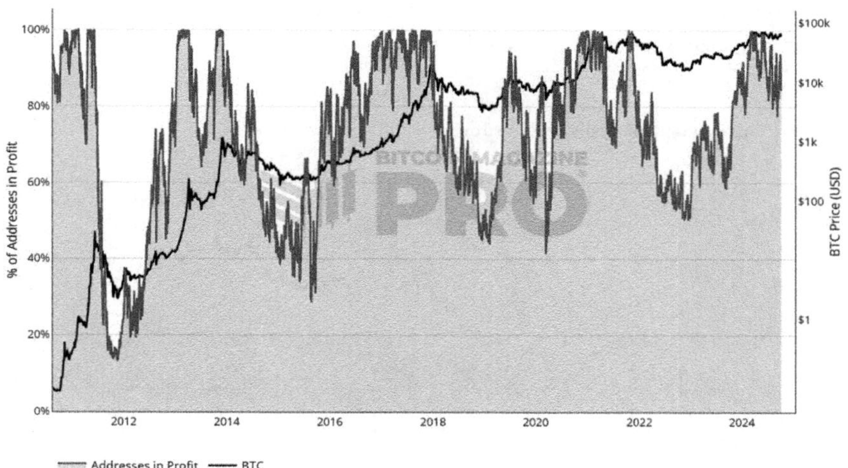

Chart 13.4 *Source* Bitcoin Magazine Pro

This metric is useful for understanding market sentiment and tells us whether the market is holding onto Bitcoin at a profit or a loss.

13.4 Onchain Movement

13.4.1 Supply Adjusted Coin Days Destroyed

Supply Adjusted Coin Days Destroyed quantifies the total BTC moved, weighted by how long it was held, and standardizes that data by the circulating supply. It divides CDD by the total number of bitcoins that have been issued into the market.

Coin Days Destroyed (CDD) is the number of coins that have been moved multiplied by the number of days since those coins were moved.

For example:

- 1 BTC held for 100 days → 100 Coin Days Destroyed
- 0.1 BTC held for 1000 days → 100 Coin Days Destroyed

This metric is invaluable for detecting whale activity and institutional profit-taking. When long-dormant coins suddenly move, it often signals large holders exiting positions. Historical data confirms that spikes in this data point align with major market tops and bottoms, reinforcing its value in cycle analysis, as shown in Chart 13.5.

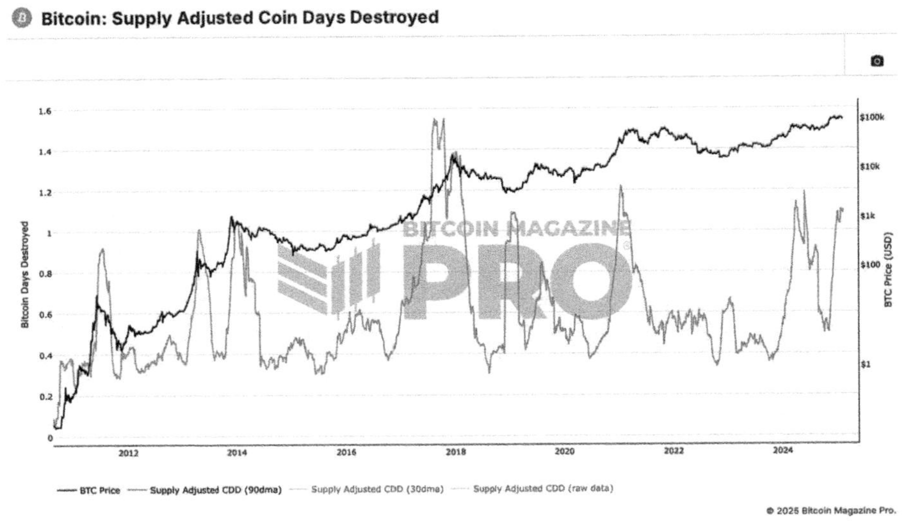

Chart 13.5 *Source* Bitcoin Magazine Pro

13.4.2 Value Days Destroyed (VDD) Multiple

Coin Days Destroyed (CDD) is calculated by taking the number of coins in a transaction and multiplying it by the number of days since those coins were last spent.

Value Days Destroyed (VDD) multiplies CDD by the $BTC price.

Value Days Destroyed Multiple divides a 30-day average of VDD by a 365-day average to compare near-term spending velocity with a yearly average.

VDD Multiple aims to identify when Bitcoin's price may be close to topping out at major cycle highs.

As illustrated in Chart 13.6, when these red wicks appear, it indicates that the market is near a potential top. A reversal could occur, possibly leading to a drop in Bitcoin's price.

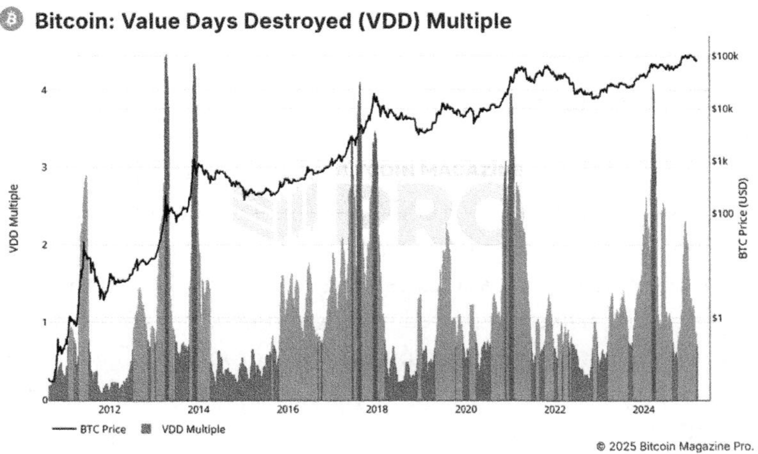

Chart 13.6   *Source* Bitcoin Magazine Pro

13.4.3 Bitcoin Cycle Master

It combines on-chain metrics, including Coin Value Days Destroyed and Terminal Price, to identify where Bitcoin's price is valued relative to its cycle peaks and lows. They can locate where Bitcoin price is valued relatively within its cycles. You can use these levels to identify **good entry points,** as shown in Chart 13.7.

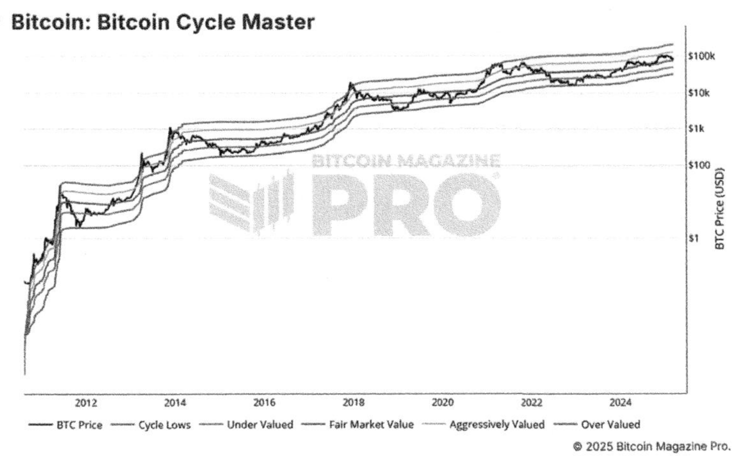

Chart 13.7   *Source* Bitcoin Magazine Pro

13.5 Miners

13.5.1 Bitcoin Hashprice

Hashprice is the expected daily value of 1 TH/s of power per day. That value can be expressed in BTC (sats) or USD. This metric is illustrated by Chart 13.8.

Hashprice refers to the dollar value of revenue miners earn for each unit of computational power expended to secure the Bitcoin network.

Rising hashprice reflects improved mining profitability and network strength. As miners adopt more efficient equipment, costs drop, reducing the need to sell BTC. This supply reduction may drive upward price pressure. Investors can view this as a sign of a stronger, more resilient network, supporting long-term price growth.

It shows how much a Bitcoin miner can expect to earn from a specific amount of hash rate power.

It is calculated by taking the ratio between total USD or BTC-denominated miner income (subsidy and fees), and dividing by the current hash rate (in EH/s).

Hashprice has a positive correlation with Bitcoin price and transaction fees.

Hashprice has a negative correlation with changes to Bitcoin mining difficulty.

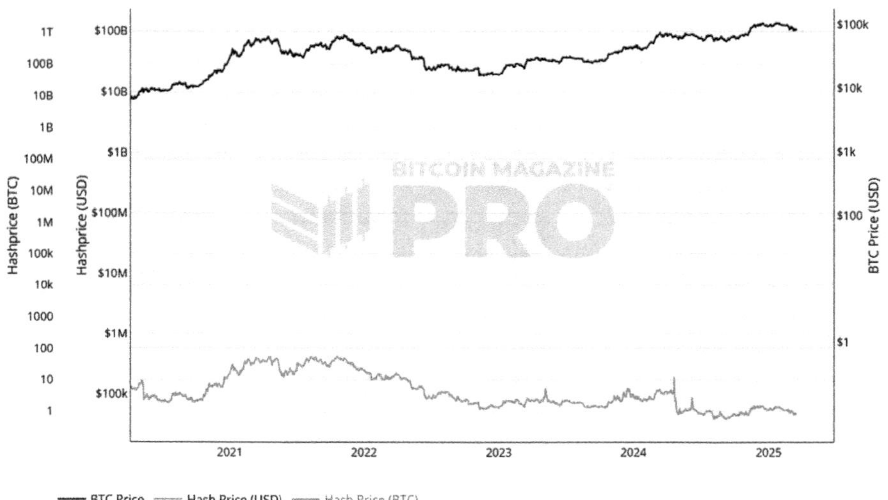

Chart 13.8 *Source* Bitcoin Magazine Pro

13.5.2 Puell Multiple

The Puell Multiple, which measures miner revenue relative to historical averages, provides insights into market cycles. Historically, when miner profitability is strong, Bitcoin tends to be in a favorable position.

It is named after David Puell, who created the metric to track Bitcoin miners' revenue and the effect it has on market behavior.

The indicator helps identify periods where the market is either over-extended or undervalued based on the relative profitability of miners.

The Puell Multiple is calculated by dividing the daily issuance value of bitcoins (in USD) by the 365-day moving average of daily issuance value.

When miners' revenue drops, they may sell their Bitcoin holdings, potentially leading to price declines.

Historically, the Puell Multiple has identified market tops and bottoms, helping investors spot potential entry and exit points.

It provides a long-term perspective on the market by comparing miner revenue over time, which is useful in gauging whether the current Bitcoin price is overheated or undervalued, as shown in Chart 13.9.

A good way to determine miner sentiment is how much money they're making. The Bitcoin Puell Multiple tracks USD-denominated miner earnings daily. It compares that Charture to the previous yearly average to gauge whether miners are making more or less than their historical norm. A Puell Multiple (orange line) value greater than 1.00 will indicate miners are making more than before, whereas a value less than that will indicate miner earnings are down.

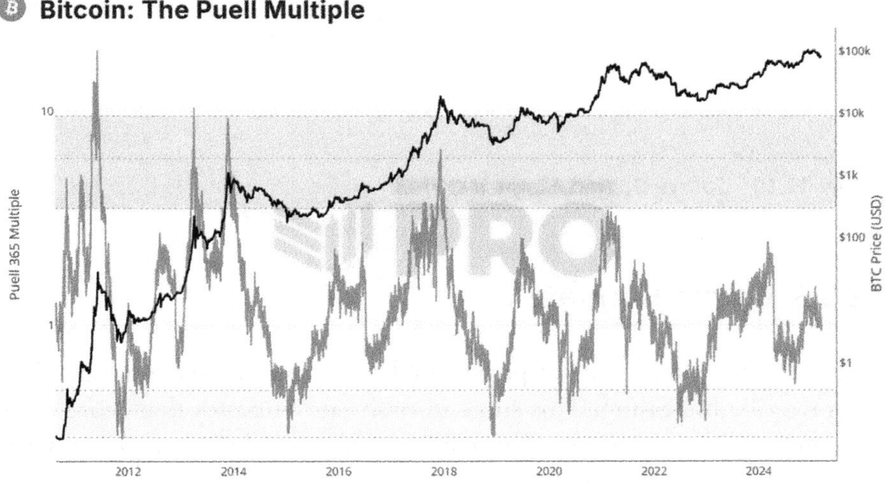

Chart 13.9 *Source* Bitcoin Magazine Pro

We can see that when miners are making a lot of money, and the Puell Multiple reaches the upper red boundary, indicating a considerable multiple on their typical incoming capital, it often aligns with a BTC bull market peak. On the contrary, when miners earn considerably less than usual and the Puell Multiple reaches the lower green region, this has historically been a great time to accumulate, coinciding with bear cycle lows.

When the value is high, it can indicate miners are earning more than the historical average, potentially signaling a good selling opportunity.

When the value is low, it can indicate miners are earning less than the historical average, potentially signaling a good buying opportunity.

Previous cycles show that after halving (2012–2016–2020–2024), crossing and retesting the value of 1 often precedes major price rallies. This pattern is repeating, signaling strong market support from mining activity, as shown in Chart 13.10.

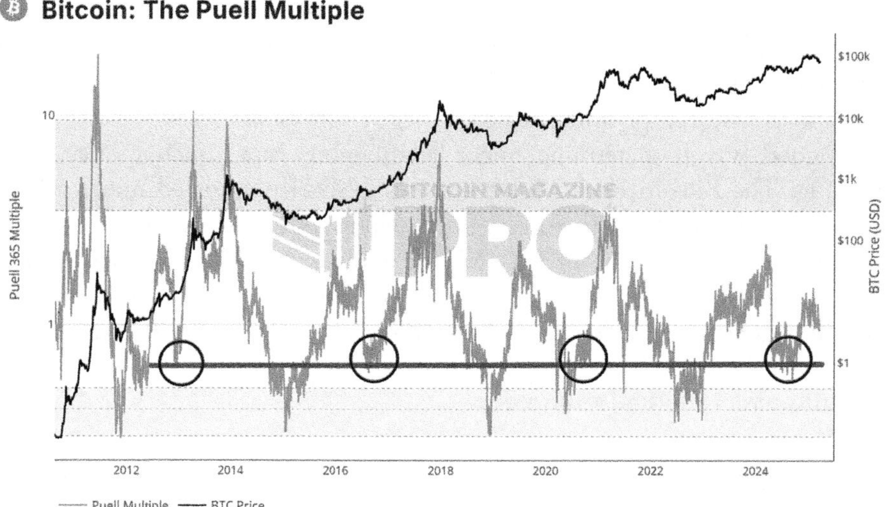

Chart 13.10 *Source* Bitcoin Magazine Pro

13.5.3 Bitcoin Hashrate

It is the total computational power used to secure the network, and it has been steadily increasing. This surge in hash rate indicates that more miners are entering the network or existing miners are upgrading their equipment to compete for block rewards.

The greater the levels of hashing operating on the network, the harder it would be for someone to overpower and attack it.

If hashrate on the Bitcoin network is high, then this indicates that the network is secure and healthy.

The BTC hashrate is typically calculated as hashes per second (h/s). Table 13.1.

Table 13.1 Illustrates that the hash unit can be expressed by size

Hashrate units	Hash size	Hashes per second
H/s (Hash)	1	One
kH/s (KiloHash)	1,000	One Thousand
MH/s (MegaHash)	1,000,000	One Million
GH/s (GigaHash)	1,000,000,000	One Billion
TH/s (TeraHash)	1,000,000,000,000	One Trillion
PH/s (PetaHash)	1,000,000,000,000,000	One Quadrillion
EH/s (ExaHash)	1,000,000,000,000,000,000	One Quintillion
ZH/s (ZettaHash)	1,000,000,000,000,000,000,000	One Sextillion
YH/s (YottaHash)	1,000,000,000,000,000,000,000,000	One Septillion

Chart 13.11 Illustrates the appearance of this metric vs Bitcoin price:

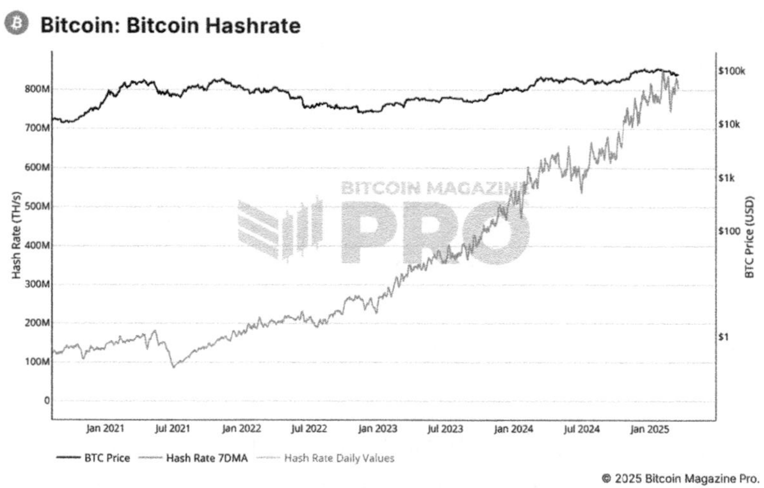

Chart 13.11   *Source* Bitcoin Magazine Pro

13.5.4 Hash Ribbons Indicator

Rather than tracking earnings, it tracks miner hashrate, or the computational power used to find a complex solution to secure the network and be rewarded with the BTC block reward and transaction fees.

It comprises two moving averages: a **30-day moving average** of Bitcoin hashrate (blue line) and a **60-day moving average** (purple line).

When the 30DMA crosses above the 60DMA, it generates a 'Buy' signal.

As illustrated in Chart 13.12, we can see that almost every time this crossover has occurred, it has been followed by a bullish rally.

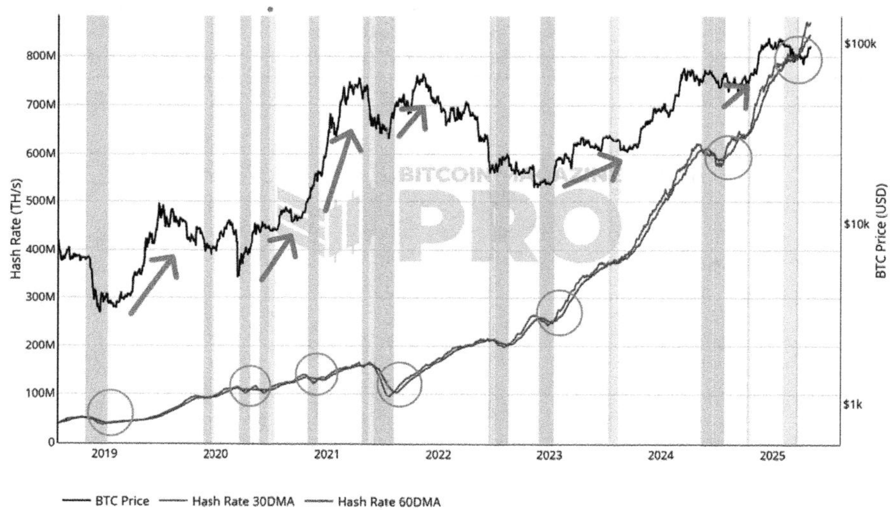

Chart 13.12 *Source* Bitcoin Magazine Pro

This metric, like the Puell Multiple, is also quite heavily impacted by the BTC halving event, which occurs every four years and reduces the block rewards of new blocks by 50%. This has a substantial and immediate impact on earnings, which then usually results in miner capitulation.

When the 60-day average rises above the 30-day average, it historically points to miner capitulation, a time when miners, under financial stress, shut off their equipment.

Until we see a bearish crossover, there's no immediate sign of bearishness. One positive is that every time this happens, it has been followed by a period of accumulation, which typically precedes a rise in Bitcoin prices. Investors often consider these capitulation periods great opportunities to buy BTC at lower prices.

13.5.5 Hashprice Volatility

One of the most interesting metrics to watch is Hashprice Volatility, which tracks how stable or volatile miner earnings are over time. Historically, periods of low hash price volatility have preceded significant price movements for Bitcoin, as shown in Chart 13.13.

Chart 13.13 *Source* Bitcoin Magazine Pro

13.5.6 Blocks Mined

A Bitcoin block is mined approximately every 10 minutes; given that there are 1440 minutes daily, we should see around 144 blocks daily. This number constantly fluctuates due to hash rate and randomness to some extent, but when we see significant divergences from this point, you can almost view it as a real-time miner sentiment check.

Disproportionately high daily blocks indicate a bullish miner sentiment and usually price peaks.

Disproportionately low daily blocks indicate a bearish, miner sentiment and usually price bottoms.

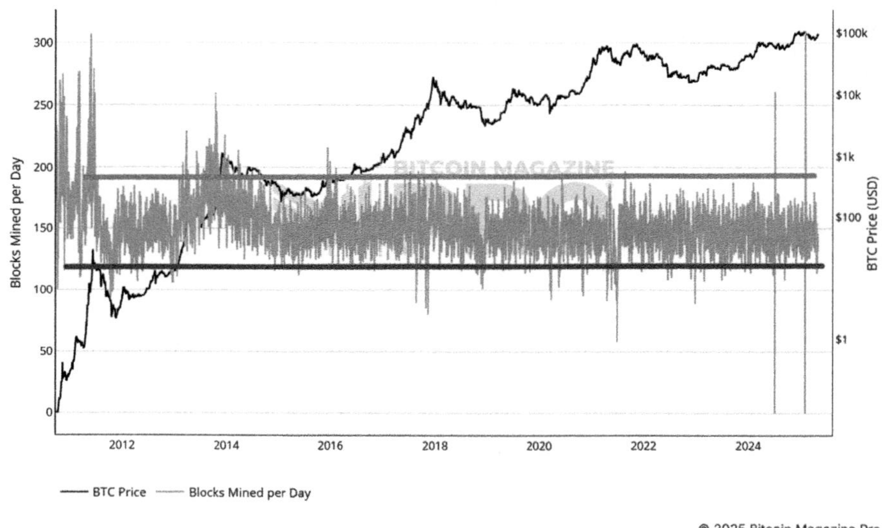

Chart 13.14 *Source* Bitcoin Magazine Pro

As illustrated in Chart 13.14, we can see that if blocks mined in a day are 20% lower than usual (so 115 blocks or lower), indicating fewer miners mining has historically marked a turning point in price. Similarly, if we see blocks mined 25% higher than usual, or 180 blocks or more, it has also often marked a price peak. The upper threshold is greater as, historically, blocks have been mined slightly faster than the 10 minutes on average, as hashrate has practically always increased.

In summary, all of these miner tracking metrics are proven to work well individually, but they all have their faults. The **Puell Multiple** may not be as reliable going forward, as halving events have a lessened price impact, and hashrate cycles will become less extreme as we move further away from retail mining. The **Hashribbons** work great for accumulation but don't necessarily provide the best profit-taking opportunities, and the **new Blocks Mined** metric may be too susceptible to external factors and be a little 'twitchy', sending a lot of signals.

13.6 Derivatives

13.6.1 Funding Rates

It indicates how much a trader has to pay or receive for being long or short on a perpetual contract. The amount they must pay or receive is the difference between the perpetual contract and the spot price.

When funding rates are positive (green bars on the chart) and the market is bullish, traders who are long pay those who are short. When funding rates are negative (red bars), traders who are short pay those who are long.

A positive funding rate means traders are taking long positions and are bullish, expecting the price to increase.

A negative funding rate means traders are taking short positions and are bearish, expecting the price to move lower.

We must pay attention when funding rates are at extreme levels, as this can indicate a trend reversal.

As shown in Chart 13.15, it may signal a local bottom if they are highly negative, and an upward rally could soon begin. If they are highly positive, it may signal a local top, and a downward rally may follow.

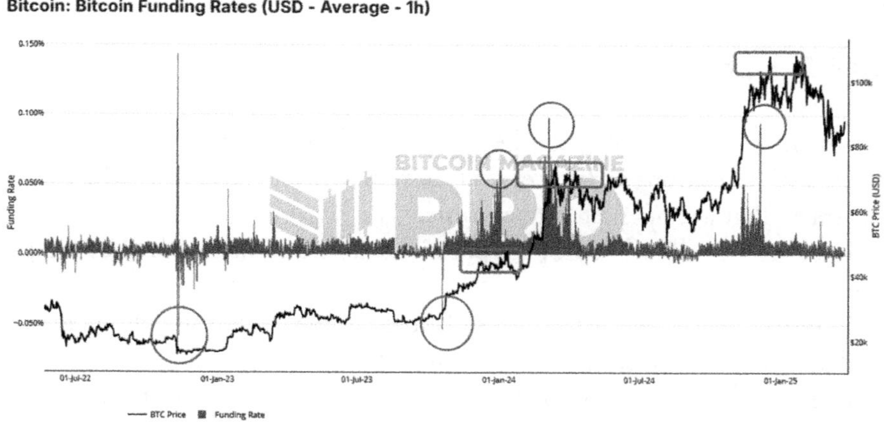

Chart 13.15 *Source* Bitcoin Magazine Pro

When the funding rate reaches these extremes, it may provide an opportunity for traders to consider positioning against the prevailing trend.

If funding rates start to decline, that would signal that excessive long leverage is starting to ease out of the market, while a re-acceleration could signal additional risk is being added to the long side.

Funding rates reflect trader sentiment in futures markets.

Negative Funding rates during bull cycles are a strong signal for accumulation during dips, making them a good buying opportunity, as shown in Chart 13.16.

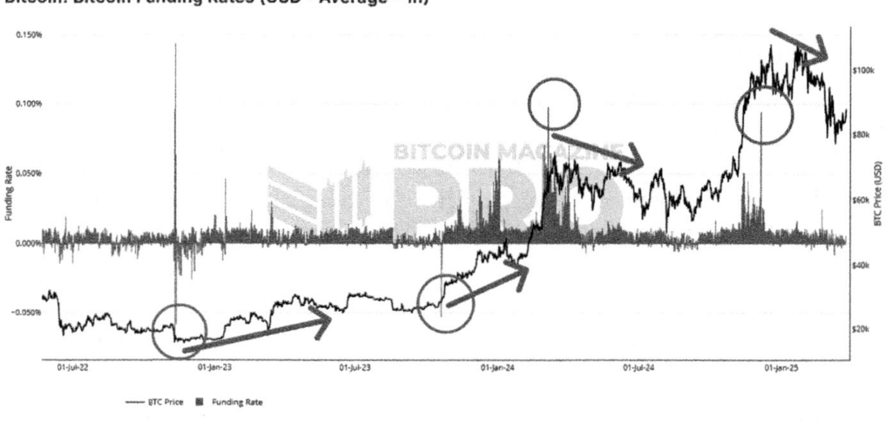

Chart 13.16   *Source* Bitcoin Magazine Pro

Funding rates must be used with other data, such as trading volume and price trends, to avoid misinterpretation of a singular signal.

13.6.2 Open Interest

Open Interest is the total number of outstanding derivative contracts for an asset, such as options or futures, that have not been settled. It is the value of contracts that are open at a given time.

It sums up all of the open positions at that time, whether long or short.

If more traders open positions, Bitcoin Open Interest will increase; if traders close positions, open interest will decrease.

It gives an overall view of how much money moves in and out of the Bitcoin derivatives market.

Chart 13.17 Illustrates the appearance of this metric.

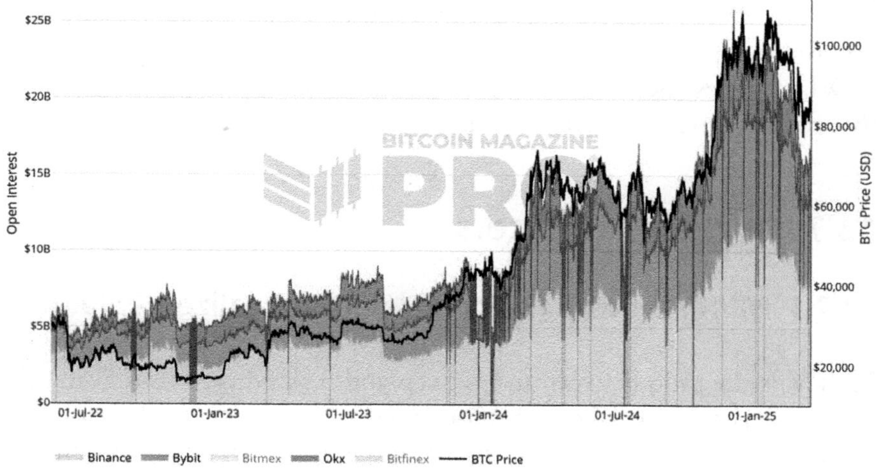

Chart 13.17   *Source* Bitcoin Magazine Pro

I'm attaching the following table to help you better understand the concept of open interest. I have already discussed it in Chap. 12, which is under the section on volume indicators. Table 13.2 and Table 13.3.

Table 13.2 Illustrates the relationship between the buyer and seller, along with its interpretation in terms of open interest

Buyer	Seller	Change In OI
New	New	Open interest up
New	Old	No change OI
Old	New	No change OI
Old	Old	Open interest down

Table 13.3 Illustrates the relationship between open interest and price, along with its interpretation

Open Interest	Price	Interpretation
Up	Up	New long positions: Bullish
Down	Up	Move up will retrace. shorts are covering and buying to exit their position. squeeze up in price
Up	Down	Selling pressure. Long positions are at risk.
Down	Down	New short positions: Bearish

The most optimal approach is to use **both metrics** to determine where the market is heading:

When the price is falling, but funding rates and open interest are climbing, it can suggest that many derivatives traders are attempting to buy the dip.

When prices rise, but funding rates and open interest fall, it can suggest that many derivatives traders are attempting to sell at the top.

13.7 Onchain Indicators

13.7.1 MVRV Z-Score (Market Value to Realized Value)

MVRV is the ratio between market cap and realized cap. It indicates if the spot price is below or above the fair value.

MVRV Z-Score is then calculated by taking the ratio of the difference between Bitcoin's market cap and realized cap, and dividing it by the standard deviation of all historical market cap data.

This metric identifies when Bitcoin is **overvalued or undervalued** relative to its fair value.

When the market cap price is much higher than the realized price, you're approaching the red zone, which indicates that the market is overheated/overvalued and signals a potential market top.

On the other hand, if the market cap is much lower than the realized price, you are near the green zone, which suggests the market is oversold/undervalued, and we may be at a market bottom.

As we can see in Chart 13.18, the peak in the 2018 cycle was 10.04, whereas in the 2021 cycle it was 7.13.

This indicates that, over time, market cycles are becoming less extreme. This is due to the growing number of participants in the market and its maturing and less volatile nature.

Bitcoin: MVRV Z-Score

Chart 13.18   *Source* Bitcoin Magazine Pro

13.7.2 Spent Output Profit Ratio (SOPR)

It is the realized value (in USD) divided by the value at creation (USD) of a spent output. It is the price sold divided by the price paid.

This metric was created to monitor Bitcoin transactions on the network, comparing the USD value of Bitcoin at the time of purchase versus when it's sold. This metric examines Unspent Transaction Outputs (UTXOs), or the BTC balances that haven't yet been spent, to assess whether investors are selling at a profit or a loss.

For example, if an investor bought Bitcoin two years ago and sells it now, the SOPR will capture the price change and track whether the sale was profitable or resulted in a loss.

It reveals the profitability of BTC transactions. A SOPR value above 0 indicates that the average Bitcoin being moved is profitable, while a value below 0 means the average sale is at a loss.

As shown in Chart 13.19, when SOPR reaches extreme levels, it often corresponds to market tops or bottoms.

Bitcoin: Spent Output Profit Ratio (SOPR)

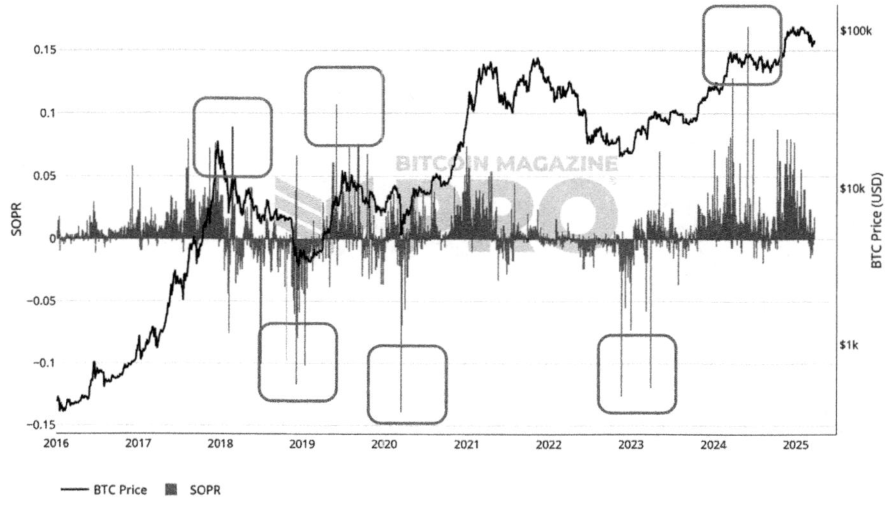

Chart 13.19   *Source* Bitcoin Magazine Pro

SOPR has the ability to identify critical turning points in Bitcoin's price cycle. It is a useful tool for detecting market sentiment.

13.8 Key Reversals

13.8.1 MVRV Momentum

Market Value to Realized Value Momentum is an indicator that compares the current market capitalization (Market Value) with the realized capitalization (Realized Value), a measure of the average price at which each bitcoin last moved.

Chart 13.20 Shows the ratio between these two metrics (orange line), then has a yearly moving average applied to it (purple line).

The orange line (MVRV) below the purple line (1 yr avg) indicates a market downtrend and bearish conditions. When this situation occurs, the indicator appears red, and the price can rally downwards.

When the orange line is above the purple line, it indicates market uptrends and bullish conditions. When this happens, the indicator appears green, and the price can rally upwards.

This metric helps investors understand whether Bitcoin is overvalued or undervalued compared to its "fair value".

MVRV Momentum

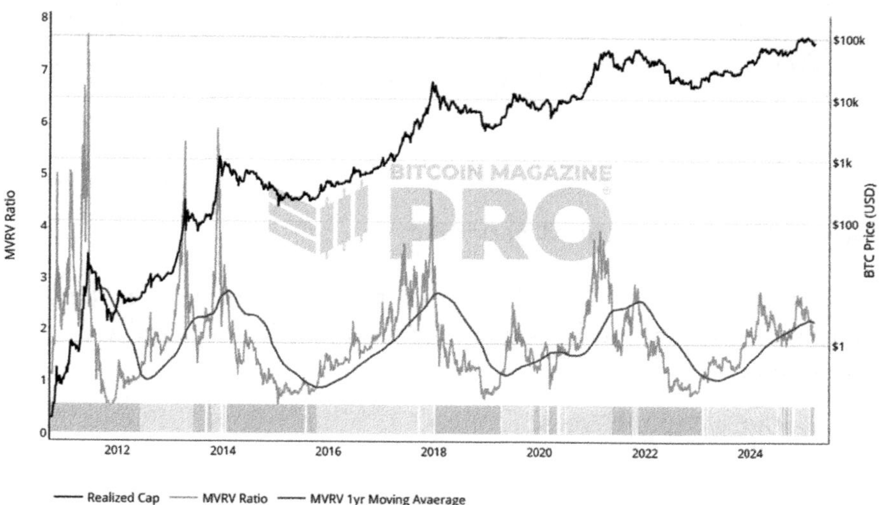

Chart 13.20   *Source* Bitcoin Magazine Pro

13.8.2 Cycle Capital Flows

This metric compares realized cap held by new investors (less than one month) vs. long-term holders (1–2 years). It shows the capital rotation from longer-term investors to newer investors.

As shown in Chart 13.21, the realized cap of short-term holders peaks when we are at the tops of a bull market, and therefore, the realized cap of long-term holders hits its lows.

Bitcoin Cycle Capital Flows

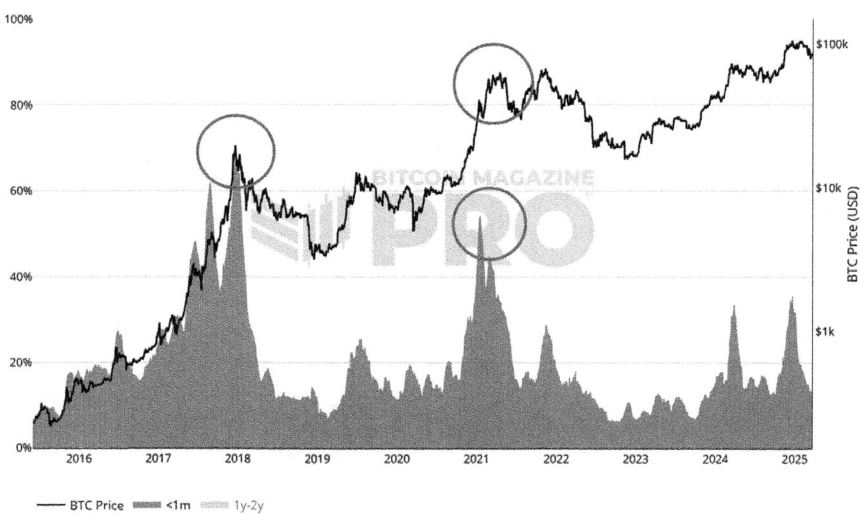

Chart 13.21 *Source* Bitcoin Magazine Pro

As illustrated in Chart 13.22, the bottom of a bear market, long-term holders' realized cap peaks, while short-term holders' realized cap hits its lowest point.

Bitcoin Cycle Capital Flows

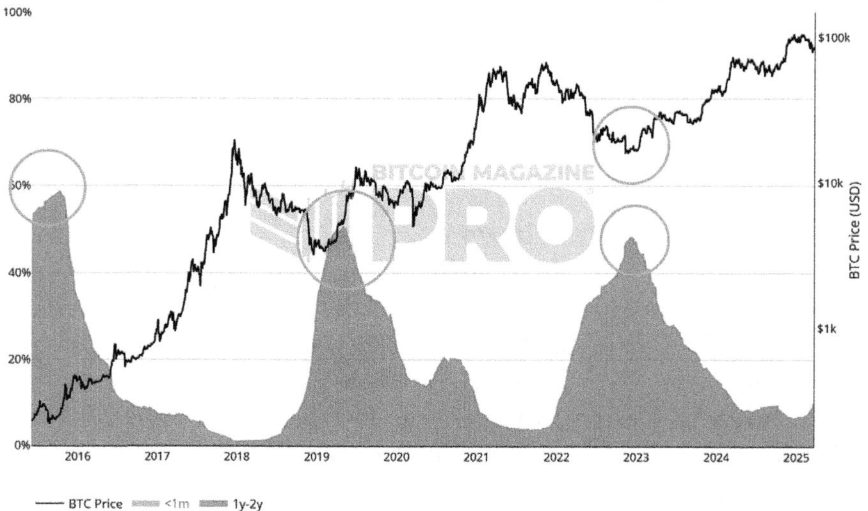

Chart 13.22 *Source* Bitcoin Magazine Pro

14

Softwares and Websites

In this chapter, I'm going to list all the **websites** I use so that you have all the necessary information readily available whenever you need it.

14.1 Brokers and Wallets

- CENTRALIZED EXCHANGES (CEX):

    - Kraken.com
    - Binance.com
    - Kucoin.com

- DECENTRALIZED EXCHANGES (DEX):

    - Pancakeswap. finance
    - Uniswap.org
    - Uniswap V3 Calculators:

        https://defi-lab.xyz/uniswapv3simulator
        https://uniswapv3.thechun.dev/

- COLD WALLETS:

    - Trezor.io
    - Ledger.com

- HOT WALLETS:

  – Metamask.io (desktop)
  – Trustwallet.com (mobile)

- TOKEN SWAP FROM ONE NETWORK TO ANOTHER:

  – Chainport.io

14.2 Market

- IMPERMANENT LOSS CALCULATOR:

  – https://dailydefi.org/tools/impermanent-loss-calculator/

- MARKET DATA:

  – Coinmarketcap.com
  – Coingecko.com

- ON-CHAIN METRICS:

  – Glassnode.com
  – Bitcoinmagazinepro.com
  – Cryptoquant.com

- RESEARCH/INDICATORS:

  – Messari.io
  – https://alternative.me/crypto/fear-and-greed-index/

- OFF-CHAIN METRICS:

  – Moonpass.ai
  – Coinmarketcal.com: proyectos

- RISK MANAGEMENT:

  – Rinasystems.com

- NEWS:

  - Cryptopanic.com

14.3 Technical Analysis

- CRYPTO TECHNICAL ANALYSIS:

  - https://www.tradingview.com/gopro/#plans

- INDICATORS:

  - https://www.decentrader.com/indicator-page/?ref=51&campaign=Predatorwidget

- POINT AND FIGURE:

  - https://www.bullseyebroker.com/
  - https://www.multicharts.com/net/features/chart-analysis/
  - https://www.esignal.com/add-ons/most-popular

- MARKET PROFILE:

  - https://www.esignal.com/add-ons/most-popular
  - https://www.prorealtime.com/en/new-features-ProRealTime-v11-1
  - https://www.tasmarketprofile.com/

- ORDER FLOW:

  - https://atas.net/es/
  - https://orderflowanalytics.com/
  - https://motivewave.com/
  - https://ninjatrader.com/es/Order-Flow-Trading

14.4 Automated Trading Systems

- BROKER:

  - Fusionmarkets.com: 24/7, variety of crypto, 1:5 leverage, spread, commissions.

- COPY TRADING:

  - Fusion +: https://fusionmarkets.com/en/Platforms/Fusion-plus
  - Pelicantrading.io

- SOFTWARES:

  - Strategyquant.com
  - Forexrobotacademy.com

- EA LAUNCH:

  - Metatrader.com
  - EA Launcher

    https://www.forexrobotacademy.com/mymt4book-ealauncher

- EA ANALYSIS:

  - Mymt4book

- DEDICATED SERVER:

  - https://www.vpsforextrader.com
  - https://www.velia.net
  - https://www.tradingfxvps.com/dedicated-server/

14.5 How to Find a Gem

- HOW TO AVOID SCAMS:

  - Bscscan.com: token tracker (transacciones- wallets-holders-liquidity)
  - Etherscan.com: token tracker
  - Bscheck.eu: tipo scam-contract owner-holders-liquidity-funciones mint
    & self-destruct
  - Tokensniffer.com: smell test—bubble map

- TRANSACTIONS:

  - Dextools.io
  - Poocoin.app

- DOMAIN REGISTRATION:

  - Whois.domaintools.com

- LOCKED LP TOKENS:

  - Deeplock.io/safe
  - https://app.unicrypt.network/amm

- AUDIT:

  - Certik.org

- SCAM FILTER:

  - Listingspy.net

14.6 DeFi

Decentralized Finance (DeFi) refers to a growing ecosystem of financial applications built on blockchain networks, primarily Ethereum, that aim to recreate and improve traditional financial services without relying on centralized intermediaries, such as banks or custodial exchanges.

These applications are governed by smart contracts, which execute transactions automatically and transparently based on code.

On these DEXs, you can earn yields through staking, farming, or lending. Some interesting websites could be:

- COIN SELECTION WITH GROWTH POTENTIAL:

  - Cryptorank.io: venture capital coins (Selection of high-potential cryptocurrencies)
  - Defillama.com: Total Value Locked: High TVL y Mcap/TVL < 1
  - Dappradar.com: games with a larger user base and low market cap.

- DEFI STAKING FARMING: Apy, protocol, TVL

  - Nanoly.com

- DEFI TOOLS:

  - Tokenterminal.com: analyze six blockchains, 115 decentralized projects
  - Eigenphi.io: MEV transaction data is the most reliable liquidity data. You can track it on this website
  - App.blockpour.com: liquidity analysis, arbitrage opportunities, new token pairs, trade reports

14.7 Others

- TRANSACTION TRACKING (Wallets Investigation):

  - Real-time tracking of crypto transactions
  - Trace the flow of crypto funds between wallets (origin and destination)
  - Over 50 million ETH and BTC wallet addresses identified
  - Token holdings of the largest wallets (whales)
  - https://www.breadcrumbs.app/our-tools
  - https://www.nansen.ai/
  - https://www.walletscan.info/

- **Thekingfisher.io:** hidden liquidity/derivatives trading
- **Openbb.co:** investment research platform (free)
- **V3app.everrise.com/everrevoke**: Protect your wallet by locking it.
- **App. intotheblock.com**: NFT collection analysis, crypto predictions, exchange TVL, over 50 indicators across 800 coins.
- **Marketcapof.com:** shows how much a coin would be worth if it had the market cap of another (useful for comparing a newly launched coin vs. the leader in its sector).

15

How to Manage a Crypto Portfolio

In this chapter, I will outline the most important points to consider when managing a crypto portfolio. These are aspects you must be clear about before investing and setting up your portfolio.

First of all, you need to consider which phase of the market we are in. For example, if we are in a bear market, the least volatile and most stable cryptocurrency would generally be Bitcoin. Being the largest cryptocurrency, it has the greatest influence on the market's price movement and overall direction.

Another important factor is understanding the correlation between the coins selected for your investment portfolio. For instance, Ripple (XRP) is a cryptocurrency that is uncorrelated with Bitcoin and is often used in portfolios to diversify risk.

You should also be clear about:

- The returns you aim to achieve,
- The maximum drawdown you are willing to accept,
- Your investment time horizon, and
- Your risk tolerance, as cryptocurrencies are not suitable for everyone due to their high volatility.

Lastly, it's essential to understand which market narratives are trending, since cryptocurrencies aligned with those narratives tend to be more liquid and have greater upside potential. For example, during the 2024–2025 bull cycle, the most promising narratives are: AI/AI Agents, RWA (Real World Assets), Layer 2s (such as Base, Arbitrum, Linea), blockchains (like SUI, HBAR), memecoins, etc.

15.1 Crypto Portfolio: Correlations

As mentioned earlier, when building a crypto portfolio, you need to clearly understand the current phase of the crypto market. Based on your risk tolerance and desired returns, you should create a portfolio including Bitcoin, big altcoins, mid-cap altcoins, and small-cap altcoins. It's important to consider the factors previously mentioned, especially the correlation between the coins.

Every portfolio should always include Bitcoin since it is the main cryptocurrency and the one that moves the market. A portfolio during a bull run might look like this:

- Bitcoin: 40%
- Big Altcoins (market cap > $1.5 billion): 35%
- Mid-cap Altcoins (market cap between $1.5 billion and $500 million): 15%
- Small-cap Altcoins (market cap < $500 million): 10%

Among the big altcoins, for example, XRP is quite uncorrelated with Bitcoin, making it a good candidate for selection, as shown in Table 15.1.

Table 15.1 *Source* Wisdomtree from 31 December 2013 to 31 January 2025

	Bitcoin	Ethereum	Solana	Cardano	Polkadot	XRP	Mega cap	Large cap	Altcoins
Crypto vs. crypto									
Bitcoin	1.00								
Ethereum	0.71	1.00							
Solana	0.64	0.54	1.00						
Cardano	0.55	0.56	0.46	1.00					
Polkadot	0.54	0.66	0.40	0.76	1.00				
XRP	0.35	0.33	0.24	0.59	0.52	1.00			
Mega cap	0.56	0.63	0.41	0.38	0.44	0.23	1.00		
Large cap	0.54	0.59	0.43	0.46	0.53	0.31	0.96	1.00	
Altcoins	0.41	0.43	0.41	0.53	0.55	0.45	0.73	0.88	1.00

15.2 Themes

Regarding themes, if you consider RWA (Real World Assets) an interesting narrative, within this theme, we would have, for example, Mantra (OM) and ONDO (ONDO).

An altcoin that has grown significantly, mainly because its network is widely used by memecoins, is Solana.

Another interesting narrative is AI Agents. For example, a selected small-cap coin could be AI16z.

Finally, another narrative with potential that I see is Decentralized Science.

The trends currently showing the most potential are AI Agents and Real World Assets (RWA).

15.2.1   AI Agents

What are AI Agents?
An artificial intelligence (AI) agent is a software program that can interact with its environment, collect data, and use it to perform defined tasks to achieve predetermined goals autonomously. Humans set the goals, but the AI agent independently chooses the most appropriate actions to execute to reach those goals.

The link between AI Agents and blockchain lies in decentralization and transparency. By operating in a blockchain environment, these agents can perform their functions without relying on a centralized entity, ensuring data integrity and traceability of actions.

Moreover, smart contracts on the blockchain allow AI Agents to autonomously and programmably interact with DeFi protocols, token marketplaces, and even DAOs.

AI Agent tokens are the financial component that enables the ecosystem of these agents on the blockchain. They act as fuel for AI Agents to operate within their respective platforms, pay for access to data, services, and computing power, and reward users or nodes participating in the network.

With blockchain's cryptographic security, AI agents can transact seamlessly without intermediaries, unlocking a future of **decentralized, self-sufficient financial ecosystems**.

The best-known are AI16Z (Solana network), VIRTUAL (Base network), and AIXBT (Base network).

15.2.2   Real World Assets (RWA)

Another very interesting narrative where we have projects like Mantra (OM), Plume (PLUME), Ondo (ONDO), etc.

What Are Real-World Assets (RWA)?
Real-world assets (RWAs) refer to tangible or financial assets in the physical world (outside of the blockchain). These assets include real estate, government bonds, private credit, commodities (like gold), and even art. Tokenizing RWAs allows investors to trade them digitally, just like cryptocurrencies, but with the added benefit of backing from physical or financial instruments.

What Is Tokenization and How Does It Work?
Tokenization is the process of converting real-world assets into digital tokens on a blockchain. These tokens represent ownership or a stake in the asset, allowing investors to buy, sell, or trade them more efficiently than in traditional markets. The process typically involves:

* **Asset Identification and Legal Structuring**: Determining the asset to be tokenized and ensuring compliance with regulations.
* **Token Creation**: Using blockchain technology to issue digital tokens that represent ownership or value. This breaks down large, illiquid assets (e.g., real estate) into smaller, tradable tokens.
* **Smart Contracts and Automation**: Enabling automated transactions, such as revenue distribution and ownership transfers.

RWA Tokenization Sector Key Metrics
RWA tokenization emerged as one of the most transformative trends of 2023–2024, mirroring the rapid rise of AI. Beyond individual users,

institutional giants like BlackRock and Franklin Templeton have fueled this sector's expansion by actively exploring and investing in blockchain-based asset tokenization.

The involvement of institutional clients is driving spectacular growth and adoption in this sector.

Chart 15.1 illustrates the trend of this market over the past five years.

Tokenized RWA Marketcap

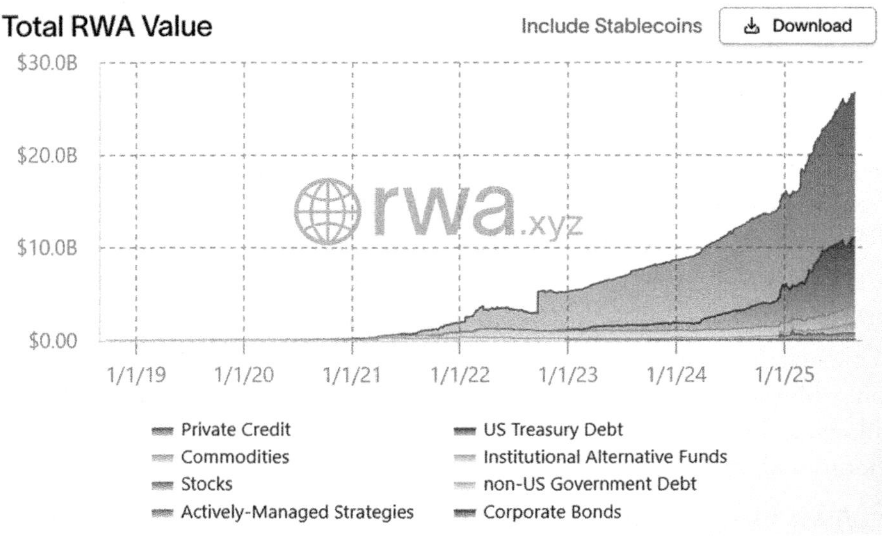

Chart 15.1   *Source* rwa.Xyx—Aug'25

Since early 2023, the market capitalization of tokenized RWAs has surged from $5.2 billion to over $19.5 billion as of early April 2025, representing a 375% increase. As illustrated in the chart above, Private Credit and U.S. Treasuries dominate the space, with market caps of $12.2 billion and $5.1 billion, respectively. Real estate is absent from the chart, highlighting that its tokenization is still in its early stages, as illustrated in Fig. 15.1.

Monthly On-chain RWA Issuance

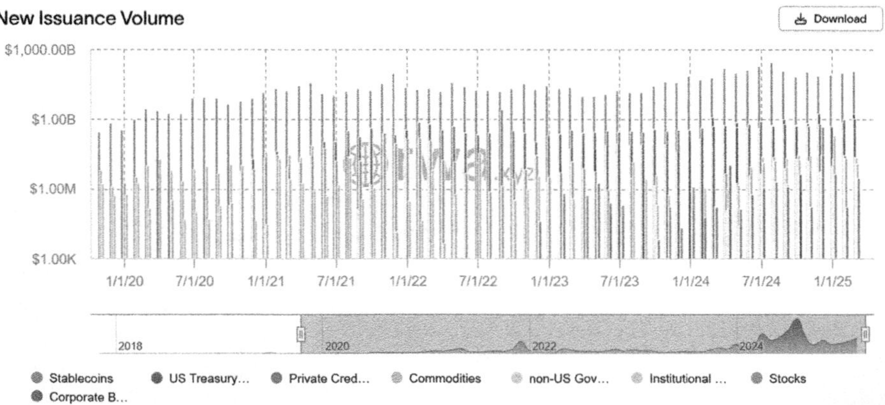

Fig. 15.1 *Source* rwa.Xyz

The issuance of tokenized RWAs across various blockchains has shown steady growth since 2019. Notably, the above chart also includes stablecoins, which, as tokenized representations of fiat currency, are inherently a form of RWA.

Currently, the total tokenized RWA market cap, including stablecoins, stands at $120 million, a staggering figure that underscores the sector's potential. Several research reports from leading institutions predict that this industry could evolve into a multi-trillion-dollar market.

The most notable development has been the emergence of three asset types that did not exist before 2022: US Treasury debt, Non-US government debt, and Stocks. Another significant highlight is the increase in Institutional Funds.

Crypto is approximately a $3 trillion asset class, while BlackRock alone manages $12 trillion in assets. If we sum up all the relevant sectors in RWAs, it amounts to over $3000 trillion in assets that need to come on-chain. With this data, we can clearly see the enormous potential that the RWA theme holds, as shown in Fig. 15.2.

Per industry in USD trillion

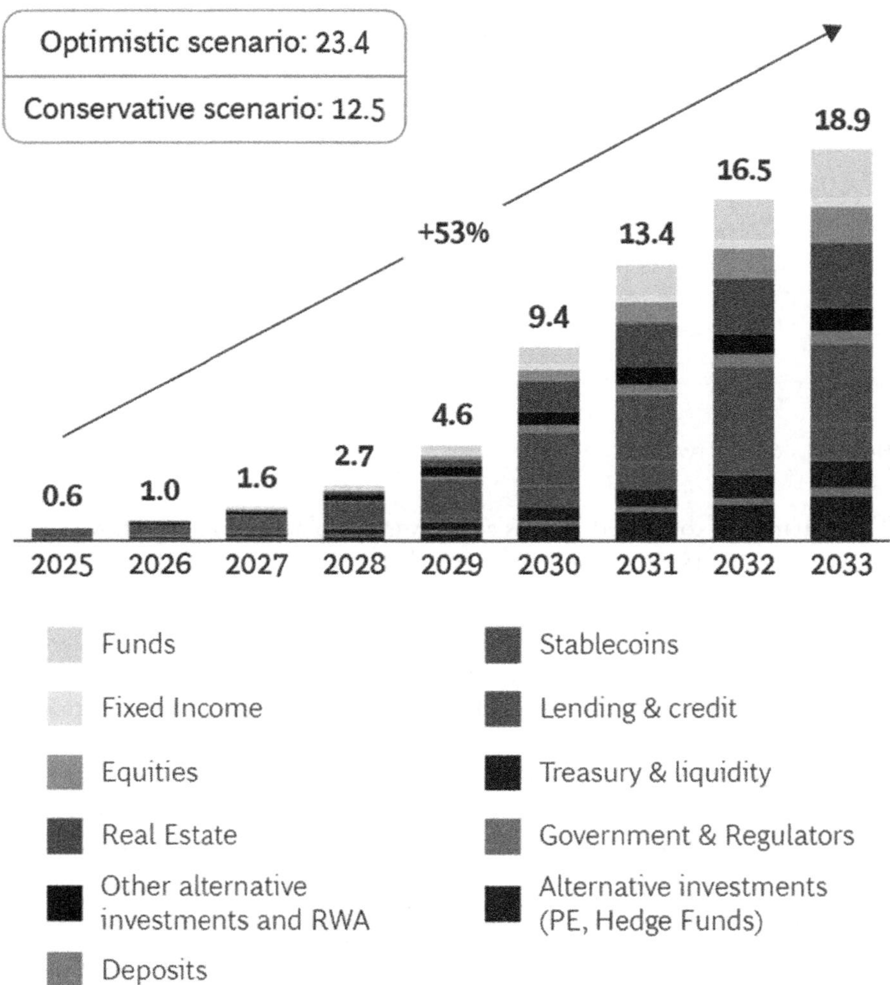

Fig. 15.2 *Source* Ripple and BCG

Example of RWA:

I would highlight three projects within this thematic area: Mantra, Ondo, and Plume.

There are two sides of the business: the buy side and the sell side.

The **buy side brings the capital—they are the demand, providing funds to invest in projects, buy assets, and so on. Then there's the sell**

side that brings the assets—issuers that bring various asset classes, financial instruments, and more to the market for the buy side to potentially purchase.

Ondo would be the sell side, and Plume the buy side because Ondo works with many institutions, while Plume is focused on the community. Plume is a distribution.

Both coins are working together to create a new global financial ecosystem, combining Ondo's institutional sell-side ecosystem with Plume's on-chain **buy-side ecosystem**.

Ondo Chain represents a new financial ecosystem designed for institutions. It has been a trailblazer in bringing institutional-grade RWAs to the blockchain. They pioneered the introduction of US Treasury Bills onchain and have been instrumental in helping BlackRock's money market fund attract liquidity from funds, foundations, and more to purchase these assets.

Figure 15.3 illustrates Ondo Ecosystem.

Fig. 15.3   *Source* Ondo Finance

The Plume community is made up of more than 3 million users: over 1 million on X (formerly Twitter), more than 450k on Discord, and over 240k on Telegram. It has over 18 million unique addresses, more than 280 million transactions, over $4 billion in assets available, and more than 180 protocols.

Plume is the first modular Layer 2 blockchain dedicated exclusively to **Real-World Assets (RWA)**. It integrates asset tokenization and compliance providers directly into the chain, **providing a unique network connecting traditional finance and blockchain technology**.

Plume offers a composable, EVM-compatible environment for onboarding and managing diverse real-world assets.

MANTRA:

It is a Layer 1 blockchain designed specifically for tokenizing real-world assets (RWAs) while ensuring regulatory compliance at the protocol level. Built using the Cosmos SDK, it is compatible with IBC and supports CosmWasm.

The platform's technology stack includes a native decentralized exchange (DEX) and various other applications. It supports a high transaction throughput of up to 10,000 TPS, secured by a Proof-of-Stake (PoS) consensus mechanism.

The project has secured significant partnerships, including a $1 billion deal with DAMAC Group to tokenize assets in the Middle East, as well as collaborations with major players like BlackRock, SwissBorg, Ondo, Chainlink, and Google Cloud. These partnerships, combined with strong investor backing, have driven the project's growth, with the $OM token reaching a peak market capitalization of $5.9 billion and a fully diluted valuation (FDV) of $10.8 billion.

Mantra's focus on integrating real-world assets into the blockchain with regulatory compliance positions it as a leader in the growing RWA sector.

The MANTRA Chain architecture is built on a five-layer structure, each playing a vital role in making MANTRA a highly efficient and unique Layer 1 blockchain. These layers are: Staking, Interoperability, Execution, Module, and Application.

Figure 15.4 Illustrates Mantra Architecture.

MANTRA Architecture

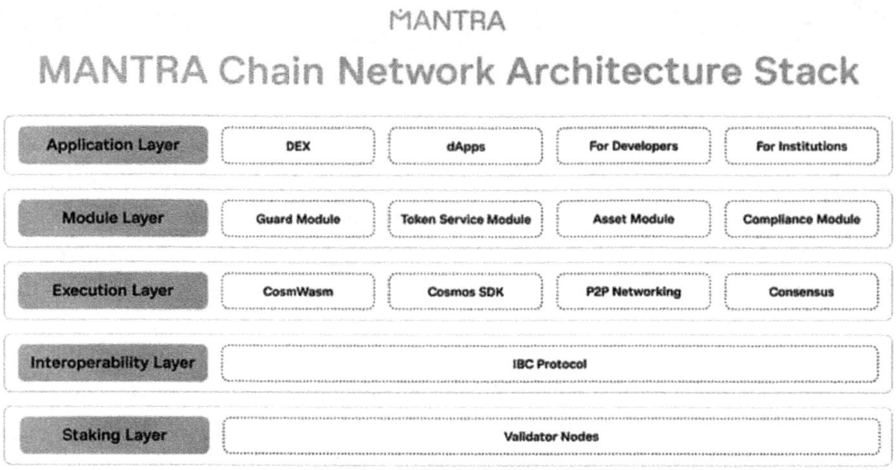

Fig. 15.4   *Source* http://www.Mantrachain.Io

A competitor of Mantra is **Ondo,** which is more focused on tokenizing traditional finance instruments, particularly U.S. Treasury Bills and other fixed-income securities. Their flagship product, OUSG, allows investors to gain direct exposure to U.S. Treasuries on the blockchain, bridging DeFi and traditional finance.

Another competitor is **Centrifuge,** which is more focused on on-chain credit loans.

In April 2025, on a Sunday night, Mantra's price plummeted from $6.30 to $0.50. It was a top 20 project with a market cap of over $4 billion, and in just 15 min, it lost more than 80% of its value. What happened, and what is important to know when investing in a coin?

At first, it was believed to be a rug pull (when project founders abandon the project and withdraw liquidity, taking users' funds), but later it became clear that the incident was unrelated to the leadership. Instead, it was due to a poor decision made earlier.

Coins often hire market makers to provide liquidity on centralized exchanges (CEX). Instead of paying a monthly fee, Mantra signed a contract called a loan option model, under which the market maker (Falcon X) had the right to buy 1 million tokens at $1 each when the agreement expired. Once the contract matured, Falcon X sold the million tokens on the market, causing the price to collapse.

Market makers are necessary because they provide liquidity and ensure there are always buyers and sellers to avoid price gaps. However, it's crucial that they are aligned with your project; otherwise, they can become your worst partner.

The lesson: if you launch a token, choose a retainer model—pay for the service, align incentives, and make sure no one can leave you without liquidity and destroy your project when stability is most needed.

Therefore, when investing, it's very important to understand how concentrated the token supply is and what contracts exist between market makers and the project leadership.

15.2.3   Decentralized Science (DeSci)

DeSci emerged from the convergence of open science and Web3 in the early 2020s.

DeSci is one such emerging narrative in the Web3 ecosystem that merges blockchain's disruptive power with global scientific research and innovation.

DeSci leverages blockchain, decentralized autonomous organizations (DAOs), and tokenization to reimagine scientific research. Unlike traditional science, which often operates within siloed institutions and centralized funding models, DeSci democratizes access to resources, data, and collaboration.

DeSci uses blockchain, smart contracts, and DAOs to decentralize scientific processes, from funding to data sharing. It is a movement to make science open, transparent, and community-driven. Core concepts include tokenization, which incentivizes contributions (e.g., research, peer review), and immutable data storage, ensuring verifiable results. For example, cryptocurrencies like OriginTrail (TRAC) secure data provenance, creating a trustless ecosystem for innovation.

Traditional science relies on centralized institutions like universities and government agencies, where funding is often tied up in slow, bureaucratic grant processes. In contrast, DeSci leverages blockchain to empower researchers and create opportunities for crypto investors. Platforms like LabDAO use transparent, token-driven crowdfunding to fund projects directly, reducing reliance on intermediaries and providing capital.

With a market cap exceeding \$500 M as of 2025 (per CoinGecko), DeSci tokens like \$BIO, \$TRAC, \$RSC, and \$VITA signal growing traction. Beyond economics, DeSci addresses systemic inefficiencies, like losing billions of dollars annually to irreproducible research, by offering solutions that resonate with Web3's ethos of transparency and ownership. DeSci also presents diversified exposure to biotech, AI, and tokenized economies for investors.

As we can see in the following image, the ecosystem of this narrative is quite large, but the biggest projects by market cap are: TRAC (OriginTrail), VITA (VitaDao), and BIO (Bio Protocol).

Figure 15.5 shows the DeSci ecosystem as of December 2024.

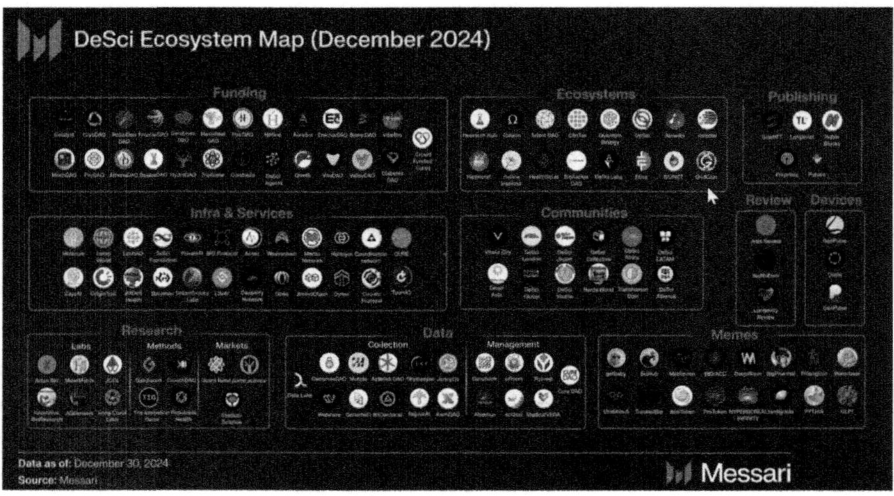

Fig. 15.5 *Source* Messari

15.3 Key Aspects

Aspects to consider before investing in a cryptocurrency:

* **The whitepaper**: it is a comprehensive document outlining the technical and economic aspects of a specific cryptocurrency.

  The whitepaper outlines the purpose of cryptocurrency, its features, how it works, and what it achieves. It includes essential technical details such as the consensus mechanism, mining process, and network architecture. It typically also outlines the economic objectives and rationale behind the cryptocurrency and its development.
* **Performance of similar projects: Verify that the sector has future potential and assess whether** other projects in the same sector are performing well.
* **Is this an original idea?**
* **Total addressable market**: to assess the level of support the project has.
* **Programming language**: whether it uses a programming language similar to other projects or one that is rarely used. It's always better if it's a language commonly used by other projects, like C++, Rust, Solidity, etc.
* **Number of developers**: This metric shows how many developers are behind the project and whether it is actively being worked on or not.
* **Ease of use**: To ensure rapid and easy adoption, it is important that the project be easy to use and not complex.
* **Roadmap**: shows the project's development phases and whether they are meeting their planned milestones.
* **Team**: It is crucial that the website clearly shows who the team members are, including their background and experience in the crypto market.
* **Social media**: check on X (Twitter) if there is a large community supporting the project or not.
* **Tokenomics** refers to the **token distribution** (how and to whom the tokens are allocated, e.g., team, investors, community).
* **Circulating Supply**: it's essential to check how much it represents of the total supply, because if only 30% is in circulation, it's a risk, new tokens could be released and devalue its price. Ideally, the circulating supply should be 70% or more of the total supply.

15.4 Investment Methods

Staking and **yield farming** (or farming) are two ways to earn rewards with cryptocurrencies, but they differ in approach and risk.

- **Staking** involves locking cryptocurrencies to validate transactions on a blockchain network, receiving fixed rewards in return.
- **Yield farming**, conversely, involves lending cryptocurrencies on DeFi platforms for others to use, seeking higher and variable returns.

Yield farming involves investing crypto assets in smart contract-based liquidity pools. The pool reuses the invested cryptocurrencies to provide liquidity in DeFi protocols and distributes some of the fees collected to users as rewards.

Regarding profitability, yield farming is generally more profitable than staking because it involves higher risk. Staking carries lower risk since the cryptocurrencies are locked in an established network. Yield farming carries more risk because it depends on the solvency of DeFi platforms and market fluctuations.

Regarding tokens, staking usually involves only one token (the one you deposit and the one you receive as a reward are the same), while yield farming often requires two tokens—one for the loan and another for the reward.

Another difference is the platform where each is performed: staking is usually done on centralized exchanges (CEX), whereas farming typically happens on decentralized exchanges (DEX).

Table 15.2 illustrates the main differences between staking, lending and farming.

Table 15.2 Comparison between Staking, Lending, and Farming

	Staking	Lending	Farming
Concept	Lock up coins	Lend coins for others to borrow	Lend coins to liquidity pool
Platform	CEX	CEX-DEX	DEX
Risk	Low	Medium	High
Performance	Low	Medium	High
Token	One	One	Two

- **Staking and Farming can only be done on PoS blockchains**
  - Bitcoin, for example, belongs to a PoW blockchain and cannot be used for staking. That's why wrapped coins like Wrapped BTC (WBTC) were created.
  - Ethereum also couldn't be staked initially, but since Ethereum 2.0, staking is possible because it transitioned from PoW to PoS consensus.

Finally, an investment method that lies between staking and farming in terms of risk and return is Lending. It involves lending crypto tokens to borrowers and earning interest. Smart contracts help eliminate risks commonly associated with traditional finance lending and remove collateral requirements. However, most lending platforms do not perform background checks, which are essential to mitigate credit and fraud risks.

In Summary:
- **Yield farming** involves providing liquidity to a DeFi protocol to earn rewards, often paid in multiple tokens.
- **Staking** involves locking up cryptocurrency to support network operations like block validation and earning fixed or variable rewards.
- **Lending** refers to providing your crypto assets for others to borrow in exchange for interest payments.

15.4.1 Staking

Staking consists of locking specific crypto assets to support the operation and security of a blockchain network, earning rewards in the process. In other words, it involves holding a certain amount of cryptocurrency locked to verify transactions and support the network. In return, you receive a reward similar to an interest payment.

Staking originates from the Proof of Stake (PoS) mechanism, which uses validators to validate blockchain blocks in exchange for rewards.

In general terms, the investor uses their existing coins or tokens to make them available and contribute to the functioning of a blockchain network. In return, the owner receives a payment for this.

The deposited coins are stored in a wallet. In this way, the cryptocurrencies back the security and operation of the blockchain network.

The most commonly used cryptocurrencies for staking are: ETH 2.0, ADA, DOT, and MATIC.

TYPES OF STAKING:

- **Proof of Stake (PoS)**

In this model, users must allocate an indefinite portion of their coins to the network, locking them outside their control as security. The probability of finding a block—and thus the reward for the staker—is calculated based on the number of coins staked, along with other factors such as random block selection or the age of the coins held.

- **Delegated Proof of Stake (DPoS)**

DPoS allows users to set their coin balances as votes, granting voting rights proportional to the number of coins they hold. These votes are then used to elect delegates who will manage the blockchain on behalf of their voters, ensuring security and consensus. Typically, staking rewards are distributed to these elected delegates, who then share a portion of the rewards with their voters proportionally to their individual contributions.

Since voters maintain a DPoS system, delegates are motivated to be honest and efficient, or they get excluded.

PoS systems make attacking a blockchain more costly, as a successful attack would require owning at least 51% of the total existing coins.

DPoS blockchains are more scalable and able to process more transactions per second (TPS) than PoW and PoS.

STAKING RISK:

- **Market Risk:** If the value of a coin crashes while you have coins locked up, you might be in a worse position than if you had sold your coins and taken profits from price gains.

- **Liquidity Risk**: If you choose a very small cryptocurrency that is hardly available on exchanges, when it's time to sell, you may be unable to convert it to fiat money or another cryptocurrency like Bitcoin.
- **Lock-up Period**: While the coins are locked, you cannot unlock them without flexible staking.
- **Validator Risks**: If you run a node, there is a risk that it may malfunction, and in that case, you can be penalized, affecting your earnings or even losing all your staked cryptocurrencies. For this reason, it's better to trust a centralized exchange (CEX), preferably one of the largest like Binance.

15.4.2 Farming

- Farming is when you provide liquidity to a protocol in exchange for an annual percentage yield (APY). This protocol generates fees when it is used, such as a decentralized exchange when you make a transaction, and part of those fees go to the liquidity providers. This is where the annual percentages you receive come from.
- The more people providing liquidity, the lower the annual percentage will be because the total pool size increases, so your share of the percentage within the pool decreases.
- If there are more transactions involving the pair to which you provided liquidity, the annual percentage will increase.
- Farming is usually done with what are called LP Tokens, which combine two cryptocurrencies in a 50–50 ratio. Once you create the LP Token, you stake it on the platform and start earning an annual percentage, receiving rewards from the moment you stake your LP.
- An example of an LP Token would be if you provide $100 in CAKE and $100 in USDT. Although LP tokens have different proportions, the most common is to contribute 50% of each cryptocurrency. Generally, the higher the risk (in more volatile cryptocurrencies), the higher the annual percentage yield, as well as the risk of impermanent loss, which we will explain later.
- With the profits earned (the tokens you receive from farming), you can reinvest them into a pool (compound interest) or sell them for a stablecoin and withdraw the money.

FARMING RISKS:
Besides the Market Risk, Liquidity Risk, and Lock-up Period Risk (similar to staking), there are the following additional risks:

1. **Hacks**: Since these are decentralized exchanges (DEX), they are not responsible for stolen funds. Diversify your investments or choose centralized exchanges (CEX).
2. **Rug Pull**: Project founders abandon the project and withdraw liquidity, taking all users' funds. This risk occurs mainly in newly launched platforms. Try to avoid projects that have just launched. Also, follow the project on Twitter and check if the community is active.
3. **Impermanent Loss (IL)**: This measures the difference between simply holding your two tokens in your wallet versus depositing them in a liquidity pool (creating an LP token), where half of the investment is in one token and the other half in the other token. For example, CAKE/BNB. Choose a pool paired with a stablecoin to reduce your risk, and pick reliable platforms or CEX.

Impermanent Loss is only realized when the tokens are withdrawn from the liquidity pool.

IMPERMANENT LOSS EXAMPLE:

Liquidity Pool CAKE/BNB:

- Deposit:

    - CAKE price: $10, amount: 100 CAKE → total $1000
    - BNB price: $200, amount: 5 BNB → total $1000
    - Total investment: $2000

- Withdrawal:

    - CAKE price rises to $20, BNB price drops to $100
    - Instead of receiving back 100 CAKE and 5 BNB (what was deposited), you receive 50 CAKE and 10 BNB
    - Total value received: $2000

- **Impermanent Loss Calculation**:

    - If you had just held your 100 CAKE, it would now be worth 100 * $20 = $2000
    - Your 5 BNB would be worth 5 * $100 = $500

- Total value if held: $2500
- Therefore, **you missed out on $500 in gains. This is not a direct loss; it is just a missed profit**

- **Details to Consider:**

  - The pool's yield or fees earned should be subtracted from this "loss" of $500.
  - Different scenarios exist: one token might not rise a lot while the other falls, both can rise or both can fall, and how much one token appreciates relative to the other matters.

- CALCULATOR:

https://dailydefi.org/tools/impermanent-loss-calculator/

- HOW TO AVOID IMPERMANENT LOSS:

  - Invest in coins that always maintain a value of around $1, i.e., stablecoins. Obviously, these will have lower returns than more volatile coins.
  - Invest in stable or less volatile coins like Ethereum.

- APR vs APY:

  - **APR (Annual Percentage Rate)** is the annual return you receive if you do nothing more than simply stake or provide your cryptocurrencies.
  - **APY (Annual Percentage Yield)** is the return you would get by reinvesting the rewards you earn every few hours or days, meaning the percentage gain on your investment generated by compound interest over a full year.
  - Since rewards are usually distributed frequently, you can reinvest them to generate a higher annual percentage. Some platforms now automate this process for you, so you don't have to manually reinvest daily.

- TRICK TO PAY LESS SLIPPAGE ON PANCAKESWAP:

  - Slippage: The difference between the price when you place the order (the quoted price) and the price at which the trade actually executes.

– How to reduce slippage fees:

> Set slippage tolerance to 1%.
> Enter the amount of BNB you want to use to buy the token.
> Modify the default amount of the token you want to swap by adding a "1" or "9" at the end, or add ".00" at the end.

This helps pay the minimum slippage possible. If 1% doesn't work, increase slippage gradually, but avoid setting it to 10 or 12% initially, as that is the common default used by many tokens on PancakeSwap.

15.4.3   Uniswap V3

In 2022, Uniswap revolutionized staking and farming with its latest update, Uniswap V3:

- V1: Created liquidity pools of ETH versus other coins.
- V2: Created liquidity pools between pairs of coins other than ETH.
- V3: Concentrated liquidity.

V3 is the latest version of Uniswap. Currently, V2 is still in use.

V3 updates the smart contracts and is the most important version to date.

It is the only DEX that uses these smart contracts. For example, PancakeSwap is not using them yet because Uniswap holds the patent and has created a license for their use. In the future, PancakeSwap will allow its use.

The change is minimal when it comes to buying and selling.

The differences lie in liquidity providers.

It is compatible with other blockchains like Optimism and Polygon.

Users can choose between three fee tiers: 0.05%, 0.3%, and 1%, depending on whether they want exposure to more or less volatile pairs and thus take higher or lower risks.

For more stable pairs, the best option is to choose a low fee to ensure traders use your liquidity, while higher fees are recommended for more exotic and volatile pairs.

When farming, it allows you to select a price range, as shown in Fig. 15.6.

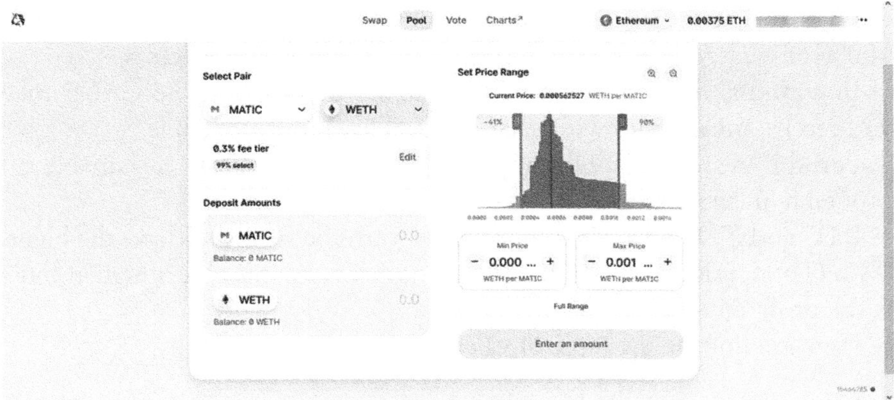

Fig. 15.6 *Source* Uniswap

Until now, when you provided liquidity, you did so without limiting the price range. Now, you can set a price range to concentrate your liquidity. By concentrating your liquidity within a specific price range, you will earn more because your liquidity is focused where the majority of trades happen.

Uniswap provides a calculator that shows how much higher returns you can expect thanks to this new version, as illustrated in Fig. 15.7.

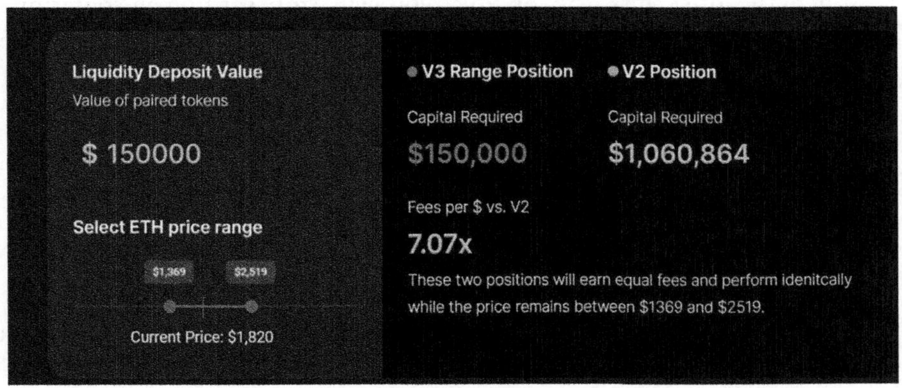

Fig. 15.7 Comparison between V3 and V2 positions

https://uniswap.org/blog/uniswap-v3#capital-efficiency

On Pancakeswap (a DEX on Binance Smart Chain), you earn money because they give you an inflationary token issued to each block.

Uniswap V3 works more like a centralized exchange. You only earn money from the fees users pay. You provide liquidity (yield farming) and get paid the fees that users pay. They do not give you UNI tokens on each block. 100% of what you earn on Uniswap V3 comes from user fees.

In contrast, on Pancakeswap, profitability depends on the CAKE token you receive inflationary with each block. This is unsustainable.

For this reason, the Uniswap V3 system is the most sustainable and profitable in the market.

BTC and ETH pairs yield the lowest returns because they have the highest TVL (Total Value Locked). If you go to other pairs, the risk is higher, but so is the profitability.

Here are links to a couple of calculators:

- https://defi-lab.xyz/uniswapv3simulator
- https://uniswapv3.thechun.dev/

Disadvantages of Uniswap V3:

- Although it is a very secure protocol with the safest smart contracts on the market, the impermanent loss (IL) is much more pronounced, meaning that just as the yield is concentrated, so is the IL.
- For example: BTC-USDC farming between BTC prices 15k and 25k. When the price hits 15k or 25k, you will stop earning yield farming rewards. When the price goes beyond those levels, you receive zero fees because it's outside your chosen range, and trades won't generate profits for you.
- When the price hits 25k, all your capital will be in USDC.
- When the price hits 15k, all your capital will be in BTC.
- Therefore, the impermanent loss is more accentuated because on the price drop, you hold BTC, and on the rise, you hold USDC, not the asset that's going up (BTC).
- This also happens in current yield farming, but limits are from 0 USD to infinity USD—so if the price hits 0 USD, all your capital is BTC, and if it hits infinity USD, all your capital is USDC. That doesn't actually happen. But now with V3, this can happen because the limits are set to 15k and 25k.

Uniswap V3 Strategy:

- If the price falls below $15k, all your capital will be in BTC. If you are a long-term holder, this acts as an automatic dollar-cost averaging (DCA) on the dip, while you continue to earn fees from yield farming. Gradually, your capital converts into BTC, so you are buying more BTC over time while generating passive income.

- When the price rises above $25k, all your capital shifts into USDC. This means you are effectively dollar-cost averaging sales. You will be selling gradually, generating USD income from BTC's rise while continuing to earn passive income.

Finally, note that after a few years, this patent will no longer be exclusive to Uniswap, and other DEXs will be able to adopt it.

On January 31st, 2025, **Uniswap launched Uniswap V4**, the most customizable and lowest-cost version of the Uniswap Protocol:

- **Unlimited Customizability**: With the introduction of hooks, anyone can create new types of market structures, add more assets, and implement new functionality on top of the Uniswap Protocol.
- **Low Cost**: Uniswap V4 offers gas savings for both traders and liquidity providers through lower pool creation costs, more efficient multi-hop swaps, and native ETH support. Pools are 99.99% cheaper to create, and gas costs for managing liquidity positions are significantly reduced.
- **Developed in Public**: The V4 codebase has received hundreds of pull requests from the community and undergone rigorous review, including a $2.35 million security competition organized by Uniswap Labs, Uniswap Foundation, Certora, and Cantina. Uniswap V4 has passed nine security audits by six independent firms, with no critical vulnerabilities found during the security competition or bug bounty programs.
- **Security and Transparency**: Developed with the same commitment as V2 and V3, which have processed over $2.75 trillion without a single hack.

The key difference between V3 and V4 is that Uniswap V4 is a developer platform. While Uniswap V3 took a fixed, opinionated approach to the automated market maker (AMM), Uniswap V4 is the first protocol to make the AMM fully customizable by developers. This is enabled through hooks, which act like plugins, allowing developers to create custom logic for how pools, swaps, fees, and liquidity provider positions interact.

15.5 Cycle Phase

When investing, we must consider which phase of the Bitcoin cycle we are in. If we are in a bear market, the safest and least volatile currency is the largest one, Bitcoin. Therefore, the optimal strategy in that phase is to hold only Bitcoin or stablecoins.

If we are in the halving phase, an accumulation period, it makes sense to start accumulating Bitcoin. Then, when we see Bitcoin's dominance decrease, we buy the larger altcoins.

Finally, if we are in a bull market, the more volatile mid-cap and low-cap altcoins have the greatest growth potential and highest profits.

Table 15.3 shows the strategy to follow based on the cycle phase.

Table 15.3 Best strategy based on market cycle phase

Cycle phase	Buy
Bear Market	Bitcoin/Stablecoins
Halving	Bitcoin and Altcoins top 10
Bull Run	Altcoins mid and low caps

A very important aspect when investing is knowing the current level of Bitcoin dominance. If dominance is high and not decreasing, even if Bitcoin's price is rising, it is not favorable to invest in altcoins. This is because the price increase and inflow of money are not being redistributed to other coins. In other words, investing in Ethereum and other altcoins is essential not only for Bitcoin's price to rise but also for its dominance to decrease.

Looking at the returns from the bear market lows (November 2022) up to early April 2025:

- Bitcoin has appreciated by 347.70%
- Smaller market cap tokens (OTHERS) by 104.77%
- Altcoins excluding BTC & ETH (TOTAL3) by 119.90%
- Ethereum only by 46.94%

As we can see in Chart 15.2, since the bear cycle lows, Bitcoin has outperformed Ethereum and altcoins. When, during a bull run, Bitcoin's dominance decreases while its price rises, the capital entering the market flows into altcoins, triggering an altseason, where these coins outperform Bitcoin significantly. As of early April 2025, this phase has not yet occurred in this cycle.

Typically, during altseason, large-cap altcoins lead the rally strongly, followed by mid-caps, and finally small caps. When the small caps surge, the bull run is usually nearing its end, and the market starts to reverse. Fear then drives money back into Bitcoin, causing the prices of other coins to fall.

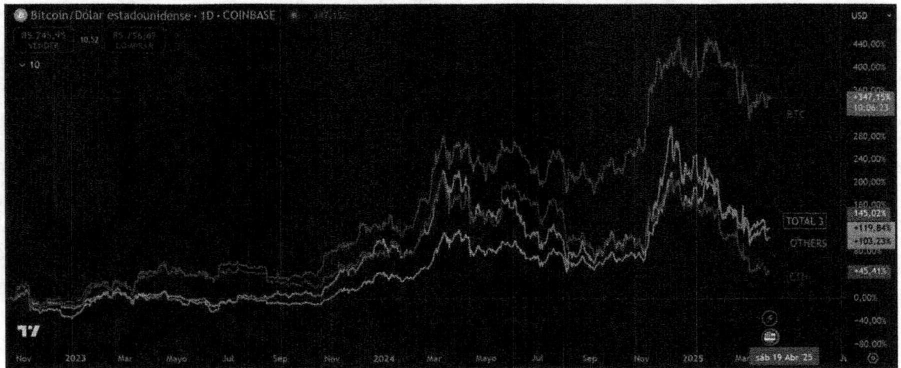

Chart 15.2 *Source Tradingview. *Total3: crypto total market cap excluding Bitcoin and Ethereum, *Others: crypto total market cap excluding top 10 cryptocurrencies*

As the bull run progresses, capital tends to flow into the most volatile projects and coins, as these offer higher returns than Bitcoin and more established cryptocurrencies. When the smaller and more volatile projects begin to reverse, money flows back to the largest and safest asset in the market: Bitcoin.

Historically, when the ETH/BTC pair shows strong returns over a three-month period, it signals that capital is moving deeper into altcoins. It is advisable to exit altcoin positions shortly after Bitcoin shows signs of peaking, since altcoins tend to follow Bitcoin's price trajectory with a slight delay.

During the 2021 bull run, we can see in the Chart 15.3, how the ETH/BTC pair surged strongly from the beginning of the year, indicating the start of the bull run.

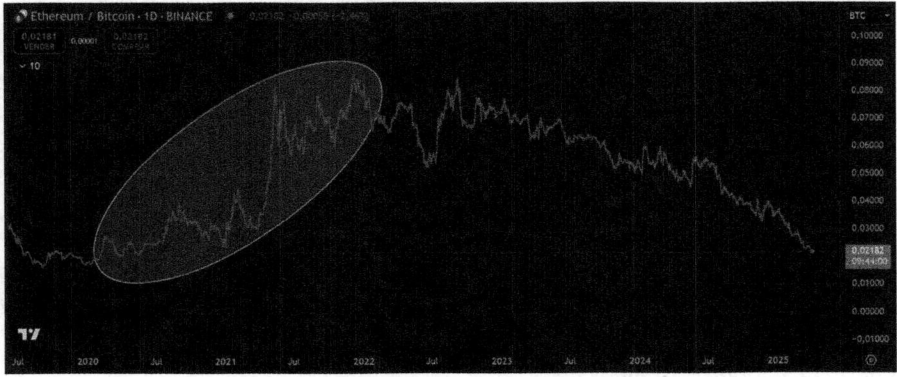

Chart 15.3 *Source Tradingview*

As we can see in Chart 15.4, in this cycle (April 25), the capital transfer from Bitcoin to Ethereum has not yet occurred, and Bitcoin remains stronger.

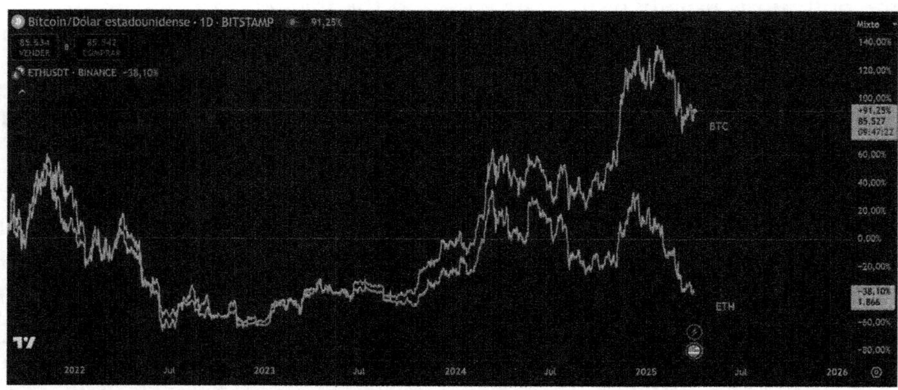

Chart 15.4 *Source* Tradingview

It is important to know whether money is flowing into stablecoins or not. When the market is fearful and seeking refuge, inflows into stablecoins increase; when greed dominates, outflows from stablecoins rise. For this reason, it is important to watch the following indicator: Aggregated Stablecoin Dominance, which comprises the four largest stablecoins: USDT, USDC, BUSD, and DAI.

It is composed of a fast-moving average (21 periods) and a slow-moving average (50 periods). When the fast MA crosses below the slow MA, it indicates that money flows out of stablecoins, and consequently, the market is appreciating. Conversely, when the fast MA crosses above the slow MA, it signals that money is entering stablecoins to seek refuge from market volatility and fear, which typically causes the price of Bitcoin and other altcoins to fall, as shown in Chart 15.5.

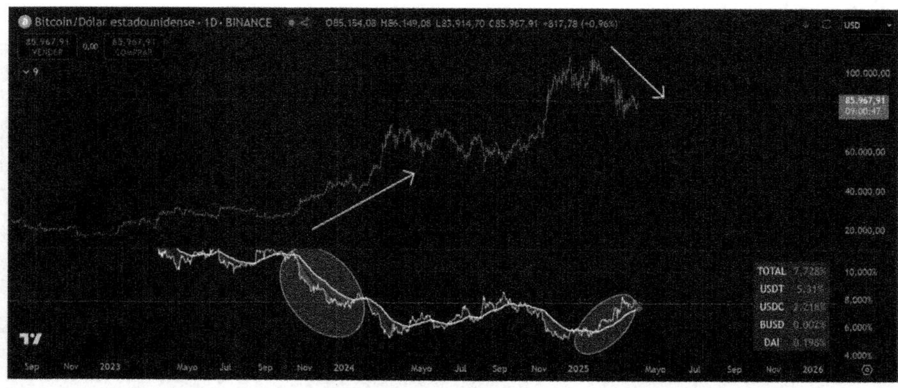

Chart 15.5 *Source* Tradingview

One aspect we need to consider is the phase of the **market's psychological cycle** we are currently in. Figure 15.8 illustrates the different phases of the cycle.

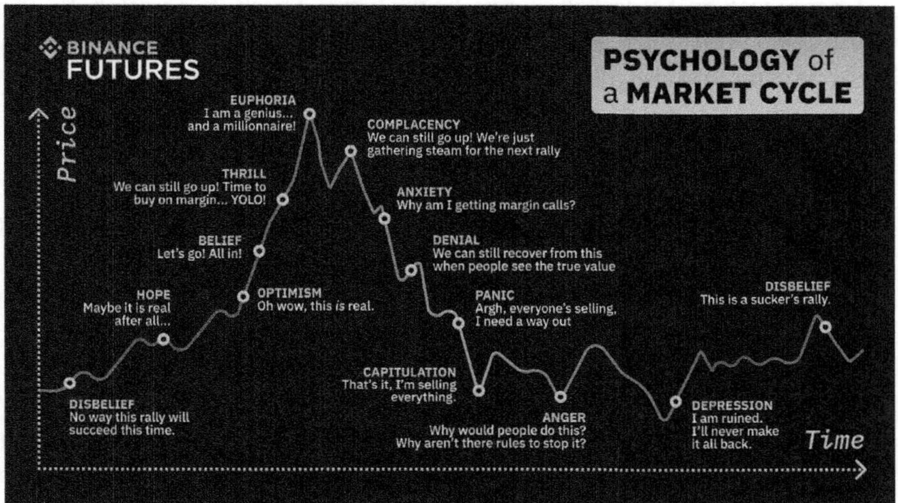

Fig. 15.8 *Source* Binance

It is crucial to have a clear understanding of the 14 stages of the psychology of a market cycle to be aware of how your emotions may be controlling your trades.

Disbelief: This is the first stage of the market cycle. After a bear market, traders tend to disregard the first rallies into a bull market because they believe the uptrend will fail to gain strength.

Hope: After a significant price recovery from the lows, traders think that the uptrend can hold.

Optimism: Traders become more confident about the strength of the uptrend as prices start trending higher, and early investors take the asset seriously due to its potential.

Belief: Traders have faith that the uptrend will hold and start entering the market with the expectation that prices will continue to surge. Many investors take this as a bullish confirmation.

Thrill: As profits pile up, market sentiment turns bullish, and traders are more vocal about the positions they are entering.

Euphoria: After a parabolic price increase, FOMO starts kicking in among traders who feel that the uptrend will continue, there is more money to be made, and nothing can go wrong. Everyone is optimistic about the market.

Complacency: Traders often mistake the first pullback after a parabolic price increase for a brief retracement, using it to collect liquidity before new all-time highs. Investors believe this is a temporary retraction before the price rises again.

Anxiety: As prices continue to drop without a significant recovery, traders become concerned about the state of the uptrend.

Denial: Traders become long-term holders because they believe prices will eventually reverse, and the market will correct, allowing them to recover their profits. The bear market has set in.

Panic: As prices continue to fall, traders panic and sell their holdings to cut losses short and keep some capital to buy at the bottom.

Capitulation: Nothing seems to stop prices from declining, generating further panic among traders, and even long-term holders are selling.

Anger: Traders cannot believe that they never realized profits when the market was trending up, and they become angry at themselves because of their losses.

Depression: All hope is lost, and traders feel foolish for not exiting the market at the right time and believing that prices will continue to increase.

Disbelief: After a prolonged downward trend, or bear market, traders tend to disregard the first rallies into a bull market because they believe the uptrend will fail to gain strength.

The level of adoption according to the phases of the cycle would be:

- During the Disbelief and Hope stages, representing the early market, the investors entering are developers and venture capitalists—the whales and long-term holders.
- Between the Hope and Optimism stages, the investors entering are the early adopters.
- Between the Optimism and Thrill stages, the early majority enters.
- And between Thrill and Euphoria, the investors entering the market are the late majority—that is, short-term holders and retail investors. The entry of these investors coincides with the exit of whales and long-term holders, as we saw with the Bitcoin Cycle Capital Flows metric in section 13.8 Key Reversal.

15.6 Metrics

Although there are many metrics, as we saw in Chap. 13, I will discuss the ones I use most when managing a cryptocurrency portfolio:

15.6.1 Short-Term Holder Realized Price

The Short-Term Holder Realized Price represents short-term bitcoin investors' average entry price cost basis. This metric measures new Bitcoin investors' average price for their Bitcoin. It's crucial because it often acts as a strong support level during bull markets and as resistance during bear markets.

When Bitcoin trades below this metric in a bull market, it is often considered a buying opportunity before the price bounces, as shown in Chart 15.6.

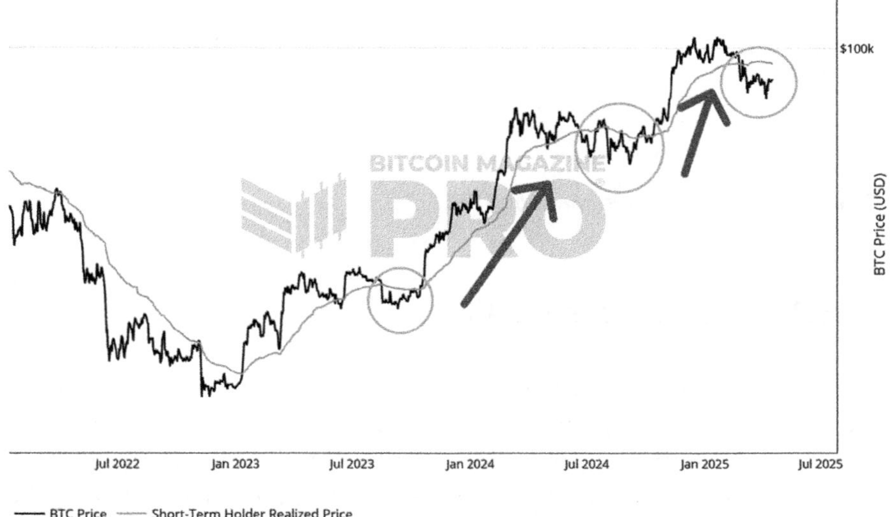

Chart 15.6 *Source* Bitcoin Magazine Pro

Throughout this bull market, the Short-Term Holder Realized Price has acted as a broad area of support. Any dips below have presented great buying opportunities.

15.6.2   Fear & Greed Index

Another metric is the **Fear and Greed Index**. When it is below 30, it indicates that a bullish rally is likely to occur soon. This reaction is normal because when sentiment is very negative, a bullish rally usually follows in the coming weeks, as shown in Chart 15.7.

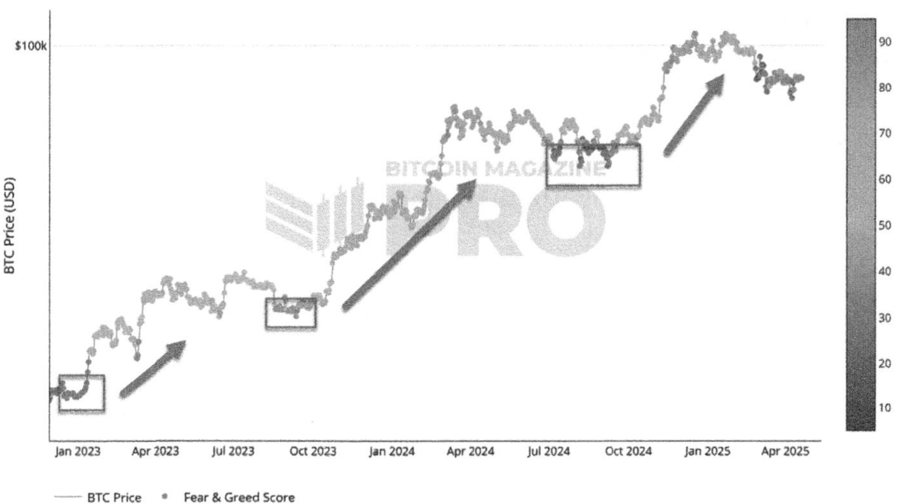

Chart 15.7   *Source* Bitcoin Magazine Pro

15.6.3   Bitcoin Crosby Ratio

I use the **Bitcoin Crosby Ratio** because it is a very effective tool for identifying major low points within a cycle. It is a volatility-based indicator that detects extremes in downside volatility. As illustrated in Chart 15.8, when the orange indicator dips below − 10 (red line), it signals that $BTC is ready to reverse upwards in the current cycle. The opposite occurs when it rises above + 10, entering an overbought zone.

Bitcoin Crosby Ratio

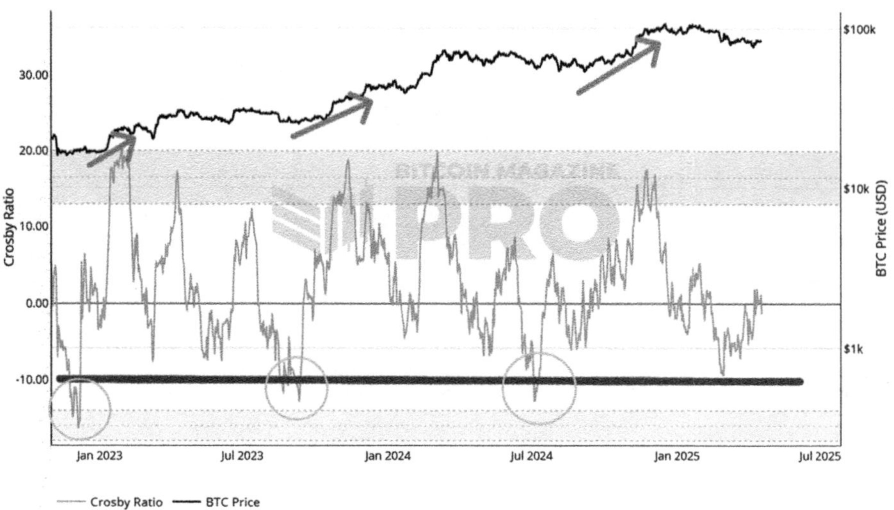

Chart 15.8   *Source* Bitcoin Magazine Pro

When this metric enters the overbought band (red zone), it is because upside volatility is uncharacteristically extreme across medium time frames. This often indicates that Bitcoin's price acceleration needs to slow down or reverse in the short term.

15.6.4   MVRV Z-Score

The MVRV Z-Score is an indicator that gives us a global perspective of where we are in the cycle. When Bitcoin's Market Cap is significantly higher than Bitcoin's Realized Cap (the average cost basis of investors), this indicator moves up toward the red zone, signaling that the cycle is becoming overheated, with scores above + 7, as shown in Chart 15.9.

Bitcoin: MVRV Z-Score

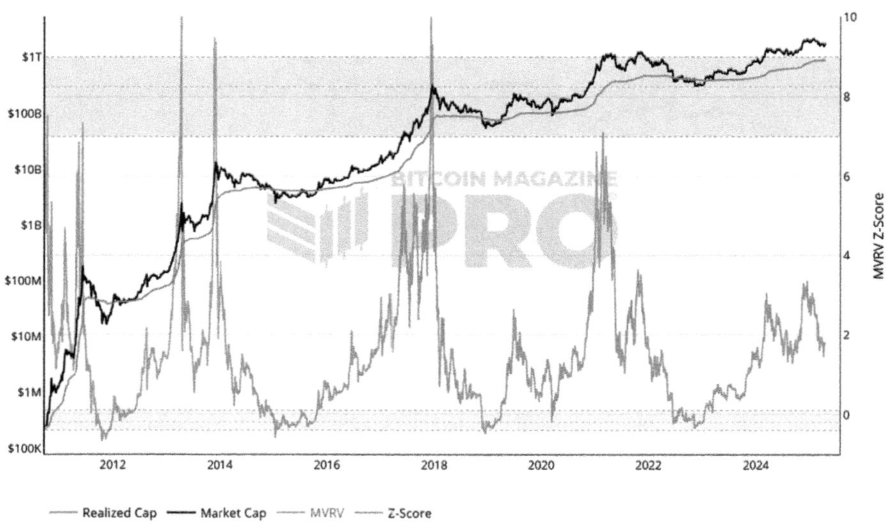

Chart 15.9 *Source* Bitcoin Magazine Pro

It should be noted that over successive cycles, this indicator has become less extreme and enters the red zone less frequently, signaling that lower average unrealized profit multiples are being reached.

Therefore, the cycle highs have been decreasing, and in this cycle, we may not even enter the red zone.

This decline describes a gradual reduction in volatility and speculative intensity as the market grows in scale and liquidity. It also suggests that, whilst Bitcoin remains cyclical, each peak becomes relatively less exaggerated, aligning with a more mature and efficient market structure. In summary, what I want to highlight is that the crypto market is becoming more mature, the cycles are less extreme than before, and volatility is decreasing.

This indicator measures the market value relative (current network valuation) to the realized value (average cost basis of Bitcoin holders). Standardized into a Z-Score to account for the asset's volatility, it's been highly accurate in identifying cycle peaks and bottoms.

Peaks in the red zone signal overvaluation, suggesting optimal profit-taking opportunities. Bottoms in the green zone indicate undervaluation, often marking strong accumulation opportunities. Historically, this metric has been remarkably accurate in pinpointing major market cycle extremes.

As we have seen, the MVRV Z-Score has limitations. Due to the market's maturation, the extremes are less pronounced, and it is increasingly difficult for the indicator to enter overbought or oversold zones.

15.6.5   MVRV Z-Score 2 yr Rolling

The MVRV Z-Score standardizes the raw MVRV data using Bitcoin's entire price history, including its early years' extreme volatility. As Bitcoin matures, these early data points may distort its relevance to current market conditions. This metric only considers data from the previous two years to avoid considering the volatility from Bitcoin's early years.

As we can observe in Chart 15.10, when the indicator falls below -1.5, the price tends to rebound upwards, and when it exceeds $+4$, the price typically enters a bearish rally. This metric helps identify market cycle tops and bottoms, providing good selling and buying levels.

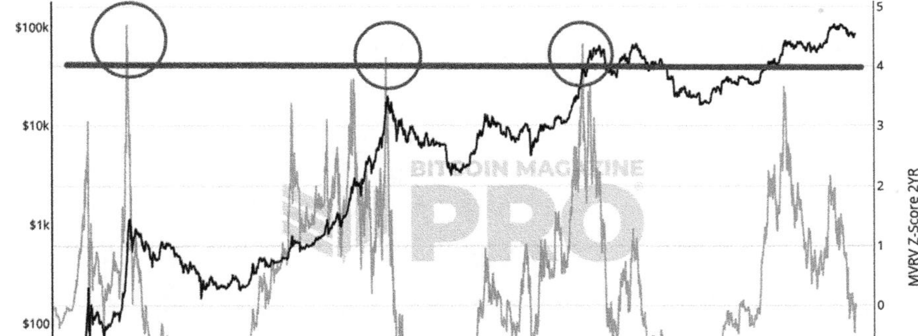

Chart 15.10   *Source* Bitcoin Magazine Pro

Focusing on just one metric when making investment decisions is not advisable. It's always better to have several metrics aligned simultaneously. For example, a good buying opportunity occurs when:

- MVRV Z-score is in the green zone (undervalued)
- SOPR indicates high realized losses (capitulation)
- Realized Cap HODL waves in short-term holders hit lows, indicating selling exhaustion

15.6.6   SOPR

The Spent Output Profit Ratio (SOPR) measures realized profits from Bitcoin transactions.

When Bitcoin holders realize massive profits, it often signals a market peak, whereas high losses indicate a market bottom. When there are many losses, the price tends to bottom out and reverse, initiating a bullish rally, as shown in Chart 15.11.

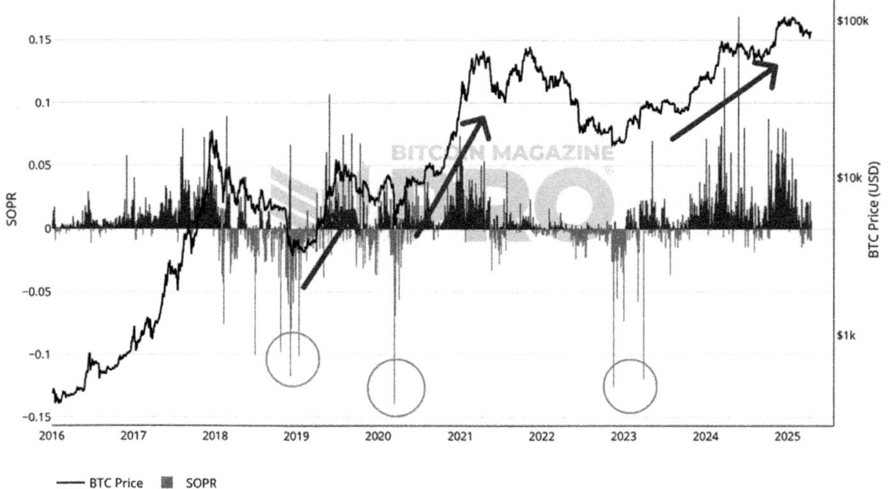

Chart 15.11 *Source* Bitcoin Magazine Pro

15.6.7   Realized HODL Waves

Short-term holders increase as the bull market develops, and consequently, long-term holders decrease. Conversely, when the bull cycle peaks, short-term holders reach their maximum while long-term holders hit their minimum.

Short-term holders typically represent retail investors, whereas long-term holders represent smart money or institutional clients/whales.

As illustrated in Chart 15.12, when this metric falls to its lows (yellow band), the price tends to surge strongly upwards at those levels (green square).

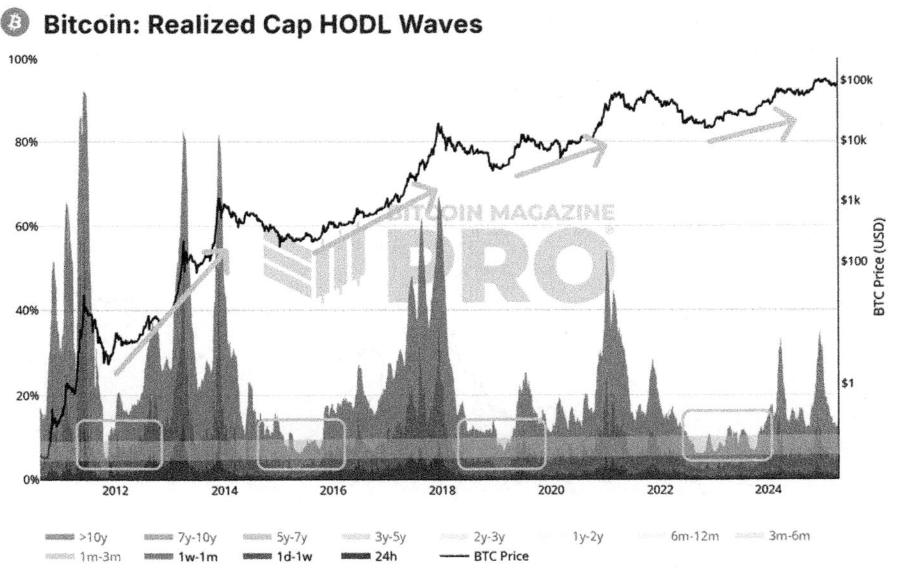

Chart 15.12   *Source* Bitcoin Magazine Pro

15.6.8 Short-Term Holder MVRV

MVRV is the ratio between Market Value (price multiplied by bitcoins in circulation) and Realized Value (the price of UTXOs when they last moved onchain).

Short-Term Holder MVRV (STH-MVRV) is an MVRV metric that only analyzes UTXOs younger than 155 days, focusing exclusively on short-term holders.

This metric acts as dynamic support in bull markets and resistance in bear markets.

When this metric dips below 1 (red line), indicating that many recent buyers are underwater, it often serves as a precursor to a local bottom during bull cycles.

Typically, when this metric is around 0.60 (indicated by the orange line), it tends to signal an optimal entry point, as it often suggests a market bottom. Resistance typically occurs at levels of 1.70 (green line) and above, as shown in the Chart 15.13.

Chart 15.13 *Source* Bitcoin Magazine Pro

15.6.9 Long-Term Holder MVRV

Long-Term Holder MVRV analyzes Bitcoin holders who have held for more than 155 days. As we can see in the Chart 15.14, with each cycle, this metric increases less and less. We are seeing a trend of declining multiples.

By drawing a downward trendline, we could estimate that the peak for this cycle would be around 8, which would imply a Bitcoin price of $320 K. Currently (June 2025), we are far from that level, which suggests there is still significant upside potential before reaching a new peak.

Chart 15.14 *Source* Bitcoin Magazine Pro

These two metrics I just mentioned (Short-Term and Long-Term Holder MVRV) should be analyzed together. One should not rely on a single metric to predict tops or bottoms in isolation; instead, they should be considered jointly to gain a clearer overall view.

15.6.10 US Dollar Strength Index (DXY)

One strong indicator with which Bitcoin has an inverse relationship is the US Dollar Strength Index (DXY) YoY.

As shown in Chart 15.15, the decline since January 2025 has not yet been reflected in Bitcoin's price as of April 2025. Still, this indicator should be closely monitored because Bitcoin tends to experience a strong rally when this inverse relationship occurs.

Chart 15.15   *Source* Bitcoin Magazine Pro

By analyzing BTC alongside the year-over-year (YoY) change in the DXY, we can identify support and resistance levels. In Chart 15.16, we can see that it has broken a support level that had held for several months, which indicates a bullish rally in BTC.

Chart 15.16   *Source* Bitcoin Magazine Pro

15.6.11 ETF Inflows

Another indicator to consider is ETF inflows. Since their inception, they have gradually grown in importance due to the magnitude of investment flowing into Bitcoin through these products, reflecting institutional demand.

At the beginning of 2025, Bitcoin ETF inflows slowed significantly during this period of low volatility. This suggests that major players await a confirmed breakout before adding to their positions. Once volatility returns, we could see renewed interest from institutions, driving Bitcoin even higher.

When volatility compresses significantly (a squeeze), a rally usually follows, which can be bullish or bearish. In this case, as shown in Chart 15.17, it was bearish.

Bitcoin: ETF Daily Flows (USD) - Total

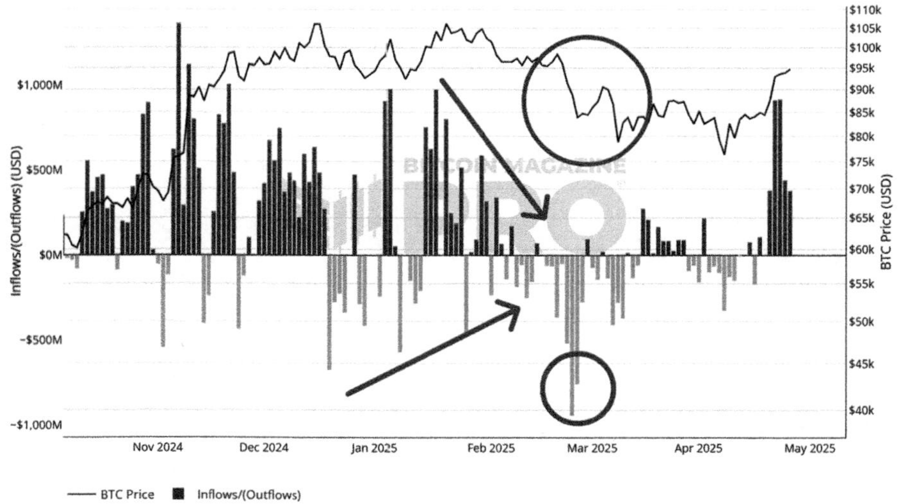

Chart 15.17   *Source* Bitcoin Magazine Pro

15.6.12 Puell Multiple

As I mentioned earlier, the **Puell Multiple** measures daily Bitcoin miner revenue (in USD) relative to its historical average over the past 365 days.

I use this metric to get a long-term view and understand which phase we are in. It reflects miner sentiment and helps us determine whether Bitcoin is overvalued or undervalued based on miner revenue trends, as shown in Chart 15.18.

A high Puell Multiple indicates miners are earning significantly more than average, while a low multiple suggests reduced miner profitability.

Identifies market extremes: Historically, low Puell Multiples (<0.5, green zone) have coincided with bottoms, while high values (>3.5, red zone) have signaled tops.

Helps in timing investments: Investors use it to accumulate Bitcoin when miners are struggling (low values) and consider profit-taking when miners are making outsized gains (high values).

Indicates miner behavior: If miner revenues are exceptionally high, it may suggest increased selling pressure, while low revenues can lead to miner capitulation and supply shocks.

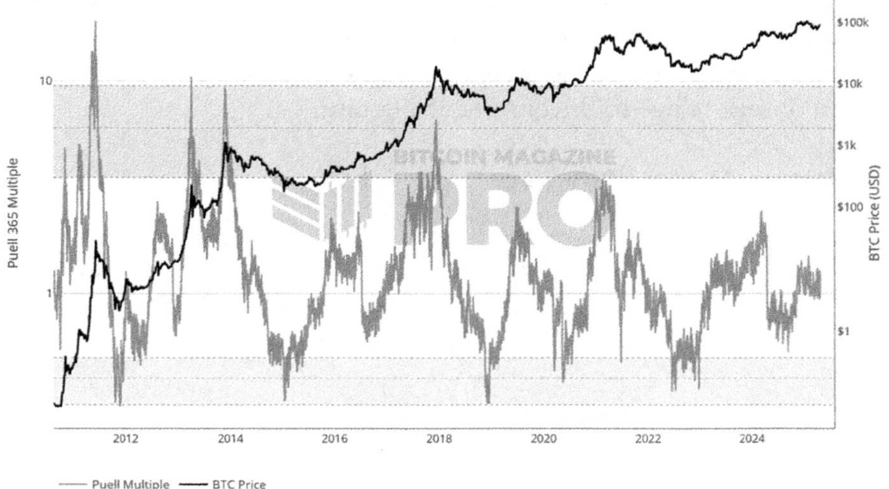

Chart 15.18   *Source* Bitcoin Magazine Pro

15.6.13 1 Year Hodl Wave

This metric indicates the percentage of BTC that has not moved on-chain for at least a year. It serves as a proxy for the "smarter money" in the system, those playing Bitcoin's market cycles.

They accumulate at the bottoms of bear markets when retail investors are exiting the market. They start selling at the tops of bull markets when retail investors are entering—new retail money FOMO late in the cycle. One-year holders sell at the end of the bull run, when the price surges past previous highs, as happened at the last all-time high.

This metric has an inverse relationship with price. When the price falls during the bear market, this metric rises, and when the price rises, this metric falls.

The metric reflects the supply that will enter the market as long-term holders sell while retail investors enter. When this metric drops sharply, it often marks the price peak, after which the bear market begins. Therefore, it is essential to monitor it.

As illustrated in Chart 15.19, in the previous cycle, the price peak was marked when the metric reached 55%; in the two and three cycles before, it hovered around 40%. As of April 2025, it stands at 64%. Once it reaches around 50%, it's crucial to watch for signs of market reversal to exit, go short, or seek refuge in Bitcoin and stablecoins.

Chart 15.19 *Source* Bitcoin Magazine Pro

15.6.14 Bitcoin Cycle Capital Flows

This metric shows the capital rotation from longer-term investors to newer investors in the Bitcoin market.

It compares the realized cap (capital) held by < 1-month holders (retail) against the 1-2-year holders (smarter money).

To classify new money, it uses a proxy of the value of bitcoins that have been in addresses for less than a month. These are likely to be newer participants rushing in to buy Bitcoin.

This metric reflects the entry levels of different participants in the market.

It is time to pay attention once the + 50% level is breached. This would signal that over half of the realized value of Bitcoins is being held in addresses that have held it for less than a month. It is a real indication of new money (FOMO) into the market on a scale.

When this metric shows an increase in short-term holders above 25%, it may indicate the beginning of a bull run, and when it rises above 50%, it signals the peak of the bull run, as shown in Chart 15.20.

Bitcoin Cycle Capital Flows

Chart 15.20   *Source* Bitcoin Magazine Pro

It is not an exact indicator, but when it rises above this level, it helps you manage risk and know that you are near the market top because hot money is entering. If you add to this the fact that the 1-year HODL wave is also declining, it's time to exit the market because these (1-year HODL wave holders) are offloading onto these (1-month cycle capital flows).

That's why these two charts are studied together.

Currently, in April 2025, the proportion of realized value in addresses that have Bitcoin for less than a month is 15%, still far from the 50% level, as shown in Chart 15.21.

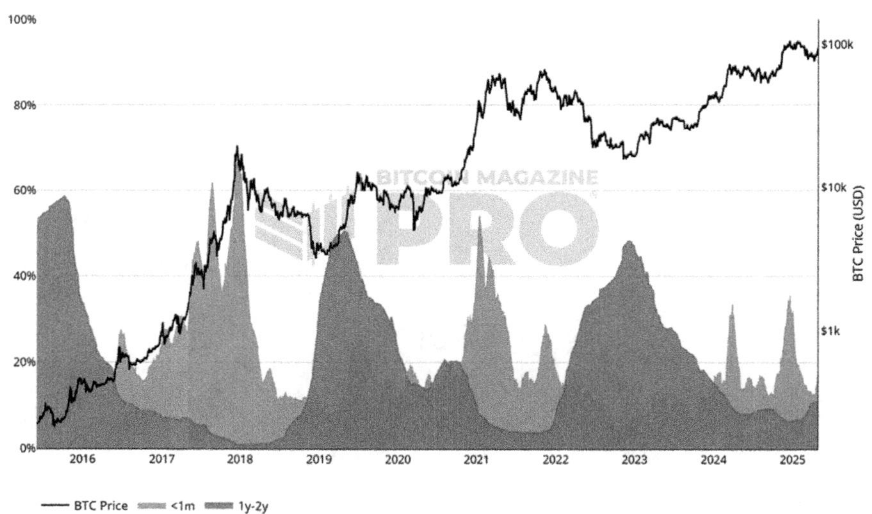

Chart 15.21 *Source* Bitcoin Magazine Pro

15.6.15 Pi Cycle Top Bottom Indicator

The Pi Cycle Top Indicator is one of the most popular tools for analyzing Bitcoin's cycles. This indicator monitors the 111-day and 350-day (multiplied by 2) moving averages, and when these two lines cross. It usually lags somewhat since it is composed of moving averages (a lagging indicator), but it tends to be quite reliable in marking cycle peaks and cycle bottoms.

Chart 15.22 illustrates that, in April 2025, the two moving averages diverged significantly, indicating that the market remained far from the cycle top.

Bitcoin: Pi Cycle Top Indicator

Chart 15.22   *Source* Bitcoin Magazine Pro

Using the Pi Cycle Top & Bottom Indicator, we can measure the difference between the two averages to better define Bitcoin's position within bull and bear cycles. As we can see in Chart 15.23, we are still far from the red zone, which would signal that we are approaching the cycle top.

Bitcoin: Pi Cycle Top & Bottom Indicator

Chart 15.23   *Source* Bitcoin Magazine Pro—Aug´25

As a curiosity, the nomenclature "Pi" arises from the ratio of these averages (350 divided by 111), which approximates 3.142. Historically, the intersection of these moving averages has corresponded with Bitcoin's market cycle peaks in 2017 and 2021.

Historically, Bitcoin's bull cycles consist of four phases:

- Phase 1: initial rapid growth
- Phase 2: a cooling-off period
- Phase 3: a second peak
- Phase 4: a significant retracement followed by a new surge

In April 2025, we are in phase 2, as shown in Chart 15.24. So, we are still far from the cycle peak.

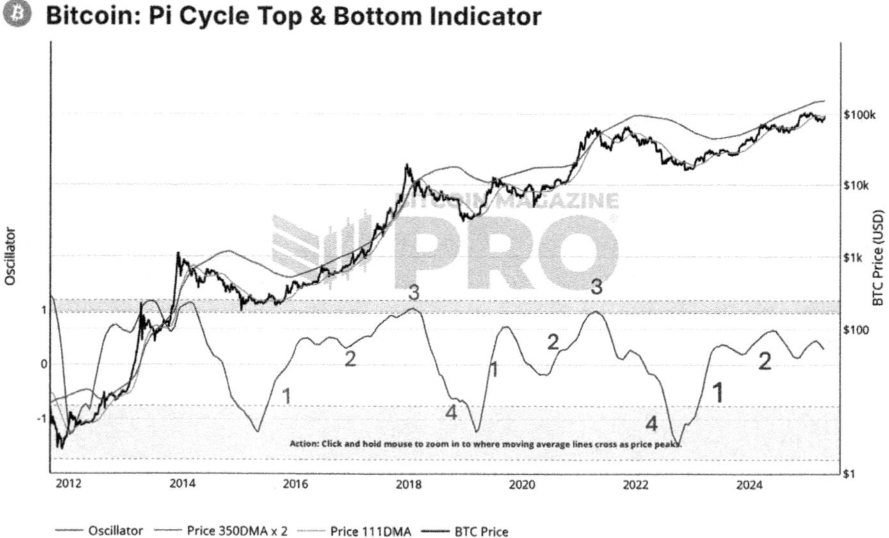

Chart 15.24 *Source* Bitcoin Magazine Pro

15.6.16 Addresses With Balance > 100 BTC

This metric indicates confidence among Bitcoin's largest investors. As we can see in Chart 15.25, it has been rising strongly since October 2024, indicating that whales trust the market and that current price levels still have significant room to grow before reaching new highs.

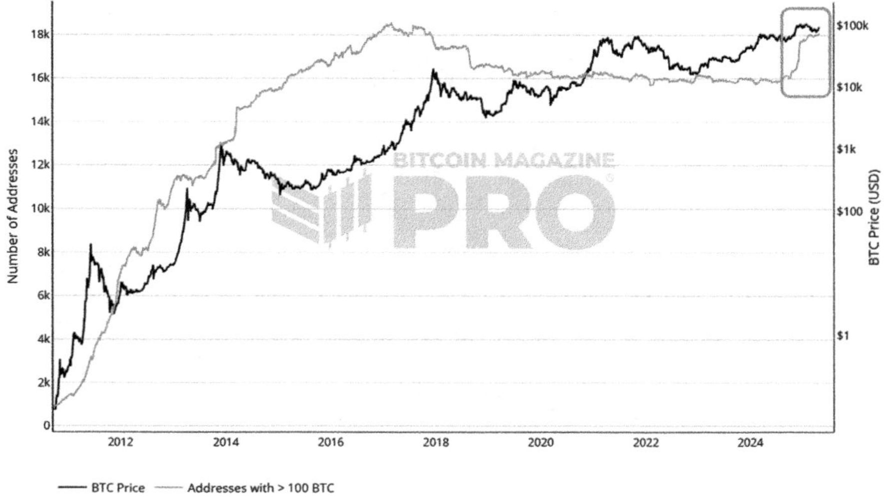

Chart 15.25   *Source* Bitcoin Magazine Pro

In past bull cycles, we saw whales exit or decrease their positions near market peaks, a behavior we're not seeing this time. This accumulation trend by experienced holders is a strong bullish indicator, suggesting faith in the market's long-term potential.

15.6.17 Value Days Destroyed (VDD) Multiple

Value Days Destroyed (VDD) Multiple aims to identify when the price of Bitcoin may be close to topping out at major cycle highs.

This measures the velocity of BTC being moved, weighted by how long the coins were held before transacting. Spikes typically indicate experienced holders taking profit, while low levels suggest accumulation.

During late bear markets or early recovery phases, the metric is usually in the green zone, meaning below 0.80.

Conversely, when it rises above 3 (red zone), as shown in Chart 15.26, it indicates that the market is at a peak. This occurs when older coins begin to enter the market rapidly for sale. Typically, this happens when longer-term participants look to take profits as prices accelerate during primary bull market cycles.

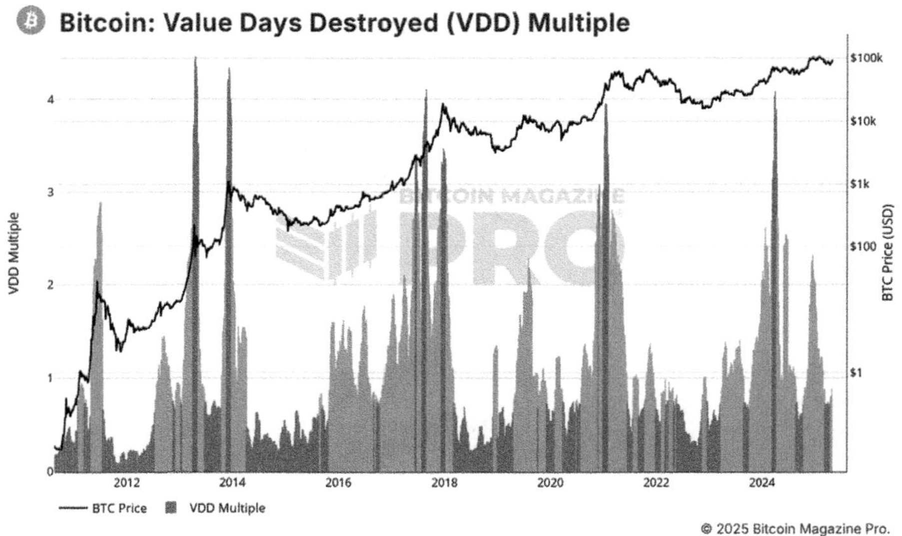

Chart 15.26 *Source* Bitcoin Magazine Pro

Coin Days Destroyed is a proxy for spending velocity that gives extra weight to coins that have not moved on-chain for extended periods of time.

Value Days Destroyed multiplies Coin Days Destroyed by the $BTC price. Then, it divides a 30-day average of VDD by a 365-day average to compare near-term spending velocity with a yearly average.

The current levels remain far from the red zones typically seen during market tops. This means whales and "smart money" are not yet offloading significant portions of their holdings and are still awaiting higher prices before beginning to realize substantial profits.

15.6.18 Terminal Price

The **Terminal Price** is the transferred price multiplied by 21 because the maximum supply of Bitcoin is 21 million.

The transferred price takes the sum of Coin Days Destroyed and divides it by the existing supply of bitcoin and the time it has been in circulation.

This Terminal Price has historically been very effective at forecasting the tops of Bitcoin price cycles, as shown in Chart 15.27.

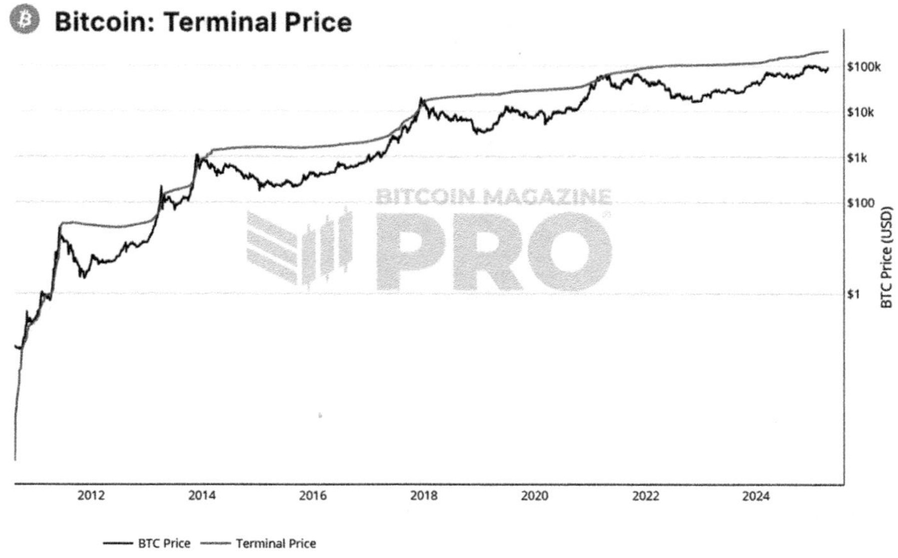

Chart 15.27   *Source* Bitcoin Magazine Pro

15.6.19 Active Address Sentiment Indicator (AASI)

AASI is a sentiment indicator for Bitcoin. In this metric, we compare the 28-day change in price (%) with the 28-day change in active addresses (%).

A rise in active addresses generally confirms a bullish trend, while stagnation or decline may signal price weakness.

To understand the graph, I am going to explain the different lines:

Grey lines on the chart show the change in active addresses. On the outer boundaries of those grey lines are standard deviation bands.

Dotted red line = upper boundary. Dotted green line = lower boundary. The orange line is the 28-day price change (%).

When the orange line reaches the upper boundary (red dotted line), it indicates that short-term market sentiment is overheated (green arrows) because the rate of price increase is outstripping the rate of increase in active addresses.

As illustrated in Chart 15.28, when the orange line reaches the lower boundary (green dotted line), it indicates that short-term market sentiment is overly bearish (red arrows).

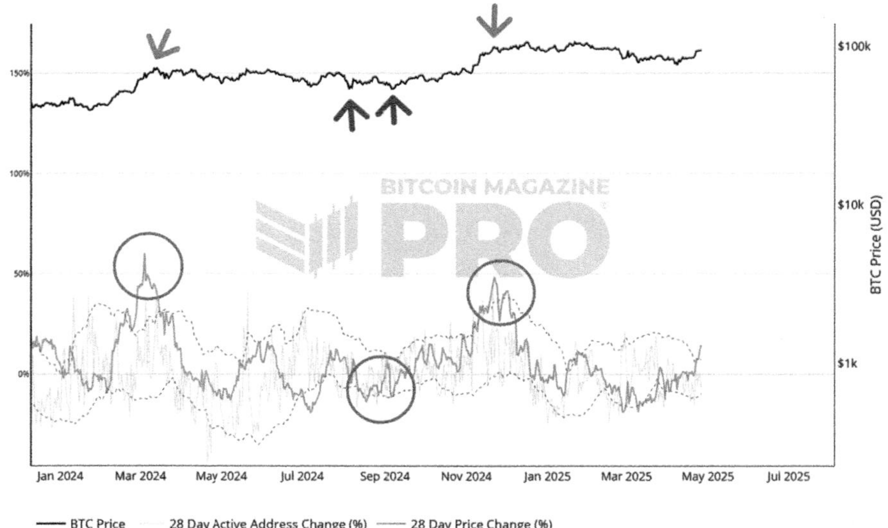

Chart 15.28   *Source* Bitcoin Magazine Pro

15.6.20 NUPL

Net Unrealized Profit/Loss estimates the total paper profits/losses in Bitcoin held by investors. This metric is calculated by subtracting Realized Value from Market Value.

When there are large unrealized profits, the market is overheated, and it will be the top of the bull run. This happens when the market cap rises much faster than profit-taking.

If there are low unrealized profits, the market is undervalued, and it will be the bottom of the bear market. This happens when profit-taking rises much faster than market cap.

As illustrated in Chart 15.29, this indicator has five phases:

- Capitulation
- Hope/Fear
- Optimism/Anxiety
- Belief/Denial
- Euphoria/Greed

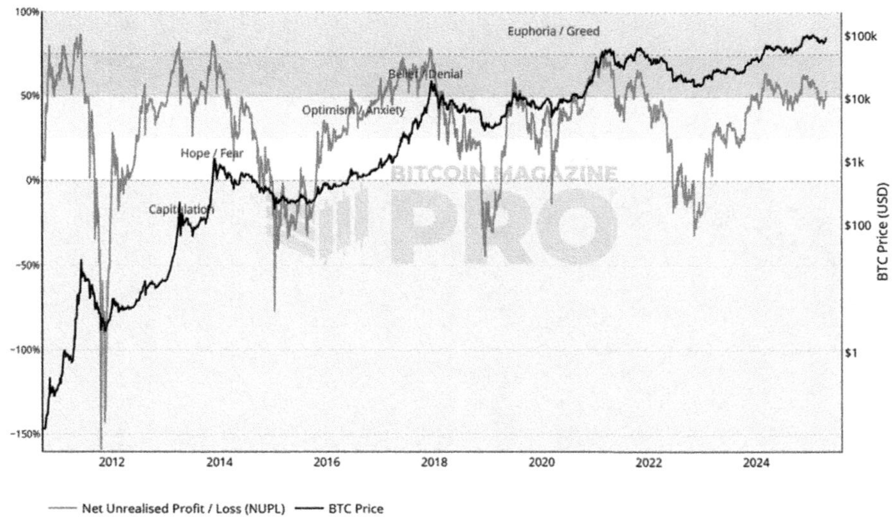

Chart 15.29   *Source* Bitcoin Magazine Pro

15.6.21 Bitcoin Cycle Master

This metric can identify major cycle highs (areas of sell opportunity) and major cycle lows (areas of buy opportunity).

Bitcoin Cycle Master combines on-chain metrics, including Coin Value Days Destroyed and Terminal Price, to identify where Bitcoin's price is valued relative to its cycles.

Chart 15.30 shows that, in April 2025, Bitcoin still has considerable room to grow before reaching overvaluation. The upper boundary is currently 210,000, and the quotation price of Bitcoin is 94k USD.

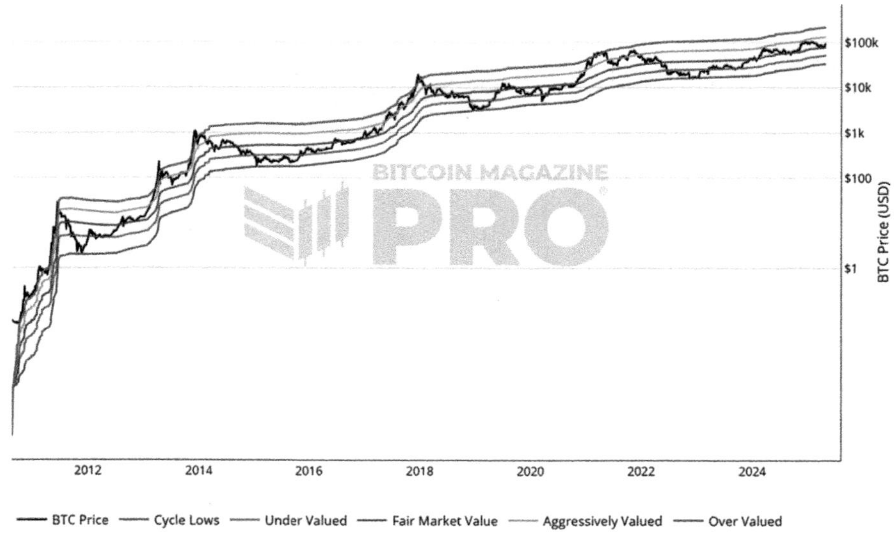

Chart 15.30   *Source* Bitcoin Magazine Pro

15.6.22 Hash Ribbons

As we discussed earlier, this metric is composed of two moving averages: the 30-day (blue line) and 60-day (purple line) moving averages of Bitcoin's hashrate.

When the 60-day average rises above the 30-day average, it historically indicates miner capitulation and a bearish outlook for the short term.

In July 2025, as shown in Fig. 15.9, the Hash Ribbons Indicator has just completed a bullish crossover, where the short-term moving average has crossed above the long-term moving average. This signal has historically aligned with bottoms and trend reversals. Since miner behavior tends to reflect profitability expectations, this cross suggests miners are now confident in higher prices.

Bitcoin: Hash Ribbons Indicator

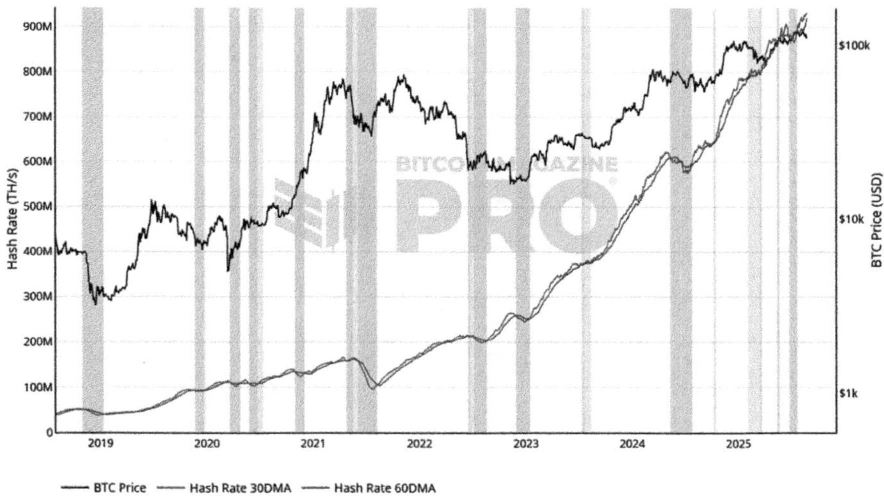

Fig. 15.9 *Source* Bitcoin Magazine Pro

15.6.23 ISM Manufacturing Index

Another important metric, due to its relationship with Bitcoin's price, is the ISM Manufacturing Index. It is a monthly gauge of economic activity in the U.S. manufacturing sector compared to the previous month.

- If the index is above 50, it indicates expansion of the U.S. economy.
- If it is below 50, it signals contraction.
- If it is above 50 but falling, it means the U.S. economy is slowing down.
- If it is below 50 but rising, it suggests a recovery in the U.S. economy.

Chart 15.31 illustrates the appearance of this metric.

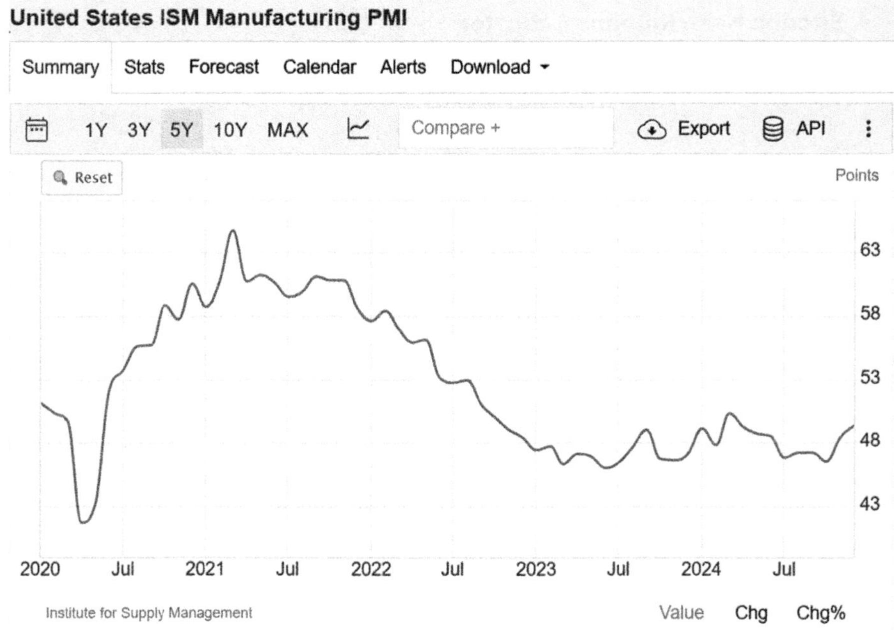

Chart 15.31   *Source* Institute of Supply Management

15.6.24 Global Supply M2

I have already discussed this metric in Chap. 9, but it is important to consider the relationship between global supply M2 and Bitcoin's price. This relationship has a lag of about 10 weeks, meaning that a rise in this metric does not imply that Bitcoin's price will increase immediately.

This metric has been rising sharply since March 2025, and as of today, April 2025, this increase has not yet been reflected in Bitcoin's price, as shown in Chart 15.32.

Global M2 vs BTC

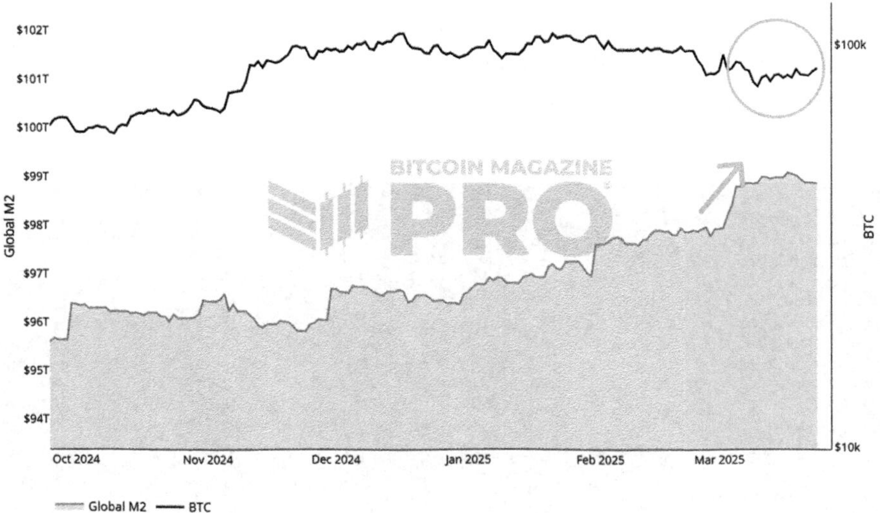

Chart 15.32 *Source* Bitcoin Magazine Pro

15.6.25 Stablecoin Dominance

When the dominance of stablecoins—that is, their weight in the market—increases, it indicates we are in a bear market or that the short-term market outlook is bearish. Conversely, when stablecoin dominance decreases, it means the short-term market outlook is bullish or that we are in a bull run, since stablecoins act as a safe haven being pegged to fiat currencies, usually USD or EUR.

This indicator reflects the combined dominance of the four major stablecoins (USDT, USDC, BUSD, and DAI). It consists of two moving averages: a short-term moving average (21 periods) and a long-term moving average (50 periods).

The thicker line is the slow-moving average (50 periods). When this MA is above the fast-moving average (21 periods), the price is rising—as we can see in the first circle on the graph—because stablecoin dominance is falling. This means money is flowing out of stablecoins into altcoins, signaling a bullish short-term outlook.

When the fast-moving average is above the slow one, the price is going down, as we can see in the second circle on the Chart 15.33, because dominance is rising. This means money is flowing into stablecoins, which act as a safe haven, and consequently, money is leaving altcoins since the short-term market outlook is bearish.

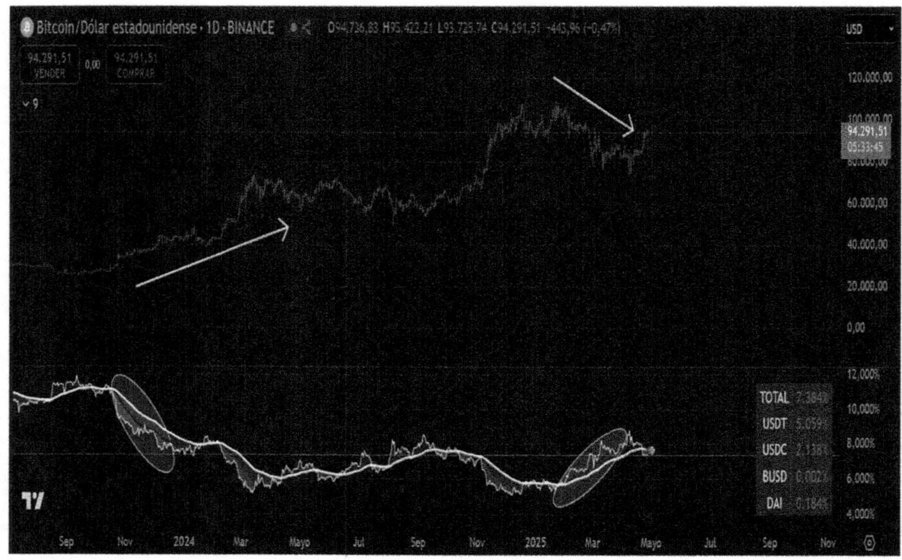

Chart 15.33   *Source* Tradingview

On-chain data is most effective when viewed on a high timeframe. Analyzing on-chain metrics on low timeframes is not very useful; for low-timeframe analysis, it is more appropriate to look at derivatives data.

15.6.26 200 Week Moving Average Heatmap

This indicator uses a color heatmap based on the % increases of that 200-week moving average. Depending on the month-by-month % increase of the 200-week moving average, a color is assigned to the price chart.

This average helps identify the bottoms of each cycle's bear market. As we can see in the different cycles, it marked the bottom during the 2015, 2018, and 2022 drawdowns.

The 200-week moving average remains one of Bitcoin's most historically reliable long-term indicators.

Historically, when the 200WMA was growing at 14–16% annualized (as indicated by the orange and red zones), Bitcoin was often near its cycle peaks, as shown in Chart 15.34. However, as Bitcoin's market cap has grown and volatility has compressed, these extremes have moderated.

Chart 15.34 *Source* Bitcoin Magazine Pro

In the current cycle, growth rates have so far topped out at around 5–6% (the blue and turquoise zones), with no major push into the yellow or green high-risk zones observed in previous bull runs. This suggests that while Bitcoin has rallied substantially, it has yet to reach the kind of parabolic phase historically associated with blow-off tops.

In previous cycles, we can observe that when the 200-week moving average (200 WMA) crosses the all-time high of the last cycle, it typically marks the peak of the current cycle. Assuming a continuation of the recent average growth rate, projections suggest this crossover could occur around May or June 2026.

As illustrated in Chart 15.35, if we consider the previous increase from the 2017 peak (around $21,000) to the 2021 peak (around $69,000), which represented a 328% rise, and apply that same percentage to the 2021 high (approximately $69,000), we get a projected level of $226,000. This would be the price at which the 200-week moving average (200 WMA) could cross the $69,000 mark.

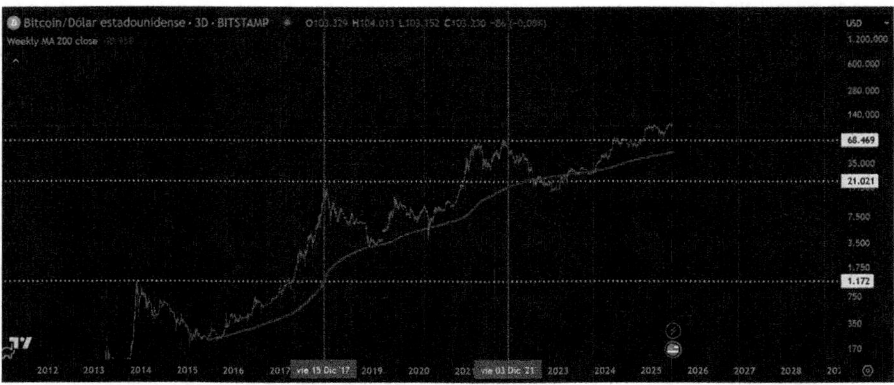

Chart 15.35   *Source* Tradingview

15.6.27 Whale Shadows

This indicator shows Bitcoins that have remained dormant for years and are now being moved. Whales are large wallets holding a significant amount of Bitcoin and are often associated with smart money, meaning that when they move, it's a meaningful signal that the market may be overheated, as those BTC are likely being brought to market for selling.

In this indicator, we can observe wallets that have been dormant for 4–5 years, 5–7 years, 7–9 years, and those that have been dormant for more than 10 years.

In my opinion, the most optimal approach is to analyze all of them together. When we see wallets with more than 10,000 BTC being activated, it's worth taking into account, as it may indicate that the market is near a top in its current phase, and a short-term retracement could follow, as shown in Fig. 15.10.

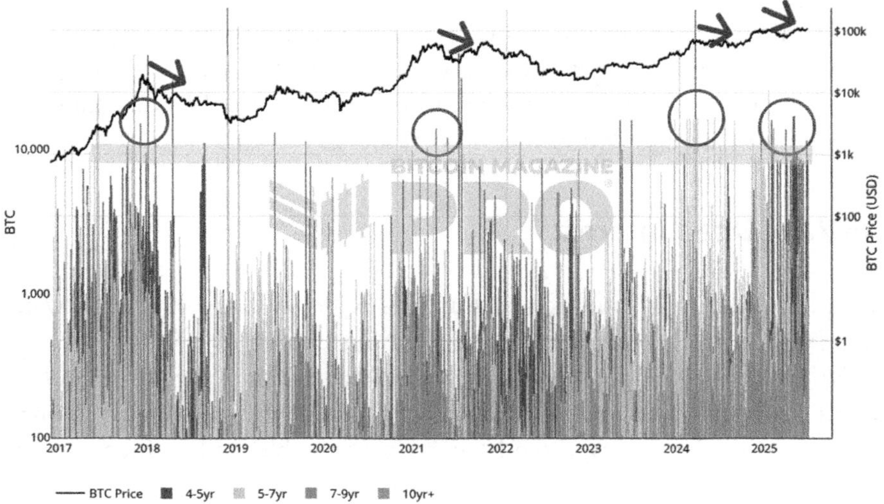

Fig. 15.10 *Source* Bitcoin Magazine Pro

15.6.28 Altseason Index

This indicator tracks Altcoins and is very useful because, as we can see, when it is at its lows, it often identifies market bottoms, and from those levels, it usually rises sharply, as shown in Chart 15.36.

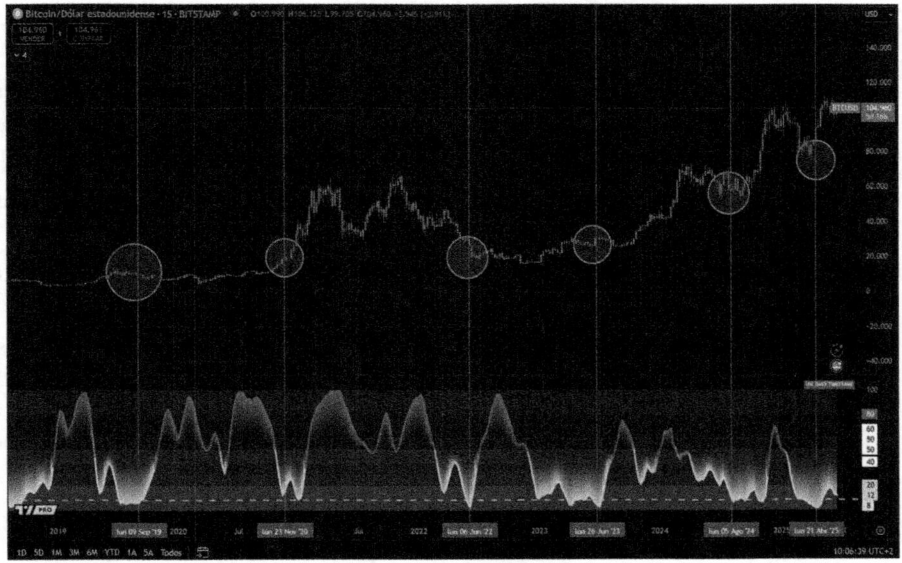

Chart 15.36 *Source* Tradingview

15.7 Derivatives & Volatility

A key differentiating factor of this cycle is the volume of derivatives, which is significantly higher than in previous cycles. Currently, derivatives account for approximately 60–75% of total crypto trading volume. For this reason, it is essential to take liquidation map into account.

15.7.1   Open Interest

I explained both this metric and Funding Rates in Chap. 13, but I want to highlight a couple of important points about them.

When derivatives positions are very high and certain levels are broken, it often leads to strong price movements. That's why a spot-driven market without excessive leverage tends to be more stable and resilient, as fewer investors face the risk of forced liquidation.

When volatility is low but volume and open interest are increasing, it indicates that traders are positioning themselves for a rally. Therefore, it's important to be cautious during volatility squeezes and to closely monitor this metric.

15.7.2   Funding Rates

Funding rates give us clues as to whether derivatives traders are heavily betting on the Bitcoin price going up or down. When they bet too heavily on one side, they have to pay large amounts of funding rates to those betting on the other side. It is typical at these points of over-confidence that the price will go against them, and they will get caught out.

Therefore, the important aspect of this metric is when it reaches extreme levels, as that can indicate a trend reversal. If it is extremely negative, it may be signaling a local bottom, and a bullish rally will soon begin. Conversely, if it is extremely positive, it may be marking a local top, and a bearish rally will start. This can provide a good entry opportunity.

Negative Funding rates during bull cycles are a strong signal for accumulation during dips. It is a good buying opportunity.

In a bull market, Bitcoin typically bottoms out when traders feel pessimistic, which we can visualize using the red bars in Chart 15.37.

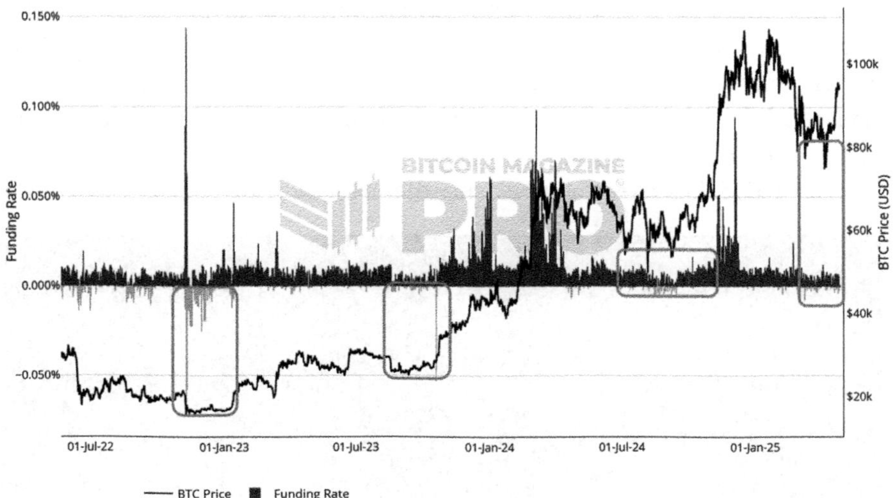

Chart 15.37 *Source* Bitcoin Magazine Pro

15.7.3 Heat Map and Liquidation Map

An important software to have access to is TheKingfisher. This software provides access to margin call levels for derivatives, which serve as supports and resistances. The derivatives market is very important because it drives the spot market. When margin call levels—which are stop levels where open derivative positions would be closed—are broken, it creates a snowball effect that tends to drag the market intensely. Therefore, it is crucial to know where these levels are located.

These areas are where a high density of liquidations will take place. They represent price zones of high liquidity.

The **Liquidation Map** and **Heat Map**, which show levels where open futures positions should close due to margin calls, are used as supports and resistances. Both display future liquidations but in different ways.

The Heat Map shows Z-Scores of liquidations, indicating how large liquidations are at each level compared to others. The Liquidation Map reveals hidden liquidity.

There are other software options like **Decentrader** that also provide Liquidation Maps, but in my opinion, Kingfisher is preferable because TheKingfisher has a custom method for calculating liquidations, making their clusters much more accurate and actionable than competitors like Decentrader, who usually use a fairly naive liquidation calculation method.

The Kingfisher employs proprietary algorithms that provide unique data and incredible accuracy, whereas Decentrader offers its data for free.

This software helps improve entry and exit timing because liquidation clusters occur when many traders close their positions simultaneously, causing a sudden price drop. With these tools, you'll be able to spot these clusters and turn them into profits.

Chart 15.38 illustrates the appearance of the Liquidation Map in this software.

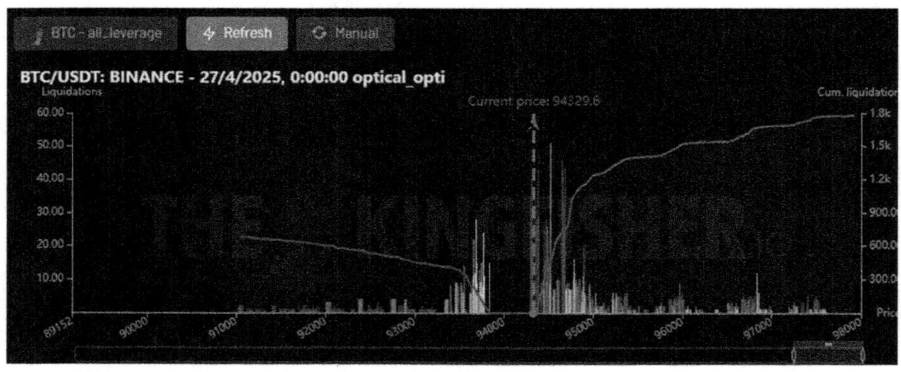

Chart 15.38   *Source* The Kingfisher

The function **Optical_opti** gives an interesting short-term view of the market's liquidations. All leverage includes all positions (short-term and long-term).

15.7.4   Bitcoin Futures

At CME (Chicago Mercantile Exchange), Bitcoin and Ethereum futures and options are traded. It is important to observe how these futures trade relative to the spot price to understand traders' expectations for these two coins.

- When futures trade at a higher price than the spot, it indicates bullish expectations and is called **Contango**.
- When futures trade at a lower price than the spot, it indicates bearish expectations and is called Backwardation.

Typically, futures positioning shows a pattern remarkably similar to ETF flows.

15.7.5   Volatility

When the one-week volatility indicator reaches levels around 1%, it is often followed by a strong double-digit bullish rally, as shown in Chart 15.39.

Bitcoin Volatility

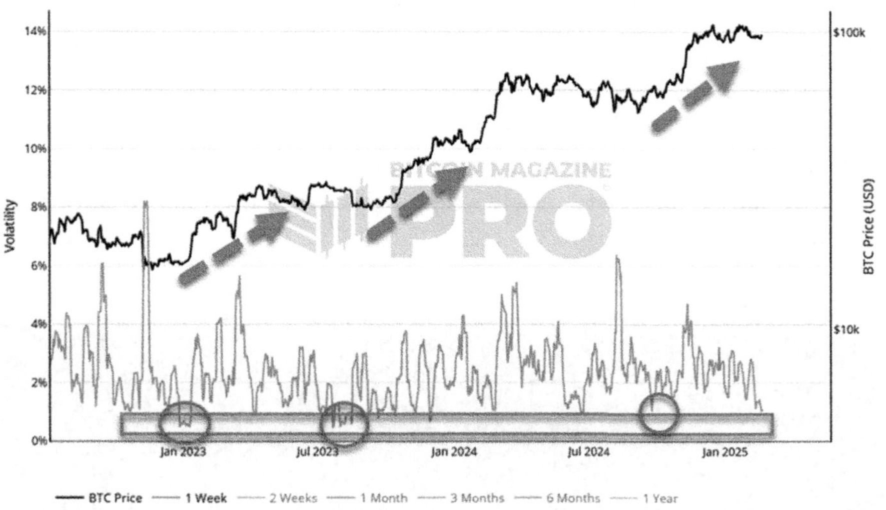

Chart 15.39   *Source* Bitcoin Magazine Pro

When the one-month volatility indicator reaches levels around **1.5% and 4.5%**, a **breakout usually occurs**, as shown in Chart 15.40. To determine the direction of the breakout, one should look at other indicators, such as oscillators.

Bitcoin Volatility

Chart 15.40   *Source* Bitcoin Magazine Pro

15.7.6   Bitcoin 7 Days Volatility

Another indicator I follow is Bitcoin's 7-day volatility. When it reaches levels around 4.0, it often precedes a rally. It doesn't tell me whether the rally will be bullish or bearish—that's why I check other indicators—but when it hits that level, I prepare for a strong move. When volatility exceeds 8, that rally may be ending.

As we can see in Chart 15.41, when it reaches that level, the price moves sharply.

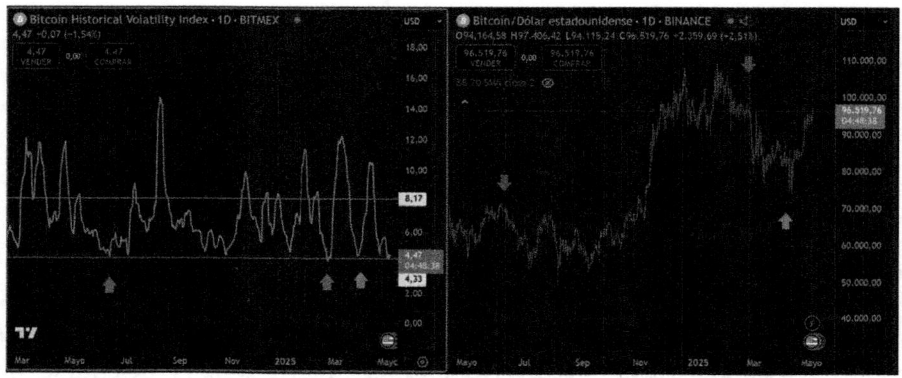

Chart 15.41   *Source* Tradingview

15.7.7   Bollinger Bands (Squeeze-bulge)

When the Bollinger Bands contract (a squeeze), they indicate that volatility is decreasing. By observing when this happens, we can anticipate the next move. Eventually, volatility expands sharply (a bulge), and that's when a rally emerges.

I have included several examples to show that a volatility squeeze doesn't necessarily mean the price will go up; rather, it signals that a rally is coming, but we don't know in which direction, as shown in Chart 15.42.

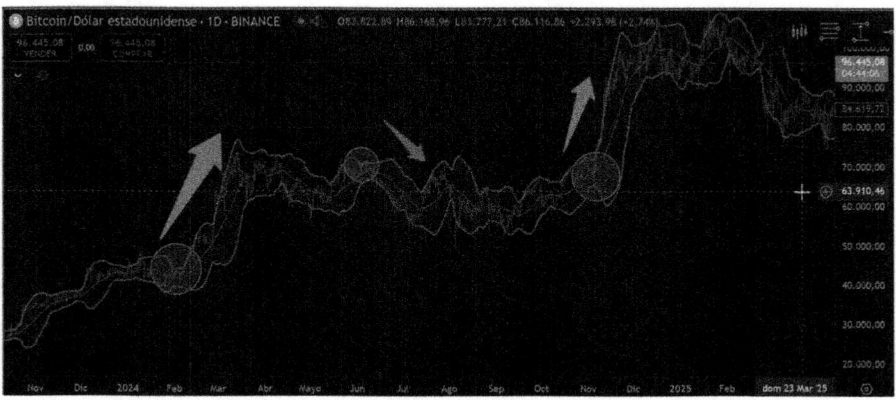

Chart 15.42   *Source* Tradingview

15.8 Summary

A summary of good **buy and sell signals** would be:

- **Good BUY Opportunities**:

  - Short term holder realized price below BTC Price (support during Bull Markets)
  - Aggregate Stablecoin dominance green (50p > 21p)
  - MVRV Z-Score green zone (undervalued)
  - Extreme Fear (Fear Greed Index)
  - Hash Ribbons just after red zone
  - Extreme net outflows ETF (local market bottom)
  - Extreme negative levels (funding rates)
  - Altseason Index < 5 (market bottom)

- **Good SELL Oportunities**:

  - Short term holder realized price above BTC Price (resistance Bear Markets)
  - Aggregate Stablecoin dominance red (21p > 50p)
  - MVRV Z-Score 5–6/red zone (overvalued)
  - Extreme Greed (Fear Greed Index)
  - Capital Flows > 50% (peak bull run)
  - Extreme positive levels (funding rates)

16

How to Find a Gem

In this chapter, we'll explore how to find a gem—that is, a coin that hasn't exploded yet but, due to its small size, may carry more risk than a well-established and widely traded coin listed on a centralized exchange like Binance.

It's important to try to identify these types of coins because they often have great growth potential, but of course, they also come with higher risk. That's why I'll explain the different steps you need to take to find them, as well as the potential dangers or risks you may encounter along the way.

16.1 Types of Scams

There are two main types of scams:

- **HONEYPOT**

  A honeypot is a cyber trap.
  Hackers insert malicious code into the smart contract of a token, allowing only them to withdraw funds from that contract.
  They launch the token, and people start buying it. Since no one can sell, the price keeps rising, attracting more investors.

J. Pineda, *Investing in Crypto with Confidence*,
https://doi.org/10.1007/978-3-032-07834-6_16

- **RUG PULL**

This happens when the project founders abandon the project and withdraw all the liquidity, taking users' funds with them.
This risk often occurs with newly launched platforms.
Try to avoid entering projects that have just launched, and follow the project on Twitter to see if the community is active and engaged.
Most scams happen on the Ethereum network (Uniswap, Sushiswap) and the Binance Smart Chain (PancakeSwap).

16.2 How to Avoid Scams

To avoid scams, follow these steps:

- Copy the token's contract address into Etherscan or BscScan to check the transaction history and view the holders.

  - https://bscscan.com/
  - https://etherscan.io/

- Go to Token Sniffer (https://tokensniffer.com) and paste the token's contract address to get an automated analysis of the smart contract and detect potential red flags:

  - Swap Analysis: Checks whether the token can be sold or not.
  - Contract Analysis: Verifies if the creator has ownership privileges over the contract's functionality. If so, they could change its behavior (e.g., disable selling, modify fees, etc.).
  - Holder Analysis: Shows whether the token is burned, locked, and how much of the circulating supply the creator's wallet holds (OK if < 5%).
  - Liquidity Analysis: Displays the percentage of liquidity controlled by the creator's wallet—a high percentage increases the risk of a rug pull.
  - Similar Contracts: Highlights other tokens with identical or similar contract code.
  - Overall Score: Gives a general rating out of 100, but keep in mind, a high score does not guarantee the token is safe.
  - You can also view the smart contract code.

- In the Bubble Map, you can visualize token transfers among the top 100 holders of that coin.

  The creator's address is shown as the orange dot.
  The burned (burn) address is shown as the red dot.
  When you hover over the dots, it shows the percentage of holdings.
  If you click on a dot, it will take you to the corresponding wallet address.

- Go to any of these websites and enter the token's contract address to monitor transactions:

  - Check that there are actual sell transactions, and that multiple wallets are selling
  - If there are no sell transactions, or if only one or two wallets are selling, DO NOT BUY
  - Etherscan/BscScan
  - https://www.dextools.io

Table 16.1 shows the transactions through the website https://poocoin.app

Table 16.1 *Source* poocoin.app

	Token tx	Wallet tx	Buyers	Sellers	
Tokens	**Price**	**Price / Token**	**Time**	**Tx**
712,063 BFT	$150.88 0.4856 BNB	$0.0002119 Pc v2	11:52:40	0x44f4 Track
307,730 BFT	$64.82 0.2086 BNB	$0.0002107 Pc v2	11:47:46	0x515b Track
410,312 BFT	$86.85 0.2795 BNB	$0.0002117 Pc v2	11:42:49	0x7d47 Track
768,038 BFT	$161.87 0.5210 BNB	$0.0002108 Pc v2	11:40:55	0xb932 Track
1,090,714 BFT	$230.78 0.7427 BNB	$0.0002116 Pc v2	11:39:07	0x2a16 Track
727,278 BFT	$154.48 0.4972 BNB	$0.0002124 Pc v2	11:38:37	0xc02e Track
126,076 BFT	$26.95 0.0867 BNB	$0.0002137 Pc v2	11:35:04	0x9066 Track
114,905 BFT	$24.55 0.0790 BNB	$0.0002136 Pc v2	11:34:16	0xa050 Track
768,038 BFT	$163.48 0.5261 BNB	$0.0002129 Pc v2	11:33:58	0x17a0 Track

16.3 Do Your Own Research

It's always important to do your own research. Here are the key aspects you should focus on:

1. Check the token's website:

- Design and appearance (Is it professional and well-made?)
- Domain registration date: Use https://whois.domaintools.com/

  If the domain was registered within 24 hours or less before the token launch, it's a strong scam warning.

2. Check the token's social media accounts: https://www.moonpass.ai/

- If the project has thousands of followers but the accounts were just created, it's a red flag for a scam.
- Legitimate projects hire professionals to manage their social media.
- Look for quality content, proper documentation, and informative articles about the project.
- Check for high-quality images that are not stolen or generic and have no grammatical errors. They should never ask you to provide personal data, such as ETH addresses or private keys.

3. Investigate their Telegram and Twitter followers:

- Detect bots and fake accounts: recently created profiles, strange usernames, no information or bio, fake profile pictures, etc.

4. Large wallet holders: Do not invest in tokens where a few wallets hold the majority of the supply.

- Do not invest in tokens with unlocked liquidity pools.
- Do not invest in unaudited tokens.

5. Mint Function:

- This function allows the contract owner to create more tokens at will.

6. Slow Rug Pull:

- Scammers create a token and distribute a large portion of the supply across hundreds of wallets, all of which they control.

- For example, they distribute 20% of the tokens to 500 wallets.
- As people start buying the token, the scammers gradually sell off the tokens from these wallets until they've dumped everything and then abandon the project.

A **Slow Rug Pull** is difficult to detect, but you can investigate using Etherscan or BscScan.

If you find many wallets holding the same percentage of tokens, it is a strong indicator of this type of scam.

16.4 Certik.org

This website performs a project audit and allows you to review the following aspects:

- Trust Score
- Social Analysis
- Liquidity and Volatility
- Top DEX and CEX liquidity pairs
- On-Chain Analytics
- Wallet Age Distribution
- Smart Money
- Token Holder Distribution Analysis
- Top Token Holders

Figure 16.1 shows the appearance of the website http://www.certik.org

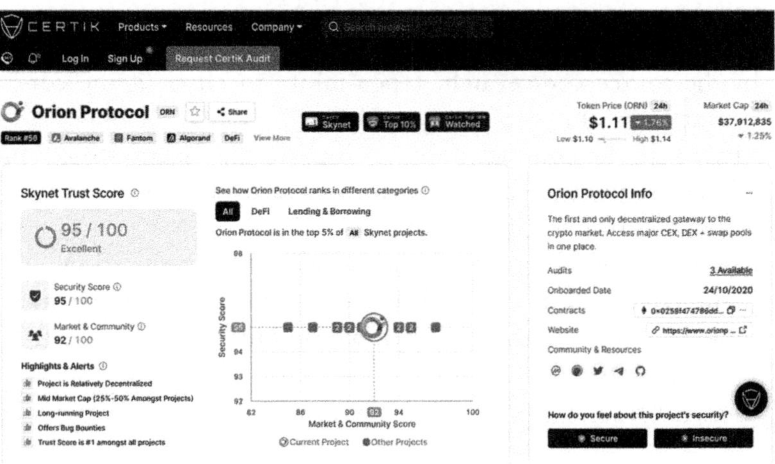

Fig. 16.1 *Source* https://www.certik.org

16.5 Tools to Detect Scams

Below are some useful tools to help detect scams:

- LISTING SPY: https://listingspy.net/

  - Suspected Scam Removed Filter:

    Filters out tokens with low trading volume, low number of transactions, and few holders.

  - Hide Low Liquidity Filter:

    Removes tokens with very low liquidity from the list.

- BSCHECK: https://www.bscheck.eu/

  - The first step is to select the token's network and paste the token wallet address.
  - Look for scams such as honeypots.
  - Check if there is an owner contract (they can change the code at any time).
  - Developer wallet information:

    How much token supply do the developers and team members hold? If they hold a high percentage, they could ruin the project by selling their tokens on the market.

- Manually review the contract:

  - On Etherscan/BscScan, check the contract's source code (contract/code).
  - In scams, the compiler version is usually old (v0.5.17/v0.6.12).
  - In the source code search, type "mint" to check if the contract has a mint function.
  - Make sure the contract does not include the "self-destruct" function. With this function, the developer can destroy the contract and replace it with a completely different one.
  - Check the date the contract was submitted for verification.
  - If the contract has two different dates, do not invest; it means they copied another contract and resubmitted it for verification.

- Check that the Liquidity Pool is secure:

  - If there are large wallets holding a significant portion of the tokens, they can manipulate the token's price.
  - If a project locks tokens or burns a large amount of tokens, it makes the project more secure, since they won't be able to perform a rug pull with their LP tokens—they don't have access to the tokens, meaning they can't remove liquidity from the DEX.

- How to know if the LP tokens are locked:

  - https://deeplock.io/safe: DeepLock Liquidity Locker shows you what percentage of the token supply is locked and for how long.
  - BscScan/Etherscan: In the "Holders" section, the wallet address should have a document icon next to it to indicate that it is locked, as shown in Fig. 16.2.

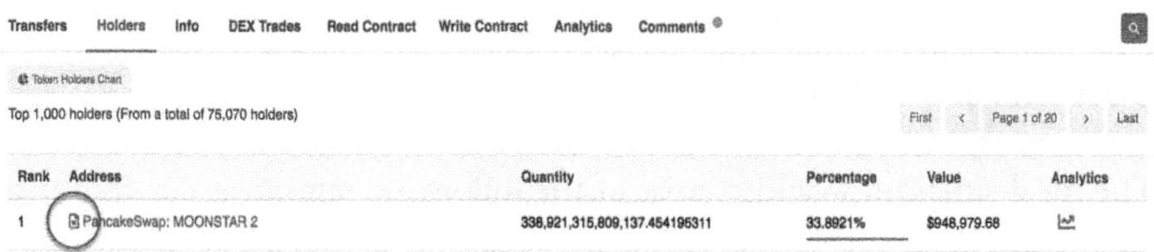

Fig. 16.2 Etherscan website showing that the LP tokens are locked

- Another tool to check if LP tokens are locked: https://app.unicrypt.network/amm

  - It lets you see if the tokens are locked across DEXs like PancakeSwap, Uniswap, and QuickSwap.

- If there was a large purchase right after the LP token was created, it's possibly a scam:

  - https://poocoin.app/rugchec

If unsure, buy a small amount and try to sell it. If you can sell it, then it's likely not a scam.

Table 16.2 shows the appearance of the website http://www.poocoin.app

Table 16.2 *Source* https://www.poocoin.app

Manual wallet address (if it didnt appear as an owner)

Enter wallet address... | Go

Token total supply: 100,000,000,000

Wallet activity for 0xCD2b070568C3b744A016c678082F777707b73c29

Date	Token	Amount	Receiver	Action	Tx
21/10/2022, 19:48:45	BFT	3,000,000.00	0xcee41df001714399c1ed620c47f5238b36d6e9ab	Send to contract	0x2a76...
13/10/2022, 18:32:49	BFT	2,000,000.00	0xcee41df001714399c1ed620c47f5238b36d6e9ab	Send to contract	0x98d3...
12/10/2022, 18:33:36	BFT	1,200,000.00	0xcee41df001714399c1ed620c47f5238b36d6e9ab	Send to contract	0x76d0...
18/8/2022, 9:03:46	BNB	0.3324	0x0fa86fe063876f93e81bded3c1ba11c4c927a3e9	Send to wallet Follow	0xb6fa...
9/8/2022, 23:53:00	BNB	0.6800	0x663c88706221477476 8de0fc6adf685e117dd236	Send to wallet Follow	0x6e96...
9/8/2022, 23:50:06	BFT	7,000,000.00	0x99c2d5977b94bdfdf91ee36f613e330e8102e326	Sell BFT	0x3ebd...
7/8/2022, 3:01:12	BFT	7,000,000.00	0x99c2d5977b94bdfdf91ee36f613e330e8102e326	Sell BFT	0xa2d6...
3/8/2022, 19:34:34	BFT	3,279,100.00	0x7178350e072c3852c2a1a931181d55ef2c43f76e	Send to wallet Follow	0xe39b...
3/8/2022, 10:25:29	BUSD	530.00	0x9e112764c31be2fdad0e5be923bd150375a2e439	Send to wallet Follow	0x4703...
3/8/2022, 10:22:47	BFT	1,063,432.56	0x99c2d5977b94bdfdf91ee36f613e330e8102e326	Sell BFT	0x438d...
3/8/2022, 10:20:56	BFT	1,062,143.98	0x99c2d5977b94bdfdf91ee36f613e330e8102e326	Sell BFT	0x1b06...
3/8/2022, 0:21:28	BUSD	400.00	0x01bc636969ae2e25addcfce02a3039d8555a7612	Send to wallet Follow	0x9a07...
6/7/2022, 13:05:35	BFT	1,000,000,000.00	0x000000000000000000000000000000000000dead	Send to wallet Follow	0x15da...

16.6 Ideal Situation

The ideal situation would consist of the following items:

- Close to 100% of the tokens were converted into LP tokens on an Exchange
- No pre-sale.
- No Mint function.
- No self-destruct function.
- Ownership of the contract has been renounced by the owner.
- 100% of the LP tokens were burned, and/or there is some form of liquidity lock for a period of time.

And always remember: DO YOUR OWN RESEARCH (DYOR).

16.7 Summary

Finally, here's a summary of the most important points:

1. Check the smart contract (etherscan/bscscan/tokensniffer).
2. Bubble Map (tokensniffer): shows token transfers among the top 100 holders of the coin.
3. Monitor transactions (etherscan/bscscan/dextools.io/poocoin.app).

4. Website: look and domain registration (whois.domaintools.com).
5. Social media (moonpass.ai).
6. No mint function.
7. No selfdestruct function.
8. Who owns the contract (OK: ownership renounced)—bscheck.eu.
9. Project audit (certik.org).
10. Listing Spy.
11. Developer wallet information (bscheck.eu).
12. Manually review the contract (etherscan/bscscan).
13. Check liquidity pool (LP tokens locked or burned)—(deeplock.io/safe).
14. Check if there was a large buy right after the LP token was created—(poocoin.app/rugcheck).

You can find potential hidden gems to analyze (and check if they're scams or not) on this site:

https://dexscreener.com/solana?rankBy=trendingScoreH24&order = desc

Set a filter for market cap between $50 K and $100 M, and daily volume greater than $10 K.

Figure 16.3 shows the appearance of the website http://www.dexscreener.com

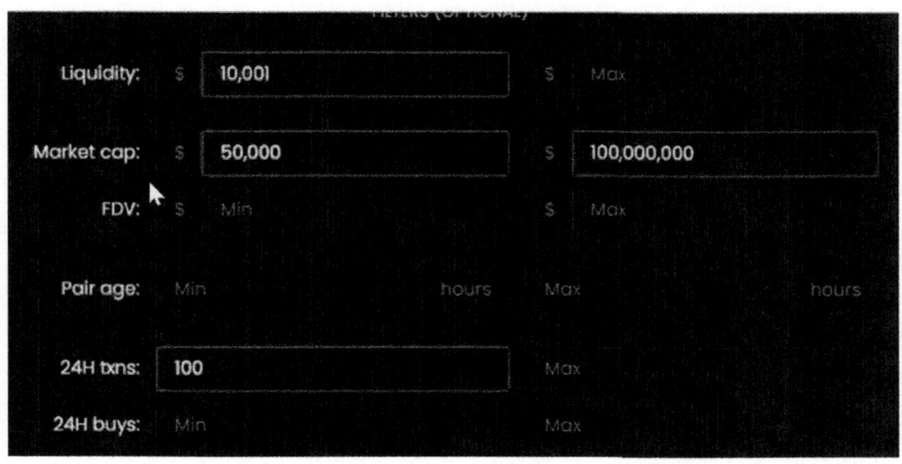

Fig. 16.3 *Source* dexscreener.com

17

Automated Trading Systems

Before we begin, I want to mention that in this chapter, I'll summarize the most important points to remember when creating automated trading systems. However, suppose you want to dive deeper into the topic. In that case, I recommend my book *Sistemas de Trading 2: Cómo crearlos por ti mismo y tener éxito*, which for now is only available in Spanish.

17.1 Definition and Advantages

I recommend this type of trading mainly because machines lack emotions—something humans do have, which often leads us to act irrationally when investing. By default, humans tend to close a position too early when it's making even a small profit, and hold on too long when it's losing, hoping the value will eventually go up to recover their investment.

This lack of discipline generally makes exit strategies in manual trading far less efficient than automated trading.

- Automated Trading System:

  - Avoids emotions
  - Improves order management
  - Enhances risk management
  - Brings discipline
  - Improves entry and exit timing

J. Pineda, *Investing in Crypto with Confidence*,
https://doi.org/10.1007/978-3-032-07834-6_17

An Expert Advisor is an algorithmic program used in the MetaTrader software to invest automatically in any type of asset (for example, Forex, cryptocurrencies, etc.).

17.2 Brokers

The choice of broker is a fundamental part of success due to factors such as product variety, data quality, slippage, spread, commissions, and trading hours.

It's important to keep in mind that both Forex and cryptocurrencies are decentralized markets, and it's the broker who provides the liquidity, not the market itself, since these assets are not regulated. For that reason, choosing the right broker is crucial and a key part of your strategy's success.

There are several brokers that meet these requirements, but you need to analyze them and see which one best fits what you're looking for. One essential aspect is that they operate 24/7. If they don't, you'll need to configure your automated system to close on Friday and reopen on Monday. Otherwise, the system might give you an entry or exit signal that can't be executed because the broker is closed.

For example, FX Open has very good data and low slippage because it offers ECN accounts, but it does not provide copy trading or demo accounts on MetaTrader 4. This means you can't use certain software, which I will explain later, that helps analyze strategies you run on a demo account.

Another broker is Fusion Markets; it does offer copy trading but lacks extensive historical data. Having ample historical data is important because the more data you have, the better your automated systems will perform, having been tested through all kinds of market situations.

Finally, another broker I like is Vantage Markets, but it does not offer copy trading with MetaTrader and has limited historical data.

Another option is that the software you use to create automated systems provides historical data from a broker like Binance. Obviously, this is not the most optimal setup, since ideally, the data you use to develop your system should come from the broker where you will actually run it. However, it's always better to have a large amount of data from a broker like Binance than to have only limited data from your broker, even if that data isn't as precise as your broker's own data.

If you create automated systems for Forex, you won't have a problem with data, since all Forex brokers have extensive historical data available.

17.3 Copy Trading

Once you have an optimal strategy, what I recommend is to make it profitable and, besides earning your own benefit by using it, also attract clients who want to replicate it and thus give you a share of their profits.

With copy trading, your master account can be replicated by other accounts in terms of timing, direction, and position size.

For example, if you choose the broker Fusion Markets, you would have two options:

- OPTION 1: Fusion Markets broker + Fusion + Platform

In this case, you would do everything with the broker. The copy trading platform at Fusion Markets is called FUSION + .

A couple of notes about this platform:

- Clients cannot modify settings
- It costs $10 USD if you don't trade at least 2.5 lots per month
- There is no public leaderboard (ranking table)

- OPTION 2: Fusion Markets broker + Pelican Trading Platform:

The Pelican Trading platform does not belong to Fusion Markets. On this platform, you can use many brokers, and their trading hours match those of your chosen broker. Essentially, they are just a platform that replicates your signals to clients who want to follow your account.

However, to connect your strategy with them, you need to have 6 months of trading history. In this case, clients can modify settings, and there is a leaderboard.

17.4 Softwares

When it comes to software for creating your automated trading systems, there are mainly two:

- **STRATEGY QUANT X (SQX)**

  - https://strategyquant.com/pricing

- **FOREX ROBOT FACTORY (FRF)**

  – https://www.forexrobotacademy.com/store

In this book, the software I will use to explain automated trading systems is FRF, as it is easier to use and requires less hardware.

- The differences between the two are:

  – In FRF, you can create a robot with 100 Expert Advisors (EAs), and by launching the robot, you deploy all 100 EAs in MetaTrader at once. In SQX, you don't have that functionality.

    This feature works with hedging accounts, as you can have a buy position on EURUSD and simultaneously a sell position on EURUSD without netting them. It does not work with U.S. brokers, as positions are netted.

  – In SQX, you have 5 data modes when creating EAs:

    Fast methods: selected timeframe, trade on bar open—used for **CREATING** strategies.
    Slow methods:
    1-minute data
    Tick simulation
    Real tick

    Slow methods are used for **TESTING/RETESTING** strategies.

- In FRF, you only have one mode: trade on bar open (it only considers the open of each candle and ignores what happens within the candle).
- With SQX, you need a powerful computer—at least 16GB of RAM and 6–8 CPU cores.
- With FRF, that's not necessary because it uses cloud computing, unlike SQX, which runs on your local machine.
- In SQX, you can add custom indicators—in FRF, you cannot.

A store specializing in trading computers is Falcon Trading Systems.

- 🌐 http://www.falcontradingsystems.com

17.5 Data

As I mentioned earlier, it is important that the data you use to build your automated trading systems comes from the broker you will use to deploy them.

Therefore, below I explain how to download your broker's data in MetaTrader 4 (MT4) and save it into your strategy software.

- **Downloading Data in MT4**:

Data is extremely important when creating an EA.

Ideally, the data used to create the EA should be provided by the same broker where you plan to launch your EAs in MetaTrader, both on demo and live accounts.

That's why it's important to choose a broker that offers several years of historical data.

- **How to download MT4 Data for use in FRF**:

1. Install the Broker Data Downloader App in MT4 (it comes free with the FRA Course).
2. Go to: Tools > Options > Charts and set both "Max bars in history" and "Max bars in chart" to 999,999,999,999.
3. Open a chart and set the timeframe to 1 minute.
4. Save the template as the default.
5. Open one chart for each FX or crypto pair you want to download data for (e.g., one chart for BTC, another for ETH, etc.).
6. Drag the Broker Data Downloader App onto each chart—this will start downloading the data.
7. A faster way to do step 6:
   Go to the "Window" > "Tile Windows" tab, click the chart window, then double-click the Broker Data Downloader App and press Enter.

- **Import data from MT4 to FRF**:

1. Download the script for MT4 located in FRF/Tools/Data Import and install it in MT4.
2. Alternatively, copy and paste it into:
   MT4/File/Open Data Folder/MQL4/Scripts.

3. Drag the Robot Factory Data Export script onto the chart and modify the commission and spread settings.
4. Commission: 7 USD.
5. Spread: 2800 for BTC and 300 for ETH (using Fusion Markets).
6. In FRF, go to: Tools/Data/Data Horizon and set Maximum Data Bars to 200,000 (default is 20,000).
7. In MT4, go to: Open Data Folder/MQL4/Files and copy the JSON files.
8. In FRF, go to: Tools/Data Import and either paste or upload the JSON files.

17.6 Expert Advisors

Expert Advisors (EAs) are the automated systems you will create. They need to have a set of important settings to increase their chances of success.

- EA Settings:

  - Make sure the FRF indicators you use for creating the EA are also installed in MT4.
  - No Martingale.
  - No scalping.
  - Always use Stop Loss and Take Profit.
  - Symmetrical rules.
  - No hedging.
  - Use Trailing Stop.

- Settings to select in FRF:

  - Go to: Tools > Settings > Trading Session and select the same trading hours as your broker, whose data you are using, so the EA you create is synchronized with the data you upload.
  - Go to: Tools > Acceptance Criteria > Complete Backtest and Set:

    Min Net Profit > 100
    Min Count of Trades > 100

  - Go to: Tools > Settings > General Settings and Set:

    Collection Capacity to 300.

- Go to: Tools > Available Indicators and choose the indicators you want for that strategy. **Always use the same indicators for both the entry and exit rules.**

17.7 Phases of Creating an EA

When creating an EA, there are several phases you need to follow. Below is a schematic overview of each phase, since the purpose of this book is not to cover automatic trading systems in detail.

- THE 5 PHASES OF CREATING AN EA:

1. **CREATION**:

- Designing the basic rules and logic of the trading system.

2. **OPTIMIZATION**:

- Improving the system's results by adjusting its parameters using historical data.

3. **ROBUSTNESS TEST (Montecarlo)**:

- Used to evaluate whether the results generated by the system are likely to repeat in the future.

4. **WALK FORWARD OPTIMIZATION**:

- The goal is to get a more realistic picture of the system's probability of success.
- It is performed after the system has passed the optimization and robustness test phases.
- This phase helps prevent overfitting.
- It consists of dividing the data into segments and checking if the parameters optimized in one period also perform well in other periods.

5. **EXPORT TO METATRADER**:

- The final step is to export the EA to MetaTrader (MT4 or MT5) for deployment.

17.7.1   Creating an EA

Let's begin with the first phase: Creating an EA. The first variables you need to set in generator section are:

- Data
- Timeframe
- Stop Loss/Take Profit (SL/TP)
- Lots
- Working Minutes: 30,000

Once you click the start button, several strategies are generated and displayed in the collection section, as shown in Fig. 17.1.

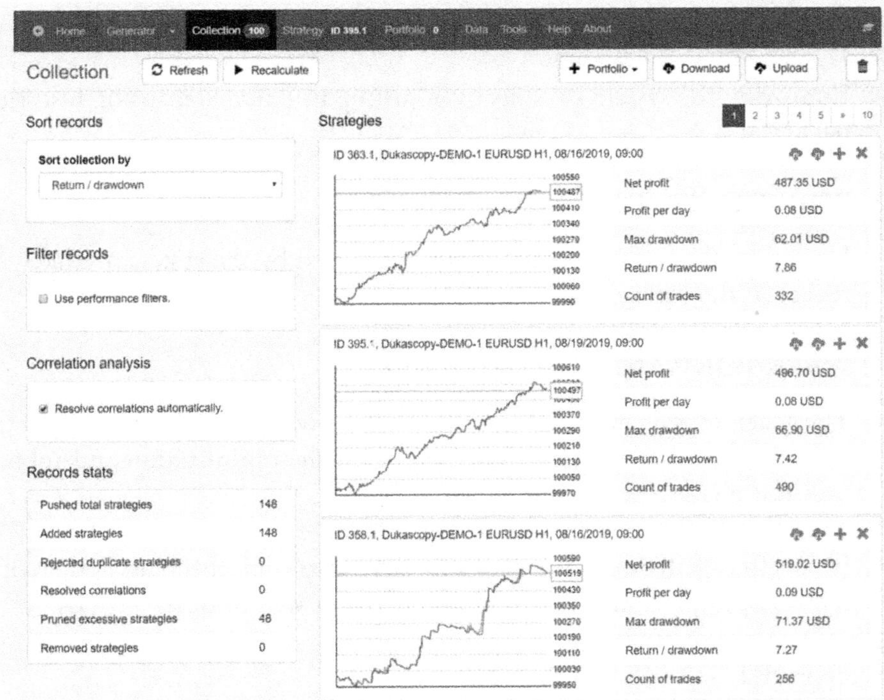

Fig. 17.1   *Source* Forex Robot Factory (FRF)

17.7.2 Optimization

- I recommend using Monte Carlo Stress Testing instead of the Optimizer, because otherwise, you risk over-optimizing the strategy, making the results look perfect but unrealistic.
- **Perform optimization only on already profitable systems, not to try to make unprofitable ones profitable**.

The most important thing is that the system passes the Monte Carlo test, which allows you to assess its robustness.

The variables I recommend using are the ones shown in Fig. 17.2.

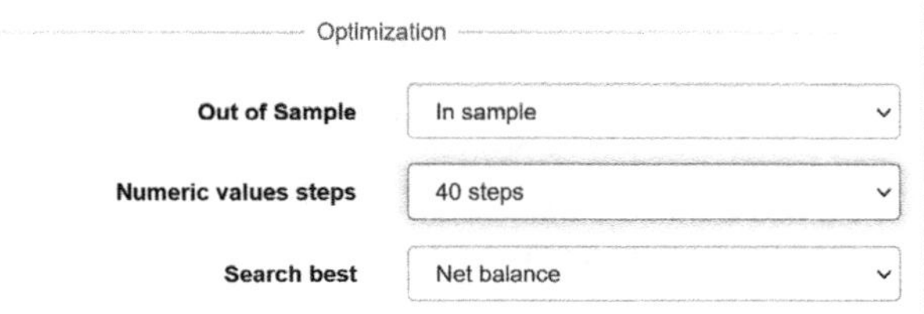

Fig. 17.2 Forex Robot Factory (FRF)

The appearance of the Optimizer section is shown in Fig. 17.3.

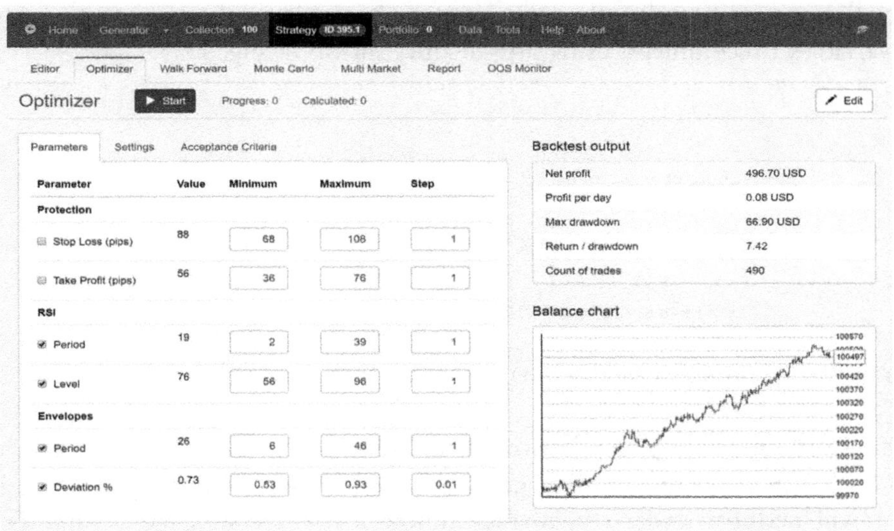

Fig. 17.3 *Source* Forex Robot Factory (FRF)

17.7.3 Robustness Test (Montecarlo)

There are several ways to carry out this phase.

I'll outline the three methods I believe are most important. If your EA passes all three, it's clearly a robust system that can adapt to different market conditions.

- **Randomize indicators parameters** (Change the parameters of the indicators to see how sensitive the strategy is to those values). The variables I recommend using are the ones shown in Fig. 17.4.

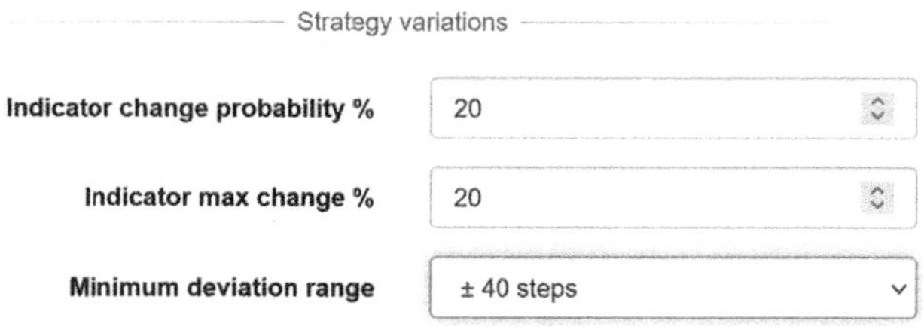

Fig. 17.4 Forex Robot Factory (FRF)

- **Randomize history data**: The price of each bar is slightly modified by a few pips. This simulates how your strategy would behave with different brokers (with somewhat different pricing).

If the backtest results remain similar to the live performance, the broker used will not significantly affect the strategy—it will work consistently. The variables I recommend using are the ones shown in Fig. 17.5.

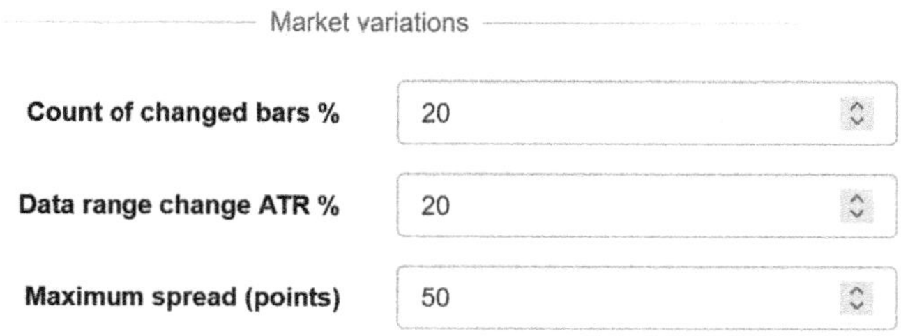

Fig. 17.5 Forex Robot Factory (FRF)

- **Randomize slippage**: This method alters each price (entry and exit) by a few pips to simulate slippage. It helps you understand how your strategy will perform under real market conditions where slippage occurs. The variables I recommend using are the ones shown in Fig. 17.6.

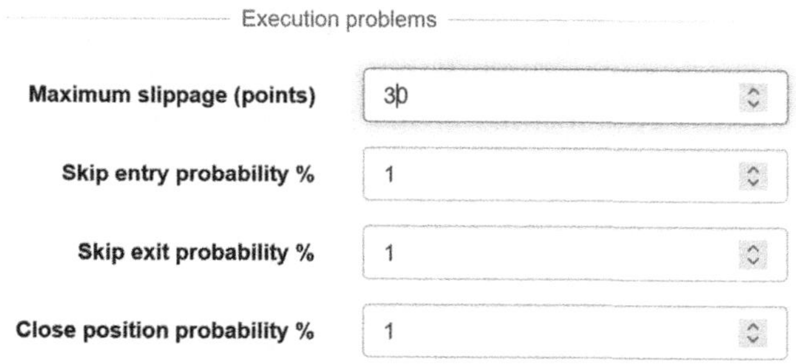

Fig. 17.6 *Source* Forex Robot Factory (FRF)

The final result of the process is shown in Fig. 17.7.

Fig. 17.7 *Source* Forex Robot Factory (FRF)

17.7.4 Walk Forward Optimization

The action of Walk Forward Optimization is to divide the data into periods and optimize each period, which includes IS (In-Sample) and OOS (Out-of-Sample) segments.

Additionally, it indicates which period is the most optimal.

- It is the most challenging process to pass, so applying it only to your favorite strategy, not to all of them, is recommended.
- It tells us which combination of runs is the most efficient and with which OOS percentage.

The appearance of the walk-forward section is shown in Fig. 17.8.

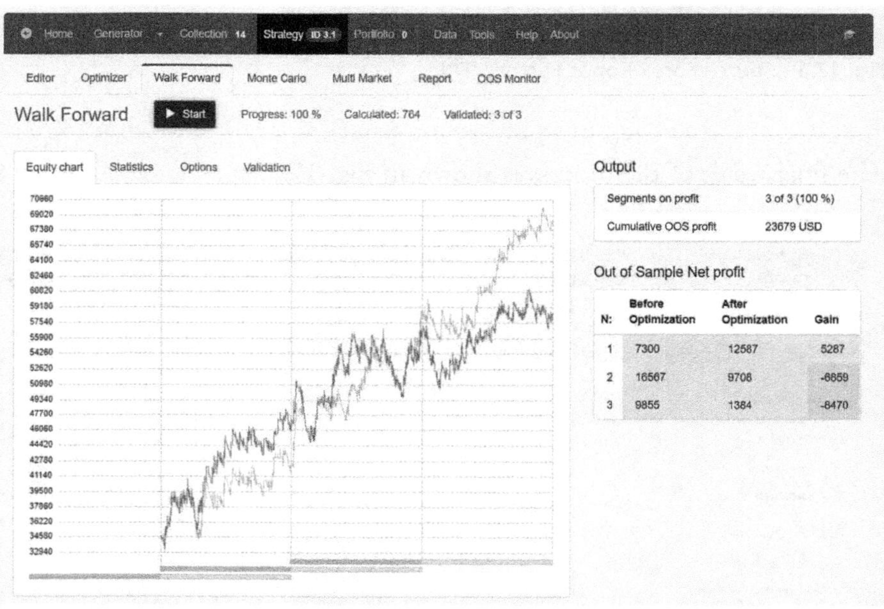

Fig. 17.8 *Source* Forex Robot Factory (FRF)

17.8 Automation of Phases

You have the option to automate all the processes using the REACTOR function.

- With the REACTOR module, you can automate all the phases so they are executed one after another.

1. Creation: Tools/acceptance criteria:

- Trades > 200
- Net profit > 100
- Return/Drawdown > 2

2. Monte Carlo(MC):

- Count of tests: 100
- Validated test 90% (90 out of 100 must pass)
- Randomized historical data
- Randomize indicator parameters

3. Optimizer:

- Out of sample: IS
- Steps: 40
- Search Best: Return/Drawdown
- Optimize Stop Loss(SL) and Take Profit(TP)
- **Run Monte Carlo multiple times**, not just once

The appearance of the Reactor section is shown in Fig. 17.9.

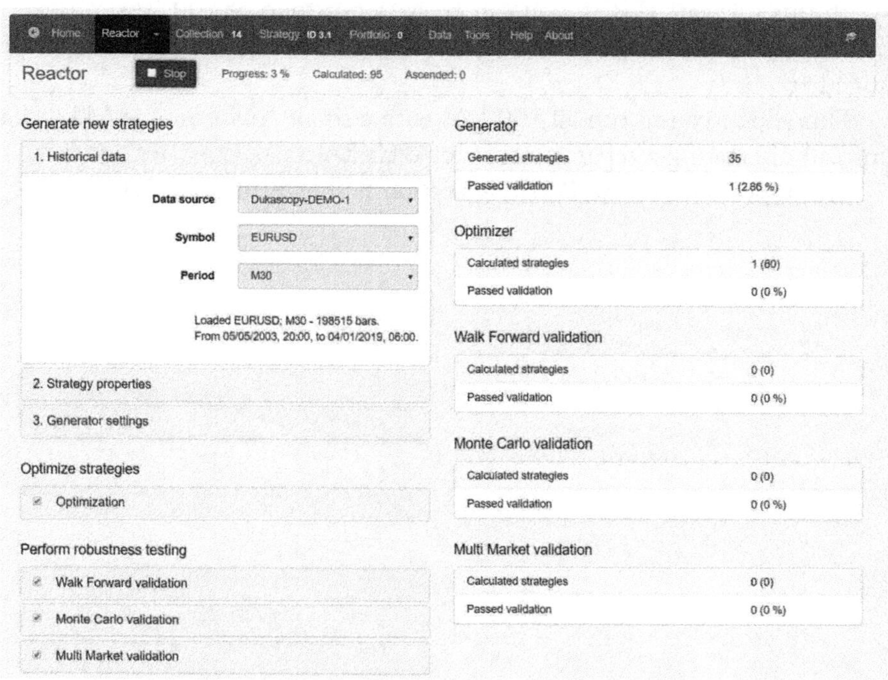

Fig. 17.9 *Source* Forex Robot Factory (FRF)

17.9 Curve Fitting

A common issue that occurs frequently is Curve Fitting.

- **Curve Fitting**: It refers to modifying the curve to make it fit the historical data too perfectly—in other words, over-optimization.

- **How to avoid Curve Fitting?**

1. Use a few variables in the Optimizer
2. Set high step values for the parameters to be optimized (e.g., steps > 5)
3. Use Monte Carlo testing (randomize historical data/randomize indicator parameters)
4. Use OOS Monitor with 30% Out of Sample

17.10 Portfolio EA Creation

With this software (FRF), you can create a portfolio of 100 EAs.

You can create a portfolio with 100 EAs to analyze all the strategies together.

This allows you to run all 100 EAs with a single robot on one MT4 chart instead of creating a separate chart for each EA.

The appearance of the Portfolio section is shown in Fig. 17.10.

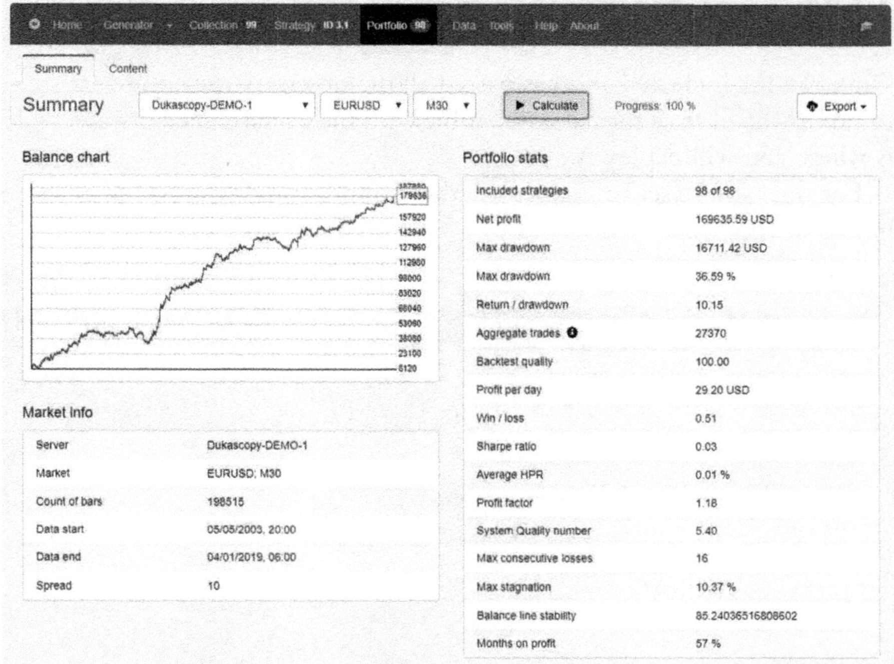

Fig. 17.10   *Source* Forex Robot Factory (FRF)

You can also use the **Multimarket** function, as shown in Fig. 17.11, which allows you to test your strategies across different markets and time-frames to evaluate the strategy's robustness.

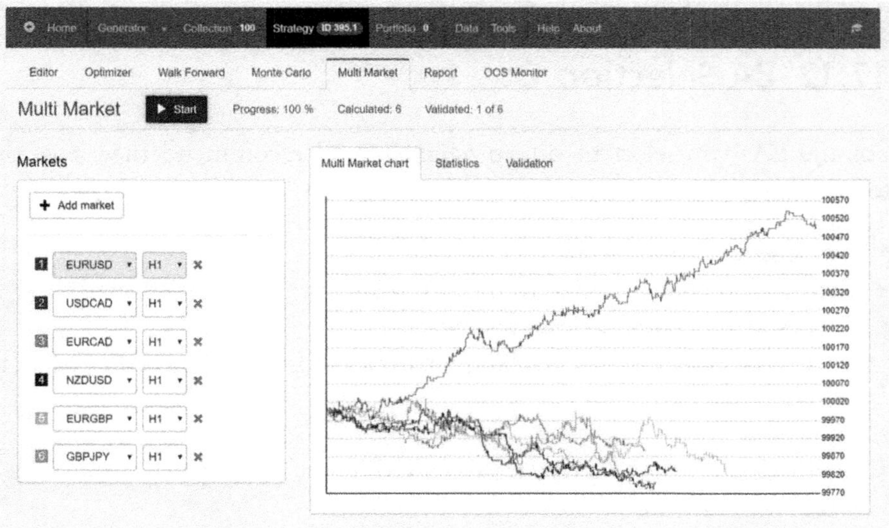

Fig. 17.11   *Source* Forex Robot Factory (FRF)

17.11 Exporting to Metatrader

Once the EA is created and has passed all the necessary tests, the next step is to export the file to a format compatible with the Metatrader software, which is where you will deploy it.

For this, you select in Export whether you want MT4 or MT5, as shown in Fig. 17.12.

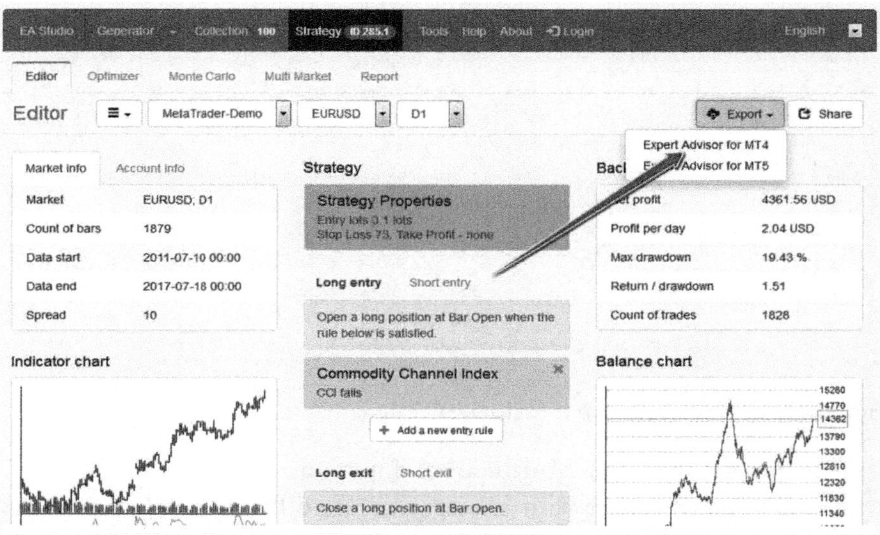

Fig. 17.12 *Source* Forex Robot Factory (FRF)

17.12 EA Selection

For the EAs you select to run in Metatrader, I recommend they have the following characteristics:

- Net Balance > 500 USD
- Return/Drawdown Ratio (RET/DD) > 3 (total profit/drawdown)
- Trades > 50 per year of backtesting
- Max Drawdown (DD) < 40% (maximum observed loss from peak to trough during a period
- Win Ratio > 50
- Stagnation < 30% (days your strategy did not make profits; those days were without gains

- SQN > 2 (System Quality Number, measures the quality of an automated system)

  - From 1.6 to 1.9: below average
  - From 2.0 to 2.4: average
  - From 2.5 to 2.9: goo
  - From 3.0 to 5.0: excellent
  - From 5.1 to 6.9: super

Once selected and launched in Metatrader on a demo account, I recommend letting them run for about 2–3 months to see how they perform in real-time market conditions.

17.13 Metatrader 4 Vs Metatrader 5

When choosing between Metatrader 4 and Metatrader 5, you need to consider their differences, as these can affect the creation of your EA:

- **MT5:**

1. Six types of pending orders and two types of spot orders
2. Markets: Forex, CFDs, Options, and Stocks
3. Timeframes: 21
4. Indicators: 55
5. Economic calendar
6. Multi-currency strategy tester
7. MT5 is superior for testing and optimizing. It is faster than MT4

- **MT4:**

1. Four types of pending orders
2. Markets: Forex and CFDs
3. Timeframes: 9
4. Indicators: 47
5. Requires less storage space than MT5
6. Most widely used among brokers (larger community support)

- **EAs created for MT5 are incompatible with MT4 and vice versa because they use different coding languages.**
- **I prefer to use MT4 because the MyMT4BOOK App only exists for MT4.**

17.14 Decimals (Price)

An essential aspect is understanding the relationship between a pip and a point. This relationship varies depending on the number of decimal places used in the broker's price quotation. Therefore, the first table presents the case with 4 or 5 decimal places, as shown in Table 17.1, and the second table presents the case with 2 or 3 decimal places, as shown in Table 17.2.

- PRICE:

    - With 2 and 4 decimals in the price: 1 Pip = 1 Point
    - With 3 and 5 decimals in the price: 1 Pip = 10 Points

		1 pip	1 punto
Broker A	EURUSD 4 decimales	0.0001	0.0001
Broker B	EURUSD 5 decimales	0.0001	0.00001

Table 17.1   Scenario of the broker that uses 4 or 5 decimals

		1 pip	1 punto
Broker A	GBPJPY 2 decimales	0.01	0.01
Broker B	GBPJPY 3 decimales	0.01	0.001

Table 17.2   Scenario of the broker that uses 2 or 3 decimals

- For example, at the broker Fusion Markets:

    - The spread is always shown multiplied by 100. For example, BTC bid 20,000 and ask 20,010 with a spread of 10 points, which is displayed as 1000.
    - Therefore, when creating an EA, for SL/TP I set 10,000 pips, which would be 100 points.

17.15 Metatrader Settings

When using Metatrader software for automated systems, you need to keep in mind these settings so that they work correctly, as shown in Fig. 17.13.

- **SETTINGS Tools/Options**:

  - Events: disable
  - Server: disable news
  - In Expert Advisors, select:

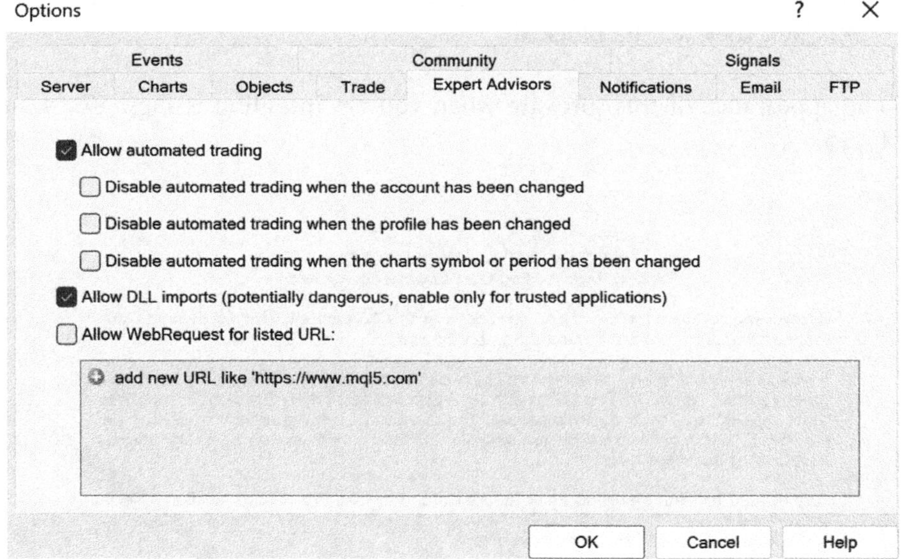

Fig. 17.13 *Source* Metatrader 4

17.16 How to Install Multiple Metatrader Platforms at Once

Since you will need to download multiple Metatrader platforms because the optimal is to run about 20–25 EAs on each, and you will be creating more, here is how you can do it in the fastest way.

- Each Metatrader platform supports 100 EAs, but it is recommended not to run more than 30 EAs per platform.

1. Go to your broker's website and click on Download Metatrader software.
2. Click on Settings.
3. In the Installation Folder, add 4–1.
4. In Program Group, add 4–1.
5. Click Next and install.
6. Repeat this process as many times as you want, changing to 4–2, 4–3, etc.
7. Open each Metatrader platform and enter your username and password. You can create as many demo accounts as you want; they are free. Ask your broker to set them as non-expiry accounts because otherwise, after 30 days, they will be blocked.

The appearance of this software when you are installing is Figs. 17.14 and 17.15.

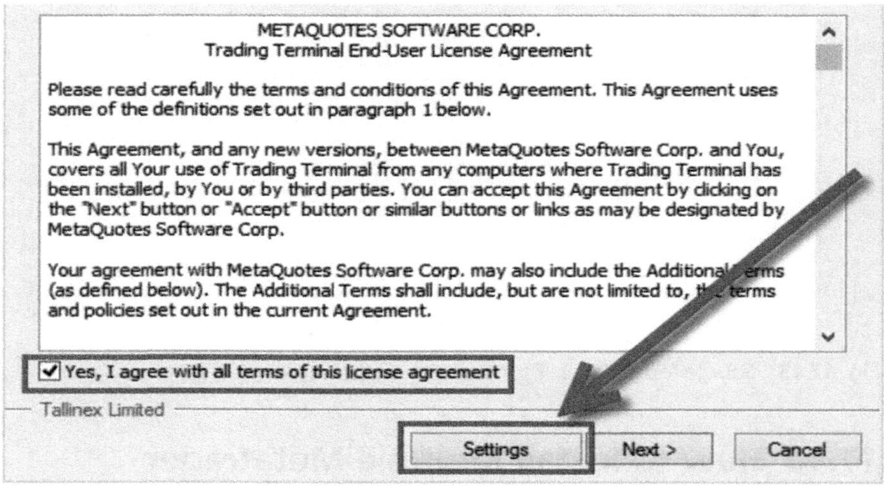

Fig. 17.14 *Source* Metatrader 4

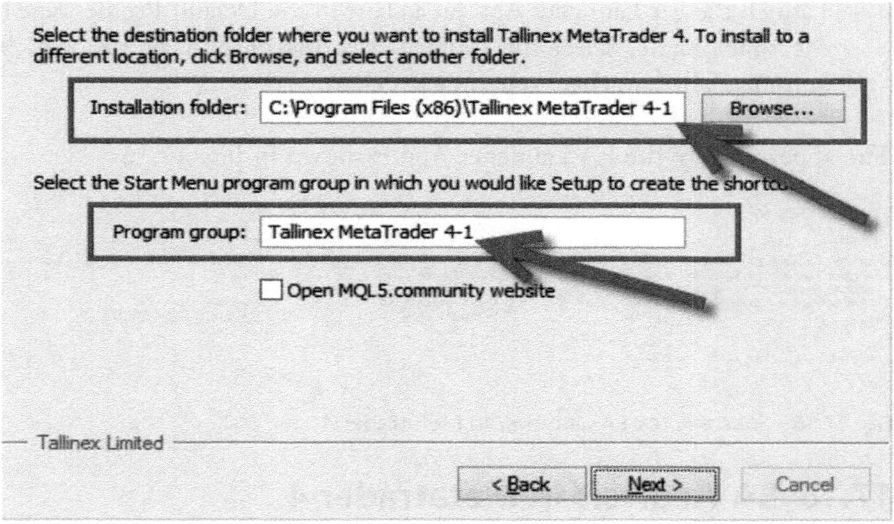

Fig. 17.15 *Source* Metatrader 4

17.17 How to Launch EAs in Metatrader 4

Once you have downloaded the MetaTrader platforms, the next step is to launch the EAs in them. This can be done either manually or automatically.

- Manual Method:

  - Save the EAs in MT4 via: File/Open Data Folder/MQL4/Experts.
  - In the Navigator window, click on Expert Advisors, then right-click and select Refresh.
  - Open a chart and drag an EA onto that chart. Repeat this step for each EA you want to launch.

- Automatic Method (using EA Launcher App):

  - Save the EAs in MT4 via: File/Open Data Folder/MQL4/Experts
  - In the Navigator window, click on Expert Advisors, then right-click and select Refresh.

– Launch the EA Launcher App on a chart in the Default Profile, type in the robot name, select the profile, click Install, and all EAs will be automatically launched, one on each chart.

The appearance of the EA Launcher App is shown in Fig. 17.16.

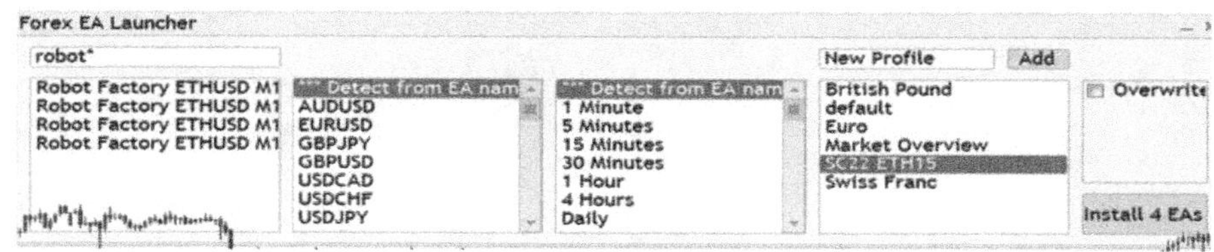

Fig. 17.16 *Source* Forex EA Launcher in Metatrader 4

17.18 EA Analysis in Metatrader 4

Once the EAs have been launched and left running for 2–3 months, it's time to analyze which ones to select. For this, there is a software called MyMT4Book, which only works with Metatrader 4 and greatly simplifies the task. Below is the link.

* https://www.forexrobotacademy.com/mymt4book-ealauncher

Figure 17.17 shows the appearance of these two software (MyMT4Book and EA Launcher).

MyMT4Book + EALauncher

Fig. 17.17 *Source* Metatrader 4/MyMT4Book

The appearance once you launch this software in Metatrader is shown in Fig. 17.18.

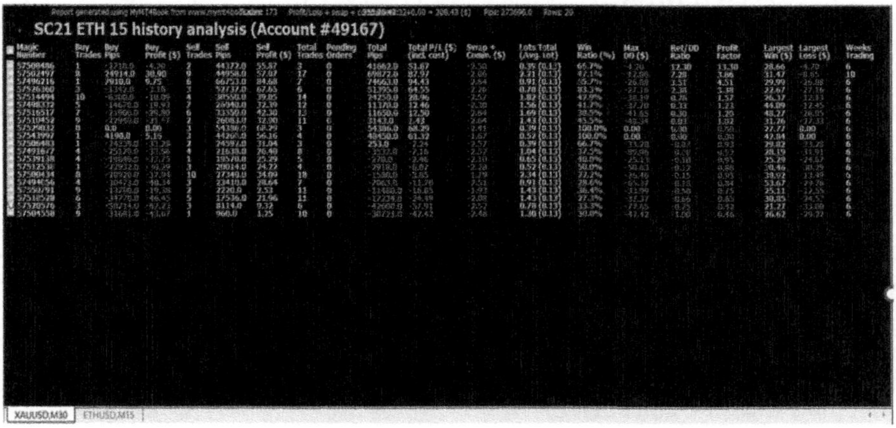

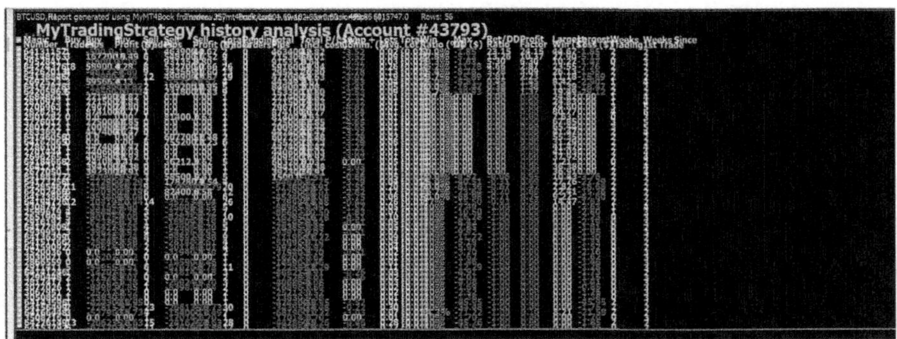

Fig. 17.18 *Source* Metatrader 4/MyMT4Book

- Once this software is installed in Metatrader, open a chart and drag MyMT4Book onto the chart, then enter the license.

If you get an error, as shown in Fig. 17.19, when installing it on the server, change the scale to 100% in the Windows graphics settings.

Fig. 17.19 *Source* Metatrader 4/MyMT4Book

The software will display the following variables for the EAs you have launched:

- MAGIC NUMBER: A random number the software assigns to each EA to identify it.
- TOTAL PIPS: The number of pips generated by the EA.
- WIN RATIO: Indicates whether the profit obtained comes from a single large trade or multiple trades, showing consistency.
- RET/DD RATIO: Return to drawdown ratio.

17.19 Selection Process

When selecting the final EAs to launch on the live account, the following variables must be considered:

- **RET/DD Ratio > 3**
- Trades > 20 over three months of deployment
- Max Drawdown < 30%
- Win Ratio > 40%
- If, after 3 months in Live, they show poor performance, they must be removed.
- **If, after 6 months in Live, they generate 30–40% profit, the lot size should be increased**
- If, when restarting MT4, MyMT4Book only shows trades from that day onwards, do the following to make all trades appear since MyMT4Book was installed:

  – Go to the Account History tab, right-click, and select All History.

17.20 Dedicated Server

A very important aspect of running EAs is ensuring they never stop working. For this reason, having a server is crucial since any power outage could cause the EA to stop functioning.

Dedicated servers are the best and most powerful servers, as they allow you to run a greater number of EAs.

When selecting one, consider the following aspects:

- You need to know where your broker's server is located, so the latency (the time it takes for your order to reach your broker's server) between your dedicated server and the broker's server is minimal. They are usually located in New York (NY).
- If the server's CPU performance exceeds 70%, do not install or open more instances of Metatrader (Table 17.3).

Table 17.3 Illustrates the four servers that I consider the best. The one I use is VpsForexTrader (highlighted in bold)

	Velia.Net	Vpsforextrader	Tradingfxvps	Forex VPS
CPU	6 cores	**6 cores**	4 cores	6 cores
RAM	64 GB	**16 GB**	16 GB	16 GB
PRICE	99 USD	**149 USD**	199 USD	175 USD

17.21 Recommendations

Finally, here are a series of important recommendations to keep in mind when creating automated trading systems:

- Think about the logic behind the system before creating your EA, and choose the type of indicators accordingly (volatility, volume, trend, etc.).
- Use the data provided by your broker to build your EA.
- The simpler the EA, the better. Don't use too many indicators during creation. The fewer the rules/indicators, the less risk of overfitting. Avoid complex systems.
- Never over-optimize an EA, as you will just be creating a system based on noise, which won't work in live trading.
- There is no perfect system, and no system will work forever. Review your system every 6 months.
- Once you've built your EA, test it on a demo account for a few months before going live.
- Start with microlots (0.01 lot), and once it has performed well in live trading, increase the position size.
- Risk-reward ratio: 3:1.
- Risk per trade: 3%.
- Use 30 min–1 h timeframes for intraday trading and daily timeframes for long-term trading.

- Save the created EAs on Dropbox on the server.
- The ATR in a bear market (BTC at 3–4k) is different from a bull market (BTC at 1–2k).
- More important than running all phases (Optimization/MC/WFO) is to launch as many strategies as possible on demo.
- Do not launch more than 30 EAs per Metatrader instance.
- There are no uniquely winning systems. You must build a portfolio of systems.
- A bad system won't work just because you apply a good money management strategy.
- If a system isn't good, don't over-optimize it.
- Don't use Martingale. Doubling your position to recover losses leads to ruin.
- A system with little capital won't behave the same as one with a lot. Volume matters.
- If you have a winning system, don't tamper with it.
- Single-indicator systems don't work.
- Systems perform better in high—but—not—extreme volatility environments.
- The optimal scenario is strong price movement in a clear direction.
- Your portfolio should include both trend-following systems (momentum, moving averages) and counter-trend systems (oscillators).
- A high number of trades in the system implies robustness.
- Only apply optimization to systems that are already profitable, not to try to make unprofitable ones profitable.
- A system that works across multiple assets is more robust than one that only works on a single asset. Try to avoid a single-asset system.
- Use low-correlation indicators to avoid multicollinearity (significant correlation between independent variables in your predictive model), thus avoiding redundant overlapping information.

METHOD:

CREATE—LAUNCH ON DEMO FOR 2-3 MONTHS—LAUNCH BEST ON LIVE—REPEAT THE PROCESS

18

Valuation Method

There are several valuation methods, but for Bitcoin, I would highlight these three:

- S2F (Stock-to-Flow)
- Metcalfe's Law (explained in Chap. 2)
- Metrics (also explained in Chap. 2)

As for the rest of the coins, I would mainly use metrics, as explained in Chap. 3.

18.1 Stock To Flow (S2F)

It is a model developed by Plan B. This model is based on the relationship between the existing supply of an asset (stock) and the amount of that asset being created (flow). If something is scarce and hard to obtain, its price rises.

It's important to note that BTC has a limited supply of 21 million, and its issuance decreases over time due to the halvings, as mining rewards are cut in half. Moreover, these characteristics are immutable and not controlled by any government, which supports the idea that their price tends to surge over time.

He has adapted his model and predictions over time, but in my opinion, the main drawback of this model is that, although its foundation is solid, the model does not take demand into account, focusing only on scarcity.

Additionally, BTC is no longer the only crypto asset in circulation, which further limits the model's ability to accurately reflect the dynamics of today's broader crypto market.

J. Pineda, *Investing in Crypto with Confidence*,
https://doi.org/10.1007/978-3-032-07834-6_18

Chart 18.1 shows the appearance of the stock-to-flow model.

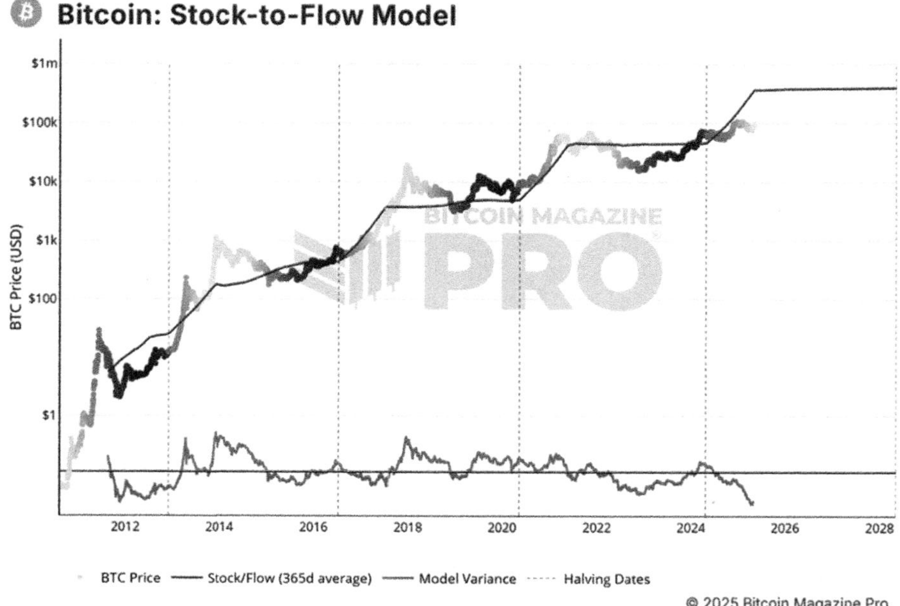

Chart 18.1 *Source* Bitcoin Magazine Pro

The SF Ratio shows an estimated price level based on the number of bitcoins available on the market relative to the number mined each year.

The colored dots on the price line of this chart represent the number of days remaining until the next Bitcoin Halving.

The line at the bottom indicates the difference between the actual Bitcoin price and the SF (Stock-to-Flow) model price.

$$SF = 19{,}714{,}581/331{,}204 = 59.524$$

$$\text{Model Price} = 0.4 \times SF^3 = 84{,}359\,USD$$

Criticism: The model does not take demand into account, focusing only on scarcity, and Bitcoin is no longer the only crypto asset in circulation.

Plan B has developed various other indicators (RSI, etc.), as shown in Chart 18.2, which you can explore through his YouTube videos or on his Twitter account:

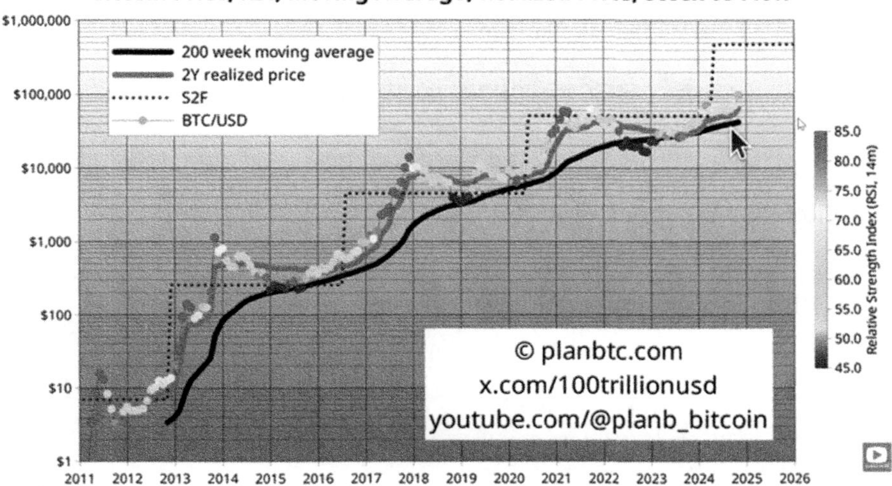

Chart 18.2   *Source* Plan B

You can find more information about this indicator on the following website:

https://charts.bitbo.io/stock-to-flow/

18.2 Metcalf Law

Used to determine the value of a telecommunications network. The value of a telecommunications network (Instagram, WhatsApp, etc.) is proportional to the square of the number of users, meaning that the network's value increases exponentially as the number of users grows.

It could be used to estimate Bitcoin's fair value, but only if users who hold Bitcoin purely for speculation are excluded, focusing instead on those who genuinely believe in it as a payment network. In the future, the number of active users will be more representative for calculating Bitcoin's fair value, as it will be widely adopted in many countries.

The number of active wallets is the closest approximation to the number of active users (although a single user can have multiple wallets): currently between 900 K and 1 M wallets, as shown in Chart 18.3.

Circulating Supply: 20 M
Bitcoin's Fair Value calculation:

$$(950\,\text{K} \times 950\,\text{K})/20\,\text{M} = 45{,}000\,\text{USD per Bitcoin}$$

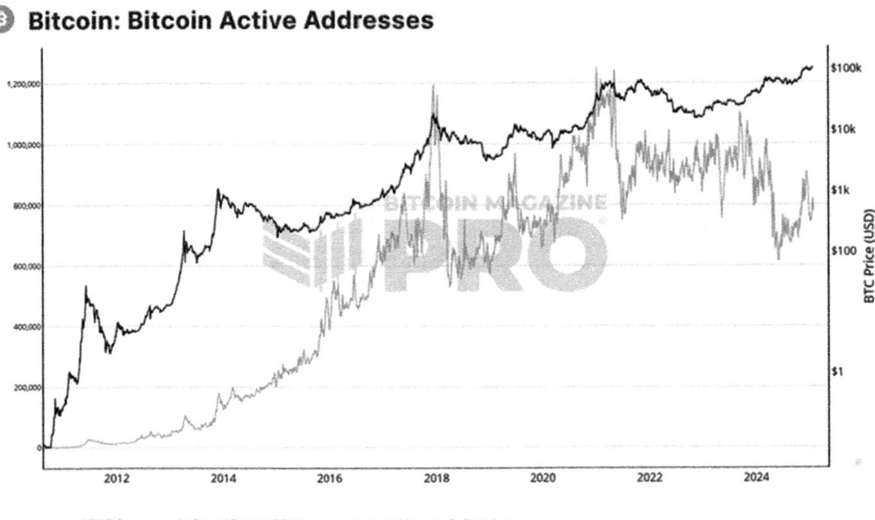

Chart 18.3 *Source* Bitcoin Magazine Pro

An increasing number of users boosts the number of connections, and consequently, the value of the network.

The main disadvantage of this method is that it values retail investors and whales equally, as it does not consider the transaction amount, only the number of active wallets.

The **Network Value** is calculated as:

$$(\text{active addresses} * \text{active addresses})/\text{circulating supply}$$

The Network Value to Metcalfe Ratio is calculated by dividing the market cap by the network value calculated using Metcalfe's Law. If the ratio is greater than 1, it means that the market is valuing bitcoin more than its network value per Metcalfe's Law, and if the ratio is less than 1, it means that the market is valuing bitcoin less than its network value.

18.3 Metrics

To evaluate a crypto project using metrics, you have two options:

1. Use a set of individual metrics.
2. Create a custom indicator that combines several of them.

Here are some metrics you can consider when evaluating the Bitcoin network:

- The **Network Value-to-Transactions Ratio (NVT)** is calculated by dividing the market cap by transaction volume. A high NVT means the bitcoin price is quoting at a premium, and a low NVT means the bitcoin price is quoting at a discount.
- The **Market Value-to-Realized Value Ratio (MVRV)** is calculated by dividing the market cap by realized capitalization. If the ratio is greater than 1, the average cost for all bitcoins is lower than the market cap, and all investors will be profitable. If the ratio is lower than 1, the average cost for all bitcoins is higher than the market cap, and all investors are incurring losses.

    You can apply a standard deviation to this ratio to determine when the market is overvalued (red zone) or undervalued (green zone) relative to its fair value.

    This calculation gives us the MVRV Z-Score. Chart 18.4 shows the appearance of this metric.

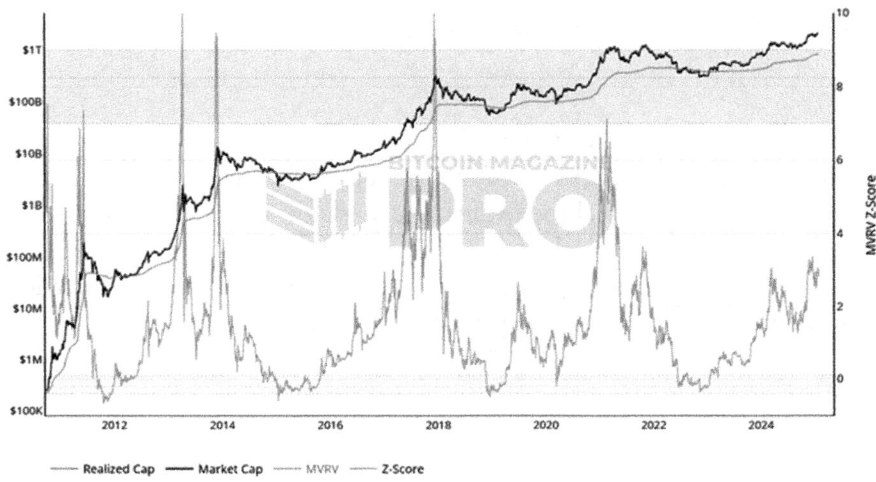

Chart 18.4 *Source* Bitcoin Magazine Pro

- **Net Unrealized Profit Loss (NUPL)**: calculated by subtracting Realized Value from Market Value, we calculate Unrealized Profit/Loss.

  Market Value is the current price of Bitcoin multiplied by the number of coins in circulation.

Realized Value takes the price of each Bitcoin when it was last moved, i.e., the last time it was sent from one wallet to another. It then multiplies that price by the total number of coins in circulation.

Chart 18.5 shows the appearance of this metric.

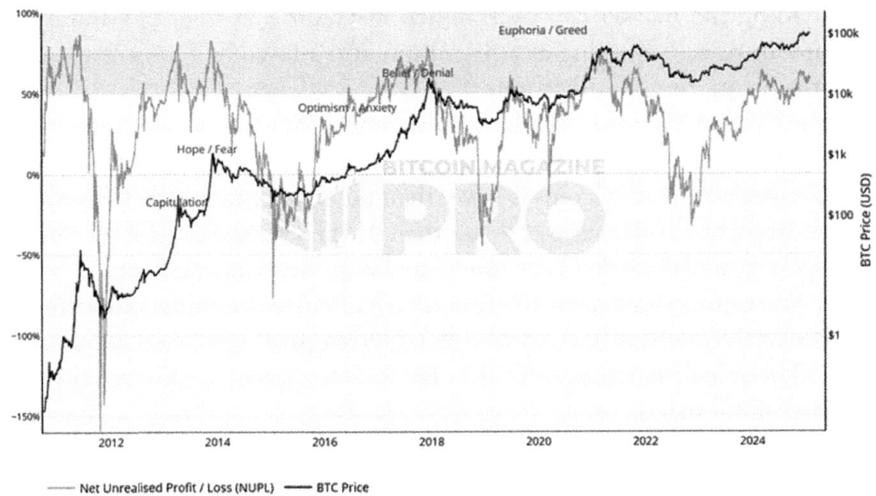

Chart 18.5   *Source* Bitcoin Magazine Pro

If there are large unrealized profits and potential for profit taking, then the market is overheated, and it will be the top of the bull run.

If there are low unrealized profits, the market is undervalued and will be at the bottom of a bear market.

As we have seen in the previous chapters, there are many more metrics that can be used to determine the price of a cryptocurrency.

18.3.1 Market Indicator V1

Using API data, I have created a **MARKET INDICATOR** based on various metrics, as shown in Chart 18.6, which helps identify whether the market is near the top of a bull run or the bottom of a bear market.

The indicator includes the following metrics:

- NUPL
- MVRV Z Score
- Terminal Price
- VDD Multiple
- Puell Multiple

As we can observe, when the market is at a bull run peak or a bear market bottom, the indicator enters the green/red zones.

- If it enters the green zone, it indicates that the market is overbought, which is typically when bull market tops occur.
- If it enters the red zone, it indicates the market is oversold, which is usually when bear market bottoms take place.

As of January 2025, we are still far from those levels, which suggests that we have not yet reached the bull run peak, and the market is not ready to reverse.

- The overbought zone is between 25 and 35.
- The oversold zone is between −5 and −15.

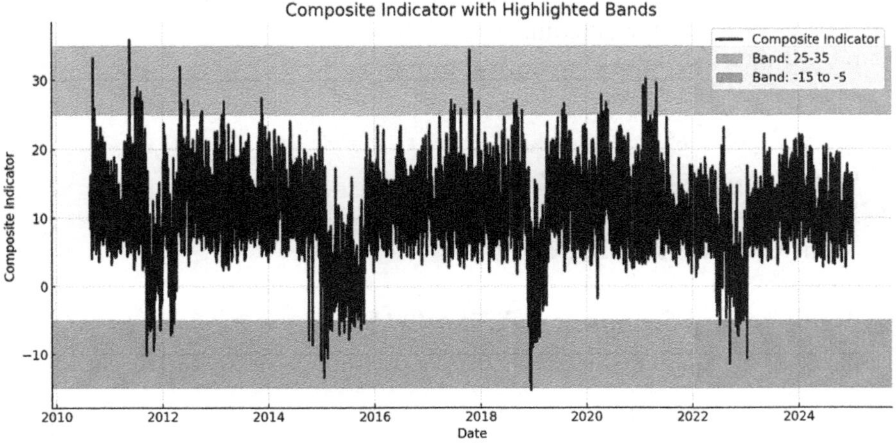

Chart 18.6 *Source* ChatGPT with Bitcoin Magazine Pro data

I'm attaching the Bitcoin price chart in a weekly timeframe to show that when it reached bull run peaks (Dec'17–Apr/Nov'21) or bear market bottoms (Dec'18–Nov'22), this indicator was in overbought or oversold territory, as shown in Chart 18.7:

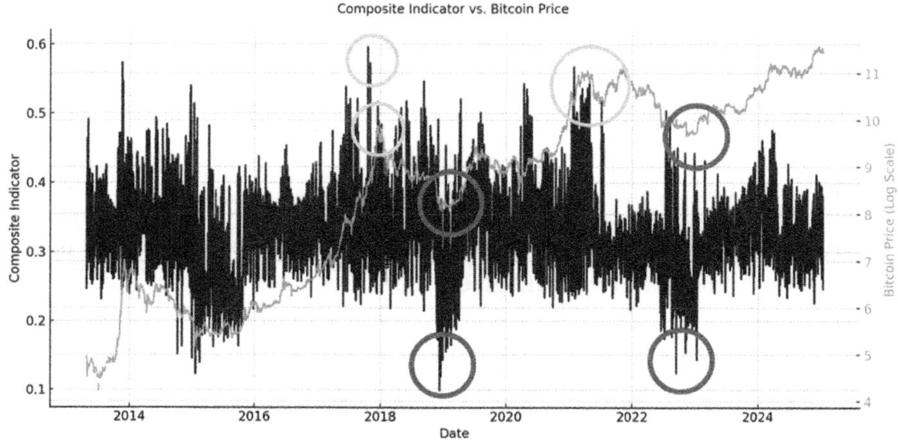

Chart 18.7   *Source* ChatGPT with Bitcoin Magazine Pro data

18.3.2 Market Indicator V2

Another indicator could be composed of the following metrics, which I have named MARKET INDICATOR 2, as shown in Chart 18.8.

The result is a reactive, historically reliable oscillator that identifies market peaks and bottoms for Bitcoin.

It combines the following critical inputs:

- MVRV Z-Score
- Global M2 Money Supply
- Puell Multiple
- Spent Output Profit Ratio (SOPR)
- Crosby Ratio
- Active Address Sentiment Indicator (AASI)

In the following chart, we can see this indicator alongside Bitcoin's price on a weekly timeframe, showing that when the market reached the bull run peak (Apr'21) or the bear market bottoms (Dec'18–Nov'22), the indicator was in overbought or oversold territory, as shown in Chart 18.8:

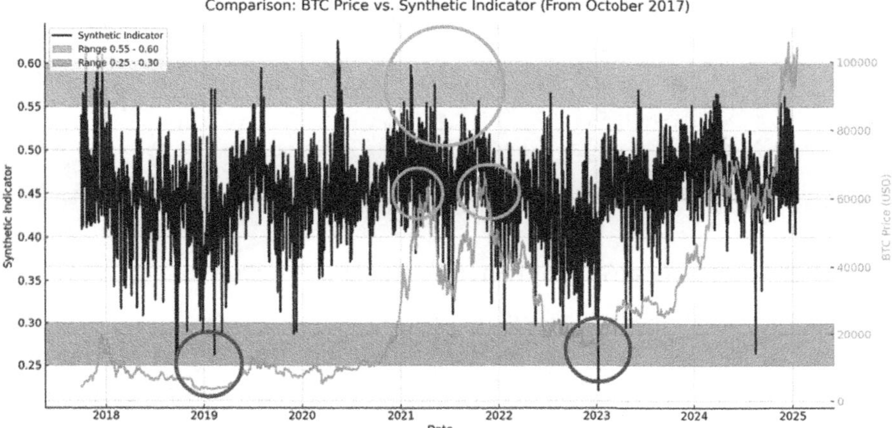

Chart 18.8   *Source* ChatGPT with Bitcoin Magazine Pro data

18.3.3 Volatility Indicator

I have also created a Volatility Indicator, based on the following metrics, since periods of volatility compression or expansion often have a strong relationship with the direction of the price:

- Funding rates Average
- Hashprice Volatility
- Advanced NVT Signal
- Bitcoin Volatility

As can be seen in Chart 18.9, when the Volatility Indicator enters the lower zone, it is usually followed by a bullish rally. When it enters the upper zone, it is typically followed by a bearish rally.

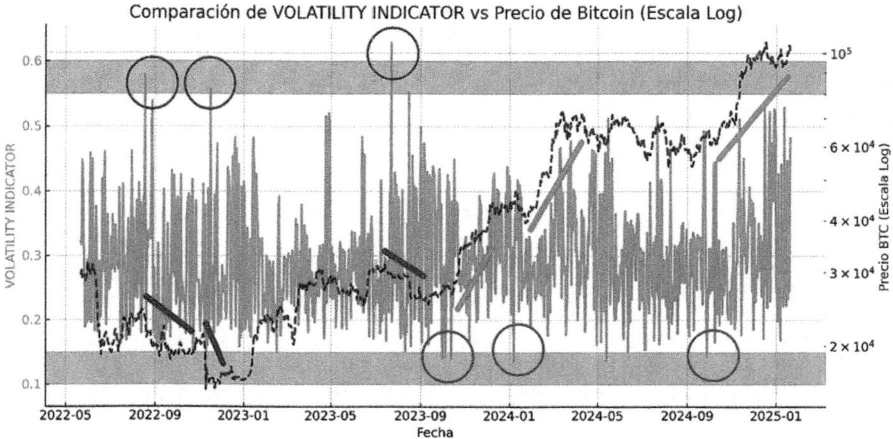

Chart 18.9   *Source* ChatGPT with Bitcoin Magazine Pro data

You can also calculate a Z-score for the indicator, as you are analyzing cycles, historical highs, and lows. This allows you to represent it in a way that highlights unusually high or low values compared to the historical average. It would be displayed on a scale from -1 to $+2$, where zero indicates average behavior, values near $+2$ suggest overheating, and values near -1 indicate a potential buying opportunity.

I also added two SMAs: one with 34 periods (blue) and another with 144 periods (red) to observe the crossover between them. As of June 2025, we can see in Chart 18.10 that the short-term average is above the long-term average.

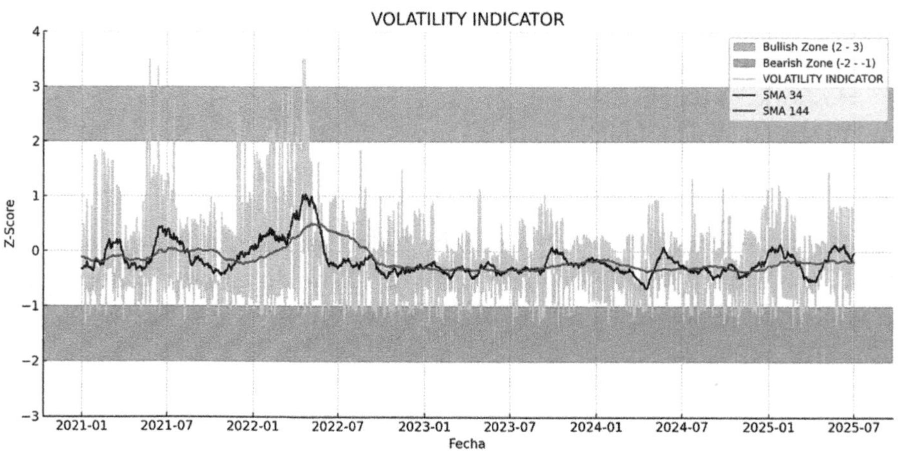

Chart 18.10   *Source* ChatGPT with Bitcoin Magazine Pro data

18.3.4   Final Evaluation of a Cryptocurrency

You need to take several aspects into account when evaluating a crypto currency:

1. Phase of the market cycle we are in
2. Macroeconomic data (U.S. employment, U.S. GDP, Fed interest rates, Global M2 Money Supply)
3. Bitcoin fundamentals
4. On-chain metrics
5. Technical analysis

I recommend creating a table and assigning a weight to each of these factors in order to help guide your decision regarding the project you're evaluating. For example:

- Market cycle phase—30%
- Macroeconomic data—10%
- Bitcoin fundamentals—20%
- On-chain metrics—20%
- Technical analysis—10%
- Social media & roadmap—10%

If the total score is:

- Above 0.7 → Buy
- Between 0.4 and 0.7 → Hold
- Below 0.3 → Sell

Note: If the project you are evaluating is Bitcoin, the fundamentals and on-chain metrics are essentially the same, and you would not take social media or roadmap into account. In that case, the weighting could be as follows:

- Market cycle phase—30%
- Macroeconomic data—20%
- On-chain metrics—25%
- Technical analysis—25%

18.4 Valuation Method

To develop a valuation method, you must consider the following five key areas. The proposed weighing and composition of these main areas would be:

On-Chain Metrics/Cycle – 30%
This area defines whether the market is undervalued, neutral, or overvalued. Depending on market conditions, portfolio exposure will be more aggressive or more conservative.

Within this area, you can select the following metrics:

Puell Multiple, VDD Multiple, Bitcoin Cycle Capital Flows, NUPL, Hash Ribbons, Short-Term Holder Realized Price, etc.

Momentum – 25%
This area defines trend and timing, i.e., when to enter, exit, and position size.

Within this area, you can select the following metrics:

Stablecoin Exchange Net Position Change, SMA 365–720p, ETF Flows, Long-Term Holder Supply, Stablecoin Dominance, etc.

Sentiment – 15%
This area defines who is positioned in the market and how.

Within this area, you can select the following metrics:

Liquidation Map, Total Futures Liquidations, Funding Rates, CME Open Interest, etc.

Macro – 15%
This area defines risk appetite and global liquidity.

Within this area, you can select the following metrics:

Federal Reserve Balance Sheet, DXY, M2, etc.

Altcoin Index – 15%
This area indicates internal market rotation, i.e., whether more weight should be allocated to Bitcoin, Ethereum, or altcoins.

Within this area, you can select the following metrics:

ETH/BTC, ETH MVRV Z-Score, Altcoin Season Index, etc.

This area is never given weight if Bitcoin momentum is not positive.

Finally, you assign the weighting you consider appropriate to each individual metric.

MARKET SCENARIOS:

Based on different market scenarios, the following alerts and example portfolios can be defined:

Early Bull Market

ETH/BTC starts to rise, BTC momentum is positive with low volatility, and on-chain metrics are undervalued.

A possible portfolio allocation would be:

- BTC 60%
- ETH 25%
- Altcoins 10%
- Stablecoins 5%

Altseason

ETH/BTC in an uptrend, with strong BTC momentum, and neutral on-chain metrics.

A possible portfolio allocation would be:

- BTC 30%
- ETH 30%
- Altcoins 35%
- Stablecoins 5%

Bull Market Peak (Euphoria)

Extreme bullish sentiment, BTC momentum remains positive with high volatility, and on-chain metrics indicate overvaluation.

A possible portfolio allocation would be:

- BTC 40%
- ETH 15%
- Altcoins 5%
- Stablecoins 40%

Bear Market

Restrictive macro conditions, negative BTC momentum, and on-chain metrics signaling capitulation.

A possible portfolio allocation would be:

- BTC 25%4
- ETH 0%
- Altcoins 0%
- Stablecoins 75%

19

NFT

19.1 Definition of NFT

An NFT is a Non-Fungible Token, meaning it is not divisible.

It represents intellectual property, which is:

* Unforgeable
* Transparent
* Immutable

The term 'minting' refers to the process of creating or issuing a digital asset on a blockchain. If it is not minted, the NFT is not recorded on the blockchain, and it will not be possible to verify its authenticity, ownership, or origin.

Minting usually refers to the moment when an entire NFT collection is released at once, and one is assigned to you randomly.

You can view upcoming mints on this website:

* whatsminting.live

19.2 Ways to Access an NFT

There are three ways to gain access:

© The Author(s), under exclusive license to Springer Nature Switzerland AG 2026

J. Pineda, *Investing in Crypto with Confidence*,

https://doi.org/10.1007/978-3-032-07834-6_19

- WHITELIST: This is the launch phase of an NFT collection that allows projects to reward early supporters by letting them mint the first pieces of the collection.

  - Via Raffle: https://www.premint.xyz

- PUBLIC SALE: The phase where the collection is launched on a marketplace.

If you increase the gas fee, you can move ahead of other users in the minting queue and secure a better position (auction-style).

- SECONDARY MARKET: Buying from another user who previously acquired the NFT.

19.3 NFT Markets

- Opensea.io(Eth Wallet):

  - Top 1
  - Metamask Wallet
  - Lazy minting (minting fees are paid by the buyer, not the creator)
  - You can upload a collection for free using the Polygon network
  - Free NFT collection creation without needing to know how to code
  - Create, buy, and sell NFTs on a single platform

- Magiceden.io (Sol):

  - Leader in Solana-based NFTs (90% of the market)
  - Also offers Ethereum-based NFTs
  - Easy to use
  - Low transaction fees (2%)
  - No listing or offer fees, only a transaction fee
  - Popular collections: quickly view the most popular and trending collections
  - Create, buy, and sell NFTs on a single platform
  - However, it uses closed-source software

- Solanart (Sol):

  - No fees
  - Marketplace

- Rarible.com (ETH):

  - Artwork
  - No listing fees
  - Transaction fee: 2.5%
  - Royalties up to 50% (the amount the creator receives after the initial sale of an NFT; others offer only 15%)
  - Lazy minting (you create your NFT without paying gas fees upfront)

    (*) With lazy minting, you don't actually create the NFT right away; the item appears on the marketplace and is only minted when the sale occurs.

  - Marketplace

- SuperRare.com(Eth): Art

  - One-of-a-kind pieces
  - Transaction fee: 3%
  - You fill out a form, and they decide whether you're accepted
  - Creators receive 85% of their first sale (SuperRare keeps 15%)
  - 10% royalty on secondary sales

- Foundation.app(Eth):

  - Digital art collections
  - Invitation required to join
  - Creators receive 85% of their first sale (15% goes to Foundation)
  - 10% royalty on each subsequent transaction

- Niftygateway.com:

  - Art
  - Hard to get into
  - Best reputation
  - They partner with artists and brands to create exclusive and limited-edition collections

- For every secondary sale, the artist earns 10%
- The platform charges a 5% commission on the sale price

• Ethernity.io (Eth):

- Sports
- A-NFTs: Authenticated NFTs verified by their creators and endorsed by popular figures, allowing users to know the NFT's origin, minting date, and the celebrity backing it. This enhances the collectible value of the artwork

19.4 Analytics Tools

These tools are used to analyze new collections, trending collections, statistics (volume, sales, floor price), and minting collections.
Among them we have:

• Nftnerds.ai:

- Alerts to detect a new listing from a collection
- Customize filters to follow only the collections you're interested in
- Provides information to identify the rarest (most valuable) NFTs. Rarity Ranking
- Trending collections (volume, sales, floor price)
- Real-time statistics

• Traitsniper.com:

- Detects NFTs with incorrect prices that are bargains
- Identifies the most desirable NFTs in a collection
- Scans collections and ranks NFTs by rarity level

• Dune.com:

- Open-source platform specialized in on-chain data analysis (NFTs, DeFi apps, etc.)
- Supports data from Ethereum and Binance Smart Chain networks
- Free real-time data provider for DeFi projects, NFTs, and crypto ecosystems
- Offers tools to perform complex queries

   – Plans available for private queries, CSV export, or faster search speeds.

- Flips. finance
- Icy tools: find whale wallets and track them on Dune

19.5 NFT Investment Strategies

- **TRENDING:**

To find out which collection is trending the most, you can use the web https://www.nftnerds.ai:

- Pay attention to the most active collections:
  - 5 min volume
  - 5 min sales
  - Increasing number of sales
- Go to Opensea.io, click on the collection, and select the Activity (sales) tab.
- Whales usually make sales with high volume. Go to their account and check what they're buying.

Figure 19.1 shows the appearance of the website https://www.nftnerds.ai

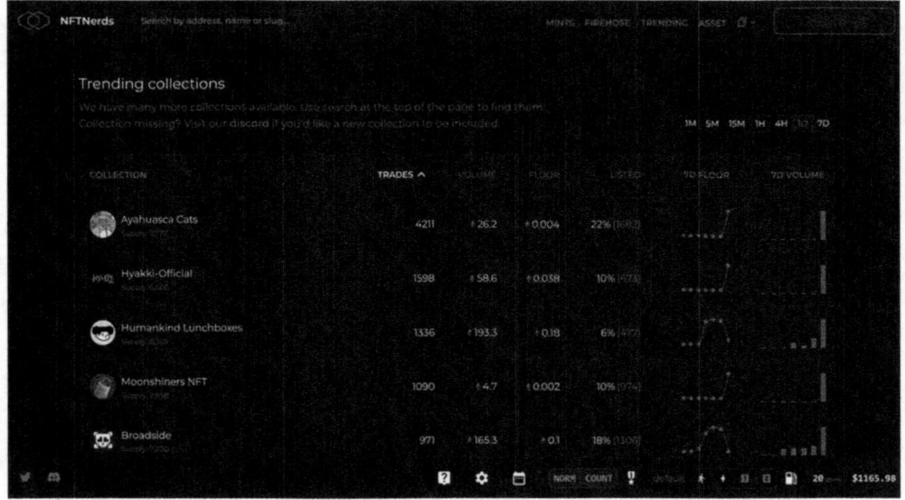

Fig. 19.1 *Source* nftnerds.ai

- **FLIPING:**

This strategy involves buying an NFT below its actual value and reselling it. To do this, go to the following website:

- **Web traitsniper.com**

  - Alerts for any relevant changes
  - NFT search by trait, rank, and price
  - Platform integrated with Metamask and OpenSea
  - Notifications for new listings
  - Launchpad for small new NFT projects (advisory, contract creation)
  - Whitelist marketplace

19.6 Wallets

- SOLANA Network:

  - Phantom
  - Solfare

- ETHEREUM Network:

  - Metamask
  - Myetherwallet

19.7 Scams

1. Discord Scams

- They trick you into giving up your password or access to your collection.
- They impersonate your friends or official collections, sending you direct messages asking you to mint your NFT, and then steal it. Always use the official channel of the collection.

2. Minting on Fake Websites/Fake Marketplaces (Phishing)

- They create a website identical to the official one. You might think it's real, lose your NFT, and in some cases, they drain your entire wallet.

3. Rug Pulls

* Very hard to detect. Example: Evolved Apes—the founder disappeared with \$2.7 million USD.

4. Fake Profiles/Identity Impersonation

* Scammers impersonate known collectors or influencers to gain your trust.

5. Fake Giveaways, Gifts, and Offers

* Too-good-to–be-true airdrops or offers often aim to get access to your wallet.

6. Pump and Dump Schemes

* The collection is concentrated in a few wallets. They artificially inflate the price through social media hype, then sell everything, crashing the value.
NEVER Share Your Passwords or Wallet Seed Phrases.

19.8 NFT Collection

The first thing you need to be clear about is the characteristics your NFT should have:

* It should feel relatable
* It must be original
* Avoid large/complex backgrounds
* Use flat backgrounds without strong colors
* The illustration should have one color on the top and another on the bottom
* No highlights or shadows
* Example: Krapopolis Krap Chichenks was unsuccessful because it wasn't engaging as a profile picture—it didn't feel relatable, the image was small, etc.

Once you're clear about the characteristics of the NFT you're going to create, you need to define the Niche and the Format.

19.8.1 Niche and Format

- Niche:

  - Art: You need to have strong drawing skills
  - Avatars: A very saturated market (e.g., CryptoPunks, Bored Apes, etc.)
  - Digital Trading Cards: Collectibles, like sports or fantasy cards
  - Memes
  - Digital Toys
  - Digital Food: e.g., sushi-themed NFTs
  - Merchandising
  - Objects (unique or conceptual digital items)

- Format:

  - 2D
  - 3D
  - Video
  - Pixel Art

Mistakes that can lead to a collection's failure:

- Not understanding what collectors in that niche are looking for
- Not knowing how many people are actually interested in that niche (use tools like Google Trends)
- The collection fails to generate interest, emotion, or connection
- Copying other existing collections

19.8.2 Community

To make your collection successful, you need community support:

- TWITTER:

  - The most important community platform
  - There must be regular activity
  - How to Build a Community:

    Search for NFT collections
    Follow them, retweet their content
    Send them private messages inviting them to check out your collection

- DISCORD:

  – Once you've built a community on Twitter, create a Discord server.
  – Try to move your Twitter community over to Discord.
  – If you don't have a community on Discord, your collection will likely fail—anyone who joins your channel and sees no engagement or support will not feel confident enough to buy.

19.8.3 Launch

When launching your collection, keep the following in mind:

- Have everything ready (website, completed collection, etc.)
- Launch it on the Ethereum network (ETH)—it's the most professional and stable (with fewer network outages).
- Launch with a low gas fee, making it cheaper for you to mint and for buyers to purchase.

  – Gas fees depend on the network's congestion level.
  – Check the current gas fee on https://www.etherscan.io → More → Explore → Gas Tracker.
  – Ensure there isn't a major product launch that day.
  – Check nftcalendar.io.

- Ideal Market Conditions:

  – Launch when the market is **sideways but volatile**.
  – Avoid launching when BTC is going up (holders won't sell their crypto to buy NFTs) or going down (buyers fear losing value after purchasing).

One piece of advice I can give you is to look for references:

- Look at the top-selling collections on OpenSea and use them as inspiration. Don't copy.
- Find design references on https://www.behance.net
- Choose one collection reference and one design reference to guide your style.

19.8.4 NFT Price

When deciding what price to set for your NFT, keep the following in mind:

- Key Factors:

    - Whether or not you're well-known in the community
    - If the royalty fee is high, the base price can be lower, and vice versa
    - The platform where you'll be selling:

        OpenSea is cheaper due to the high number of collections
        SuperRare is more expensive but harder to get into

    - The level of detail in the artwork
    - The number of pieces in the collection

        The more pieces, the lower the price should be

- The price must at least cover your basic costs:

    - Web 3.0 setup
    - Artwork and design
    - Smart contract development
    - Graphic designer
    - Community/social media moderator

- Suggested Pricing (for collection of 5–10k items):

    - If you're not well-known and haven't invested much in marketing or influencers, your price should be around **0.1 ETH—0.2 ETH**

19.8.5 Minting Strategies

- **Minting on a Marketplace**

    - You need a large community for this to be successful
    - Avoid this strategy if you've invested a lot of time and effort in your collection, as you'll be competing with many others and may go unnoticed

- **Public minting on your own website:**

  - Ideal for large collections
  - You need a Web 3.0-enabled website
  - You must have a smart contract created and linked (typically $20,000)

- **Pre-sale + public minting on website:**

  - To sell NFTs at a lower price during the pre-sale than in the public sale, you need:

    > A well-developed strategy
    > A Discord server with an active community
    > Pre-sale buyers get a discounted price compared to public buyers
    > To access the pre-sale, users must join a whitelist, which requires doing promotional tasks such as:
    > Making YouTube videos
    > Inviting friends
    > Retweeting and liking posts on Twitter

  - This gives your collection free publicity
  - You collect wallet addresses and allow only whitelisted users to mint
  - Leave a few days between pre-sale and public mint
  - You must already have the smart contract created

- **Two Pre-sale + Public Mint**

  - Used for very large collections
  - Allows you to split launches into phases (e.g., Whitelist 1 and Whitelist 2)

- **Free Minting:**

  - You don't earn anything from the initial sale, but reach Sold Out status quickly
  - Your profit comes from secondary sales (typically 5–7% royalties)
  - Requires a strong Twitter community to generate traction
  - Users are willing to mint for free and then resell to recover the gas fee
  - Risk: There may be no secondary market sales, and you earn nothing

- Strategy to increase Price: Price Manipulation

  Buy NFTs on Opensea from original minters to raise the floor price

  Launch a new collection and let holders swap two old NFTs for one new one

  You then buy NFTs from the new collection yourself to increase the floor price

  Users migrate from the old to the new collection and start trading again—you earn royalties on the new trades

19.8.6 Naming—Branding

- Naming:

  - Use words like crypto or NFT
  - Do not copy existing names
  - When choosing a name for your collection, check if the domain is available so you can create a website with the same name

- Branding:

  - Define your brand image
  - Choose the right typography
  - Use resources like https://www.dribbble.com for design inspiration

19.8.7 How to Create a Website

- Information your website should include:

  - Explanation of the collection
  - Links to Twitter and Discord
  - Roadmap
  - Core team (photos and real names)
  - Blockchain network (ETH/SOL)
  - Marketplace where the NFTs will be listed
  - FAQ (Frequently Asked Questions):

    How to join the whitelist

    Will there be a pre-sale?

    Public minting cost

    NFT price during pre-sale

    Which blockchain network will be used

The site must be Web 3.0 compatible and have a smart contract in place, allowing users to mint NFTs directly from your website.

19.8.8 Roadmap

The roadmap is the strategic plan outlining the milestones your project will achieve.

- Avoid using fixed dates; use percentages (%) instead
- Each time a milestone is reached (e.g., 25%, 50%), unlock a goal
- Include donations, e.g., "At 25% completion, we will donate XX BTC to a charity
- Host in-person events for holders
- Connect your collection to the metaverse (e.g., buy land or build a virtual space)
- Include collaborations with other NFT collections and their communities

19.8.9 Twitter Strategies

- Your NFT collection must have a Twitter account

  - Optimize your profile: include the name of the collection, profile picture, banner, and a bio with key details (blockchain, number of items, and Discord link)

- Follow top NFT influencers and users in the space
- Don't follow more than 20–30 accounts per day to avoid getting your account restricted
- Use hashtags to increase visibility
- Create three unique hashtags for your collection—they should be catchy, recognizable, and reflect your project
- Also use popular industry hashtags (e.g., #NFT, #NFTdrop, #NFTCommunity)
- Retweet your own tweets, reply to users, and start conversations
- Do collabs and promos with other NFT creators (shilling)—e.g., "I'll give you an NFT if you talk about my collection
- Organize giveaways and contests

- Use NFT slang/language, such as:

  - GM (Good Morning)
  - DM (Direct Message)
  - GMI (Gonna Make It)
  - AMA (Ask Me Anything)
  - DYOR (Do Your Own Research)
  - MINT (to mint an NFT)

- Content Calendar:

  - Use tools like hootsuite.com
  - Example schedule:

    3–5 tweets per day
    Share a preview image of a new NFT
    Announce whitelist dates

19.8.10 Instagram Strategies

- Optimize your profile (use the same profile picture and branding as on Twitter)
- Highlight important dates (giveaways, whitelist openings, mint date, etc.)
- Showcase NFTs from your collection
- Go live to engage directly with your audience
- Upload eye-catching videos
- Repost content from your Instagram Stories
- Posting frequency: 1 post per day leading up to the mint date
- Follow people in the NFT space on Instagram

19.8.11 Discord Strategies

- Information Group:

  - Rules channel (no racism, no pornography, no insults, etc.)
  - Announcements channel
  - Official links channel
  - Utilities and benefits channel
  - Roadmap channel
  - Giveaways channel

- Community Group:

  - Chat channel (with a moderator)
  - Sneak-peek channel: for sharing new NFT designs from the collection
  - Fan art channel: followers can create their own designs inspired by your collection, post them on social media, and you can retweet them. They can also upload them to the sneak-peek channel
  - Memes channel

- Voice Channel Group:

  - AMA voice channel (Ask Me Anything sessions)

- Support Group:

  - FAQ channel: include the same questions and answers as on the website
  - Support channel: The moderator must filter spam from real issues
  - Suggestions channel

19.8.12 Smart Contract

- To Hire People for the Project (artists, etc.):

  - https://www.fiverr.com
  - https://www.behance.net
  - https://www.artstation.com/?sort_by=community

- To create an NFT:

  - https://www.bueno.art (Ethereum network)—they charge a 5% fee
  - Go to "Manage" and create the different parts of the character separately
  - Then go to "Create Collection" and drag and drop all those individual parts
  - Upload the collection to IPFS

- To Create a Smart Contract:

  - https://www.bueno.art
  - https://www.manifold.xyz

19.8.13 Photo

- Choose a Photo and Resize It:

  - https://www.canva.com
  - https://www.resize-image.net

- What size should you choose?

  - NFT Pixl Art: 32 × 32px
  - NFT Art Dimensions:

    Twitter: 600 × 600px, max file size 5Mb
    Facebook:
    Cover photo: 820 × 312px
    Profile Picture: 640 × 360px
    Instagram:
    Square 1080 × 1080px
    Portrait 1080 × 1350px
    Landscape 1080 × 608px

  - Recommended sizes: 640px, 840px or 1080px
  - Maximum NFT Art File sizes by platform:

    Rarible 10mb
    Opensea 100mb
    Mintable 300 mg

- **PIXILART.COM**
- **NFT-GENERATOR.ART**
- **FOTOR.COM/NFT-CREATOR**

19.8.14 Recommendations

Tips for Launching a Successful NFT Project:

- Study a successful project: Look at how it started on Twitter and Discord, analyze the evolution of its posts—this will give you a clear idea of what successful projects actually do
- Create your collection on the Ethereum network
- Research what type of art is most in demand

- Launch the collection with low gas fees, and when the market is moving sideways
- Build a community on Twitter and Discord before launch
- Set a reasonable price between 0.1 and 0.2 ETH
- Create a solid website
- Follow through with your roadmap
- Be active on social media and engage with your community

19.9 Other NFT Websites

Other interesting websites would be the following:

- SCHEDULE SOCIAL MEDIA POSTS:

  - Hootsuite.com

- CALENDAR OF UPCOMING COLLECTIONS:

  - Nftcalendar.io

- LIST OF AIRDROPS:

  - Airdrops.io: Free NFT distribution in exchange for social media marketing

- DISCOVERY TOOLS (whitelist):

  - Cryptoscores.io: upcoming projects give you an idea of where the NFT market is heading and current trends. A quantitative NFT analysis tool.
  - Nftgo.io: whale tracking tool.

- AUTOMATION TOOLS:

  - Nft Pirates.io:

    Bid Bot: The goal is to get a discount on the floor price by placing multiple automatic offers below the floor price.
    Sniper Bot: Buys NFTs listed at a significantly lower price than they should be due to the owner making a pricing mistake.

  - Rarity.tools: rarity tracker.

- SNIPING TOOLS:

  - Nftnerds.ai: shows floor price of new listings before OpenSea, and trending collections.
  - Traitsniper.com: rarity rankings, mispriced NFT.
  - Ninjalerts.com (Red Eth): tracks whale and influencer wallets and sends real-time mobile notifications. Includes analytics tools for each wallet and highlights trending NFTs.

    https://opensea.io/collection/ninjalerts-lifetime-license

- NFT PORTFOLIO VALUATION:

  - NFT Bank.ai
  - Wgmi.io

    https://opensea.io/collection/wgmi-premium-membership

  - Dappradar.com
  - Zerion.io
  - Zapper.fi

20

Criticisms of Bitcoin

I will mention the three most representative criticisms made of Bitcoin, especially by its detractors.

20.1 Criticism Number 1

Bitcoin has no intrinsic value:

It's true that Bitcoin does not have intrinsic value in the traditional sense, as it doesn't generate cash flows or pay dividends, since it's not a company. The same applies to gold.

The value of an asset is determined by its ability to serve these three functions:

- Medium of Exchange
- Store of value
- Unit of account

Gold is often considered to have intrinsic value because it has uses beyond being a store of value. However, the percentage of gold used for jewelry, electronics, etc., is minimal compared to its use as a store of value. Its price mainly depends on that role.

Therefore, the fact that Bitcoin doesn't have intrinsic value doesn't diminish its importance or value.

J. Pineda, *Investing in Crypto with Confidence*,
https://doi.org/10.1007/978-3-032-07834-6_20

Although one of Bitcoin's functions is as a medium of exchange, **its primary function is actually as a store of value,** which is why it is often referred to as digital gold.

20.2 Criticism Number 2

Bitcoin cannot scale or process the number of transactions required in the case of mass adoption:

BTC processes an average of 3 to 5 transactions per second (TPS). Clearly, this is not sufficient for global mass adoption or for its use as a medium of exchange, especially considering that VISA processes 40,000 transactions per second.

The limiting factor of the Bitcoin network is determined by:

- Block size
- Block time

The solution is not to simply increase the block size or reduce the time between blocks, as this would lead to the centralization of the network. Only a few users or entities would be able to run the software due to the high hardware and bandwidth requirements.

The solution to increase the scalability of the Bitcoin network would be the creation of a second layer (Layer 2), where users can make payments to each other on a peer-to-peer network without needing to publish every transaction on the Bitcoin blockchain.

Only the initial deposit of bitcoins and the final settlement would use the Bitcoin blockchain, meaning that only these two transactions (deposit and final state) need to be validated and stored by Bitcoin nodes.

20.3 Criticism Number 3

Bitcoin wastes a lot of energy:

Bitcoin consumes a significant amount of energy, which is true. However, many other industries consume even more, and no one questions them. For example, household air conditioning or clothes dryers are accepted because they serve valuable functions in our daily lives.

The difference is that Bitcoin has not yet become a socially accepted tool that performs an essential function, at least not for those living in developed countries.

It is estimated that over 300 million people worldwide own Bitcoin, and not all of them live in developed countries.

For those living in developing nations, Bitcoin has become essential. Access to the traditional financial system is very limited, and many individuals are excluded because they do not meet the minimum requirements.

According to studies by MicroStrategy, Bitcoin mining accounts for less than 0.08% of global CO_2 emissions and is the fastest-growing industry in terms of clean energy adoption.

Chart 20.1 shows that Bitcoin's energy consumption is lower than that of many other industries, which allows it to remain secure and decentralized.

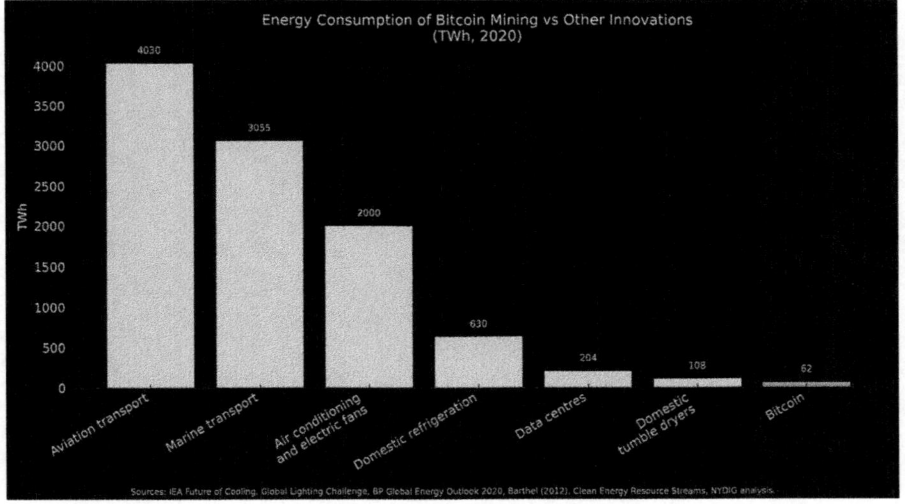

Chart 20.1 *Source* IEA Future of Cooling, Global Lighting Challenge, BP Global Energy Outlook 2020, Barthel (2012), Clean Energy Resource Streams, NYDIG analysis

One mistake is to lump all cryptocurrencies together with Bitcoin. Bitcoin is more energy-intensive than other cryptocurrencies because its mining method, Proof of Work (PoW), requires much energy.

However, over 90% of cryptocurrencies are mined or validated using a different method called Proof of Stake (PoS). It is not energy-intensive since it requires very little electricity to validate transactions.

For example, Ethereum, which initially used PoW and later transitioned to PoS, reduced its electricity consumption by more than 99%.

21

Recommendations

In this chapter, I will provide a summary of the most important aspects to consider when investing in cryptocurrencies.

21.1 Aspects to Consider Before Investing

- Know which MARKET PHASE you're in
- Identify and follow TRENDING NARRATIVES (AI/AI Agents, RWA, Layer 2—Base, Arbitrum, Linea—, Blockchains like SUI, HBAR, Memecoins, etc.)
- Choose the RIGHT TOOLS FOR ANALYSIS:

  - General market analysis: CoinMarketCap, CoinGecko
  - Technical analysis: TradingView
  - On-chain metrics: Bitcoin Magazine Pro, Glassnode, CryptoQuant
  - DeFi protocol analysis (TVL): DeFiLlama
  - ETF behavior and metrics analysis: Coinglass, Farside Investors
  - Social analysis and project marketing impact: LunarCrush, Santiment

- Know WHEN TO SELL: Use all the abovementioned tools to identify when the bull run top is nearby. Sell your initial investment plus some profit and let the rest ride with tightly adjusted take profits. Use averaged exits when selling.

J. Pineda, *Investing in Crypto with Confidence*,
https://doi.org/10.1007/978-3-032-07834-6_21

21.2 Method for Selecting a Cryptocurrency

- Make a list of crypto projects to research. Focus on one category.

    - https://cryptorank.io/categories

- Follow Venture Capital companies and see which projects they are investing in.

    - On cryptorank.io/search, look for "ventures". Example: https://cryptorank.io/funds/coinbase-ventures
    - On cryptorank.io, click on filters, and under fund, select ventures.

- Select the projects with the lowest market cap within the sector/category.
- On Defillama.com, select those with high TVL and a Mcap/TVL ratio below 1. These are undervalued, and their market cap should grow.
- On Dappradar.com, select games with many users and a low market cap.

    - Click on the game and check the 30-day stats trend: (increasing/decreasing)

        Active wallets (users)
        Transactions
        Volume
        Balance

Figure 21.1 shows the appearance of the website https://www.dappradar.com

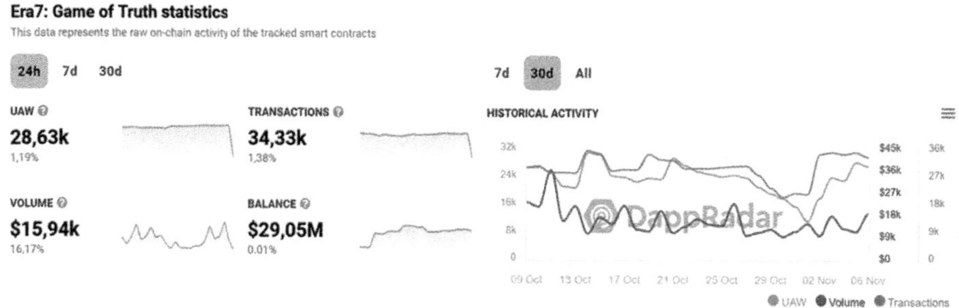

Fig. 21.1 *Source* Dappradar.com

- Analyze social media growth (Twitter, Telegram, and Discord):

  - Go to Coingecko.com → Overview → Social
  - Check if they are active on social media
  - See if their follower count is increasing
  - Check if they update their website with news

- Analyze transactions and holders:

  - Go to CoinMarketCap → More Info → Analysis

- Check Bitcoin sentiment:

  - Use the Fear and Greed Index

- On-chain metrics to determine what kind of market we're in:

  - Net Unrealized Profit/Loss (NUPL)
  - Realized Price
  - Dormancy
  - Exchange Balance
  - Pi Cycle Indicator

- Timing
- Which exchanges is it listed on
- Check upcoming projects on coinmarket**cal**.com

21.3 Aspects to Analyze in a Cryptocurrency

- Website:

  - Quality
  - Information
  - Token utility
  - Roadmap (are they meeting their goals?)
  - The management team is visible on the website

- Social media:

  - Twitter followers (are they active?)
  - Discord (is the community active?)

- Which brokers it is listed on:

  - DEX = less secure (scam?) than CEX
  - More upside potential if it's not yet listed on a CEX
  - Check whether it's going to be announced on Binance soon—buy the rumor, sell the news

- The listed projects, which you can see on CoinMarketCal, as shown in Fig. 21.2.

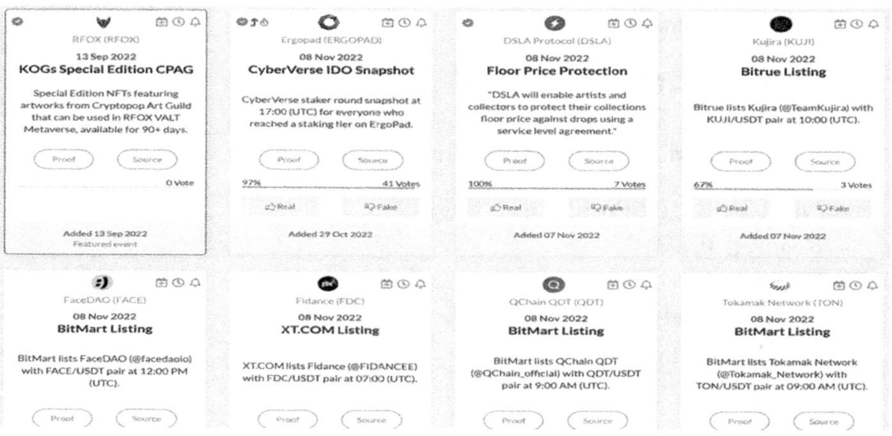

Fig. 21.2   *Source* CoinMarketCal

- Assess the growth potential:

  - Fully diluted market cap is the price multiplied by the maximum supply.
  - Fully diluted cap vs. market cap indicates potential:

    Example: Gamium
    Fully Diluted Market Cap: $29 M
    Market Cap: $6.7 M
    Potential: 4.3x

- Circulating Supply should be more than 60%.
- Tokenomics refers to the token distribution, especially in terms of marketing and the incentives used to drive the development of the project.

21.4 Risk Management

- Risk management is very important for the success of your investment.
- **Money Management:**

  - It is the mathematical algorithm that determines how much money to invest in the next trade.
  - Software: RINASYSTEMS—https://www.rinasystems.com/index.html
  - It is independent of the trading system being applied.
  - The goal is to improve the risk–reward ratio.
  - There are two types of strategies:

    Martingale: increase position size as losses accumulate. DO NOT USE.
    Anti-Martingale: increase position size as profits are made in the market.

- ANTI-MARTINGALE STRATEGIES:

  - **KELLY FORMULA:**

    Determines the percentage of capital to allocate in the next trade based on the probability of success or failure, considering the average gain and loss.
    K = (% winners—% losers)/Payoff.
    Payoff = average gain/average loss.

  - **FIXED FRACTION:**

    Allocates an amount depending on whether your system is in your favor, based on the maximum tolerable loss and the expected maximum drawdown.
    K = (max tolerable loss × account value)/max drawdown.

  - **OPTIMAL F:**

    Indicates the optimal percentage of capital to expose in a trade to achieve the highest possible return.

  - **SAFE F:**

    Similar to Optimal F but introduces a maximum drawdown limit you can tolerate.

  - **FIXED RATIO:**

    You set a fixed percentage of account equity per trade. Recommended: **2%–3% per trade**.

21.5 Important Tips

1. DIVERSIFY, but not too much, because otherwise you'll generate more risk: Over-diversifying is not ideal in the crypto market, as it adds more risk than concentrating your investment in the most profitable, secure, and sector-leading protocols.
2. Consider whether the token is inflationary. If it is, its price will gradually dilute unless new capital flows into it.
3. Check if the coin has a very low circulating supply. If so, its price could slowly dilute over the coming years as more tokens are released. You need to take into account when those token unlocks are going to happen, because they can put downward pressure on the price, as the investors who had them locked may go to the market and sell them. The unlock increases the circulating supply but does not increase the total supply if it was already pre-mined.
4. Never set a stop loss or take profit at round numbers, as those often act as strong support or resistance levels.

    a. For short positions, place your stop loss above resistance.
    b. For long positions, place them below support.
    c. For take profit, set it below resistance if you're long, and above support if you're short.

5. When trading on a DEX, it is very important to ensure the smart contract you're selecting is correct and not a scam.

    a. Websites like CoinMarketCap or CoinGecko do not guarantee that the listed smart contracts are legitimate.
    b. Be cautious when trading on a DEX.
    c. My recommendation: if the contract doesn't appear directly in the DEX, don't trade that token, because even going to the project's official website could lead you to a fake contract. For this reason, the safest option is always to trade on CEX.

In Summary, before investing in crypto:

- Phase of the market cycle we are in:

    - **From bottom bear market to Halving:** Buy btc
    - **From the beginning of the bull market:** Buy Altcoins (4 phases)
    - **From the top of bull market:** Buy stablecoins (seeking refuge)/DCA (dollar cost averaging) into BTC if you are a long term holder

- Macroeconomic data (U.S. employment, U.S. GDP, Fed interest rates, Global M2 Money Supply)
- Bitcoin fundamentals
- On-chain metrics
- Technical analysis
- Stablecoin Dominance
- Look for:

  - leading projects in their sector (for example, Chainlink as an oracle), that are robust
  - with good token distribution (tokenomics)
  - high circulating supply
  - low token unlocks
  - preferably listed on CEXs

- Diversification in crypto is not always beneficial.
- Be careful when trading on DEXs (fake contracts). Don't fully trust CoinMarketCap. **Example: Squid Game.**

  - The hacker created a backdoor in the smart contract through which he could withdraw all the money that came in. It was only possible to buy but not sell.
  - The smart contract was listed on **CoinMarketCap** and **CoinGecko**, meaning that these websites **do not perform thorough verification** of the coins that get listed. Therefore, it is always important to **do your own research**.

- Take circulating supply into account.
- Watch for upcoming unlocks (which increase supply), as they can create downward pressure on price.

And remember, for example, the case of **Mantra (OM)**: it once reached the **Top 30** and had a **market cap of 5.5 billion USD**.

- Market makers to provide liquidity on centralized exchanges (CEX).
- Mantra signed a contract called a **loan option model**, under which the market maker (Falcon X) had the right to buy 1 million tokens at $1 each when the agreement expired.
- Market makers are necessary, but they must be aligned with your project; otherwise, they can become your worst partner.
- Solution: choose a **retainer model**—pay for the service. Chart 21.1.

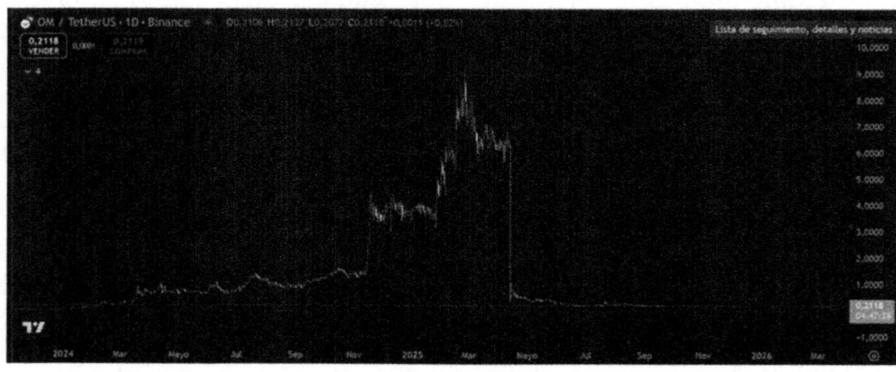

Chart 21.1   *Source* Tradingview

Bibliography

Antonopoulos, Andreas (2019). *Mastering Bitcoin.* O´Reilly Editorial.

Suarez Bravo, Álvaro (2023). *Fundamentos de Bitcoin.* Private Editorial.

Van Wirdum, Aaaron (2024). *The Genesis Book.* Bitcoin Magazine Books Editorial.

Leinweber, Willig, and Schoenfeld (2024). *Mastering Crypto Assets.* Wiley Editorial.

The only Altcoin investing book you will ever need (2023). Freeman Publications.

The only Ethereum investing book you will ever need (2023). Freeman Publications.

Antonopoulos, Andreas (2018). *Mastering Ethereum.* O´Reilly Editorial.

Black, Keith (2025). Investing in Cryptocurrencies and Digital Assets. Wiley Editorial.

Pineda, Javier (2024). Sistemas de Trading 2. Como crearlos por ti mismo y tener éxito. Editorial Ceefi.

Index